The Tide of Empire

By the same author

To Gettysburg and Beyond
A Ruined Land: The End of the Civil War
William Faulkner A to Z
Encyclopedia of North American Exploration

The Tide of Empire

America's March to the Pacific

Michael Golay

WILEY

John Wiley & Sons, Inc.

This book is printed on acid-free paper. ∞

Copyright © 2003 by Michael Golay. All rights reserved

Published by John Wiley & Sons, Inc., Hoboken, New Jersey
Published simultaneously in Canada

No part of this publication may be reproduced, stored in a retrieval system, or transmitted in any form or by any means, electronic, mechanical, photocopying, recording, scanning, or otherwise, except as permitted under Section 107 or 108 of the 1976 United States Copyright Act, without either the prior written permission of the Publisher, or authorization through payment of the appropriate per-copy fee to the Copyright Clearance Center, 222 Rosewood Drive, Danvers, MA 01923, (978) 750-8400, fax (978) 750-4470, or on the web at www.copyright.com. Requests to the Publisher for permission should be addressed to the Permissions Department, John Wiley & Sons, Inc., 111 River Street, Hoboken, NJ 07030, (201) 748-6011, fax (201) 748-6008, e-mail: permcoordinator@wiley.com.

Limit of Liability/Disclaimer of Warranty: While the publisher and the author have used their best efforts in preparing this book, they make no representations or warranties with respect to the accuracy or completeness of the contents of this book and specifically disclaim any implied warranties of merchantability or fitness for a particular purpose. No warranty may be created or extended by sales representatives or written sales materials. The advice and strategies contained herein may not be suitable for your situation. You should consult with a professional where appropriate. Neither the publisher nor the author shall be liable for any loss of profit or any other commercial damages, including but not limited to special, incidental, consequential, or other damages.

For general information about our other products and services, please contact our Customer Care Department within the United States at (800) 762-2974, outside the United States at (317) 572-3993 or fax (317) 572-4002.

Wiley also publishes its books in a variety of electronic formats. Some content that appears in print may not be available in electronic books. For more information about Wiley products, visit our web site at www.wiley.com.

Library of Congress Cataloging-in-Publication Data:

Golay, Michael, date.
    The tide of empire : America's march to the Pacific /
Michael Golay.
        p.   cm.
    Includes bibliographical references and index.
    ISBN 0-471-37791-0 (cloth : alk. paper)
        1. Oregon—History—To 1859. 2. Columbia River Valley—History—
19th century. 3. Oregon—Discovery and exploration. 4. Columbia River
Valley—Discovery and exploration. 5. Frontier and pioneer life—Oregon.
6. Fur traders—Oregon—History—19th century. 7. Pioneers—Oregon—
History—19th century. 8. Missionaries—Oregon—History—19th century.
9. Overland journeys to the Pacific. I. Title.
    F880 .G65   2003
    978'.02—dc21
                                                            2002154132

Printed in the United States of America

10 9 8 7 6 5 4 3 2 1

For my parents

Would not one say, on seeing what takes place in the world, that the European is to men of other races what man himself is to the animals? He makes them serve his use, and when he cannot bend them, he destroys them.

—Alexis de Tocqueville, *Democracy in America*

West is where we all plan to go someday. It is where you go when the land gives out and the old-field pines encroach. It is where you go when you get the letter saying: *Flee, all is discovered*. It is where you go when you look down at the blade in your hand and see blood on it. It is where you go when you are a bubble on the tide of empire. It is where you go when you hear that thar's gold in them-thar hills.

—Robert Penn Warren, *All the King's Men*

Contents

Illustrations

Maps

Author's Note

This narrative is at once an adventure story, a cautionary tale, and a lament. It chronicles, although it does not celebrate, the transformational power of American energy. It might just as well have been subtitled "How a Nondescript Band of Trappers, Missionaries, and Junior Army Officers Seized a Pacific Empire for the United States."

The Tide of Empire is an expression, too, of my fascination with the local and the particular—never more compelling to me than now, as our increasingly standardized world hurtles on toward globalization. Here character is plot. The westering Americans were at once idealistic, greedy, visionary, solipsistic. They played for high stakes. They were builders; just as certainly, they were destroyers. I admire their dash, their creative intensity, and their mother wit even as I deplore the destructive consequences, unlooked-for and otherwise, of their deeds and good intentions.

Contemporary political and opinion leaders—the Manifest Destiny lobby, if you will—claimed to be the catalysts of the American conquest of the Pacific Slope. In the event, miscellaneous bands of itinerant traders, Protestant Christian missionaries, and freelance explorers made certain the United States would advance to the Pacific anyway, more or less on schedule, even without an expansionist victory in the presidential election of 1844 and the subsequent war with Mexico. The flag followed their penetration, their colonizing schemes, and their domination of rival claimants to the land.

At least since the 1880s, historians have debated the motives and actions of the first Americans to settle permanently along the Pacific littoral, the vanguard of the great folk movement that by 1860 would carry a quarter-million men, women, and children over the great transcontinental trails and across the Rocky Mountains. Were the aggressively entrepreneurial missionary Jason Lee and his associates colonizers manqué? At what point did the missionary Marcus Whitman become a conscious agent of American expansion? American merchant-adventurers openly lusted after the Mexican province of California as early as the 1820s. Did John Charles Frémont carry secret government orders to ignite a revolt in California, or did he merely reach the scene in time to claim credit for a settler fait accompli?

In the end, questions of causation and motivation are speculative. Americans executed their schemes of imperial expansion in Oregon and California instinctively, even though most held an explicit conviction of their right to occupy and exploit the country. "What Americans desire they always effect," Dr. Whitman wrote in the spring of 1844, "and it is equally useless to oppose or desire it otherwise." Whether their motives were pure or tainted, Americans were violent, domineering, self-absorbed, and blindly certain of their values, missionaries no less than traders and soldiers. American first principles—the free market economy, the extension of the commercial frontier, and political democracy with rough equality of opportunity for white men—were fatal to the Native Americans and Mexicans of the Pacific Coast. The Americans' assumptions—that their ways were always superior—were catastrophic.

A few words of acknowledgment. *The Tide of Empire* is based on personal histories drawn from published and unpublished primary sources: letters, diaries, memoirs, and other documentary material. My thanks go to librarians and special collections archivists at the Beinecke Library of Yale University; the Oregon Historical Society; Wesleyan University; the University of Puget Sound; and Phillips Exeter Academy. I gratefully acknowledge, too, the patient support of my agent, Ed Knappman, of Chester, Connecticut; my editor at John Wiley & Sons, Hana Lane; and especially my wife, Julie Quinn.

Prologue

Columbia's River

WORK PARTIES FERRIED over the last of the gear from the log fort and workshops ashore, and the watch on deck made ready to unmoor ship. The skies were clear for a change and a warm wind blew from the southeast—a harbinger, perhaps, of a prosperous 1792 trading season for *Columbia*. Winter along this far shore of North America struck mild and humid, "never Ice thicker than a Spanish dollar," according to *Columbia*'s fifth mate, John Boit. But rain fell ceaselessly and the sun, when it appeared at all, hovered so low on the horizon in those high latitudes that only a wan twilight filtered down through the pines. Whortleberries and blueberries were available deep into the cool season; fish, fowl, and venison were plentiful; and drafts of spruce beer, a noxious drink brewed from evergreen boughs and sweetened with molasses, kept off the scurvy. *Columbia*'s fifty officers and men were in tolerable health, and their ship—83 feet long and 212 tons, built at Plymouth, Massachusetts, in 1787—lay taut and eager after six months in winter quarters in a secluded cove of Clayoquot Sound, an inlet of the Pacific along the western coast of present Vancouver Island.[1]

With a final volley of orders, *Columbia* came to sail on March 26, 1792, and stood down the sound in company with the trim little *Adventure* sloop. *Columbia*'s captain, Robert Gray, intended violence that soft spring day. Word had reached Gray in mid-February that a war party of Clayoquot Nootka (Nuu'chah'nulth) Indians planned an

1

assault on the ship. Gray judged the aggression unprovoked, even though he had, in a show of bravado, named his rough-built strong-hold on the foreshore Fort Defiance and mounted two of the ship's great guns there. Relations between the traders and the Amerindian natives had been cordial, or so it seemed to Gray. Men had drifted down from the Indian village to watch the sailors bringing up the sloop's frame from *Columbia*'s hold and assembling it onshore. In turn, Robert Haswell, Gray's first lieutenant, admired the Nootkas' efficient way of seining sardines, driving shoals of fish inshore on the ebb tide and trapping them in an enclosure of pine boughs. There were brisk exchanges in otter skins, salmon, and geese. Village girls offered wild parsley and a root resembling leek. Gray had invited the principal chiefs to dine aboard on Christmas Day, and he fired off a cannon salute to celebrate the occasion. All seemed calm, even if a great deal about the natives remained hidden to Gray and his officers. "We have never been able to gain much information as respects their Religion," Boit observed, "but they certainly pay adoration to the *Sun*, and *Moon*, and believe in Good and evil Spirits." The Nootkas were often bewildered, too. They could not comprehend, for instance, why the Bostons (as they dubbed the visitors) dressed the ship and buildings ashore in festoons of greenery at the time of the solstice.[2]

Boit and a few others returned the call on New Year's Day, visiting the village of Opitsat, the seat of the Nootkas' paramount chief, Wickanannish. Equerries led them into a large dwelling eighty feet long and forty feet wide and then into the throne room. "The *king* was elevated about two feet higher than the company, with a Canopy over his head, stuck full of animals' teeth," Boit recorded in his journal. Nearly a hundred men, most of them far gone in years, milled about. Young women, whom the traders found comely and modest, were nowhere to be seen. ("Nothing could even tempt them to come on board the ship," remarked *Columbia*'s supercargo, John Hoskins, who had heard the women sometimes offered to swap sexual favors for iron.) One of the attendants proffered Boit a concoction he described as "Fish spawn mixed with Berries and train oil," served in a wooden bowl. He declined, on account of the smell.[3]

Boit's lack of enthusiasm for this compote did not appear to offend Wickanannish. The lesser chiefs continued to visit the ship as the winter advanced and Captain Gray himself went to Opitsat to doctor ailing villagers. But the Nootkas suddenly began driving a harder bargain for their pelts, demanding muskets, powder, and shot instead of copper and cloth. And, evil omen, Gray's gun accidentally discharged on the path to the village, grazing an Indian in the arm. The piece had been loaded with birdshot and no harm done; Wickanannish laughed it off, assuring Gray that he knew the Bostons came in peace.

There *had* been an affront, though, an incident the previous June when *Columbia* first dropped anchor in Clayoquot Sound. The ship's boy, a Sandwich Islander called Attoo, jumped ship and found temporary asylum on the island among the Indians. Gray briefly held the head chief's brother aboard as ransom against the boy's return. Wickanannish promptly seized Attoo and remanded him to Gray for the inevitable flogging. But the kidnap angered Wickanannish, outraged him in a way the New Englanders failed to comprehend.

The matter doubtless struck Gray as trifling, if he remembered it at all. It did not occur to him to consider the possibility that he had offended the natives. Gray was trespassing, after all, or—in the Indian view anyway—present only on sufferance. For all their appreciation for the country, its astonishingly rife vegetation, the antediluvian cedars of the rain forest, the seven-inch-long mussels, and the shimmering silvery-gray of the pelt of a mature otter, the Americans were obtuse about Indian customs and slow to penetrate Indian patterns of thinking. They did not catch on at first to the natives' belief in a form of collective responsibility. If the Indians could not strike out against the actual offender, they were content to wait months to retaliate against the first convenient ship or exploring party to come within their ambit.

Such had been the case in August in the Queen Charlotte Islands, where Gray lost a valuable officer, Joshua Caswell, the second mate, along with two sailors. With the captain's permission, they had gone fishing in the jollyboat. When they failed to rejoin the ship, Gray dispatched a search party. The pinnace presently returned with the jollyboat in tow, its colors at half mast and Caswell's corpse in the bottom, slashed about and stabbed in twenty places. One of the sailors had been found dead upon the beach; the other had vanished without a trace. The explanation came a day or two later, when *Columbia* fell in with the brig *Hancock* out of Boston. Its master, Samuel Crowell, had fired on the natives—Haidas or possibly Tlingits—for some minor infraction, killing several.

"Perhaps this same fray was the means of our losing our worthy 2nd officer as the places are not 20 leagues distance and mayhap they reck'd their vengeance upon us, us all of one tribe," Boit speculated. "If it was so, bad *luck to Crowell, Amen.*"[4]

As it happened, the Sandwich Islander, recovering his morale, sounded a warning of the Nootkas' attack. Gray and the others realized the Indians had deceived them all along in urging the Bostons to sell them arms for a raid on the enemy village of Highshakt. "This name possibly applied to us," Haswell figured, "or was fictitious, to delude us." Gunfire had sounded, too—target practice, John Hoskins learned, with warrior marksmen firing at a board on which had been traced the outline of a man. A Nootka subchief, Attoo said, had asked him to dampen the ship's powder stocks and steal powder and balls for him. The Indians offered an otter skin for every musket ball he procured. A war party would storm *Columbia* at night and kill everyone aboard.

Gray ordered the swivel gun loaded and warped the ship in closer to the fort. The warriors did mass for an assault, at about midnight on February 18. They found the Bostons watchful and, after whooping and shrieking dismally in the starlight for a couple of hours, called off the affray. "After this," Boit noted, "no more of the Natives visited Adventure Cove except some old women and young girls, who brought us berries and fish, and most probable they was sent as spies." When Wickanannish himself turned up finally, Gray brusquely ordered him to keep out of his way. A few days later the chief's aged mother came alongside with otter skins to sell. She told Gray that the moon had informed Wickanannish that he would be killed if he approached the ship.[5]

So Gray resolved to exact his revenge as he sailed away that late March day. In a premeditated tantrum, he sent the seventeen-year-old Boit with three boatloads of heavily armed men ashore with orders to burn Opitsat. Boit recoiled. "I am grieved," he wrote, "to think Capt. Gray shou'd let his passions go so far," but he had no choice but to obey. The villagers had fled, leaving household goods and other possessions scattered among the pines. Opitsat contained two hundred or so well-constructed houses. "Ev'ry door that you entered was in resemblance an human and Beasts head, the passage being through the mouth, besides which there was much more rude carved work about the buildings, some of which was by no means *innelegant,*" Boit recorded. All the same, the sailors went to work with torch and tinderbox, leaving the village, dwellings, storehouses, and totems a charred desolation.[6]

With Gray's arson, the all-too-familiar cycle of outrage and retribution played itself out. Gray and his officers never deciphered the motive for the attack: the insult of the captain's arrest of Wickanannish's brother. In Haswell's view, the traders all along had treated the natives humanely and hospitably. Even Hoskins, whose highly developed mercantile instincts led him to blur almost any disagreement in pursuit of profits, felt aggrieved. "Had we treated them ill or as some people have an idea savages ought to be treated had we ravaged their women spoiled their towns, destroyed their fisheries or committed any depredations whatsoever they would have just grounds," he allowed. "But the contrary of this has been the case." Still, the Indians had done them no actual injury. Why, Haskins wondered, risk making a permanent enemy of a potentially profitable trading partner?[7]

This was not the outcome *Columbia*'s investors envisioned. They had seen the ship off with high hopes; the first voyage to the Northwest and China, from 1787 to 1790, had not been profitable, even though Gray's *Columbia* became the first vessel to circumnavigate the globe under the new American nation's colors. With the second voyage, Joseph Barrell and his partners sought a tangible reward, in the form of first-quality otter skins for the Canton trade. Success would depend on the traders' relations with the Indians. "It is of importance, and we therefore enjoin it upon you," Barrell had written Gray on September 25, 1790, "that the most friendly intercourse be observed in all your traffick with the Natives and [that you] endeavour, by your honorable conduct, to impress them with a respect for Americans." That meant fair dealing with the tribes, Barrell went on, and an equable temper in the face of provocation.[8]

Gray had barely been ashore in New England six weeks when he set out on the second expedition to the Pacific. "If the wind is fair on the morrow, we desire and expect you will embrace it and proceed on your voyage," Barrell wrote in his farewell. *Columbia*, laden with blue cloth, copper, and iron trading goods valued at fifteen hundred pounds sterling, sailed out of Boston Harbor on September 28 on what the supercargo Hoskins described as "a voyage of trade and discovery"— "discovery" a euphemism for the search for Amerindian nations that had not yet encountered whites and so had no conception of how highly they valued furs. On November 25, fifty-four and a half days out, *Columbia* crossed the equator. The ship doubled Cape Horn on February 25, 1791. Toward the end of March the first signs of scurvy appeared: soft gums and weak legs in two or three of the people. Hoskins blamed the captain for refusing to alter course and seek land for a supply of antiscorbutics. Boit reported seven men off duty with scurvy on May 19. The ship made a landfall on the Northwest coast between Nootka and Clayoquot Sounds on June 4, a fast passage of eight months.[9]

Columbia ventured north beyond the Queen Charlotte Islands over the trading summer of 1791 and as far south as the Strait of Juan de Fuca, swapping metal and cloth for otter skins, and beads, fishhooks, and other gadgets for greens, fish, and meat. Hoskins, a merchant-shipowner's son who owed his place not to Gray but to a family connection with Joseph Barrell, found fresh occasion to find fault with the captain, this time for recklessness and inept shiphandling as *Columbia* sought an entrance to the strait in the encircling fog. "We were hourly in the most imminent danger," Hoskins wrote. "Yet Captain Gray could not be induced to stand off but seemed rather to preferr this distressful situation. There was not the least chance of the natives coming off with skins." On this occasion, anyway, Boit took Hoskins's part. "Damn nonsense," Boit thought, "beating about among rocks in foggy weather." Off Tatoosh Island a few days later, the watch sensed the loom of the land through the murk. Gray ordered out all the boats and just managed to see the ship towed clear. The next midnight, an officer roused Gray to report the roar of the surf perilously near. He emerged on deck, listened intently for a moment, then issued urgent orders to claw off the fatal shore.[10]

The unsettled winter mood of the Clayoquot Nootka, the aborted attack and punitive expedition to Opitsat: *Columbia* left these troubles in its wake with the opening of the 1792 trading season. Gray ranged as far south as Cape Blanco, along the coast of southern Oregon, before doubling back and putting in to trade at present Bayview, Oregon, and at the mouth of the Umpqua River. From the ship's rail, Boit's eager glance embraced an irresistible country—soft, temperate, and cultivable. "The Shore made in sandy beaches, and the land rose gradually back into the high hills, and the beautifull fields of grass, interspersed among the wood lands, made itt delightfull," he wrote. Working unhurriedly north, *Columbia* stood inshore frequently to meet

Indian trading canoes laden with otter skins and fish and to scout for safe harbors. A promising opening appeared at about latitude 46°, but strong currents, rain squalls, and the unquiet surf barred a closer examination. "However," noted Boit, "Capt. Gray is determin'd to persevere in the pursuit." Before dawn on April 28 or 29, near Cape Elizabeth on the Washington coast, the masthead lookout bawled out a report of a sail, two sails: HMS *Discovery*, it turned out, the flagship of Captain George Vancouver's Northwest coast surveying and exploring expedition, and with her, HMS *Chatham*.[11]

In the complacent way of his kind, Vancouver regarded these lonely stretches of the North Pacific as British waters. He had sailed with Captain Cook as a midshipman, and Cook himself in 1778 had become the first European known to set foot on the 285-mile-long island that eventually would bear Vancouver's name. A British trading vanguard had arrived in the Pacific Northwest in 1785, drawn by Cook's enthusiasm for these rain-drenched coasts as a prime untapped source of furs. *Discovery* signaled the stranger to bring to. "This was a very great novelty," Vancouver wrote, "not having seen any vessel but our consort during the last eight months. She soon hoisted American colours, and fired a gun to leeward." Vancouver sent his second lieutenant, Peter Puget, and the expedition's naturalist, Archibald Menzies,* across to board the Yankee vessel.[12]

Gray told the Britons that *Columbia* had wintered in Clayoquot Sound (he supplied details of Wickanannish's plot), and that he had dispatched *Adventure* north to trade in the Queen Charlotte Islands while the larger vessel cruised the Oregon coast. He added what he knew about the inland sea that separated Vancouver Island and the mainland. *Columbia* had penetrated only fifty miles up this passage, Gray said, although his Indian guides claimed it extended considerably farther to the north. He also informed Puget and Menzies that he had been, a few days earlier, off the mouth of what he took to be a substantial river in latitude 46°10'. Given this intelligence later, Vancouver dismissed it, certain as he was that *Discovery* could not have overlooked any important inlet along that coast.

---

*Menzies doubled as expedition surgeon. A protégé of Sir Joseph Banks, longtime president of the Royal Society, Menzies may have been a model for the fictional physician-naturalist Stephen Maturin of Patrick O'Brien's Aubrey-Maturin novel cycle.

"This was, probably, the opening passed by us on the forenoon of the 27th; and was, apparently, inaccessible, not from the current, but from the breakers that extended across it," Vancouver wrote. "I was thoroughly convinced, as were also most persons of observation on board, that we could not possibly have passed any safe navigable opening, harbour, or place of security for shipping on this coast."[13]

In fact, *Discovery* and *Chatham* had cruised past the mouth of the fabled Great River of the West. The Jesuit missionary Charlevoix speculated about its existence in the 1720s. Frontiersman Robert Rogers in 1765 confused it with the upper reaches of the Missouri and called it "Ouragon." Ten years later, the Spanish explorer Bruno Hezeta sailed into the river's mouth and assigned names to the estuary and the two capes at the entrance. Captain John Meares scouted the Oregon coast for England in 1788, declared pedantically that the great river did not exist, and renamed the northerly headland Cape Disappointment. Vancouver had been instructed not "to pursue any inlet or river further than it shall appear to be navigable by vessels of such burthen as might safely navigate the Pacific Ocean."[14] He judged this opening not worth trouble or delay, a confirmation of Meares's report. Nothing Puget and Menzies heard from Gray raised any question in his mind.

As John Boit remarked, Gray was intent on finding a good anchorage along the Oregon coast. Here, perhaps, his single-mindedness and obstinate courage—his foolhardiness, Hoskins and Boit might have put it—served him well. Possibly Lieutenant Puget had expressed skepticism, kindling a desire in Gray to prove the Briton wrong. Possibly the Yankee resented what he took to be Puget's smug, know-it-all air. A native of Tiverton, Rhode Island, Gray had served in the American navy during the Revolution, then sailed as a merchant officer. Thirty-seven years old in 1792, he had a lot of maritime experience to consult. Whatever his impulse, Gray watched *Discovery* disappear over the horizon, then ordered *Columbia* to crack on sail and double back to the south.

The ship ghosted along, standing in from time to time to meet Indian trading canoes. On May 1 Boit reported "a brisk trade for furs." On the seventh, Gray sent the cutter to reconnoiter an inlet, perhaps two miles broad, that appeared to lead to a good anchorage. The cutter sounded and signaled the results to *Columbia*, which slowly approached the weather bar. The ship scraped over the shoals and glided to anchor in a placid bay at about five o'clock in the afternoon.[15]

This was present-day Grays Harbor, Washington. Canoes flashed out from shore, filled with startled natives armed with bows and arrows. "Without doubt we are the first Civilized people that ever visited this port," Boit decided, "and these poor fellows view'd us with the greatest astonishment." The men were naked, the women nearly so, except for "a small apron before, made of rushes." The Bostons did not recognize their language. All the same, the Indians, probably of the Chehalis tribe, seemed eager enough to sell fish and furs for blankets and iron. And, through gestures and signs, they may have told Gray of a great river not far to the south.[16]

Sometime after sunset, a flotilla of canoes closed on the ship with evident menace. Gray ordered musket shots fired overhead, and the canoes withdrew. The Indians, possibly raiders from beyond the Chehalis frontier, returned at midnight, whooping it up under a bright moon. Gray called for warning shots from the nine-pounders. A lone canoe, carrying twenty or so men, continued to come on fast. One of the great guns flashed, and an instant later the canoe exploded in a cloud of spray and splinters.

"I do not think they had any Conception of the power of Artillery," Boit wrote in his journal. "I am sorry we was oblig'd to kill the poor Divells, but it could not with safety be avoided."[17]

Columbia beat down Grays Harbor on the evening of May 10, cleared the bar, and ran southward just offshore. Gray hauled wind in the morning for what looked like a spacious roadstead opening out beyond a shoaling passage between two headlands. The captain launched the pinnace, and the ship followed its lead under short sail. *Columbia* shot the passage into "a large river of fresh water." Indians crowded the beach, skipping along the foreshore abreast of the ship, which kept to the channel a quarter-mile or so distant. Then twenty or so canoes pushed off, carrying salmon and furs. They were Chinooks, a trading tribe perhaps seven hundred strong inhabiting the country behind the northern shore of the estuary. Chinooks may have dealt with Spanish castaways before *Columbia* arrived, although tribal elders would later assert that Gray had been the first white man to enter the great river. Certainly Gray was the first Euroamerican to report the existence of the Chinooks. Whether or not the Chinook traders had met whites before now, they seemed to grasp at once what the strangers prized. They offered salmon two for an iron nail and accepted copper and cloth for pelts. The ship crept upstream and came to anchor off a large village that straggled along the northern shore a few miles from the entrance.[18]

Hard, wind-driven rain fell more or less continuously for the next two days. The gales and the short, choppy seas did not discourage the Chinooks. The Bostons acquired four otter skins for a sheet of copper and paid two spikes each for beaver skins. Other "land furs" went for one spike. Noting that canoes from upstream never brought otter pelts, Boit deduced that "the Otter constantly keeps in Salt water." On the third day, the wind abating, *Columbia* came to sail and stood upriver, course northeast by east through a narrowing channel. By late afternoon the ship had proceeded a dozen or so difficult miles—far enough, Gray decided, for a seagoing vessel in confined waters among islands, rocks, and sandbars.[19]

Columbia lay in the river for nine days. With Boit, Gray went ashore for a scout and, in a journal entry Boit added later for posterity, "to take possession" of the country, though no evidence survives of any formal ceremony or flag-raising. "Found much clear ground, fit for Cultivation, and the woods mostly clear from Underbrush," Boit wrote. The natives—there were, perhaps, 180,000 Indians in the Pacific Northwest before the whites arrived in force—were numerous, civil, and, on first impression, anyway, honest. "The men are straight limb'd, fine-looking fellows, and the women are very pretty," he went on. "They are all in a state of Nature, except the females, who wear a leaf Apron (perhaps 'twas a fig leaf)." Some of the men, on closer examination, reported the covering wasn't a leaf at all, but a sort of woven mat. "And so we go—thus, thus—and no Near!"[20]

Dropping downstream to the Chinook village, Gray put the people to work refilling the water casks, paying the ship's sides with tar, and caulking the pinnace. Hoskins brought the accounts up-to-date: a tally of 150 otter skins and 300 beaver skins. On May 19, according to the ship's official log, "Captain Gray gave this river the name of *Columbia's River*." The next day, after a near-disaster on the sandspits (the wind lapsed at just the wrong moment, stranding the ship briefly on the bar), *Columbia* cleared the entrance and stretched away to the northward.[21]

So concluded the first contact between Euroamericans and the Indian first nations of the lower Columbia River. The New Englanders had cast a practiced eye over the country of the coastal Indians and deemed it ripe. "The river abounds with excellent *Salmon*, and most other River fish, and the woods with plenty of Moose and Deer ... and the Banks produce a ground Nut, which is an excellent substitute for either bread or Potatoes," Boit observed. There were fine stands of oak, ash, and walnut, and sufficient open ground for cultivated plots to sustain a colony. All in all, Boit judged the lower Columbia an excellent place for a trading post that might (who could predict?) evolve into a civilized settlement of importance.[22]

Columbia sailed for Nootka Sound, stopping to trade here and there along the way and falling in again with Robert Haswell in *Adventure*. With the end of the trading season at hand, Gray sold the sloop to the Spanish authorities at Nootka for seventy-two prime sea otter skins (said to be worth $55 apiece in Canton), and Haswell resumed his old place as first lieutenant. The captain also reported his discovery of the Great River of the West to Juan Francisco de la Bodega y Quadra, the Spanish governor, and left a sketch of the river's entrance with Quadra. On October 3, 1792, *Columbia* sank the Northwest coast and shaped a course for China. After an uneventful passage via the Sandwich Islands, the ship arrived at moorings at Whampoa in the Canton River on December 12.

With fifty or more European and American competitors crowding the anchorage, worry about profits assailed Hoskins. "Furs are very cheap and almost impossible to get rid of for money," he wrote Joseph Barrell in Boston. "The ship is considerable leaky and must undergo repair. However, we shall be as frugal as possible in all expenses." In the event, *Columbia's* cargo sold for a respectable $90,000, an average of $45 per pelt, including the land furs, leaving Hoskins with ample resources to fill the hold with nankeen, sugar, and China porcelain for the homeward voyage.[23]

Meanwhile, Quadra tipped Captain Vancouver to Gray's alleged discovery. Armed with the Yankee's sketch, Vancouver sailed south in mid-October to have a belated look for himself. Judging that the 337-ton *Discovery* drew too much water for an attempt on the ferocious bar, Vancouver on October 20 sent Lieutenant William R. Broughton in *Chatham* to explore and survey *Columbia's* river. Leaving the tender at anchor in tranquil waters below the high, steep bluffs of Cape Disappointment, *Discovery* stood out to sea on the twenty-first. Basing his account on *Chatham*'s logs, Vancouver narrated Broughton's reconnaissance in his *Voyage of Discovery to the North Pacific Ocean*, published in London in 1798.

Using Gray's chart, Broughton navigated *Chatham* upstream, past a deserted Indian village toward Tongue Point on the southern shore. The tender came gently aground on the ebb and stuck fast. She floated off at high tide. The shoal had not been marked on Gray's sketch—a superficial effort that, Vancouver remarked acidly, "did not much resemble what it purported to represent." (In fact, he failed to account for the fact that Gray had done his rough chart and soundings in the spring, when the great river's flow reached its peak.) Painstaking and accurate, an experienced surveyor, the twenty-nine-year-old Broughton took it upon himself to correct the deficiencies. He seized the opportunity, too, of bestowing names on natural features of the neighborhood, many of which have been preserved.[24]

Mindful of the sandbar, Broughton shifted to the cutter. Before setting out, he named the sheltered waters under Cape Disappointment Baker Bay, after the master of a trading schooner *Chatham* had fallen in with. Crossing to Point Adams, Broughton entered a bay just east of the promontory and ascended the little river that emptied into it, naming both for a Royal Navy colleague, Sir George Young. He then turned back for the low, sandy spit of Point Adams. This was the country of the Clatsops. Like the Chinooks, the Clatsops kept slaves and flattened the heads of their infants, but they were more dependent on hunting than the fishing tribes on the northern shore and were less adept as traders. Here the cutter's men inspected an abandoned Clatsop village, finding three large burial canoes decorated with carvings at the bow and stern and filled with corpses in an advanced state of decomposition. The sailors camped ashore in the dunes. The wind blew hard over the sand all night, with rain descending steadily till daybreak.

Straining against a stiff east wind, the cutter pushed up to Tongue Point on the twenty-third, Broughton sounding all the way. He magnanimously named the bay to the northeast for *Columbia*'s captain before returning to *Chatham*. Wood and water were plentiful at the anchorage, and the Chinooks were friendly. Nevertheless, Broughton attempted to take the tender upstream. *Chatham* glided along through

This A. T. Agate engraving shows Chinook Indians in their lodge. Travelers to the lower Columbia rarely failed to note the coastal tribes' most striking physical characteristic, plainly visible here: the flattened head. "The more acute the angle, the greater the beauty," trader Alexander Ross wrote. (Library of Congress)

shoal water, touching bottom here and there. Toward the end of a trying day, Broughton decided to leave the tender at moorings and provision the cutter for a seven-day expedition.

The exploring party set out across Grays Bay in moody weather on the morning of October 25. Broughton industriously sounded near Pillar Rock, filled in blank spaces on his chart, and made an early camp. The cutter drifted into the stream with the first of the flood on the twenty-sixth. The river here narrowed to a width of half a mile, with a low, marshy shore on either hand. Broughton marked the channel as lying close to the northern shore. He named a low, wooded island on the right hand for Peter Puget, the officer who had catechized Gray at sea six months before. Just beyond, natives appeared in their coracles, offering fish for sale. The richness of *Columbia's* river awed Broughton. "The river seemed to abound with fish," he wrote, "consisting of two sorts of salmon, both very good; and sturgeon of a large size and very fine flavor, with silver bream, herrings, flat fish, and soirdinias."[25] The party camped that evening on the Oregon shore in the country of the Cathlamets. A band of Indians in nine canoes landed just down the beach. They wore deerskins and looked warlike, thought Broughton, but proved peaceable. The cutter had covered only twenty-two miles in twelve hours of hard rowing.

The Britons proceeded upstream the next day, with the flotilla of canoes as escort. On the northern shore rose "a remarkable mount, about which were placed several canoes, containing dead bodies."[26] Broughton prosaically named it Mount Coffin. The river bent sharply to the south a little farther on. On the twenty-eighth, a Sunday, Broughton stopped briefly at a large Indian village whose leaders advised him that, if he proceeded much farther, he would risk having his head cut off. Ignoring the warning, he pushed on till eight in the evening before stopping to camp in a willow grove on present Sauvie Island, near where the Multnomah Channel empties into the Columbia.

Daybreak disclosed distant views of a snowpeak lifting cold and remote to the northeast. Observing it from *Discovery*'s quarterdeck, Vancouver already had named it Mount St. Helens, for the British ambassador to Spain. The river narrowed to a quarter mile, with a tidal rise and fall Broughton measured at three feet. At the nooning near Reeder's Point, a large party of Indians stopped to trade. Here, too, Broughton parted company with a friendly old chief, probably a Clackamas, who struck out for his village upriver to arrange food and lodging for the white visitors. The cutter proceeded through fine country—meadows and dells on either bank and, far to the east, "a very distant high snowy mountain rising beautifully conspicuous" out of a broad tract of plain.[27] Declining the Indian's offer, Broughton camped for the night in isolation some miles below the Clackamas village.

By now supplies were running low, although the amiable chief turned up on October 30 with a gift of several fine salmon. As the cutter labored upriver against an increasingly strong current, the same remarkable mountain they had seen yesterday again presented itself. Broughton dubbed it Mount Hood, after the British naval hero Admiral Samuel Hood. As they approached the Cascades, the great gorge the Columbia carves through the mountain barrier on its way to the sea, Broughton consulted with the chief, who reported an impassable falls some distance upstream, explaining, "by taking up water in his hands and imitating the manner of its falling from rocks, pointing, at the same time, to the place where the sun rises." Even with the salmon, Broughton calculated that he could eke out provisions for only another two or three days. By his estimate, he had traveled a hundred miles from *Chatham*'s anchorage.[28]

The sun set at 4:59 on October 30. The moon, a day past full, cast a silvery sheen on the river. Before turning back, Broughton arranged a ceremony ashore. Robert Gray, he concluded, had not sailed into the river at all, only the estuary. The Yankee's sketch map proved it so. Broughton therefore "formally took possession of the river, and the country in its vicinity, in His Britannic Majesty's name," Vancouver wrote, "having every reason to believe, that the subjects of no other civilized nation or state had ever entered this river before." The Clackamas chief, so said Broughton, assisted with the flag-raising and enthusiastically drained a toast to the health of George III.[29]

The cutter swept downriver in the moonlight. Did the friendly chief take Broughton's ceremony seriously? Possibly it struck him as fatuous—a few pale and puny men laying absurd claim to a boundless country. Doubtless he was grateful for the drink. At any rate the chief accompanied the Britons as far as the mouth of the Willamette, the western limit of Clackamas lands. Covering the hundred miles in just three days, Broughton's party arrived alongside *Chatham* at nine o'clock on the evening of November 2. Contrary winds blocked up the tender in Baker Bay for eight days. Finally, on the tenth, a favorable breeze and a strong tide shot her across the churning commotion of the bar. "It appears to be highly adviseable, that no vessel should attempt entering this port, but when the water is perfectly smooth," Broughton wrote with understatement in his report to Vancouver. "A passage may then be effected with safety, but ought even then to be undertaken with caution."[30] In calmer water just beyond the entrance, *Chatham* fell in with HMS *Daedalus*, Vancouver's storeship.

As Boit had before him, Broughton rhapsodized over the Columbia region's potential. A "most excellent green vegetable, that ate much like mealy potatoe," grew wild along the skirts of the woods. Mint, lavender, and cranberry flourished. Supplies of fresh water and wood seemed inexhaustible. The river yielded astounding harvests of fish, prodigious in size and excellent in quality. The Chinooks—the most decorated natives Broughton had yet met, with varicolored body paints, feathers, and other ornaments—were hospitable and avid to trade. The soil, too, he felt certain, could be made productive.[31]

With Broughton's expedition, the Americans and the British had posted competing claims to the vast expanse of the Pacific Northwest. The area in contention would encompass all of present Oregon and Washington and parts of Idaho, Wyoming, Montana, and British Columbia. Robert Gray, the dour Yankee trader, and William Broughton, the obscure British naval officer, nonentities both, sailed away from the misty coasts of the Columbia in 1792, never to return. They had no way of knowing, of course, how it would all end. But the breathtaking effrontery of their claims set in motion events of fateful consequence, touching off half a century of trade and diplomatic rivalry, a flood of Euroamerican settlement, and the displacement and virtual destruction of the immemorial inhabitants of what the contestants would come to call the Oregon Country.

1

Ways West

COLUMBIA HAD BEEN sometimes a sullen ship, though invariably a lucky one; John Jacob Astor's *Tonquin* sailed into a nightmare, with a murderous and delusional martinet for a captain. Well launched upon his rise to becoming America's richest man, Astor in the summer of 1810 outfitted *Tonquin* for a voyage around Cape Horn to the Pacific Northwest, where his advance agents were to establish a depot at the mouth of the Columbia River for the collection of Rocky Mountain furs for the China market. A hard and canny buccaneer, Astor meant to challenge and ultimately dominate the two British Canadian trapping and trading firms, the 140-year-old Hudson's Bay Company and its parvenu rival, the North West Company. He dispatched two expeditions to the Oregon Country in 1810: a party of overlanders under the New Jersey merchant Wilson Price Hunt and the shipborne contingent in the star-crossed *Tonquin*.

Trade and wealth were Astor's obsessions, and he had an instinctive feel for the precise points at which his interests and those of the United States might intersect. His hired memorialist Washington Irving would write in 1836 that Astor intended the Columbia outpost as "the germ of a wide civilization" that would attract settlers from the United States. Astor may or may not have been aware of the dictum of the geographer Thomas Hutchins, an early prophet of American transcontinental destiny. "If we want it, I warrant it will soon be ours," Hutchins said in 1784, the same year, coincidentally, that the

17

German-born Astor arrived in the United States. Robert Gray had staked the first American claim to the Oregon Country with *Columbia*'s reconnaissance of the estuary of the great river in May 1792. A party from George Vancouver's British exploring expedition trumped the Americans in October of that year, venturing a hundred miles upriver and raising the British standard. In 1805–1806, the Lewis and Clark transcontinental expedition wintered over near the mouth of the Columbia, the second American penetration of "the Oregon of the Spaniards." Now Astor's American Fur Company aimed to plant a trading colony there, the first permanent white presence in the region.[1]

With foreigners controlling the fur trade in U.S. territory on the upper Mississippi and Missouri Rivers, Astor complained that he had to travel to Montreal to buy American pelts to sell to his U.S. customers—with a substantial markup to cover British profits and his own added expenses. Lewis and Clark having shown the way, Astor proposed a line of trading forts from the Missouri to the Pacific. He sought the U.S. government's blessing and assistance, adumbrating the prospect of a Pacific empire in return. "The intention is to carry on the trade so extensively that it may in time embrace the greater part of the fur trade on this continent," he wrote President Thomas Jefferson early in 1808. "Every exertion shall be made to forward the wishes of the government in these relations with the Indians & it is believed that the trade will in time . . . have advantages to the country." Jefferson responded with enthusiasm: "You may be assured that in order to get the whole of this business passed into the hands of our own citizens and to oust foreign traders who so much abuse their privileges by endeavoring to excite the Indians to war on us every reasonable facility & patronage in the power of the Executive will be afforded." Astor chartered the American Fur Company in April 1808 with the goal of forcing the British out of the fur trade and establishing a monopoly of his own.[2]

Initially Astor proposed a partnership on the Columbia with the North West Company. When the North Westers rebuffed him, he hired away a legion of the company's experienced traders and prepared to go it alone, setting up a subsidiary, the Pacific Fur Company, for the purpose. In the early days of the trade, Americans exchanging Pacific Northwest furs for Canton silks, tea, nankeens, and porcelain had returned home with fabulous profits—"an average clear gain of a thousand per cent every second year," according to one of Astor's new

John Jacob Astor, America's first tycoon. Astor's trading emporium on the Columbia established a firm U.S. claim to the Oregon Country. Washington Irving would memorialize the fur trading enterprise in *Astoria* (1836). (Library of Congress)

employees, the ex-North Wester Alexander Ross. So the prize glittered. Astor himself advanced the start-up capital, $200,000 out of his own copper-bottomed assets, and agreed to bear all expenses and losses for the first five years. Oddly for so pawky an operator, he chose Hunt, a man with no experience of the wilds, to lead the overland voyage and assigned the former North Wester Alexander McKay, a veteran of trapper-explorer Alexander Mackenzie's epic march across Canada to the Pacific in 1792–1793, to command the *Tonquin* party.[3]

Hunt's overlanders set out from Lachine near Montreal in early July 1810. Two separate parties of partners, clerks, mechanics, and voyageurs pushed south from the St. Lawrence in bark canoes, bound for New York City via Lake Champlain and the Hudson. The second band of Canadians reached the metropolis on August 4, taking the inland passage along the eastern shore of Manhattan Island to their lodgings in Brooklyn. The voyageurs in their piebald uniform—blanket coat, striped shirt, leather leggings, and deerskin moccasins—created a sensation. "We sang as we rowed," Gabriel Franchère, one of the clerks, wrote in his journal; the singing and the novelty of the canoes drew dense crowds to the water's edge to catch a glimpse of these wild exotics of the forest.[4]

Astor's people and Captain Jonathan Thorn, the master of *Tonquin*, clashed from the outset. A U.S. Navy officer on half-pay leave, the thirty-three-year-old Thorn struck the Astorians as violent, rigid, secretive, and peevish. "He was accustomed to exact obedience, being obeyed at the smallest demand," Franchère observed, "and was concerned with duty only." To Ross, he went out of his way to make everyone packed into the ninety-four-foot-long ship as miserable as he allowed himself to be. Even Irving, who out of loyalty to Astor attempted a published defense of the captain, called him "dry and dictatorial." As for Thorn, he stigmatized his passengers as dirty, boastful, noisy, lazy, and lax about discipline—in a word, *lubberly*. The journal-keeping habits of Ross and Franchère particularly grated on him. "The collecting of material for long histories of their voyages and travels appears to engross most of their attention," Thorn wrote Astor. And the Scots aboard tormented him by murmuring conspiratorially among themselves in Gaelic, raising the specter of mutiny in the captain's mind.[5]

Perhaps anticipating trouble, Astor advised Thorn before *Tonquin* sailed to take care to promote harmony aboard. "To prevent any misunderstanding will require your particular good management," he wrote. But the captain made scant effort to restrain himself when McKay, as head of the traders, challenged him for assigning the five Astorian mechanics to berths with the common seamen. They were passengers, McKay insisted, not foremast jacks. Thorn informed McKay that "he would blow out the brains of the first man who dared to disobey his orders on board his own ship," according to Alexander Ross. This set the tone for the entire voyage—rankling hatred between the partners and the psychotic Captain Thorn.[6]

Tonquin, 269 tons, pierced for 22 guns (but carrying only 10), with 21 crewmen and 33 passengers, warped away from the wharf on the morning of September 6, 1810, and floated out into the stream. The wind died presently, leaving the ship adrift under limp sails off Staten Island and unable to make an offing. A fitful southwesterly breeze finally carried *Tonquin* out to sea. With rumors of an armed brig from British Halifax lying just over the horizon, Astor had asked the senior naval officer in New York City for an escort to see his investment safely away. Franchère and Ross recalled that *Tonquin* sailed in company with the frigate USS *Constitution* for a day or so as a precaution against an encounter with the British vessel, which Astor supposed to be a North West Company hireling.[7]

In the event, the brig failed to appear. To Thorn's disgust, the restless heaving of the ship caused an epidemic of seasickness among the Canadians. Miserable and disoriented, others fell victim to the blue devils. "I found myself sailing on the open sea with nothing between the depths of the water and the immensity of the sky on which to fix my eye or attract my attention except the frail machine that bore me," wrote Franchère. "For a long time I remained with my eyes straining toward the coastline that I could no longer see and that I despaired of ever seeing again."[8] *Tonquin* struck the trades on October 4. The next morning, lookouts reported a distant view of the Cape Verde Islands to the northwest. The ship wallowed in a dead calm all day on the eighth. The men captured a shark and made a meal of it; Franchère thought it ate like sturgeon. The sun bore down with an intensity the Canadians had never before experienced, the mercury reaching 108°F on October 16. *Tonquin* crossed the equator six burning days later. Conditions gradually turned cool and rainy as the ship dropped down the map. Beginning on November 10, hard gales damaged the rigging and started several leaks. Scarcely had that fifty-hour storm blown itself out when a second struck, a true widow-maker, dismounting six guns (for a time, they rolled about on deck like thunder, according to Ross) and sending the people below to the pumps. With water running short, Thorn reduced the ration to three gills a day (about three-quarters of a pint), torture for hard-worked men on a salt-meat diet. He altered course for the Falklands so the water casks could be refilled and greenstuff taken aboard.

Tonquin dropped anchor between two bald, treeless islands on December 4. The second mate, John Mumford, led a detail ashore in search of water. He found none, though he did return with several geese and two seals. With the barometer falling, Thorn stood out to sea that evening. He discovered a safe anchorage on the sixth—Port Egmont, as it turned out. Shore parties reported a flowing spring of freshwater and abundant geese, duck, seals, and penguin eggs. One group came upon the headboards of the graves of two British whalers, the names almost obliterated. The men set to recarving them. Another scythed grass for the ship's livestock. Two of the Astor partners, Duncan McDougall and David Stuart, moved off in search of game. Then, quite without warning, Thorn flashed out the order to embark.[9]

The shore detachments did not respond to the summons promptly enough to satisfy Thorn. He ordered *Tonquin* to weigh and sailed off, stranding McDougall, Stuart, McKay, the clerks Franchère and Ross, and three or four others. The castaways raced down to the beach, wrestled the launch into the surf, and began to row furiously. An hour passed, then another. Robert Stuart, a nephew of David Stuart, persuaded himself that Thorn really intended to maroon the men. Drawing two pistols, he confronted the captain on his holy quarterdeck and demanded that he put ship about. According to Thorn, the wind shifted providentially just then and *Tonquin* lost way. Stuart sheathed the pistols. The launch closed fast and McDougall and the others heaved themselves aboard. To the end, Thorn insisted he had intended to abandon them in the Falklands, as an encouragement to the others.[10]

"Had the wind (unfortunately) not hauled ahead soon after leaving the harbor's mouth, I should positively have left them," he wrote Astor.[11]

After ten days of fog, rain, and piercing cold, Thorn doubled Cape Horn on Christmas Day. Curving northward into the Pacific, *Tonquin* caught favorable winds and sped on a great spread of sail into the new year of 1811. Fishing from the rail, the men caught several large tuna on January 17. The ship crossed the equator on the twenty-third. Thorn made landfall on February 11, raising Mauna Loa volcano on the island of Hawaii in what were then known as the Sandwich Islands, and in due course *Tonquin* glided to anchor in Kealakekua Bay. Natives in outriggers raced alongside with cabbages, yams, watermelons, and poultry for sale. Franchère, Ross, and others ventured ashore. A Hawaiian guide led them to the place where islanders had killed Captain Cook in an argument over a small boat on the same date thirty-two years before. Franchère noted the coincidence, then— to be on the safe side—returned to the ship.

With trade in pork a royal monopoly, the Hawaiian king's representative on Hawaii advised Thorn to sail for the capital on Oahu and negotiate for hogs there. A double pirogue with a crew of twenty-four ferried the king himself to *Tonquin*'s anchorage in the roadstead opposite Waikiki. Tall, robust, running to fat, and majestic of carriage, King

Kamehameha I wore European clothes and carried a sword at his side. The traders' dealings with the king, especially the pretensions of the vain, rank-conscious Duncan McDougall, spurred Thorn to new heights of churlishness. "It would be difficult to imagine the frantic gambols that are daily played off here," he wrote Astor; "sometimes dressing in red coats, and otherwise very fantastically, and collecting a number of ignorant natives around them, telling them that they are the great eris of the Northwest, and making arrangements for sending three or four vessels yearly to them from the coast with spars &c.; while those very natives cannot even furnish a hog to the ship."[12] True, Kamehameha did drive a shrewd bargain for meat, demanding payment in Spanish dollars because he wanted to buy a frigate from his brother, King George of England, to protect his coasting fleet of small schooners. Thorn took aboard a hundred hogs, some goats and sheep, poultry, and a quantity of sugarcane for fodder. To work off his bile, he had two sailors flogged for overstaying shore leave by a few minutes. A third hand, absent overnight, appeared the next day to accept his flogging; instead, Thorn had him thrown overside. Islanders fished him unconscious from the sea and returned him to the ship. Thorn refused to allow him aboard.

Tonquin departed the Sandwich Islands on March 1, 1811. Inky clouds piled up to the northeast, and the weather turned cold and stormy. Thorn denied the Astorians' request to break out warm clothing stowed with the cargo, this latest outrage touching off a mutinous colloquy in Gaelic. Cape Disappointment advanced into the sea out of a thin curtain of rain on March 22. With seas tumbling violently over the bar, Thorn called for a boat to be lowered and sent the first mate, Ebenezer Fox, and four men to reconnoiter a passage. Irving speculated that Thorn chose Fox as punishment for alleged slackness earlier in the voyage. McKay interceded, urging Thorn to recall Fox. This probably sealed the first mate's doom. He pushed off, and within moments the boat vanished into the mists.

The wind dropped, and the skies cleared on the twenty-fourth. The shock of Fox's misadventure lingered, though, and the early spring sun failed to burn off the pall that hovered over *Tonquin*. The deserted shore looked forbidding and hostile. "The country is low," Ross noted with disquiet, "and the impervious forests give to the surrounding coast a wild and gloomy aspect."[13] A chaotic sea continued to pound over the bar. Thorn sent Mumford in the longboat to sound a channel; he judged the surf too heavy and retreated to the ship. McKay and David Stuart then took to the boat to search for Fox but could find no safe place to land.

With a shift of the wind to the northwest, Thorn plotted a fresh assault on the entrance. The pinnace led the way, *Tonquin* following under light sail. The ship scraped bottom half a dozen times, breakers lifting and crashing over the stern as though in time with each bump. The breeze died with the ebb, and night closed in with *Tonquin* still caught upon the bar. Light airs sprang up out of the offing on the first of the flood and carried the ship into Baker Bay without further incident. Thorn anchored in the lee of Cape Disappointment at about midnight. Of the pinnace and its crew of five there was no trace.

Ross and others alleged later that Thorn had deliberately refused to stop as *Tonquin* swept past the pinnace on the approach to the passage. The captain himself took a search party ashore, returning presently with a sailor named Stephen Weeks. Mountainous waves had overturned the boat, according to Weeks. Clinging to the hull, Weeks and two of the Sandwich Islanders righted it with the last reserves of their strength and hauled themselves aboard. One of the islanders died at about midnight. At first light Weeks, somewhat recovered, manhandled the boat through the surf and onto the beach. After a short rest, he wandered along an Indian path for several hours before encountering Thorn. Searchers eventually found the surviving islander on the beach, half dead with cold and fatigue. The two others in the boat's crew were presumed dead, bringing to eight the number of fatalities chargeable to Thorn's attempts to enter the river.

With a Clatsop Indian guide, Thorn, McKay, and David Stuart pushed upriver in the longboat to scout a site for the trading post. The other partners remained on board *Tonquin*, doing business with Chinooks peddling sea otter and beaver skins. Despite prodding from Thorn, who seethed with impatience to land his cargo and be off, McKay and Stuart found nothing suitable along the northern bank. McDougall and David Stuart with several clerks set out on April 4 for a reconnaissance of the southern shore. They settled provisionally on a site at Point George (now Smith Point) seven miles from the river's mouth. After a courtesy call at the northern bank village of the paramount Chinook chief, Concomly, the party shoved off for the return to the ship, a Chinook canoe following at a discreet distance. A gale sprang up suddenly and—nobody could say later quite how it happened—the boat capsized, spilling its contents into the chop.

From the first, Ross had observed the Chinook watermen with something approaching awe. Robert Stuart flatly called them "the most expert paddle men any of us had ever seen." Their canoes, too, had a suggestion of classical purity about them. "If perfect symmetry, smoothness and proportion constitute beauty," he wrote, "they surpass anything I ever beheld." Even Irving regarded them with respect. "They seem," he reported in *Astoria*, "to ride the waves like sea fowl." The Indians were indifferent to the cold and as comfortable in the water as out of it. They so impressed Ross, in fact, that he half-seriously accused them of staging the accident. When the canoe tipped over, four of the Chinooks slid silently into the river, rounded up the eight flailing passengers, helped them back aboard, and steered the vessel safely to shore.[14]

"The Indians all the time never lost their presence of mind," Ross remarked. "Instead, it was supposed, from the skillful manner in which they acted afterward, that the sordid rascals had upset us willfully, in order to claim the merit of having saved us, and therewith a double recompense for their trip."[15]

A contingent from *Tonquin* landed at the bottom of a small bay along the southern edge of Point George and pitched camp in a grassy area near a stand of trees just coming into leaf. "We imagined ourselves in an earthly paradise—the forests looked like pleasant groves, the leaves like brilliant flowers," Franchère wrote in his journal.[16] It was a commanding site, the estuary here narrowing to six miles in width, with a usable harbor. The men set about taking down trees, clearing away the underwood, and burning stumps. *Tonquin* came up and anchored in the bay. Thorn landed ready-cut frame timbers from the ship and by the end of April the artisans had laid the keel of *Dolly*, a thirty-ton coasting schooner.

As the exhilaration of arrival wore off, visions of paradise dissolved in the muscle-tearing reality of the work at hand. The forest crowded in on the site, stupendous firs of astonishing girth. "Incredible as it may appear," wrote Robert Stuart, "we found some of them 7 and 9 fathoms in circumference, and 250 to 300 feet long."[17] Even with four men to a team, it sometimes took two days to fell a single tree. Stumps had to be blown apart with gunpowder, roots grubbed out by

The Astorians marveled at the girth of Oregon's rain forest pines. "Incredible as it may appear," wrote Robert Stuart, "we found some of them 7 and 9 fathoms in circumference, and 250 to 300 feet long." (Library of Congress)

hand. According to Ross, the people were two months in clearing *one* acre. Falling trees badly injured two men, and an accidental detonation of powder destroyed the hand of a third. Ross found the climate enervating: cool, overcast, rain every other day. The post's Hawaiian gardeners planted Indian corn, potatoes, turnips, and greens; the Astorians subsisted in the meantime on a monotonous diet of ship's fare, salmon and boiled camas, a native root staple—farinaceous, nutritive, with a faint taste of licorice. From mid-June, wild fruit came into more or less constant supply: white strawberries ("small but delectable," Franchère thought), then red and orange raspberries, and eventually currants and cranberries.[18] McDougall, irascible and aloof, dined in state off private stocks he had carried out from New York, Ross claimed, while everyone else looked on hungrily. There were rumors of an uprising, talk of returning to the States. Four men deserted, were taken captive upstream, and had to be ransomed from the natives.

Indians milled about the encampment, touching off confrontations and, according to Ross, a number of assaults. The Astorians lived in a constant state of apprehension. The dripping woods were haunted and sinister, so thickly grown that a man could barely see a hundred yards ahead. Ross blamed some of the trouble on the friendly Chinooks, suspecting them—rightly, as it happened—of turning the hinterland bands against the whites to reserve the trade for themselves. Still, he had confidence in Concomly, the Chinook chief. Rising fifty in 1811, one-eyed, quick-minded, tenacious of memory, wealthy, holding immense authority over the estuarine tribes, Concomly had been openhanded with Lewis and Clark in 1805 and seemed to regard the arrival of Astor's party as a business opportunity rather than an invasion.

Reports reached the Astorians that a party of white traders, doubtless North Westers, had established an outpost up the Columbia beyond a distant rapids. In early May, therefore, the Clatsop subchief Coalpo led McKay, Robert Stuart, and a small band upstream on a reconnaissance. Like William Broughton twenty years before, Franchère found the Willamette region charming: groves of oaks and poplar, spring wildflowers in bloom, glimpses of the prairie through a screen of trees. They approached fast water on May 8 just above the place Lewis and Clark dubbed Strawberry Island. Small groups of Indians were harvesting salmon below the falls; the whites amused themselves by shooting seals basking on the rocks. Coalpo refused to push on from there, saying the natives beyond were hostile. The expedition turned back for Point George, arriving on May 14 without having confirmed the existence of the rival post.

The traders laid the foundations of their first building, sixty feet long and twenty-six feet wide, on May 16 and christened the place Astoria two days later. Work parties finished unloading the ship under Thorn's surly glare. With McKay and two other traders aboard, *Tonquin* weighed on June 1 and dropped down to Baker Bay to await a breeze that would vault her over the bar. Nobody mourned Thorn's departure. Even so, the Astorians, alone ashore now, felt vulnerable, for no guns had been mounted nor palisades raised as yet, although work progressed satisfactorily on the barracks, storehouse, and powderhouse.

In mid-June two Indian messengers—both women, it turned out, although one dressed like and attempted to pass as a man—arrived with a note from the North Westers. The rumors evidently had foundation in fact; the British were on the ground, perhaps in force. McDougall decided to send a trading party under David Stuart up the Columbia as far as the Spokan country to establish a rival station. Stuart at once began to prepare for the mission, and by July 15 he was ready to set out. Just before he embarked, someone sighted a large and stylish canoe dashing around Tongue Point and bearing for the fort. The canoe carried the legendary trader-mapmaker David Thompson with a crew of seven voyageurs and two Indian guides. The Union Jack streamed out from the stern.

For Thompson, who had immigrated to Canada as a Hudson's Bay Company clerk in 1784, arrival marked the completion of the greatest of his wilderness journeys: twelve hundred miles down the Columbia from near its source in an upland lake in what is now southeastern British Columbia. Born in 1770 in London of Welsh parents, his speech in midlife still showed traces of Cambrian cadences. His widowed mother entered him for the navy but he signed articles with the Hudson's Bay Company instead, his London charity school paying five pounds for a seven-year apprenticeship. Thompson served the company at Churchill Factory and elsewhere in the Canadian interior until 1797, when he defected to the North Westers. The Lewis and Clark expedition and then the Astor venture rekindled the North West Company's interest in the Oregon Country. Thompson had discovered the true source of the Columbia on an 1807 expedition. Now he set out to become the first European to scud down the length of the great river from its headwaters to the Pacific.

Thompson had marched with twenty-four men in late 1810 for a treacherous winter crossing of the Rockies. Warlike Piegan Indians barred him from Howse Pass, so he struck northward in a long deviation for the defiles of the Athabasca River. A number of his voyageurs lost heart and drifted away. The remainder passed most of December on the eastern flank of the Rockies near the entrance to present Jasper National Park. The ascent began on December 30. The mercury dropped to twenty-six degrees below zero, too cold for the pack animals, so Thompson shifted the provender to dogsleds and turned the horses loose. He reached Athabasca Pass at six thousand feet above sea level on January 10, 1811. One of the men probed the snowpack with a twenty-foot-long pole, vainly seeking soil or rock. "I told him while we had good snowshoes it was no matter to us whether the snow was ten or one hundred feet deep," he wrote in his journal. Such assurances, no matter how rational, no longer appeased the people. Cold, eternal snows, fear of the unknown, even the towering fissured pines of the western slope: the eerie silence and the alpen strangeness unnerved them. Another five men petitioned for their release and retraced their steps eastward.[19]

The expedition wintered on the Wood River, sheltering in a snow hut reinforced with split cedar sides. Thompson oversaw the construction of a cedar canoe, its components stitched together with thread spun from pine roots. With the advent of spring he gathered the little band together for the downriver voyage, pushing out into Clark's Fork River, a Columbia tributary, on June 5, 1811. Three days later he commenced the long portage that led to Kettle Falls, reaching this landmark on the present Washington–British Columbia line on the nineteenth. Here the people—five métis, two Iroquois, and two local Indians—built a canoe large and sturdy enough for the descent to the sea.

High water and a racing current swept the voyageurs downstream. They logged seventy miles the first day, July 3, traversing agreeable country, thinly wooded with broad short-grass meadows that Thompson judged excellent for sheep. On the ninth, the expedition passed the mouth of the Snake; just below, the Columbia widened out to nearly nine hundred yards bank to bank. Thompson came ashore briefly to parley with a band of Wallawalla Indians. When they asked him to put up a trading post at the site, the self-consciously imperial North Wester nailed a proclamation to a tree pegging out a British claim to the country. Thompson caught sight later that afternoon of "a high mountain, isolated, of a conical form, a mass of pure snow without the appearance of a rock"—the dormant volcano Broughton had called Mount Hood.[20]

They approached a major rapids on July 12, the paddlemen maneuvering skillfully along a stretch of river forced between high basalt walls rising at right angles to the course of the stream. "These breaks formed rude bays," he noted; "under each point was a violent eddy, and each bay was a powerful dangerous whirlpool." Thompson had reached The Dalles, the Columbia there contracting to a width of sixty yards. He had experienced nothing like it in a quarter century in the wilds. "Imagination can hardly form an idea of the working of this immense body of water under such a compression, raging and hissing as if alive," he marveled. The north bank Wishrams and the Wascos of the south bank, traders and tollkeepers of The Dalles, impressed him as physically different, too, from the Plateau tribes, as though an ethnic as well as geographical frontier had been crossed. "They are

Three Native Americans along the shore of The Dalles, the Indian trading mart above the Columbia River Gorge. A gorge and rapids made the river unnavigable here until the end of the nineteenth century, when a canal and locks opened. This image dates from around 1855. (Library of Congress)

not so tall as the tribes above the rapids," he noted, "but strongly built, brawny, fat people." The voyageurs steered for shore and hauled the canoe out of the maelstrom, carrying craft and contents along a well-trodden path to calmer water a mile downstream. Thompson noted that the country here was softer in appearance and greener. He camped for the night near a Wasco settlement of log houses and divided two fat salmon among the people for dinner.[21]

Rounding Tongue Point, the North Westers glimpsed the broad, shining Pacific opening out before them. Thompson thought they seemed disappointed somehow. "Accustomed to the boundless horizon of the Great Lakes of Canada, they expected a more boundless view, a something beyond the power of their senses which they could not describe," he decided. At Point George, four low log huts huddled together in a rough clearing—"the far-famed Fort Astoria of the United States," Thompson, perhaps a bit let down himself, remarked with a tinge of sarcasm. The canoe nudged gently into the mud and he stepped ashore, the voyageurs, a rough-and-ready honor guard, making way for him deferentially.[22]

Thompson's journals reveal no hint that he regarded the Astorian presence as a setback. The Canadian scholar Arthur S. Morton has argued that the North West Company had aspired to dominate the lower Columbia at least since 1801, and that word of the Astor venture lent renewed urgency to Thompson's task. Morton faults him for "mistaken leisureliness and misjudgements" in his choice of route and in failing to negotiate a safe passage at Howse Pass or, failing that, to brush the bristling Piegans aside. The delay, Morton claimed, cost the North West Company—and Britain—the chance to be first in the field at the mouth of the Columbia.[23]

Thompson evidently believed that the much-discussed North Wester–Astor joint venture had finally gone through. He suggested as much to Duncan McDougall—that the North Westers were trading partners rather than business rivals. A shrewd operator, Thompson may have been practicing upon the Astorians, bluffing to cover his tardy arrival; or he may simply have been relying on outdated information. Whatever the case, McDougall greeted his old trader colleague like a long-lost brother. "Nothing was too good for Mr. Thompson," wrote Ross; "he had access everywhere; saw and examined everything; and whatever he asked for he got, as if he had been one of ourselves." Thompson wrote dismissively of Astoria in his journal; the site lay exposed and difficult to defend, and he judged the Astorians' stock of trade goods as low in quality, though doubtless "good enough for the beggarly natives about them." As it happened, Ross agreed, blaming Astor—a vulpine trader who ought to have known better and probably did—for the post's inventory of old metal pots (instead of guns), white cotton (instead of beads), and molasses (instead of blankets). "In short," he complained, "all the useless trash and unsaleable trumpery which had been accumulating in his shops and stores for half a century past were swept together to fill his Columbia shops." Still, Ross regarded Thompson as a commercial and political spy and dismissed the North Wester's warnings of the difficulties of operating in the interior as so much cant—and a feeble effort, too, as most of the Astorians had considerable experience in the backcountry trade. McDougall at any rate opted to go ahead with David Stuart's voyage, arranging for Stuart to travel in company with Thompson as far as the Spokane.[24]

Meanwhile, masses of Indians were assembling in camps along Baker Bay for the summer fishing. A band from the north brought word, nobody knew how reliable, of *Tonquin*. The ship had been destroyed, these Indians reported, together with chief trader McKay, Captain Thorn, and all the crew.

THE ASTORIANS EXHAUSTED the stores landed from *Tonquin* by midsummer. McDougall sought to buy venison from the Clatsops but discovered they were up to all the shifts of bargaining—"the ordinary cost of a stag," according to Gabriel Franchère, "was a blanket, a knife, some tobacco, a little powder, and some balls." The garden looked beautiful, yet except for radishes, potatoes, and turnips, nothing matured. In compensation, the turnips grew big as pumpkins, up to thirty-three inches in circumference and fifteen pounds in weight. All the same, these were anxious weeks as the river tribes gathered. The departure of David Stuart's expedition left the post shorthanded. The Astorians suspended all regular business to concentrate on strengthening the fort's defenses, throwing up a ninety-foot-square stockade with two bastions each mounting two four-pounder guns. McDougall launched a diplomatic offensive as well. Convening a council of the chiefs, he flashed a vial that he claimed contained smallpox and threatened to draw the cork should Astoria come under attack. (No idle threat: the British commander Henry Bouquet had distributed pox-infected blankets to Ohio Valley tribes during Pontiac's Rebellion fifty years earlier.) Disease had greatly reduced the coastal tribes since first contact with Europeans—by some estimates, tribal populations were down one-third to one-half by the first decade of the nineteenth century. The Indians felt obliged to take the man they now denominated "the great smallpox chief" at his word.[25]

The barracks were finished in late September, *Dolly* slid into the river on October 2, and on the fifth, three men returned from the interior to report the founding of a trading post on the Okanogan River some six hundred miles northeast of Astoria. David Stuart's party built a sixteen-by-twenty-foot factory out of driftwood and, according to Ross, extracted a promise from the local chiefs "to be always our friends, to kill us plenty of beavers and to furnish us at all times with provisions."[26] But there had been no sign of Wilson Price Hunt's overlanders, no word from Hunt or any of his band. And the Indians were withdrawing to their winter quarters inland now, leaving the Astorians isolated and facing famine.

With the coming of the rains, the scribblers Captain Thorn had so despised were at leisure to bring their journals up to date. Ross, Franchère, and Stuart closely observed the Native Americans of the lower Columbia and set down reports dense with ethnographic detail, much of it accurate. Even when sympathetic, though, the Astorians' accounts presented the native culture as static and primitive: Indian ways did not accord with the whites' notions of progress. The Chinooks, Clatsops, Clackamas, and the others no doubt found the traders just as compelling a study; unfortunately, they left no written record of their impressions. Accounts of weird customs, quaint rituals and beliefs, and outlandish apparel lay mostly on one side. Clatsop ethnographers did not record, for example, their reaction to the appearance of Duncan McDougall in one of the great eri costumes that had so appalled Captain Thorn at Waikiki. In the Pacific Northwest in the year 1811, the ability to shape perceptions and ultimately, perhaps, events lay with the Euroamericans and their powerful written language.

Robert Stuart noted that Captain Gray's 1792 excursion into the river had passed into Chinook folk legend. Word of *Columbia*'s appearance spread rapidly, causing surprise at first, then panic and dread when the ship ghosted over the treacherous bar. All but a few old people fled the riverfront villages. Wrote Stuart, "Some imagined that the ship must be some overgrown monster come to devour them, while others supposed her to be a floating island inhabited by cannibals, sent by the great spirit to destroy them and ravage their country." (Events in due course would show this initial suspicion to have been dolefully close to the mark.) A boat's crew from *Columbia* landed and, distributing presents, soon assuaged the old people's fears. Post-*Columbia* traders reported that shipwrecked Spanish sailors evidently had once lived among the coastal tribes. But the Chinooks told Stuart that Gray's men were the first whites they had encountered. Traders and Indians met fairly frequently after 1792. Then Lewis and Clark materialized from beyond the mountains in the autumn of 1805 and wintered among the hospitable Clatsops. By 1811 the estuarine bands were long accustomed to doing business with whites.[27]

Alexander Ross counted ten distinct tribes in the vicinity of the mouth of the Columbia, mustering a total of perhaps two thousand warriors. "All these tribes appear to be descended from the same stock, live in rather friendly intercourse with, and resemble one another in language, dress, and habits," he wrote. "Their origin, like that of the other aborigines of the continent, is involved in fable, although they pretend to be derived from the musk-rat." Stuart concluded that no two tribes spoke the same tongue, although each seemed to understand that of its neighbors on either side; thus each tribe "may be said to comprehend three different languages." All the lingual variants were "filled with gutturals like those of the Scottish Highlanders," Franchère remarked. The coastal tribes seemed, even before the regular visits of whites, to be declining in population.[28]

The native men were muscular, well made, and strong, but not tall. They let their thick black hair grow long, wearing it pleated or wound in tresses. Compulsively smooth-chinned, they plucked out such whiskers as appeared and deemed it "uncouth to have a beard, calling the whites by way of reproach long beards," according to Stuart. In summer the men often went about naked; in winter, they wore a loose skin garment draped over the body like a shift. They sallied forth in all weathers without shirt, leggings, or shoes. Concomly and some of the subchiefs dressed resplendently in robes of luminous sea otter. A broad-brimmed, cone-shaped hat of coarse grass, woven tight enough to be waterproof, surmounted the heads of men of all classes. For battle, warriors donned as body armor a vest made of round sticks the length and thickness of arrow shafts.[29]

Franchère found the men to be patient and industrious artisans. They worked with the simplest of tools, such as a two-inch chisel wrought from an old file and an oblong stone for a hammer. Wrote Franchère, "With these wretched instruments and some wedges made of hemlock knots, oiled and hardened by firing, they cut down cedars twenty-four to thirty feet in circumference, dig them out, and fashion them into canoes; or they split and transform them into beams and planks for their houses." He judged their workmanship first-rate. Ornaments such as the human or animal heads carved on the prows of canoes could be fiercely beautiful.[30]

Each village answered to its chief, chosen according to his wealth in wives, slaves, and goods. The head man presided over a portable settlement of long, narrow dwellings built of cedar. Three or four families inhabited a lodge, their quarters divided by partitions. A fire burned day and night in the middle of the building, smoke venting through an opening at the ridgepole. With the coming of spring the coastal tribes dismantled their winter villages and carried them down to the river, recycling the beams and planks to construct square sheds for drying and curing fish, roots, and berries. The movable villages were sovereign. Tribal councils settled intervillage disputes with a payment of tribute, although in more serious cases—murder or the theft of a woman—war would sometimes break out. Battles were stylized affairs with Stone Age weaponry, even if they were fierce enough in their way. When one or two men had been killed the fighting ended, the victor compensating the vanquished with gifts of slaves or other property.

Ross described the native women as stout and flabby, with handsome features, fair complexions, and prominent eyes. Along with a skin shift like the men's, they wore a fringed cedar-bark petticoat that fell from the waist to the knees. Ross found it simple, practical, and titillating. "It does not screen nature from the prying eye," he wrote. "In a calm the sails lie close to the mast, metaphorically speaking, but when the wind blows the bare poles are seen."[31] The women customarily applied fish oil to their hair and skin (it kept off mosquitoes and other stinging insects), and sometimes painted their bodies with red clay. For ornament, they favored metal wrist and ankle bracelets, glass beads (preferably blue), and three- or four-inch-long white shells (*haiqua* in the whites' transliteration). The latter served as currency as well, at an exchange rate of a six-foot-long string of shells for ten beaver skins.

Slaves drew the heaviest work. In the Chinook division of labor the women were more active than the men in trade, and they also carried water and wood, cured fish, collected camas and baked it in loaves, preserved fruit, and wove mats and baskets. To prepare fresh fish, a woman plunked a red-hot stone into a square cedar kettle filled with water. She dropped in the fish at the boil and covered the kettle with rush mats to trap the steam. (The Astorians commended this method of cooking salmon, although they noted that overindulgence in the rich, fatty fish caused an explosive diarrhea.) The women closely and affectionately attended their young, often to their cost. "Children are suckled at the breast till their second or third year," observed Ross, "and the mother, in consequence, becomes an old hag at the age of thirty-five." Stuart characterized Chinook and Clatsop women—the younger ones, anyway—as inconstant, although he did not elaborate. Ross, either more scandalized than Stuart or more inclined to gossip (perhaps both), found them coarsely sensuous and shameless. Suitors could scarcely afford to be scrupulous about a potential bride's past. "It must be admitted that few marriages would occur if the young men wished to marry only chaste young women, for girls have no qualms about their conduct and their parents give them complete liberty in that respect," Franchère wrote. (The Indians in this at least did not differ greatly from the whites. By some estimates fully a third of early nineteenth-century American brides were pregnant on their wedding day.) But once a marriage had been contracted, the spouses remained faithful. Adultery was rare—and punishable, for offending women, by death.[32]

No traveler to the lower Columbia failed to mention the coastal tribes' most striking physical characteristic. As a matter of common practice, a mother placed her baby's head into a wooden press, leaving the contraption in place long enough for "a ridge [to be] raised from ear to ear, giving the head the form of a wedge," wrote Ross. "The more acute the angle, the greater the beauty," he went on. The result shocked many whites at first, although Ross for one accepted head-flattening with cosmopolitan tolerance. "All nations have their peculiar prejudices," he remarked. "The law of the land compels a South-Sea Islander to pull out a tooth; a northern Indian cuts a joint off his finger; national usage obliges a Chinese lady to deform her feet; an English lady, under the influence of fashion, compresses her waist; while a Chinook lady deforms her head." Ross stressed that the coastal Indians alone observed the custom, never those of the interior.[33]

The river tribes organized their lives and rituals around fish. Columbia River salmon—the famous chinook *(Oncorhynchus tshawytscha)*, the best-known of the species and, according to Stuart, "by far the finest fish I ever beheld"—appeared in vast shoals from late May through the middle of August, surging relentlessly upstream toward their spawning grounds in the upper Columbia basin a thousand miles from the Pacific. David Thompson described the reproductive process in detail. "The female with her head cleared away the gravel, and made a hole to deposit her spawn in, perhaps an inch or more in depth by a foot in length; which done, the male then passed over it several times, when both covered the hole up with gravel," he wrote. Citing Salish Indian sources, Thompson reported that no salmon ever returned to the sea. He had seen, in spawning season, the riverbanks covered for miles with lean and gasping fish.[34]

The native fishermen took salmon with what Franchère described as a dart—actually a sort of harpoon, a $\frac{1}{2}$-inch iron point attached to two pieces of curved bone at the end of a shaft—or with nettle-fiber nets 80 to 100 fathoms in length. Individual fishermen generally used hook and line for sturgeon which, although large (the Astorians claimed to have landed one that weighed 390 pounds *after* the eggs and intestines had been removed), rarely put up a struggle. Flotillas of canoes harvested smelt, spearing these fish—most flavorful creatures, Stuart found, "and so fat as to burn like a candle"—on the tines of long wooden rakes.[35] Smelt ran in early spring but traveled only 50 or so miles upstream, so the lower tribes valued it for trade with the interior Indians. Sturgeon, too, were a springtime catch.

Another salmon species, dubbed the "dog-tooth," entered the Columbia in late summer. This fish *(Oncorhynchus keta)* had a double row of sharp teeth, each tooth about $\frac{1}{2}$-inch long, and, remarked Franchère, "a hooked nose like the beak of a parrot."[36] Males used the teeth to fight for a chance to spawn. The Astorians regarded the dog-tooth as inferior owing to its insipid flavor. All the same, the Columbia tribes caught it in vast amounts, smoking and storing it for the winter.

Mystically attached to salmon, the tribes of the Columbia treated it solemnly in sacrament and fetish. They believed that after the Creator set the world in motion a second divinity, sometimes represented as an immense and protean bird, animated men, taught them to make tools and canoes, and caused the salmon to gather so they could collect as many as they needed. The Indians conceived the afterlife, for the virtuous, as a country of abundant fish. They followed a strict and recondite liturgy for the first ten days or so of the salmon run. Fishermen reverently placed sand in the mouth of the first fish caught and rubbed its skin with moss. They then cut it lengthwise and removed the heart and eyes. "Salmon are never allowed to be cut crosswise, nor boiled, but roasted," Ross observed, "nor are they allowed to be sold without the heart first being taken out, nor to be kept overnight; but all must be consumed or eaten the day they are taken out of the water." In the early days at Astoria, the Chinooks and the Clatsops brought the traders only a small number of salmon at a time, "fearing that we would cut them crosswise and believing that if we did so," wrote Franchère, "the river would be obstructed and the fishing useless." The chiefs agreed to supply the Astorians with salmon in quantity only after the Astorians swore to cut it lengthwise, bake it, and not eat any before sunset.[37]

With the autumn dispersal of the tribes, the Astorians were left to shift for themselves. Robert Stuart sailed in *Dolly* to gather rations and trade with the dozen or so Clackamas villages upstream. He returned with little to show for his efforts. Although game seemed plentiful, heavy rains and the denseness of the forest made hunting difficult. Rations remained scanty. In early December, Stuart, a guide, and several voyageurs embarked on a reconnaissance of the Willamette Valley. They regained Astoria in time for a celebration of the new year. The rains ceased, the clouds dissolved, and the sun shone brightly on January 1, 1812, the Astorians marking the holiday and the mild, bright weather with an extra allowance of rum, a three-gun cannon salute at sunrise, another salute at sunset, and an evening of dancing.

TWO CANOES FILLED WITH WHITES approached the post near sunset on January 18—the advance guard, it turned out, of Wilson Price Hunt's long-overdue cross-country expedition. Donald Mackenzie and half a dozen others had split from Hunt's main body at Cauldron Linn on the Snake River in present south-central Idaho. From there the voyage had been a terrible ordeal. For days at a stretch Mackenzie and his men lived on roasted beaver skin and shoe leather. Mackenzie, wasted with hunger, skin hanging in folds, the fat that once quivered along his outsized frame all melted away, brought no word of the fate of the rest of the party. As it happened, Hunt's experiences were even more harrowing than Mackenzie's, if only because he endured them for several weeks longer.

Hunt's itinerary led him from Lachine in Quebec to the fur trading center of Mackinac in the straits connecting the Great Lakes Huron and Michigan, where he paused in the late summer of 1810 to add recruits from the transient community of trappers and woodsmen there. The quality and reliability of the labor pool proved disappointing. Most of the trappers had migrated to the island to recuperate after the rigors of a wilderness winter and were in a playful mood. "In the morning they were found drinking, at noon drunk, and in the night seldom sober," Alexander Ross wrote.[38] Along with the feckless woodsmen, the British-born printer's apprentice turned naturalist Thomas Nuttall, twenty-four years old, joined Hunt at Mackinac. The Philadelphia botanist Benjamin Smith Barton, cataloger of specimens from the Lewis and Clark expedition, sent the energetic but inexperienced Nuttall west to augment the collection with new species from the Great Lakes region and the northern Plains. Nuttall planned to travel with the Astorians into Sioux country, collecting, describing, and categorizing as far as the Great Bend of the Missouri.

Hunt pushed on to St. Louis in August via Green Bay and the Fox, Wisconsin, and Mississippi Rivers. After discharging a number of the French Canadians and replacing them with Americans, he struck north from St. Louis on October 21 in a sundry flotilla of three river craft, one of them a retired Mohawk River transport known as a Schenectady barge. The expedition settled into winter quarters a month later at the mouth of the Nodaway River, some 450 miles up the Missouri.

Nuttall and another British naturalist, John Bradbury, joined Hunt on the Nodaway when the journey resumed in April 1811. An eminent scientist, forty-four years old in 1811, Bradbury was a protégé of the venerable Sir Joseph Banks, for forty years president of the Royal Society and a veteran of Captain Cook's voyage to Tahiti to observe the transit of Venus in 1769. On Thomas Jefferson's recommendation, Bradbury had chosen St. Louis for his operational base. He met Hunt there in the autumn of 1810 and at once accepted the Astorian's offer of a place in the expedition.

Nuttall and Bradbury would be among the first trained scientists to systematically investigate the natural history of the West. Nuttall amused Hunt's Canadians with his antics as a specimen-hunter. He uprooted samples with his gun barrel, and he developed a habit of wandering far afield in his botanizing, trusting to luck and bemused Indians for his safety. "He went groping and stumbling along among a wilderness of sweets, forgetful of everything but his immediate pursuit," Washington Irving wrote of Nuttall. "The Canadian voyageurs used to make merry among themselves at his expense, regarding him as some whimsical kind of madman."[39] They designated him, inevitably, *le fou*, and he rarely disappointed them.

Like the naturalists, the twenty-eight-year-old Hunt had no experience of wilderness travel, although—as Irving noted—he could draw on a secondhand knowledge of the trade and of the Plains Indians from his years as a merchant in St. Louis. And his second-in-command, Mackenzie, a veteran North Wester, was an expert woodsman, even if he did engage in titanic struggles to heave his 300-pound body in and out of the boats. The early stages of the journey passed uneventfully. The party, now in four boats, one mounted with a swivel gun Lewis and Clark style, negotiated a safe passage of Sioux territory and reached the Arikara Villages on June 12.[40] Here Hunt broke the journey for more than a month to negotiate for horses for the overland march to the Wind River country.

The naturalists collected furiously during this interval. Bradbury, a skilled marksman, fired at prairie dogs; like the Columbia River seals, they recognized the flash "and darted with surprising quickness into their holes before the shot could reach them." He and Nuttall carefully observed Arikara manners and customs. Like most whites, Bradbury found native attitudes toward sexual matters jarring. When Mackenzie turned up in a green frock coat, Arikara women offered him sex in exchange for pieces of it. "This occasioned much mirth betwixt us, and on my part a pretended alarm that his coat should become a *spencer*," that is, a woman's garment, Bradbury remarked. Sexual transactions served two purposes, he concluded: they were a mark of hospitality as well as a means by which the Arikaras obtained goods they valued.[41]

In mid-July, Nuttall and Bradbury packed away their skins and specimens—Bradbury alone planned to travel with several thousand living plants—and prepared to turn back for St. Louis. Hunt resumed the westward trek on July 18, 1811, with sixty-one men; Marie l'Ayvoise, the pregnant Iowa Indian wife of his interpreter, Pierre Dorion; and the Dorions' two children. The peaks of the Big Horn Mountains (in present north-central Wyoming) came into view in mid-August. A three-week march brought the Astorians to the Wind River. Crossing the Rockies via Union Pass north of Gannett Peak in the Wind River Range on September 16, they arrived at the landmark of Henry's Fort, a ruined trapper post on a tributary of the Snake River, on October 9.[42]

Here Hunt calculated his next move. Against the advice of the local Indians, he elected to abandon the horses and try a descent of the turbulent Snake in canoes. Some of his own men were skeptical, too: the minor partner Joseph Miller, who had been in a state of barely suppressed rebellion for weeks, now announced his intention to desert Hunt and join a trapper detachment for the winter season. Something of a greenhorn, Miller was unlikely material for a wilderness trapper, but Hunt had no authority to prevent his going, and after a long argument agreed to outfit him with traps, provisions, and horses. Miller thus set out for the beaver streams with the veteran hunters John Hoback, Jacob Rezner, and Edward Robinson. Hunt turned to more urgent tasks, putting some of the people to work building a river fleet while directing others to prepare caches for trade goods and other impedimenta to be left behind.

Inclement weather set in, rain and sleet along the river and snow in the higher elevations. Leaving their seventy-seven horses in the care of two young Snake Indians, the Astorians pushed into the stream in fifteen canoes on October 19. Snow fell all day, the flakes dropping with a hiss into the pale green water. They made good progress: thirty miles the first day, steady going for the next couple of days, and seventy-five miles on October 23. Then the water began to foam, the first intimation of trouble ahead. Obstructions, narrows, and rapids made frequent portages necessary. The Snake entered wild and rocky country; over one two-day stretch, Hunt's band covered just eight miles. When Ramsay Crooks's canoe struck a rock and the powerful current swept a voyageur to his death, Hunt realized he would have to discard the vessels and continue on foot.[43]

The overlanders had reached the Cauldron Linn. The river here ran between two ledges of rock fewer than thirty feet apart, exploding through the cleft with terrific violence. Making camp nearby, Hunt sent a party ahead to scout the river. For forty miles or more the Snake writhed between towering ledges, all falls and rapids; except for one or two places, the scouts reported, it appeared to be impossible to descend from the ridge to the banks. Accidents to the canoes had left Hunt with only five days' rations. He now divided his command, sending detachments off in different directions in search of pack animals and provisions. Donald Mackenzie with five men pushed north and west across the plain. With the main body of thirty-one men plus Dorion's family, Hunt decided to follow the inflexions of the Snake.

The little band advanced painfully over the bare rock of the rift. The Columbia outpost—if it even existed—lay nearly a thousand miles distant still. Winter was approaching. The men had caught and dried a few fish at Cauldron Linn, working the river at night with spears by the light of cedar torches. The tails and bellies of beaver provided further sustenance. Hunt distributed the last of the provender on November 8: 40 pounds of Indian corn, 20 pounds of grease, 5 pounds of gluey portable soup, and 150 pounds of dried meat. Each man carried a 20-pound pack along with his own equipment. The Astorians now divided again. Hunt with half the party marched along the northern bank, following a rocky trace two hundred feet above the river. Crooks led the other half along the southern bank.

They survived only by the good will of itinerant Shoshones. Hunt's men managed to trade every few days for salmon and dog ("well-flavored and hearty," the men found dog meat); in the intervals they subsisted on handfuls of parched corn. Firewood, even sagebrush, was scarce. The men suffered torments of thirst. Rain fell finally on November 20—"timely," Hunt observed in his diary, "as several Canadians had begun to drink their urine." The river, though nearly always in sight, coursed far below in the canyon, tantalizingly out of reach. The spawning season had ended now; putrefying salmon lined both banks, and the odor of corruption tainted the atmosphere.[44]

Toward the end of November Hunt decided to leave the river and steer north over the lava flows. Encountering Shoshones, he traded for dogs and a pair of packhorses. Somehow Dorion contrived to acquire a nag to carry his wife. The route led through a defile toward the mountains. With only beaver and an occasional mule deer for food, Hunt ordered one of the horses destroyed. "I ate it reluctantly," he wrote, "because of my fondness for the poor beast." Snow lay waist deep in the uplands. Frozen blackberries and chokecherries supplemented what little meat the hunters managed to bring in.[45]

Regaining contact with Ramsay Crooks and his half-starved contingent on December 6, Hunt found Crooks so enfeebled he could barely walk. There seemed nothing to do but turn back for the Shoshone lodges. Hunt approached Pierre Dorion about slaughtering his crowbait horse. Dorion refused. "What was singular," wrote Irving, "the men, though suffering such pinching hunger, interfered in favor of the horse." Half dead with hunger, the band approached a Shoshone camp on the evening of December 10. Shouting and firing into the air, they drove off the startled Indians and seized five of their horses.

This engraving from an A. T. Agate drawing shows Fort Astoria with the U.S. color waving in the middle ground, the Columbia and the uplands on the far shore in the background. The British North West Company and later the Hudson's Bay Company occupied the post, known to Britons as Fort George, after the War of 1812. (Library of Congress)

Hunt refused to give up the attempt on the mountains. He had little choice, for to stay in place was to perish of hunger or exposure. With insults, flattery, and bribes, he browbeat three Shoshones into accompanying the party as guides, and in readiness for the march ordered two horses killed and their skins sewn together to make a raft for a last crossing of the detestable Snake. Leaving Crooks behind, the tattered band quit the river on December 23 and slouched north-westward toward the Blue Mountains of eastern Oregon. Marie Dorion went into labor on December 30 and delivered safely within a few hours. She rested a day, then caught up to the band. "One would have said, from her air, that nothing had happened to her," Hunt remarked.[46] The babe, however, lived only a few days.

A hard slog through deep snows under leaden skies brought Hunt and his men to the summit of the last ridge of the Blues on January 6, 1812. The sun appeared for the first time in weeks, and they could see the plain of the Columbia stretching before them, with distant views of Mount Hood to the west. After a long descent, they paused for a few days' rest in a Cayuse/Tushepaw encampment along the

Umatilla River, then pushed on to the Columbia itself, arriving on the southern bank on January 21, nine months and a precisely calculated 1,751 miles after leaving the Arikara villages on the Missouri. The river here flowed 1,320 yards wide between treeless banks. The January air struck mild, like autumn in the middle states of the Atlantic coast.

Fish and fat dogs were plentiful now. Local Indians reported a party of whites had passed some weeks before: Mackenzie's band, surely. They told him, too, of a large house enclosed in palisades the whites had built near the river's mouth—Astoria? Hunt had completed the voyage, to that extent vindicating Astor's decision to entrust the command to him. He could congratulate himself on surviving at least, and on having been the first white man to lead a party through Union Pass of the Rockies. At The Dalles he learned of the *Tonquin* disaster in Nootka Sound and of David Stuart's founding of the post at Okanogan. In tough negotiations with the relentless Wascos, Hunt bought several canoes and embarked on the last stage of the journey on February 5. The flotilla reached Astoria ten days and a series of rain- and windstorms later. A trim little shallop lay at anchor in the bay below the guns of the fort.

A SENTRY HIGH in the Astoria bastion reported a sail in the offing: J. J. Astor's ship *Beaver*, so it turned out to be, carrying provisions, trade goods, and thirty-six clerks and laborers to reinforce the Columbia depot. *Beaver*'s master, Cornelius Sowle, laid the ship in toward the bar early in May 1812 after a seven-month voyage from New York. With baffling winds, Sowle stood off the mouth of the great river till the ninth, when he launched the cutter to sound the passage. *Beaver* ground over the shoals in midafternoon, striking twice without damage, and came to anchor in Baker Bay.

Sowle brought formal confirmation, too, of the loss of *Tonquin* off the wild northern shore of Vancouver Island. True to type to the last, Jonathan Thorn had mortally offended one of the Nootka chiefs, slapping him across the face with an otter skin for some trifling offense and ordering him off the ship. Indian traders returned the next day with skins; against the advice of Donald McKay and others, Thorn permitted a crowd of them aboard. Belatedly recognizing the danger, he bawled out orders to clear the ship and come to sail. The Indians struck as though on cue, attacking with war clubs and knives. The captain, McKay, and sixteen crewmen were killed or mortally wounded in the first wave of the assault. Five survivors barricaded themselves in a cabin and held out until dark. Four of them jumped ship during the night and were caught later and put to death. The fifth, a seaman named Lewis, invited the Nootkas aboard in the morning and, in an act of self-immolation, touched a light to the powder magazine. The explosion destroyed Lewis, *Tonquin*, and, by report, upward of a hundred Indians.

The new arrivals off *Beaver* found the Astorians discouraged about prospects for the trading enterprise. Five partners, 9 clerks, and 90 artisans and voyageurs were in residence; the *Beaver* party swelled the muster roll to 140, a substantial population for an uncultivated country to support. All the same, for newcomer Ross Cox, a twenty-nine-year-old Dublin-born ex-North Wester, Astoria was a picture of luxury after thirty weeks at sea. He savored the feel of the hard, unyielding earth underfoot. The buildings—barracks, refectory, warehouses, a forge, and a carpenter's workshop—were sturdy, warm, and dry. Bateaux and canoes could unload their cargoes on the workmanlike landing stage even at low water. The kitchen garden flourished in Astoria's second spring. Cox played amateur ethnologist, touring native villages; making midnight excursions to burial places in search of specimen skulls; and venturing out to the ruins of Lewis and Clark's Fort Clatsop, overgrown now with parasite creepers. Like earlier arrivals, though, Cox found the claustral woods unnerving. "Their deep and impervious gloom resembles the silence of solitude and death," he thought. Sometimes even the birds refused to sing.[47]

Veteran Astorians were too full of business to brood. Robert Stuart had set out upriver in late March at the head of a relief party for the Okanogan post, traveling part of the way with the clerk John Reed, bound overland for New York and carrying a polished tin case with dispatches for John Jacob Astor. A party of Wasco Indians armed with bows and arrows and battle-axes ambushed Reed along the portage at the Long Narrows above The Dalles and were poised to dismember him when Stuart, hearing the war whoop, doubled back with seven or eight men and drove them off. Reed survived a thump on the head, but the Indians bolted with his rifle, pistols, and the gleaming dispatch box. Stuart detached a couple of men to escort the addled Reed back to Astoria and pushed on without further incident to the Okanogan.

Stuart found Alexander Ross recovering from a melancholy winter alone at the Okanogan station. The start had been auspicious, with the blaze of the Great Comet of 1811 across the sky. Ross observed it a handsbreadth above the horizon at twilight of evening on August 31, "a very brilliant comet with a tail about 10 degrees long." The Sinkaiekt natives of the region explained that the Good Spirit sent it to announce Ross's arrival and foretell comfort and prosperity. The omen proved faulty, or anyway untimely. In October, David Stuart with three men marched northward on a fur reconnaissance into present British Columbia, leaving Ross at Okanogan with only "a little Spanish pet dog from Monterey, called Weasel" for company for the entire winter—188 days, by his count.[48]

"Every day seemed a week, every night a month," he wrote. "I pined, I languished, my head turned gray, and in a brief space ten years were added to my age. Yet man is born to endure, and my only consolation was in my Bible."[49]

The Sinkaiekts, "the people of the water that does not freeze," were a horse tribe, subsistence hunters, fishers, and gatherers. They struck Ross as friendly at first, at peace with each other and their neighbors, and managing comfortably in their temperate surroundings. Ross improved the time working out a Sinkaiekt vocabulary and establishing a trading routine with native trappers. After a while he began to notice a change in the Indians' attitude. They loitered about the post, as though waiting for something to happen. The men neglected their hunting. The evenings were interminable and, as the winter advanced, ghost-ridden, too. Shrill whoops and enigmatic chants sounded suddenly out of the depths of the night.

Ross wondered whether the racket accompanied some ritual, or perhaps signaled the prelude to an assault. Alone, barricaded in his ramshackle hut, guns freshly primed at bedtime each night, Ross experienced a kind of slow-motion loss of nerve. He gradually worked himself up to a full pitch of terror. Yet the Indians never harmed him. In fact, once they settled into a winter routine, the Sinkaiekt trappers delivered furs regularly. At the time of David Stuart's return, on March 22, 1812, Ross had procured 1,550 beaver pelts and otter skins worth 2,250 pounds sterling in Canton, at a cost to J. J. Astor of only 5½ pence each.

He had grown accustomed to isolation, if not reconciled to it, by the time David Stuart returned from the north and Robert Stuart arrived from Astoria. Ross saw them both off with their cargo of peltries after a few days' rest. The Stuarts witnessed a minor miracle on the homebound journey when, just below the junction of the Snake and the Columbia, the wraithlike forms of Ramsay Crooks and John Day materialized out of the wilds. Stragglers from Hunt's voyage, they had managed, with Indian help, to survive the winter. The combined party reached the haven of Astoria on May 11, two days after *Beaver*'s arrival. Along with Crooks and Day, long since given up for dead, the Stuarts safely delivered some two thousand skins from the Okanogan station.

The partners met in conclave a few weeks later to fix assignments for the new trapping and trading year. The Astorians resolved to move aggressively into the interior to intensify competitive pressure on the North Westers. David Stuart would return to the Thompson's River region for the winter of 1812–1813, leaving Ross to suffer Okanogan's wind-scoured days and haunted nights in solitude for another season. Donald Mackenzie planned to penetrate the country of the Blackfeet, a brave, bellicose, and incorruptible tribe that would show scant interest in Astor's trumpery goods, still less in following trap lines along the icy streams of the Idaho high country. With Reed's journey aborted, the partners directed Robert Stuart to strike overland for St. Louis with dispatches for Astor, who remained in a state of anxious ignorance about affairs at the Columbia outpost. Stuart would carry word of the successful establishment of Astoria and the interior posts; the destruction of *Tonquin;* the belated appearance of Hunt's cross-country party; and the arrival of *Beaver*.

A brisk salute from the four-pounder cannon at Fort Astoria sent the expeditions on their way on the morning of June 29, 1812. The flotilla consisted of two barges and ten canoes, with Mackenzie and David Stuart and their clerks, voyageurs, and Sandwich Islanders occupying all but one of the vessels. Robert Stuart embarked in the tenth canoe with his small band: Ramsay Crooks, the disaffected ex-partner Robert McLellan, hunters Benjamin Jones and John Day, and the voyageurs André Vallée and François Leclerc. It became apparent at once that Day had not regained his equilibrium after the ordeal of the previous winter. He seemed morose and churlish, Robert Stuart thought, and gibbered at odd moments.

With a following wind, the canoes hurried past the mouth of the Cowlitz River on the forenoon of July 2 and reached Deer Island, opposite the Willamette, at sunset. Here Day became unstrung entirely. He prowled about the camp muttering threats of self-murder, then settled into a thundery silence. The others ostentatiously ignored him. Rising toward daybreak, he seized a brace of loaded pistols, waved one of them in the direction of his temple, and fired. Two or three of the people shucked their blankets, tackled the dazed but only lightly wounded Day, and pinned him to the ground before he could do further damage. Stuart sent him back to Astoria under an Indian escort later in the day.

The favorable breeze swept the flotilla smartly eastward toward the Columbia River gorge until the sixth, when the weather abruptly turned contrary. Heavy rains delayed the attempt on the Cascades, and the Astorians, now 153 miles from the fort, according to the penciled marginal notes in Stuart's manuscript journal, advanced just three miles in three days. The glacial pace allowed them plenty of time to admire the long, vaporous flumes of the group of cataracts east of the mouth of the Sandy River, among them a two-tiered falls (today's Bridal Veil) and another with an elegant dissolving cascade of more than two hundred yards (present Multnomah). The crags and projecting rock faces that flanked the cataracts suggested to Stuart the antique towers and fortifications of his native Scotland.

But the current raced like a mill sluice there, and the several hundred Indians camped in the neighborhood for the salmon fishing were the antithesis of picturesque. Ross Cox found them hideous, with bad teeth and sore eyes. Muskets were broken out as a precaution, and the men donned arrowproof elkskin jerkins. "They are saucy independent rascals, will steal when they can, and pillage whenever a weak party falls into their clutches," Stuart complained. As ever, the river's bounty, its surpassingly generous gifts, astounded the whites. Plying a scoop net from a doubtful-looking scaffold that extended into the stream, Indian fishermen harvested salmon in prodigious numbers. Stuart judged that an experienced hand could catch at least five hundred a day.[50]

The journey here became something of an ordeal. The ascent from the first rapid to the Long Narrows, a distance of about eighty miles, consumed fifteen days. After yet another in an interminable series of portages, the Astorians late on July 16 camped for the night on a sand beach a couple miles below the mouth of the Deschutes

River. The natives seemed friendlier here, less rapacious, and only a few carried weapons. Robert Stuart doled out tobacco and other presents to the principal chiefs. They finally cleared Celillo Falls (now vanished beneath a placid sheet of reservoir) on the eighteenth and passed into a sparser and drier country, with fewer pines and more scrub oak.

From Celillo Falls onward, the pace quickened. The expedition on July 21 made eighteen miles despite the necessity for two short portages, then covered forty-five miles with a strong wind abaft on the twenty-second. The landscape assumed a forsaken aspect, "without a stick of wood," Stuart remarked, "and the soil is an entire desert of sand, even on the top of the bluffs." Rattlesnakes appeared in quantity. On the theory that the odor of tobacco repelled them, the men slashed open a bale and strewed loose leaves around the campsites. The sun beat down relentlessly out of an immense sky, and there was a jagged edge to the torrid air. Stuart began to scout for horses for the overland journey. He fell in with a party of Indians near the junction of the Walla Walla River and the Columbia; they were cordial and inclined to trade, although they struck him as materially less well off than the fish Indians downstream. All the same, he pushed on to their village. The Wallawalla tribe, about two hundred strong, built an enormous bonfire and staged an elaborate dance that night to welcome the travelers. The next day Stuart obtained four good horses for merchandise to the value of $179.82.[51]

There, 384 miles upriver from Astoria, the parties divided, the Mackenzie and David Stuart contingents striking north for the mouth of the Snake River. Robert Stuart negotiated for another dozen or so horses, while the people prepared packsaddles and packages for the march. His band started early on July 31 for the hills southeast of the Columbia. The sun heaved up and scorched the desert landscape. A light breeze blew with just enough velocity to raise suffocating clouds of dust. To all appearances no rain had descended on these barrens since Noah's time.

A succession of dry ravines, tedious to negotiate, lay athwart the route. Early in the afternoon Leclerc, suffering terribly from thirst, paused to drink his own urine—a portent of hardships to come. Stuart drove the men on in search of water: thirty miles for the day, forty, and still nothing in view but round, gray hills and a purpling sky to the east. They raised the Umatilla River near present Pendleton, Oregon, with the last of the light. Men and horses splashed into the cool, clear stream and lapped gratefully.[52]

With the succession of weary days, the Astorians came to acknowledge the insignificance of their presence in a hostile and indifferent land. For all his Scots fortitude and high Presbyterian sense of duty, Stuart would cease to care at times whether he delivered Astor's mail, or indeed whether he lived or died. Twenty-seven years old in 1812, the acquisitive, principled, and physically indestructible son of a Scots crofter, he had no way of knowing that his ordeal would be the chief legacy of the Astor enterprise. As far as he could tell, he left no tracks in this pitiless landscape. Although the credit (or blame, depending on one's point of view) would go elsewhere, Stuart and his men would be the first known whites to follow a trace from the Pacific through South Pass of the Rocky Mountains and down the Platte River—a route that would prove practical for wagons and, eventually, for streams of ordinary travelers.

The expedition advanced through dense stands of yellow pine into the Blue Mountains of eastern Oregon. Leaving the shadows of the woods for a region of grassy hills and meadows, Stuart followed a faint track that led to the delectable Grande Ronde, a perfect green disk of rich grass, clover, and wild flax dropped among the mountain peaks. Dubbing this place, a shared grazing land for the Cayuse, Nez Perce, and Umatilla tribes, the "big flat," he chose a campsite along the right bank of the Grande Ronde River and dispatched the hunters, who presently returned with two salmon and a beaver. The men remained in camp for two days, mending saddles and recruiting their strength for the approach to the stone and sage deserts of the Snake River country.

Stuart forced the pace when the march resumed: twenty miles on August 7, twenty-three miles on the eighth, twenty-six miles on the ninth. He counted no fewer than nineteen antelope slanting along the hills above Alder Creek—so rare a sight that he did not at first trust his eyes. The creatures were bashful, the hunters' fieldcraft deficient. Nobody managed to creep close enough to squeeze off a shot. The next day brought them to the Burnt River and a rough track weaving southeasterly through rocky hills that tumbled down to the stream's edge. Stuart noted professionally that the river, here thirty yards wide and lined with willow, supported plenty of beaver.

The Astorians struck the Snake below present Farewell Bend State Park, Oregon, on August 12. Beyond the high, sandy far bank lay the country of the Nez Perces and their neighbors the misnamed Flatheads, who emphatically denied that their ancestors had ever distorted the skulls of their young. The Nez Perces seemed peaceable if haughty and imperious; they tended, too, to demand high prices for their horses. The route followed the southern bank of the Snake through broad saltwood bottomlands. Daytime temperatures soared into the nineties, sapping the people's energies. Mosquitoes swarmed at night. Stuart agreed to a steep price for an Indian guide to lead the party over the mountains: a pistol, a blue blanket, an ax, a knife, an awl, a fathom's length of blue beads, a looking glass, and a quantity of powder and ball. The guide presently disappeared, taking Stuart's horse with him.

Settling into a punishing routine, the Astorians followed a stony trace that faintly suggested the eastward route. A hot, dry wind breathed heavily over the sun-blasted Snake River Plain. The region seemed reaved of life, although in fact it carried a steady traffic of compulsively mobile Shoshones, so the sound of human voices on the sultry afternoon of August 20, voices speaking *English*, startled and unnerved Stuart and his band. It was as though the rocks had been given tongue. A moment later Joseph Miller materialized like an apparition from a narrow band of willows along the riverbank. Close behind followed Hoback, Rezner, and Robinson, who with Miller had deserted Wilson Price Hunt's expedition the year before.

The castaways emerged from the woods naked as worms, sunshriveled, and skeletal. An outlaw band of Arapaho had stolen their packaged peltries, most of their clothing, and their horses the previous winter. They had been wandering on foot ever since, living almost exclusively upon fish.[53] For all their misadventures, though, Miller and his shag-bearded companions had taken careful note of beaver stocks as they tramped along the western verges of the Rockies: they were abundant, Miller told Stuart, and prime in both size and quality. All the same, the trappers in the full flush of a joyous reunion decided to accompany the Astorians to St. Louis. Stuart thus began to negotiate for remounts. The inhabitants of these sterile hills were poor, though—even now, during the fishing season—and averse to trading away their equine capital. But they had little else to offer in exchange for the whites' alluring stocks of awls and beads. Stuart finally argued a Shoshone band into swapping two fresh animals for two of his jaded beasts and other considerations.

A two-day march over rough ground brought Stuart to "the Salmon Falls," a series of cascades (now diminished by damming downstream) in south-central Idaho east of the junction of the Big Wood River with the Snake. Here a hundred lodges of Shoshones were industriously killing and drying fish. Fishermen waded into the center of the falls at sunrise and slew the leaping frantic salmon with elkhorn spears attached to long willow poles. Miller, who had rested here briefly with Hunt in 1811, told Stuart he had seen the Indians destroy thousands of salmon in a few hours.

The trace veered cross-country away from the tortuous Snake through sand barrens and withered stands of wormwood. Stuart struck the river again on August 29 at Cauldron Linn, 1,011 miles from Astoria. He studied the frenzied channel from the high bluffs. The violence of the river's surge through the constricting rock generated a spray that Stuart likened to the ocean heaving itself upon a lee shore. The wreck of one of Hunt's canoes lay wedged among the boulders. Stuart suppressed the urge to descend, concluding that "nothing that walks on the earth" could pass between the base of the bluffs and the torrent. He pushed on for another dozen miles and pitched camp in a broad patch of good grass. With McLellan and Crooks he soon found the first six of Hunt's caches; they had been plundered, by wolves at first and later by Indians. Only a few weather-damaged books were strewn about. Nearby were three of Hunt's abandoned canoes, shattered and irreparable.[54]

The next day Stuart located the last three of the caches, these undisturbed and with a sufficient quantity of traps, dry goods, and ammunition to equip a small brigade for the winter hunt. Hoback, Rezner, and Robinson had reconsidered: they would try their chances in fur country again after all. Figuring he had seen enough of the wilderness and of Arapaho thieves to last a lifetime, Miller opted to continue on to St. Louis with Stuart. The men spent the last day of August in camp, making and mending for the onward journey. Stuart packed the greater part of the remaining trade goods he had carried from Astoria into the undamaged caches and saw the trappers off early on September 1. The country here leveled out, and the Astorians reeled off a steady fifteen and sometimes twenty miles a day. Stuart bought a dog, some dried salmon, and "an excellent sort of cake

made of pulverized roots and berries" from a Shoshone band. The
men had long ago discarded any lingering inhibitions about eating
dog flesh. It made a hearty meal, Stuart thought, and its fat proved
useful in frying the lean, flavorless trout that now had become a staple food.[55]

Reaching the fifty-foot cascade of American Falls (inundated with
the building of a dam in 1925), Stuart found grass for the animals and
wild cherries in abundance. Again quitting the Snake, the Astorians
followed the line of the Portneuf River southeasterly along an Indian
track that led through the hills to a broad sand and gravel flat. A further trek of eighteen miles bought them to the Bear River. Here,
after an arduous day's march of forty-two miles, were fresh signs of
buffalo (properly, the American bison) and rich, grassy bottoms where
they could halt to bait the horses. They sighted antelope, but the
herds, shy as ever, scampered out of range. The men continued to
subsist mainly on trout, a diet insufficient in fat and calories to fuel
the daily marches, even over tableland.

A party of Crow Indians paid a late-afternoon call on the camp,
offering buffalo meat prefatory to serious bargaining for gunpowder.
More Indians arrived as the evening advanced. There were adequate
numbers now, twenty or more men, to overwhelm the whites. Even
so, Stuart refused to trade powder for horses and doubled the camp
watch, visibly annoying the Crows. "Their behavior was insolent in
the extreme," he complained, "and indicated an evident intention to
steal, if not rob—we kept close possession of our Arms, but notwithstanding our vigilance, they stole a Bag containing the greater part of
our kitchen furniture." As a gesture of diplomacy, Stuart offered the
Indians a present of a token twenty loads of powder before breaking
camp in the morning.[56]

Partly to shake off the Crows, Stuart here decided to ignore Indian
counsel about the best route to the southerly pass through the mountains and follow Miller's imprecise directions instead. He led the party
away from the course of the Bear River—and what would become the
Oregon Trail—not much more than a hundred miles in an air line
from South Pass, the long, gentle upsweep that pierced the main
chain of the Rockies. The detour would add four hundred miles and
all but unendurable misery to the journey. Stuart struck mostly north
along today's Idaho–Wyoming border, the Salt River Range on his
right hand. Food stocks were nearly depleted and the weather had

turned cold. After a day or so Stuart began to question Miller's competence as a guide. Stuart concluded finally that the safest plan would
be to abandon the search for a southward gap and strike north to
Teton Pass, where he could pick up Hunt's track of the previous year.
The band slogged north for eleven miles on September 17, then east
for a stage, then due west. The next day, Stuart pushed fifteen miles
to the northwest, hard going, too, much of it through scenes of beaver
devastation in the upper Snake River bottomlands: quagmires and
gloomy stands of dead trees.

Stuart rose after an uneasy night at first light on September 19
and made his way down to the river to drink. As he dropped to his
knees on the muddy bank, a troop of mounted men swooped down
upon the camp, scattering the pastured horses—even the hobbled
ones. The attackers were Crows, Stuart guessed, probably the same
band they had encountered on the Bear River. Whatever their identity, the raiders were adept at rustling horses. The leader had posted
one warrior in position on a knoll commanding the route of the
intended stampede, while the main band, on signal, gave the war
whoop and charged. The initial ruckus spooked the horses. When the
lookout on the knob put spurs to his mount, causing it to bolt as
though in fright, the Astorians' skittish horses followed in hot pursuit.
Simultaneously, a second contingent threatened the camp from the
rear. Reluctantly allowing the horses to go, Stuart ordered the men to
fall back to defend the baggage. From the knoll, the raider chieftain
pointed emphatically to his backside in a taunt that required no trans-
lation. Jones, a marksman, begged Stuart for permission to bring him
down. Stuart forbade Jones to fire, knowing he would never escape
the Crows once blood had been drawn. The loss of the horses would
take some laughing off. Even so, Stuart could not help admiring the
Indians' tactical competence. In minutes they had driven away all his
livestock at no cost to themselves.

The people consumed the last of the meat that evening. Jones
trapped a beaver in the morning, and after making a meager breakfast
of it, they packed for the onward journey. Not much of value remained, but Stuart nevertheless ordered everything they could not
carry burned or dumped into the river. The route ran northwest, along
the upper Snake. Jones caught another beaver, and over the next two
evenings the men took eighty-five trout with rod and line. "They are
poor and indifferent food," Stuart lamented, "and were it not for the

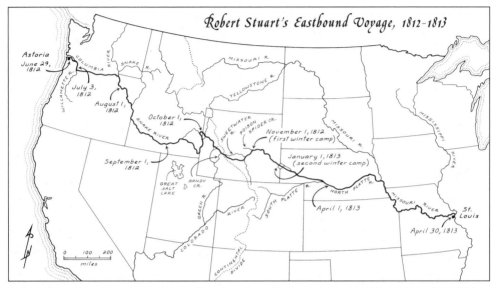

Robert Stuart's Eastbound Voyage, 1812-1813

Astoria
June 29,
1812

July 3,
1812

August 1,
1812

October 1,
1812

November 1, 1812
(first winter camp)

September 1,
1812

January 1, 1813
(second winter camp)

April 1, 1813

April 30, 1813

St.
Louis

GREAT
SALT
LAKE

0   100   200
miles

Robert Stuart's route eastbound from Fort Astoria to St. Louis, July 1812–April 1813. (© 2003 by Jackie Aher)

little meat we occasionally fall in with, I really think they would not even support life." He now changed plans again, determining to backtrack to the Snake River plain below Henry's Fort in hopes of trading for Shoshone horses. Pausing briefly to knock together hand-made rafts, the Astorians pushed out into the river, reeling off twenty miles the first day. It seemed effortless, and nobody wanted to dwell on the fact that they were moving *away* from St. Louis and that winter was coming on fast. On the twenty-third, afloat on the swift and twisting stream, they made ten miles northwest, two miles northeast, another six miles northwest, a mile north, and another mile northeast. André Vallée shot a fat beaver, but it sank to the bottom before he could haul it aboard.[57]

By the last week of September, Stuart's erratic course brought the Astorians as far north and west as the verges of today's Yellowstone National Park. One of the hunters wounded an elk; the creature took to the river and drifted a mile downstream before they could finish it off and tow it to the bank. Skinning the carcass, they extracted a rifle ball and an arrow point, both fresh, thought Stuart, indicating the presence in the neighborhood of Blackfeet—a tribe to be avoided at all hazards. The meat was good, though, and Stuart called for a day's halt to jerk and package it. Rain and hail clattered down through the afternoon, turning to snow with nightfall.

They lay in camp all day on September 28 to make ready for the resumption of the foot march. Stuart decided they had gone as far as they could go on the rafts, some ninety miles; the next day's trek carried them fifteen miles north over rough ground, still on course for Henry's Fort. By now the band had begun to show signs of disintegration. Stuart banned the use of firearms for fear of alerting the Blackfeet, so there was no fresh meat. With Ramsay Crooks feverish, Stuart's decision to abandon the Blackfeet walks and strike directly over the mountain they had been skirting meant that the others would be obliged to take up Crooks's burdens, perhaps even carry him, too. Complaining of bruised feet, the fractious McLellan mutinied, flatly refusing to haul the beaver trap any longer or its equivalent in dried meat. He abruptly announced that he would proceed on his own. As they labored uphill, the men caught glimpses of McLellan in his solitary progress across the plain below. They reached the snowclad summit in early afternoon. Willows lined a silvery river that coursed through a broad valley below. After a painful descent, they made an early camp along the stream.

Crooks's fever ran dangerously high despite regular dosings of castor oil; soon he would be too weak to walk. McLellan's defection seemed to embolden the others. Gathering in a circle around Stuart, they ticked off the perils of western travel: the inhospitability of the country, the murderous Blackfeet, lack of food, the harshness of the climate. Then they proposed going on without Crooks. As nothing else had done, the petition to abandon one of the party forced Stuart to confront not only the perils of the moment but larger questions of courage, duty, and endurance—as well as humankind's chronic inability to rise to the occasion.

"The phantoms which haunt a desert are want, misery and danger," he reflected, "the evils of dereliction rush upon the mind; man is made unwillingly acquainted with his own weakness, and meditation shows him only how little he can sustain and how little he can perform."[58]

Ben Jones killed five elk on October 2. With Crooks unfit to march, Stuart made a virtue of necessity and pitched camp near the carcasses. Having used up the last drops of castor oil, he subjected the invalid to an "Indian sweat," hoping to broil the fever out of him.

It seemed to help. When the march resumed on the fifth, Crooks managed to stay on his feet. The course lay south-southeast, for now Stuart had given up on Henry's Fort and meant to try Teton Pass before the snows blocked it. One of the hunters shot a grizzly bear with 3½ inches of fat on the rump—a life-sustaining supplement to the lean, tough elk.

The Astorians trudged southeast by east, camping near present Jackson, Wyoming, on October 7. They finished off the last of the elk on the eighth and made a paltry breakfast the next morning of a few trout and a small duck. Two days later they came upon Robert McLellan's camp and traces of his dinner of the night before—a bony wolf. Stuart and his men could not even manage that much, and they rolled themselves up in their blankets, hungry. An exhausting climb on the morning of the eleventh brought them to a ridge overlooking the Green River, a wide, shallow stream with a thin line of willows shivering along the banks. They had hoped for buffalo here, but there were no signs—and no supper on October 12 nor yet breakfast in the morning, for Jones found nothing but a beaver's forepaw in his trap. At daybreak Stuart espied a thin column of smoke on the horizon and sent Leclerc to investigate, praying it rose from an Indian camp. It turned out to be McLellan's halt; it had caught fire while he was off fishing. Like the main band, McLellan had eaten little or nothing for five days.

"He was lying on a parcel of straw," Stuart wrote, "emaciated and worn to a perfect skeleton, hardly able to raise his head or speak."[59]

Stuart distributed McLellan's things among the others, and they dragged him along a level, sandy track. With the people nearing the end of their strength, he signaled an early halt on the Green River north of the site of Daniel, Wyoming. There was no game, no prospect of a meal. Some of the men had been talking among themselves, and after a while one of the Canadians approached Stuart. Rifle in hand, he suggested they cast lots—Stuart, as leader, would be exempt—to determine which of the men would die to provide flesh so the others might live.

The notion froze Stuart's blood. When he found speech, he emphasized the man-eating taboo: crime upon mortal sin, premeditated murder, and cannibalism. Besides, the killing might well be purposeless: When the time came, would anyone actually be able to force human flesh down? The Canadian—Leclerc it was, although Stuart did not name him—seemed to carry the others along with him. They were, after all, lost, stupid with fatigue, and raddled with hunger—and perhaps they had heard that a man ate like pork. The lifeless plain stretched away forever, and all of them would starve before they could clear it and enter abundant country. Stuart's words, his natural air of command, had failed to persuade. He reached for his rifle and leveled it at Leclerc's chest.

This broke the spell. The Canadian realized all of a sudden that if he persisted he might just as well draw the short end, so far as his own well-being was concerned. "He fell instantly on his knees and asked the whole party's pardon," wrote Stuart, "solemnly swearing he should never again suggest such a thought." All the same, Stuart relieved Leclerc of his rifle and placed him under guard. The incident deeply disturbed Stuart. Wrapped in his blanket, he mused resentfully upon the heedlessness of the comfortable and affluent. "Let him visit these regions of want and misery; his riches will prove an eye sore, and he will be taught the pleasure and advantage of prayer," he wrote later. Banal reflections, perhaps, yet Stuart was hungry, too, wasted, his stomach shrunken and in knots.[60]

In the event, his prayers proved effectual. The route of October 14 led east over a range of low hills, a spur of the Wind River Mountains. Buffalo bones piled up near old Indian encampments mocked the Astorians' hunger. Then, in the early afternoon, they stumbled upon deliverance in the form of an ancient buffalo bull. They killed and flayed it and hurled themselves on it in a frenzy, tearing at the flesh and consuming it raw. With the most violent pangs satisfied, they butchered the creature and carried the cuts to a proper camp along a stream. Stuart ordered a thin soup to be prepared and consumed before he would allow the people to attack the barbecued flesh.

The Wind River peaks nicked the eastern horizon, the main ridge vaulting up high, rugged, and treeless, masses of dark rock covered in places with snow. Famine still threatened. "Our living is of the meanest kind," Stuart wrote, "being poor Bull meat and Buck antelope, both too bad to be eat, except in cases of starvation." Yet again an encounter with Indians postponed disaster. The Astorians fell in with a band of Shoshones on October 18 and followed them to their encampment on a creek northeast of present Big Sandy, Wyoming. Although they themselves were short of animals—Crow raiders had come calling—the Indians agreed to exchange a horse for a pistol, a breechcloth, an ax, a knife, a tin cup, two awls, and a few beads. Stuart also arranged to trade for a five-day supply of buffalo meat and much-needed leather moccasins.[61]

Stuart led a hard march of eighteen miles the next day in cruel weather, a bitter northeast wind blowing a snowstorm in his teeth. Vallée and Leclerc killed a young bull in the twilight. Snow fell steadily overnight, covering its clean-picked bones. Pushing southeast in the morning, Stuart realized he had reached the neighborhood of the Continental Divide. He made camp the night of October 22 at the western end of South Pass, 20 miles wide, a series of gently rising hills 7,550 feet above sea level at the summit. The men found enough dry aspen for a good fire against the numbing cold, but no water. At daybreak on the twenty-third Stuart ascended for 3 miles, then called a halt for breakfast at a spring of sweet water. A further climb of 5 miles brought him to an eminence he dubbed "big horn." The snow had drawn off. Below him stretched a broad, level plain, its reds, browns, and ochers glowing dully in the wintry morning light. Before long thousands of emigrant wagons would come crawling along these flats in a final approach to the South Pass gateway to the farther West.

ROBERT STUART'S BAND went into winter camp in early November near the junction of Poison Spider Creek and the North Platte River in central Wyoming. Wood, water, and game were plentiful there: hunting parties killed thirty-two buffalo on November 5 and another fifteen on the eighth. Then heavy snow fell and severe cold clamped down. The men hunkered down in their rough-built hut, six feet high, eight feet wide, and eighteen feet long, with "the fire in the middle, after the Indian fashion" and thick buffalo hides covering the roof and sides.[62]

The appearance of a party of Arapaho raiders in mid-December took Stuart unaware. They had other prey in mind, as it turned out: a band of Crows who had stolen their horses and abducted a number of their women. The Astorians fed them and sent them off with a quantity of jerked meat, although once again Stuart firmly rejected requests to trade weapons and ammunition. With two bands of potentially hostile Indians in the neighborhood, he reluctantly decided on a shift of base. Abandoning the improvised shelter that Stuart dubbed "our chateau of indolence," the Astorians set out two hours before sunrise on December 13 and slogged across North Platte barrens lying under fifteen inches of powdery snow: twenty-two miles that first day; twenty-seven miles on the fourteenth, with only cottonwood bark as fodder for the horses; and twenty-six blister-raising miles on the fifteenth. Two weeks of arduous travel brought them to today's Wyoming–Nebraska border near the site of Torrington, Wyoming. When Leclerc, returning from a reconnaissance, reported he had found three trees large enough for canoes, Stuart resolved to pass the winter there. The men at once threw up scaffolds for drying meat—no need to fire-cure it; the sun and the pure, dry air of the high plains would jerk it for them—and commenced to build a hut. Stuart proclaimed a feast day for January 1, 1813, to mark the occasion.

"We destroyed an immoderate quantity of Buffalo Tongues, Puddings, and the choicest of the meat," he wrote in his journal. "Our stock of Virginia weed being totally exhausted, Mr. McLellan's tobacco pouch was cut up and smoked as a substitute, in commemoration of the New Year."[63]

As Stuart and his men were settling into quarters along the Platte, Astor partner Donald Mackenzie encountered a North West Company wintering party deep in the Oregon interior. The North Westers cheerfully passed along the news that the United States and Britain had been at war since the previous June, and that British warships were heading for the Columbia with orders to seize Astoria. Mackenzie at once turned back for the coast, reaching Astoria in mid-January 1813. He and Duncan McDougall went into emergency conference. Stocks of trade goods and rations were low, and with American ports presumably blocked up there would be faint hope of resupply. The partners decided to discontinue trade with the natives except in provisions—in any case, they already had more furs in the warehouses than they could carry away. Anyhow, McDougall had been skeptical for some time about Astoria's prospects. Mackenzie's report spurred him to act. They agreed between them to abandon the depot in the face of the British threat and shut down Pacific Fur Company operations by early summer. Mackenzie retraced his steps north and east to the outposts to inform David Stuart and John Clarke of the decision to fold the enterprise.

So passed the winter of 1813. Robert Stuart set out down the Platte in mid-March, on the last stage of his trek to the Mississippi. After a few days the country began to take on a settled look. In the Indian villages, spring planting had begun—corn, beans, and pumpkins, a crop that, by the end of May, could be laid by while the tribes followed the seasonal migrations of the buffalo. They would return in August for the harvest, then move off again in pursuit of "black cattle" in the fall and winter. Crooks and Vallée visited an Otoe village on April 12 and returned with word of the nearly year-old war between the United States and Britain. Two itinerant French Canadian traders confirmed the news the next day. The pace quickened once the band reached the Missouri, the powerful spring current sweeping the boats along at the dizzying rate of sixty and more miles a day.

The Astorians arrived in St. Louis just before sunset on April 30, Astor's dispatches intact after a meandering voyage of 3,768 miles and 306 days.[64] Stuart pushed on to New York bearing optimistic reports for the chief. Astor by now had learned of the loss of *Tonquin* and of lesser disasters. The British, too, were on the prowl at sea, with blockade vessels off New York and a squadron rumored to be headed for the Pacific Northwest. Stuart delivered happier news: the safe arrival of Hunt's overland party and the establishment of a thriving trapping/ trading network in the interior. With luck and resolution, Astoria might to be able to ride out the crisis.

In the event, the British—the frigate HMS *Phoebe* and the armed merchantman *Isaac Todd*—failed to turn up at the mouth of the Columbia on schedule in the early spring of 1813. Still, when the partners convened at Astoria in late June for the annual meeting, McDougall and Mackenzie once again pressed the issue of dismantling the operation. Ross Cox arrived from Spokane House in June to discover that "a total revolution had taken place in the affairs of the company." David Stuart, Clarke, and others put up a strong dissent, but in the end McDougall and Mackenzie carried the meeting. The partners voted to bring Astor's affairs on the Columbia to a close no later than June 1, 1814.[65]

The peripatetic Hunt reached Astoria from Oahu on August 20 in the chartered resupply brig *Albatross*. The partners' resolve to withdraw chagrined him, yet he may have been partly responsible for it. Hunt had judged the Snake country unsuitable for settlement and of modest value as a trapping ground. This view doubtless deepened McDougall's pessimism about long-term prospects in the Oregon country. In any case, Hunt reluctantly fell in with McDougall's scheme, announcing he would sail away in *Albatross*, which had business else-where, hire another ship in the Sandwich Islands, and return to carry off the bundled furs and other property stored in the Astoria warehouses.

The collapse of the enterprise devastated Alexander Ross, Gabriel Franchère, Cox, and the other young clerks. "After having sailed the seas and having suffered all sorts of fatigue and privation, I lost in a moment all my hopes of a fortune," Franchère lamented. He decided to return to Canada with the spring express. Ross and Cox would seek positions with the North West Company. Ross blamed Astor for failing to support the operation adequately, and faulted McDougall and Mackenzie for backing down from the British without a fight. In his last assignment for the Pacific Fur Company, he padlocked the lonely post on the Okanogan. When he returned to Astoria early in 1814, Hunt gave him a $500 cash reward for his efforts. It was slight comfort; Ross hadn't joined Astor for a salary, but for the chance of a partner's profits.[66]

A flotilla of North Wester canoes rounded Tongue Point on Octo-ber 7 and slid alongside the landing stage under Astoria's light cannon. The rival traders came as conquering heroes. Saying they expected the *Isaac Todd* letter of marque any day now, they hoisted a Union Jack over their camp and congratulated themselves on their forbear-ance in not slaughtering the garrison to a man and confiscating the goods. Some of the younger Astorians urged resistance; McDougall chose to bargain instead. By October 16 he and North Wester John McTavish had struck a deal: all Pacific Fur Company assets would go to the British firm for the sum of $58,291.02. McTavish acquired Astoria at a steep discount—he picked up 907 otter skins, for exam-ple, for 50 cents each, perhaps 10 percent of their market value. In the final tally, McDougall recouped no more than a third of Astoria's worth, by Irving's calculation; he estimated the value of the furs alone at $100,000.[67]

As McDougall and the North Westers signed off on their settle-ment, Astor continued to press—without success—for U.S. govern-ment protection for the Columbia trade: a naval presence and a small garrison for Astoria. After all, he expected a generous return on the millions he and several associates were raising for the U.S. Treasury to support the underfunded American war effort. "I hope yet the gov-ernment will do something," Astor wrote ex-president Jefferson in mid-October. "In the meantime I am fearful that our people will be driven off and perhaps dispersed and it may not be easy to get them together again." By then, they indeed had begun to scatter. Jefferson offered sympathy but nothing else. "It would be afflicting indeed should the English be able to break up the settlement," he wrote Astor. "They would not lose the sale of a bale of furs for the freedom of the whole world." Jefferson consoled Astor with the conceit that his name ultimately would be coupled with those of Columbus and Raleigh as the founder of a great empire.[68]

McDougall claimed that he negotiated the best deal he could, given the anticipated arrival of British forces. He never managed to persuade Astor. "Had our place and our property been fairly captured, I should have preferred it," he told Irving later. "I should not feel as if I were disgraced." The agreement, it turned out, also included a North West Company partnership for Duncan McDougall.[69]

It remained for the Astorians, the North Westers, and the long-awaited British naval forces to ring down the curtain on Pacific Fur Company affairs with a slapstick finale. A British warship swept over the Columbia bar on December 1 and dropped anchor in Baker Bay—the *Raccoon* sloop of war, twenty-six guns, Captain William Black commanding. Adverse weather confined Black to the sloop, and several days passed before he learned that the North Westers had baulked him of his prize. *Raccoon's* barge finally put in below Astoria on December 12 and landed Black with a guard of five marines and four sailors.

"They had looked forward to finding several American ships loaded with furs and had counted in advance upon their share in the Astoria prize," Franchère remembered. "They found nothing, and their astonishment reached its peak when they discovered the establishment had been transferred to the North West Company and was under the British flag."[70]

Black had been doubly deceived, for he could see at once that even had the Americans opted to defend the fort, taking Astoria offered no prospect of glory. "Good lord," he said with disgust, "I could knock it over in two hours with a four-pounder!" All the same, Black made the most of his conquest. "Country and fort I have taken possession of and left in possession and charge North West Company," he reported to the Admiralty. "Enemies party quite broke up they have no settlement whatever on this River or Coast." Black arranged a formal ceremony to claim possession of the region for the British crown, summoning the paramount chiefs, running up the Union

Jack, and breaking a bottle of Madeira (the accounts are conflicting; it may have been port) over the flagstaff. His sailors fired a three-gun salute, the chiefs drank a toast to the king, and the captain renamed the place Fort George.[71]

So concluded Astor's venture. There was nothing farcical in the final toting up of accounts, material and moral. Some years afterward, Alexander Ross recapitulated Pacific Fur Company casualties from 1810 to 1814: eight men lost upon the Columbia bar; five lost during land expeditions; twenty-seven lost in the *Tonquin* explosion; eight lost when the supply ship *Lark* went down in a gale south of the Sandwich Islands; nine lost in various Snake Country excursions; one lost in the final departure; and so on—sixty-one dead altogether, "a tragical list."[72]

As for gain, the Astorians could boast of the plant and animal collections of Bradbury and Nuttall, the basis of a future U.S. claim to the Columbia, and Robert Stuart's discovery of South Pass. But Astor regarded Stuart's find as proprietary, although he did offer Jefferson a copy of Stuart's account of his adventures. "You may have seen by the publick papers the arrival of Mr. Stuart & others from the Columbia," he wrote. "He kept a journal of his voyage . . . which he left with the President [James Madison] should you feel a desire to read it."[73] A loyal soul, Stuart said nothing, then or later, about Astor's suppression of the journal. Another decade would pass before the mountain man Jedediah Smith broadcast word of a viable cross-mountain route to the Pacific.

2

The Road to India

THE AMERICANS RETURNED circumspectly to Astoria, now Fort George, in 1818. The special U.S. commissioner, John Baptist Prevost, arrived on the Columbia on October 1 aboard a British naval vessel, the *Blossom* sloop of war, and in a brief ceremony floated the Stars and Stripes over the fort. That signified Britain's nominal restoration of the prize four years after the Treaty of Ghent brought the War of 1812 to a close. There was, in fact, no actual change of possession. After all, Prevost only managed to reach Fort George courtesy of the Royal Navy. "He could not man the fort himself," the American expansionist Thomas Hart Benton would say, "and had neither soldier nor sailor to do it for him." Prevost signed a receipt for the property and sailed away in *Blossom* on October 6. The North West Company garrison hauled down the American colors, hoisted the Union Jack, and resumed business as usual.[1]

Two weeks after Prevost's departure, American and British negotiators in London reached agreement on a ten-year joint occupation of the Oregon Country. The accord opened a vast area, stretching south from British Columbia to Spanish California and east to Idaho, to trappers and traders of both countries. But it left larger issues involving British, American, Spanish, and Russian territorial pretensions unresolved. British and Spanish claims dated to the sixteenth century. The Russians had been trading in the Aleutian Islands since the second quarter of the eighteenth century. The late-eighteenth-century expeditions of Cook, Vancouver, and Mackenzie reinforced the British case. The United States claimed the entire Columbia basin on the strength of Robert Gray's 1792 rediscovery of the river's mouth, the Lewis and Clark expedition of 1804–1806, and J. J. Astor's trading post of 1811. Then there were the first nations, scattered, nomadic, essential for traders, convenient for missionaries, obstructive for settlers: some 125 distinct tribes with a population, as the third decade of the nineteenth century approached, considerably in excess of a hundred thousand.

The Spanish and the Russians eventually dropped their claims, Spain ceding its rights north of the forty-second parallel (the California border) in 1821 and the Russians withdrawing beyond latitude 54° 40' in 1825. That left the British and the Americans as the only contestants for the virgin lands of the Pacific Northwest, a political, diplomatic, and mercantile rivalry that would wax and wane for another quarter century. The British proposed a permanent boundary along the forty-ninth parallel to its intersection with the Columbia, then south and west down the Columbia to the sea. The United States countered with the 49° line through to the Pacific. The dispute thus centered on an area of seventy thousand square miles—present Washington State, including the San Juan Islands in the northern reaches of Puget Sound. The British regarded free navigation of the Columbia as essential to their interests. Judging the Columbia with its treacherous bar and upriver rapids unsuitable for heavy commercial traffic, the Americans insisted on acquiring the accessible deepwater harbors of Puget Sound in any final settlement.

With neither side willing to force a final issue, the question of sovereignty remained in abeyance. For some years, anyway, the game seemed hardly worth the candle. The coastal fur trade had played itself out by 1820. The once-profitable triangular trade Gray founded in the early 1790s—New England manufactured goods to the Columbia, furs to China, nankeen, silk, and porcelain to New England—had fallen into desuetude. Overtrapping had so depleted the fur-bearing population that the North West Company considered pulling out of the lower Columbia altogether after 1818. And with the collapse of Astor's venture the Americans had withdrawn from the interior. Distance and difficult terrain confined the Yankees to the eastern flank of the Rockies.

The British strengthened their position with the merger of the Hudson's Bay Company and the North Westers in March 1821. With the end of their long-standing, sometimes violent trade war, the British government granted the Honourable Company of Adventurers of England Trading into Hudson's Bay a twenty-one-year commercial monopoly in the trackless region of western Canada known as Rupert's Land. The company absorbed the extensive, if not particularly lucrative, North Wester trading network in the Oregon Country. Company governors doubted the Oregon trade could be made profitable, although they did judge the country worth retaining, if for no other reason than flank protection for more valuable holdings to the north. The government-business partnership gave the coalition civil and criminal jurisdiction over British subjects west of the Rockies. If the Joint Occupation Agreement guaranteed U.S. trading rights in Oregon, merger and monopoly handed the Hudson's Bay Company a powerful competitive advantage.[2]

With its immemorial traditions, precise business methods, trim wilderness outposts, and gilt-edged record of dividend payouts, the company commanded immense prestige. Established by royal charter in 1670, with armorial bearings of beavers in quarters, fox sejant proper, and elks supporting, the enterprise collected furs and distributed manufactured goods—its trademark blankets, ironwork, and firearms—from the western shore of the eponymous bay to the rain forests of the Pacific Northwest. The company's agents kept order, too, enforcing peace among the tribes and mediating trade disputes. (As the British statesman Lord Palmerston once defined it, the company's mission was to strip the local quadrupeds of their furs and keep the local bipeds off their liquor.[3]) It was a profit-sharing venture, with 40 percent of the net divided among the agents in the field. Servants, trappers, and even agents were regarded as itinerant. As an article of policy, the Hudson's Bay Company discouraged settlement of the West; officially, anyway, the governors deemed the Pacific Coast unfit for colonization.

Over the horizon massed the restless, ever-westering Americans. George Simpson, the field governor of the company's vast domains, resolved to take full advantage of the monopoly and either block American competition or, should it materialize, annihilate it. Tough, despotic, and ambitious, a short, square-built, fair-haired, and blue-eyed Scot, Simpson sailed for Canada in 1820 after desultory years as a clerk in the London house of a sugar-broker uncle.[4] With the coalition, Simpson ascended to the governorship of the Northern Department of Rupert's Land—the senior officer in charge of the Hudson's Bay Company field operations, at a salary of £1,000 a year. Before long, his understrappers were calling him "the Little Emperor."[5]

Himself born of unwed parents, Simpson fathered a number of children—at least three and possibly as many as six—with Indian women, whom he called his "bits of brown." Evidently craving a more decorous domestic life, he arranged to return to England in 1824 to marry. From London, the Hudson's Bay Company governor Andrew Colville bluntly advised him to wait. "A wife I fear would be an embarrassment to you until the business gets into a more complete order," Colville wrote. "I think that having taken the settlement in hand that you should not leave it until you see it is on the right road." Diplomatic as well as trade issues were pending, for the Foreign Office had pressured the company to give up Fort George to reduce the risk of conflict with the Americans, who were sensitive about the place. Simpson, naturally, put duty before love. (He would marry his first cousin, Frances Ramsay, in 1827.) So he set out from York Factory on Hudson Bay on August 15, 1824, for Fort George and a firsthand examination of operations on the Columbia.[6]

Simpson's newly appointed chief factor for the Columbia department, Dr. John McLoughlin, preceded him, with a three-week head start. Simpson set out in high wilderness style, seated regally amidships in a twenty-five-foot-long North canoe with the company standard, the Union flag embroidered with the initials HBC, streaming from the stern, and kept his nine powerful voyageurs at their paddles for eighteen hours a day. Simpson learned at Frog Portage on August 30 that he had already made up ten days on McLoughlin; Simpson reached the provisioning post of Isle La Crosse on September 5 after only twenty-two days—"the quickest passage ever made," he boasted. By September 16 he had cut the doctor's lead to six days. To McLoughlin's unconcealed vexation, Simpson overtook him at seven o'clock in the morning of the twenty-sixth in the swamps of Rivière la Biche. The Little Emperor had shoved off before daybreak; McLoughlin had not yet broken camp when he arrived. Not disposed to minimize the moral advantage he thus gained, Simpson resumed the march at a reduced speed "in order," he gloated, "to give the Dr. an opportunity of keeping up with us."[7]

Forty years old in 1824, born in Quebec to an Irish father and a Scots Canadian mother, McLoughlin trained as a physician in Scotland, joined the North West Company in 1803, and stayed on after the coalition as head of the important post of Fort William on the northern shore of Lake Superior. For all his leisurely approach to travel, the splendid doctor impressed even the famously hard-to-please Simpson. McLoughlin's powerful build, six and a half feet of height, flowing hair, and colossal beard gave him an air of wild ferocity. For all his toughness, even Simpson found the doctor more than a little alarming. "He was such a figure as I would not like to meet on a dark Night," Simpson wrote, "dressed in clothes that had once been fashionable, but now covered with a thousand patches of different Colors; his beard would do honor to a Grizzly Bear."[8] Although there would be trouble between them later, he and McLoughlin traveled companionably enough through the abbreviated days and sharp frosts of early autumn, piercing the Rockies at Athabasca Pass, reaching the Columbia, and sweeping down the great river toward the Pacific at a pace approaching a hundred miles a day.

Simpson blamed North Wester mismanagement, extravagance, and dissension for the decline of the Oregon trade. Agents in the field, especially former North Westers, came to dread his scalding evaluations. They had learned, in his three years as virtual dictator of the Hudson's Bay Company's Canadian affairs, that the ledgers had better be in perfect order, the shelves well stocked, the trade brisk, and the living spartan.

The Little Emperor dismissed the clerk at Split Lake as scatterbrained and utterly unfit for wilderness work. "He can neither venture on Snow Shoes nor in a small canoe, cannot provide a Meal for himself with his Gun and it would be certain Death to trust him out of doors in the severity of the winter," observed Simpson.

He accused the agent at Fort Nez Perce of sticking too close to the bottle in private hours. "Were he to drink a pint of Wine with his Friends on extraordinary occasions, get up earlier in the morning, eat a hearty breakfast and drink less Tea I should have a much better opinion of him," Simpson wrote.

Besotted with their women, two of the three chief traders in the Columbia department were seriously neglecting their work. "They cannot muster sufficient resolution in themselves or confidence in their Ladies to be 5 Minutes on end out of their presence and even

Hudson's Bay Company grandee John McLoughlin ruled the Oregon Country as a benevolent despot during the 1820s and 1830s, overseeing the development of a thriving commercial center at Fort Vancouver on the Columbia River. American settlers sloughed off company rule with a democratic coup that established the first provisional government in 1843. (Library of Congress)

for that short time keep them under Lock & Key," Simpson remarked wickedly, "altho they have more than once discovered that 'Love laughs at Locksmiths.' "[9]

Alexander Ross, the former Astorian and North Wester in charge of Spokane House, impressed Simpson in October 1824 as frivolous and self-indulgent, an untrustworthy agent "whose reports are so full of bombast and marvellous nonsense that it is impossible to get at any information that can be depended on from him." More troubling still, Ross had befriended the energetic and ambitious American trapper Jedediah Smith—the vanguard, Simpson had cause to suspect, of an American trading initiative west of the mountains.[10]

Representing legendary mountain man William H. Ashley's Rocky Mountain Fur Company, Smith, with seven veteran trappers, pene-trated the Rockies in March 1824, making what Smith's biographer Dale Morgan called the "effective discovery" of South Pass. Following Robert Stuart's example, Smith approached a band of Crow Indians for directions; the Crows sent him up the Popo Agie River to the southern flank of the Wind River Range, then west through the broad pass. He crossed the Continental Divide sometime during the second week of March, reached the Green River on March 19, and began trapping northward, eventually making contact with Ross's Snake River expedition. Smith accompanied Ross to the Flathead post in southwestern Montana, where Smith had a close-up look at Hudson's Bay Company operations. Parting company with Smith, Ross reached Spokane House a few days ahead of Simpson. The Little Emperor sacked him on the spot—charge: collaborating with the enemy—and handed responsibility for the Snake River territory to the veteran trapper Peter Skene Ogden, with explicit instructions to deplete beaver stocks along the eastern marches of the Oregon Country to keep the Americans out. As for Ross, Simpson banished him to the Red River colony in Manitoba, where he presently took up the sedentary trade of schoolmaster.

Simpson and McLoughlin resumed the downriver journey on October 31. At The Dalles they indulged in the familiar white-water sport of shooting at basking seals. Below the Cascades, Simpson paused to allow the *métis* to shave, change clothes, and don their gaudy red sashes and multicolored hat ribbons, then pushed on through the night to reach Fort George the next day.

Battling headwinds all day, Simpson arrived to the blast of bugles just before sunset on November 8, "having performed the Voyage from Hudson's Bay across the continent of America to the Northern Pacific Ocean in 84 days thereby gaining twenty days on any craft that ever preceded us." He took against Fort George at once. The stockade, the bastions with eighteen-pounder cannon, and the complex of warehouses, shops, and dormitories struck him as too elaborate entirely for an Indian trading post. "Everything to me appears on the Columbia on too extended a scale *except the trade*," he wrote. From Astor's time to the present, he estimated, the entire return did not amount to twenty thousand beaver and otter pelts.[11]

Simpson moved promptly to impose economies on the Columbia department. He slashed the workforce nearly by half, from 151 to 83, and ordered a drastic reduction in expensive European "Eatables Drinkables and other *domestic comforts*," telling the agents they could live off the country or go hungry. Ross's sumptuousness particularly exasperated him. "I do not know of any part of the Country that offers such resources in the way of living as Spokane District," he confided in his journal; "they have abundance in the finest Salmon in the World besides a variety of other Fish within 100 yards of their

Door, plenty of Potatoes, Game if they like it, in short everything that is good or necessary for an Indian trader; why therefore squander thousands uselessly in this manner?"[12]

The governors could expect substantial gains from self-sufficiency alone; at any rate, cutting expenses would free up resources to meet the American challenge. Simpson prepared to evacuate Fort George, mostly because the Foreign Office had virtually ordered him to, but also because the post seemed ill-suited for the sustaining gardens, orchards, and pastures he envisioned for the Columbia post. In his search for a new site on the northern bank, he set out to learn as much as possible about the lower Columbia. His reconnaissances led him finally to the Belle Vue Plain on the north shore, opposite the mouth of the Willamette. A stronghold here would command the Columbia, Willamette, and Snake River Valleys.

Simpson and McLoughlin sited the factory on rising ground a quarter mile from the river's edge. Fresh water and timber were conveniently near. "The pasture is good and innumerable herds of Swine can fatten so as to be fit for the Knife merely on nutricious Roots that are found here in any quantity and the Climate so fine that Indian Corn and other Grain cannot fail of thriving," Simpson observed. Work on the post proceeded through the winter of 1825. "The buildings already completed are a Dwelling House, two good Stores an Indian Hall and temporary quarters for the people," he wrote in mid-March. "It will in Two Years hence be the finest place in North America, indeed I have rarely seen a Gentleman's Seat in England possessing so many natural advantages and where ornament and use are so agreeably combined." Simpson presided over a flag-raising ceremony at sunrise on March 19, with a genial group of "Gentlemen, Servants, Chiefs and Indians" in attendance. Breaking the neck of a bottle of rum over the flagstaff, he christened the place Fort Vancouver, in the name of King George IV. Imperial purpose animated the decision to honor Captain Vancouver. "The object," Simpson wrote, "is to identify our claim to the Soil and Trade with [Vancouver's] discovery of the River and Coast on behalf of Gt. Britain." He distributed a couple of drams to the people and took his leave of McLoughlin. By 9 o'clock he had settled into his palanquin amidships in the North canoe for the return voyage across the mountains.[13]

The Little Emperor had seen enough to persuade himself that the Oregon Country was worth contending for. The Russians, despite their ukase barring foreigners from trading in regions they claimed, were about to recede to the north, leaving only the Americans to confront. With the Vancouver outpost, Simpson had strengthened the British title to the country north of the Columbia. And he had given McLoughlin and Ogden categorical orders: By whatever means necessary—overbidding, underselling, and overtrapping—they were to maintain the Hudson's Bay Company monopoly over the interior trade north and east of the river.[14]

With business matters arranged to his satisfaction, Simpson turned to imperial affairs. The ambiguous boundary rattled investors, so the company lobbied His Majesty's government for a clear demarcation, preferably along the Columbia. As the deadline for expiration of the 1818 convention approached, company governor J. H. Pelley urged the Foreign Office to reject the U.S. proposal for a boundary along latitude 49° to the sea and press for the Columbia frontier. "This Line would leave to America the Trade and Possession of an extensive and valuable Country, and would furnish fewer opportunities of collision between the Traders of the two Nations, than any other Line that could be suggested," Pelley wrote Foreign Secretary George Canning.[15] Simpson followed up with a note of his own arguing for the retention of Puget Sound and the northern bank of the Columbia.

"I will further altho' unasked take the liberty of giving it as my opinion that if the Navigation of the Columbia is not free to the Hudson's Bay Company, and that the Territory to the Northward of it is not secured to them, they must abandon and curtail their Trade in some parts, and probably be constrained to relinquish it on the West side of the Rocky Mountains altogether," he wrote the senior British diplomat responsible for the boundary negotiations.[16]

Meanwhile, John McLoughlin developed the post at Vancouver. Salmon had proved impractical as an article of trade, owing to the length of time it had to soak in pickle, but lumber and cattle offered prospects for diversification. In March 1826, a year after Fort Vancouver's christening, the doctor's livestock inventory totaled twenty-seven cows, five three-year-old heifers, eleven year-old heifers, three bulls, eleven steers, and two oxen. Almost as an afterthought, McLoughlin reported an 1825 harvest of nine hundred bushels of potatoes. Although the 1826 potato crop proved a slight disappointment, with only six hundred bushels from two hundred bushels planted, he remained optimistic about the livestock.

"Our Cattle thrives well, we lost no Pigs by poison since last year, but the Wolves have destroyed several of them," the doctor wrote Simpson early in the spring of 1827. "It is a pity the Pumpkin seed I requested was not sent, Potatoes and Turnips in this warm climate are subject to fail; if we could raise a sufficiency of Pumpkins it would enable us to feed our Pigs in house all Winter. They would thrive better and none would be devoured by the Wolves."[17]

McLoughlin passed along troubling news, too: the Americans were filtering into the Oregon Country. Ogden reported Snake country trapper defections to Jedediah Smith's Rocky Mountain Fur Company brigades. The governors kept up the pressure on Simpson to use the company's advantages of experience, stability, and capital to smother the American competition. "We can afford to pay as good a price as the Americans and where there is risk of meeting their parties it is necessary to pay as much or something more," Simpson's London superiors wrote. "By attempting to make such expeditions too profitable the whole may be lost."[18] The question had taken on a new urgency with the reopening of Anglo-American boundary talks in London in November 1826. Simpson in turn sent orders the following July to his senior commanders in the field: strip the country of furs, especially that part of it lying south of the Columbia. As it happened, negotiations were nearing a conclusion by then. With no agreement on partition, the United States and Britain in August 1827 settled on a renewal of the joint occupation convention, with a one-year notice of termination from either side. The decision to postpone a final reckoning left Hudson's Bay Company all the more determined to maintain a trading presence south of the Columbia, if only as a potential bargaining concession.

Wrote the governors to Simpson, "If the American Traders settle near our Establishments, they must be opposed, not by violence, which will only be the means of enabling the Traders to obtain the interference of their Government, but by underselling them, which will damp their sanguine expectations of profit, and diminish the value which they at present put upon that Trade. It will be useful to give the Americans full occupation by active and well regulated opposition on the South of the river to prevent them advancing towards the North."[19]

By now the Americans knew a fair amount about the Rocky Mountain country as far west as the Great Salt Lake, but remained largely

A romantic view of Jedediah Smith's crossing of California's Mojave Desert in 1826. Mexican authorities detained Smith briefly in southern California before allowing him to push on north to the American River. Smith and his men were the first whites to cross the Sierra Nevadas from west to east. (Library of Congress)

ignorant of the territory beyond. Jedediah Smith set out in August 1826 to sketch in some of the blank spaces on the map. Striking south and west with sixteen men over Utah's sand and rock barrens, he advanced through the rugged Black Mountains of northwestern Arizona into the Mojave Indian country of the Colorado River Valley. The expedition paused for two weeks in the Mojave villages, trading and refitting, before pushing west along an old Indian caravan route that followed the intermittent Mojave River (Smith designated it the Inconstant) toward the Pacific. Piercing the San Bernardino Mountains late in November, Smith and his band dropped down in easy stages into the bewitching pastoral valleys of California, rich and green with the autumn rains.

The Mexican authorities, however, were suspicious. They detained the Americans near San Gabriel through December and the first half of January in a hospitable house arrest, with the weeks-long Christmas fiesta and ample quantities of wine and *aguardiente* to amuse them. Two of Smith's men adapted to southern California well enough to decide to stay on after the Mexicans reluctantly granted Smith leave to travel. He set out on January 18, 1827, cleared the Tehachapi Mountains, and headed north through the San Joaquin Valley, the foothills of the High Sierras on his right hand, trapping along the main stream and its tributaries as he advanced.

The party fetched the American River in northern California early in May. Smith's first attempt on the rampart of the Sierra Nevada foundered in deep snow and intense cold. Leaving all but two of the men behind in camp along the Stanislaus River, Smith attacked again, making the crossing via today's Ebbetts Pass and the descent along Walker's Fork to the edge of the Great Basin in eight days. By the time he reached the trapper rendezvous on the Bear River, Smith had traced much of what would become the Old Spanish Trail to California. He and his band were the first whites to penetrate the Great Basin and the first to cross the Sierra Nevada from west to east.[20]

Smith moved quickly to assemble a new expedition for a return trip to California to pick up the trapper party on the Stanislaus. The Mojaves proved hostile this time, still resentful after a clash with a Taos trading caravan some months earlier that left several of their number dead. A Mojave war party bushwhacked Smith's party during a crossing of the Colorado, killing all ten men stranded on the eastern bank. With eight survivors, he marched southwest along the Mojave and through Cajon Pass for the relatively safe haven of the San Bernardino Valley. The Mexican authorities again held him in light captivity for a while, then finally allowed him to travel north to San Francisco by sea. After a brief pause there to rest and recruit reinforcements, Smith pushed slowly northward along the coast, bound for the Hudson's Bay Company domains of the upper Willamette.

The Americans reached the Umpqua River in southern Oregon in mid-July 1828. With two of the hunters, Smith set out in search of game while the others settled into bivouac. In his absence, a party of Umpqua Indians fell on the camp, slaughtering fourteen of the party. Only one man survived in what the historian William Goetzmann calls "the worst disaster in the history of the fur trade."[21] Together with the Colorado River debacle, Smith in twelve months had lost a total of twenty-six men killed in the service of the Rocky Mountain Fur Company.

With three survivors, he retreated down the Willamette to Fort Vancouver. McLoughlin hospitably took in the Americans and dispatched a Hudson's Bay Company punitive expedition south to chastise the Umpquas and recover some seven hundred beaver pelts, thirty-nine horses, and Smith's expedition journal. The doctor magnanimously waived the company's expenses for the Umpqua operation and invited Smith to winter over at Vancouver. Simpson addressed Smith in sharper tones. In a letter, he accused the Americans of bringing the disaster upon themselves with their harsh treatment of the Indians. He went on to harangue Smith about the perils of his projected overland march to the Great Salt Lake. "Your total ignorance of the Country, the difficulty you would have in finding your way across the Blue Mountains, the inexperience of your people in Snow Shoe traveling and the danger of starvation" all argued against the attempt, Simpson wrote. Still, he did agree to buy Smith's pelts at $3 apiece, even though he judged them to be "of very bad quality, the worst indeed I ever saw"; and he also made an offer for Smith's horses.[22]

Smith improved the time by observing company business routines and reconnoitering the Vancouver hinterland. In a report to the secretary of war in October 1830, he would characterize Oregon as a settlers' paradise—hardly the sort of advertisement to delight the Hudson's Bay Company. Smith himself had led a caravan of ten five-mule-team wagons and two Dearborn vehicles up the Platte as far as the eastern flank of the Wind River Range, making a steady fifteen to twenty-five miles a day. With little difficulty, he went on, travelers could drive wagons and livestock over South Pass as far as the Great Falls of the Columbia and into a country that offered sunny prospects for farmers and ranchers. Buffalo were plentiful, the route "almost all open, level and prairie," and the country on both sides of the Continental Divide rich in grass for horses and mules. Goetzmann calls Smith's report, together with those of Billy Ashley and trapper Joshua Pilcher of the Missouri Fur Company, "the first emigrant guide to the Far West."[23]

McLoughlin saw Smith off in March 1829 with a Hudson's Bay Company draft for £550 and a private conviction that the British had seen the last of the Rocky Mountain Fur Company. "If we do not relax," Simpson wrote the doctor, "there is little doubt that we shall soon be left Masters of the Field, as those people we know to be needy adventurers existing on bad credit who cannot afford to follow up a losing business." As it happened, Simpson was in the right of it. The Missouri Fur Company withdrew in 1830. The Rocky Mountain Fur Company would dissolve in 1835. Yet Simpson failed to foresee another kind of American invasion. He himself had called for a missionary presence in the Columbia country as early as 1824. "The praise worthy zeal of the [London] Missionary Society in the cause of Religion I think would here be soon crowned with success," he wrote from Fort George. The American Methodists would answer the call to Christianize the Indians, eventually succeeding where Smith had failed in gaining a footing for the United States in the Oregon Country.[24]

The industrious McLoughlin continued to develop Vancouver. The settlement flourished under his management: the doctor reported an 1830 harvest of 927 bushels of wheat, 609 bushels of peas, 600 bushels of Indian corn, 150 bushels of oats, and 86 bushels of barley to supplement the previous year's surplus of 1,100 bushels of wheat and 300 bushels of barley. "In short," he wrote, "we have wheat and flour for two years, and more than a year's stock of peas and corn." McLoughlin had a sawmill in the works, too, at a site south of the Columbia on the falls of the Willamette that he and Simpson had scouted together. On the debit side, though, the doctor conveyed the melancholy news that an epidemic of the intermittent fever—malaria—had devastated the local Indian population, carrying off three of every four natives in and around Fort Vancouver in 1830. By 1834, by some estimates, nine of every ten Chinooks had died of European diseases.[25]

IN HIS IMPERIAL MUSINGS, Thoms Jefferson envisioned a North American road to India. Jefferson's disciple Thomas Hart Benton arrived in Washington, D.C., from St. Louis in December 1820 with the ambition of converting the sage's expansionist idea into action. He took rooms at Brown's Hotel where, so it happened, the Virginia congressman John Floyd and two veterans of J. J. Astor's Columbia venture also boarded. Floyd had read Benton's *Missouri Enquirer* essays on the Oregon Country. Ramsay Crooks and Russell Farnham represented Astor's interests in the capital. They entranced Benton and Floyd with tales of the country beyond the Rocky Mountains. The four made Brown's Hotel the headquarters of the Oregon boomers, projectors of an American empire on the Pacific. A statue of Benton would rise one day in a St. Louis park, a towering likeness that cast a brazen gaze and pointed a brazen hand eternally westward.

"There lies the road to India," ran the legend carved into the pedestal.[26]

Missouri Senator Thomas Hart Benton (1782–1858) embraced Thomas Jefferson's vision of America's Pacific destiny. This daguerreotype dates to the mid-1840s (possibly later), when Benton's explorer son-in-law John Charles Frémont was the toast of Washington. (Library of Congress)

Benton's personal history typified the westward sweep of American ambition. He was born in comfortable circumstances in 1782 along the edge of the Piedmont in Hillsboro, North Carolina. His father, a farmer-lawyer with a passion for speculation, left eight offspring and a mountain of debt when he died of consumption in 1791. Fleeing scandal, his widow moved with seven of the children to Tennessee in 1801, settling with her slaves on good cotton land twenty-five miles south of Nashville. Soon enough, trouble of his own compelled young Thomas to follow the family. Expelled from the University of North Carolina at sixteen for allegedly stealing from his roommate, he crossed the Great Smokies to start anew in frontier Tennessee.

He read law and entered Tennessee politics as a protégé of Andrew Jackson. They soon fell out spectacularly in a murky series of events that involved Benton's younger brother, a barroom brawl, a challenge, and a duel in which Benton shot and wounded his mentor. With Jackson's indestructible bulk athwart his path in Tennessee, Benton took another bound to the west and landed in St. Louis, the gateway to the Louisiana Territory and the Rockies. He practiced law there and edited the *Missouri Enquirer*, serving the territory's powerful fur trade combinations out of conviction as well as self-interest. The legislature of the newly admitted state of Missouri voted him into the U.S. Senate in 1820.

Benton assailed the Joint Occupation Agreement for the Oregon Country in the *Enquirer*, arguing that the Northwest belonged to the United States by right of law and discovery. Inattentive leaders were letting this incomparable country fall to a rival power. "American statesmen should have constantly before their eyes . . . a trade to *India* by the Columbia and Missouri Rivers," he wrote. Instead, as though sleepwalking, they acquiesced in a British presence on the Columbia— an admission that Britain had a viable claim to the country. "We shall be driven out," fretted Benton, "and the British remain sole possessors." Traders with British government backing could employ the slow but certain tactic of underselling, he warned, or they could accelerate the Americans' eviction by inciting the Indians to violence.[27]

With Crooks's coaching, Benton's alter ego in the House introduced the first formal legislation proposing the U.S. occupation of Oregon. John Floyd had lived in Kentucky briefly and so regarded western questions as his special province. Few, perhaps, took his puffery seriously, although it did draw attention to the cause. Floyd did not scruple to stretch the truth—or invent data when it suited his purpose. "The route to the mouth of the Columbia is easy, safe and expeditious," he famously told his House colleagues in December 1822. With steam navigation, he calculated the journey from the Ohio to the falls of the Missouri at twenty-four days; thence fourteen days by wagon to the Snake; and the final promenade an easy seven days down the Columbia to Astoria, "making the time necessary for that trip 44 days." The return, with a strong current carrying the steamboat down the Missouri, could be completed in only thirty-nine days.[28]

In concise form, Floyd expressed the ethos of the westward movement. He regarded Oregon as essential to the future of American democracy. It would draw off surplus population and offer new fields for the pursuit of wealth. It would serve as a sort of magnet to attract the disorderly, the restless, and the unlucky from the crowded places of the settled East, where they were likely, sooner or later, to cause trouble for their betters. The Oregon Country would be safe; protected; and, with its manifest advantages of climate, soil, and resources, eminently exploitable.

"I am persuaded (perhaps this ought to be taken with some grains of allowance), that Oregon is destined to be the great place of North America," wrote Floyd. "It is more distant from any probable war than any point on the globe; it more completely looks over the whole commerce of the world than any other. . . . Wherefore, he who can go, and grow with the country, will, and must, in three or four years, possess wealth and influence, and greater security, than can be obtained anywhere else."[29]

Benton and Floyd pursued a more practical issue as well, a campaign to dismantle the government system of managing trade with the western Indians. In an effort to win the loyalty of the tribes, the United States had introduced a system of trading forts where goods were offered for furs at fair rates of exchange. Government traders eventually auctioned off the furs to private interests. This rasped against every entrepreneurial instinct. Traders such as Ramsay Crooks wanted free play of the market and the government out of the fur business—except, of course, when it came to providing protection to private fur brigades from Indian hostility and Hudson's Bay Company competition. In congressional testimony, Crooks stigmatized the government system as a "pious monster." Last glimpsed in 1812 emerging dazed and naked from the Idaho wilderness, Crooks had risen in a decade to become Astor's right-hand man. Benton produced Crooks as a star witness against the government factories in Senate debates in the spring of 1822.

The system evolved out of a clause in Jay's Treaty of 1794 that granted Britain trading rights among Indians within U.S. territory. Benton regarded the treaty as a calamity and blamed every subsequent outbreak of Indian warfare on British intrigue among the tribes. Washington designed the factory system to counteract British influence and conciliate the natives. In practice, Benton charged, the nine factories in operation in 1822 were a collective failure on political, diplomatic, and commercial grounds. Government agents abused and mismanaged the trade, purchasing inferior goods at extravagant prices and palming them off on baffled and credulous natives. Indians wanted arms, ammunition, ornaments, and liquor. Government inventories were more adapted to a common country store than to the Indian trade, Benton charged: silk, velvet, nankeen, muslin, cambric, tea, stockings, and—inexplicably—Jew's harps.

"Do they protect Indians from the extortions of traders?" he asked his Senate colleagues. "So far from it they are the greatest extortioners, selling the meanest goods for the highest prices."[30]

The Senate voted to abolish the government trading system. Benton proposed replacing it with a line of government forts stretching from the Missouri to the Pacific, with mounted troops available to watch over the endless caravans that would carry American goods along the road to India. With protection from the Indians all else would fall into place, for the problem of communications had been resolved. "It had been done; it was done by the company which crossed the mountains in 1811, and there was no difficulty in it," Benton told the Senate in April 1822, carefully editing out the gruesome details of Wilson Price Hunt's voyage. "The Columbia river was of easy navigation, a good harbor in its mouth, and the Pacific Ocean void of peril. The region of the mountains, so formidable to the progress of Lewis and Clark, is now traversed by various and easy passes. The first and main ridge is crossed upon a good road, made by buffaloes and Indians."[31] Benton's roseate picture of western geography omitted the wind-flayed Platte Valley, the mountain barrier that separated the Missouri from the Columbia, the pitiless Snake River Plain, the turbulent waters of the Columbia from The Dalles to the Cascades, and the sandbar that had nearly wrecked *Tonquin*.

In a message to Congress in March 1824, President James Monroe recommended that the United States establish a military post at the mouth of the Columbia, and Benton early in 1825 introduced an occupation bill that called for the dispatch of naval and military forces to Oregon. The Missourian asserted that the measure would secure for American business interests a fur trade worth $1 million a year, prevent the British and the Russians from controlling Indian tribes in the Columbia watershed, give the United States a naval station on the Pacific, and attain Jefferson's object of opening communications between the Mississippi Valley and the western ocean. Besides, the country would hardly "remain longer without civilized white inhabitants," he told the Senate, and by all rights the inhabitants ought to be Americans.[32]

Benton's bill aroused the conscience of New Jersey Senator Mahlon Dickerson, who savaged it as an indecent land grab that would bring on a holocaust for the natives and cause friction, possibly even war, with Britain. He asserted—heretically, to most of his listeners—that the

Indians' rights to beaver were "as sacred as our rights to our property." Negotiations, not military force, should decide the issue. "It ought to excite no regret," Dickerson said of the prospect of extended boundary talks, "as it would give the unhappy natives of that region a little more time to breathe upon the face of the earth before the final process of extermination, by means of a white and civilized population, shall take place." Finally, Dickerson suggested that Oregon lay too distant from the United States to ever be more than an imperial dependency—a notion that cut against the American republican grain.[33]

As a Westerner and a Jacksonian (expediency heals most political wounds, and he and Jackson were reconciled in 1824), Benton had scant sympathy for the natives. They could assimilate, move out of the way, or be destroyed. "The earth was designed for man," he said, meaning Euroamerican man. "Fifty years ago and the valley of the Mississippi was like the present condition of the country of the Oregon. It is now teeming with a mighty population—a free and happy people. Their march onward, therefore, to the country of the setting sun, is irresistible." Benton had more difficulty with Dickerson's argument about colonization. To skirt it, he suggested that the Rocky Mountains formed a natural western boundary for the United States, and that Oregon might eventually develop into an independent republic.[34]

As he no doubt intended, Monroe's 1824 proposal caught the attention of the British government. The British invited the United States to reopen the Oregon boundary talks; Monroe's successor in the Executive Mansion, John Quincy Adams, accepted the offer. As Monroe's secretary of state, Adams had negotiated the 1818 agreement that Benton found so objectionable. The diplomatic historian Walter La Feber regards the accord as a coup for Adams; he rescued a weak American claim, La Feber says, by winning a British pledge to open the Oregon Country to citizens of both nations. In fact, as secretary of state and then as president, Adams pushed as aggressively for U.S. continental supremacy as ever did Benton, and with greater effect—especially in Oregon. Adams expressed his views with perfect clarity: "That the United States should form establishments there, with views of absolute territorial right and inland communication, is not only to be expected, but is pointed out by the finger of nature," he wrote.[35] When boundary talks resumed in 1826, Adams instructed the American negotiators to insist on the 49° line.

The British ministry of the late 1820s showed little passion for imperial expansion, still less for commercial affairs in the Pacific Northwest. United States negotiator Albert Gallatin concluded that the British were willing "to let the [Oregon] Country gradually and silently slide into the hands of the United States." All this, however, passed over Benton's head. He continued to regard the British as "simply working for a division . . . and waiting for *time* to ripen their joint occupation into a claim for half" of Oregon. He failed, however, to persuade the Senate to reject the boundary accord. The renewal, with the termination clause, took effect in 1828. Even so, Benton kept up the pressure. His Committee on Indian Affairs called for a firm international boundary along latitude 49° as soon as possible, together with the exclusion of all British traders from U.S. territory.[36]

NOTHING IN THE JOINT OCCUPATION AGREEMENT restricted American trade or, for that matter, settlement in the Oregon Country. Anyone with the temerity to try conclusions with the Hudson's Bay Company could seek his fortune there. Thus the Oregon idea cast a spell upon a dreamy New Hampshire–born Bostonian named Hall J. Kelley. The son of a physician and raised a Baptist, Kelley graduated from Middlebury College in Vermont, married one woman named Mary and then another, and fathered four sons. He taught school in Boston and promoted the moral reform of fallen women as founder of the Penitent Female Refuge Society. His textbook *The American Instructor* (1820) sold well, and continued to support him after his exit from the Boston schools in 1823.

Nicholas Biddle's edition of the Lewis and Clark journals touched off Kelley's Oregon *idée fixe*. A vision revealed his destiny: "The word came expressly to me to go and labor in the field of philanthropic enterprise and promote the propagation of Christianity in the dark and cruel places about the shores of the Pacific."[37] Kelley organized a colonization society and set about recruiting settlers. The fact that he had never seen the Oregon Country did not deter him from publishing *A Geographical Sketch* of the region in 1830. From the start, his energetic propagandizing outpaced his executive ability. An unstable character, erratic and impractical, he eventually would abandon the second Mary and all four sons and live out a long life as a hermit— hallucinatory, virtually blind, and dependent on his neighbors' handouts.

Kelley's plan to replicate the original Puritan Massachusetts Bay Colony in Oregon inspired a New Englander of an altogether more practical bent, Nathaniel J. Wyeth, the son of a Cambridge, Massachusetts, hotel keeper. To improve the time in slack season, Wyeth cut ice from Fresh Pond in Cambridge for shipment to U.S. southern ports and the West Indies. Inventive and ambitious, he designed a horse-drawn ice cutter for the Boston merchant Frederic Tudor that sharply reduced ice harvest time and expense. Wyeth's efforts netted him a comfortable income of $2,400 a year in 1830, when Kelley's Oregon appeals first caught his attention. They "operated like a match applied to the combustible matter in his mind," his nephew John Wyeth would write.[38]

Ice could wait. There always would be ice. "I cannot divest myself of the opinion that I shall compete better with my fellow men in new and untried paths than in those to pursue which require only patience and attention," Wyeth wrote. Applying to Kelley "for a scituation in the first expedition" to the Oregon Country, he concluded almost at once that the visionary schoolmaster would never pull off a successful emigration. Besides, trade interested him more than settlement. His letters record a swift disillusionment with Hall Kelley. With equal swiftness, a scheme of his own began to take form. "If the colonization society go through with their project I shall go out in their service if not I shall get up a Joint Stock Trading Concern (if I can) and go with a similar plan but on a smaller scale," he wrote his brother Leonard Wyeth in mid-November, only two weeks after his first approach to Kelley. By year's end he had given up on Kelley altogether and rounded up twenty recruits for a profit-sharing trading venture that would deal not only in furs but in Columbia River salmon, too.[39]

Wyeth put together his project from Cambridge over the winter of 1832, a proposition to collect furs and cure salmon to send to New England markets in ships that would return to the Columbia with supplies for sale or trade to American trappers in the Rockies. Wyeth drew his family into the scheme: his rackety older brother Jacob, a Harvard-trained physician with a drinking problem; his nineteen-year-old nephew John; and a New Hampshire cousin, also nineteen, named Thomas Livermore. Wyeth studied routes. He gathered information. "What I wish to know is how salmon are pickled and how smoked and how taken," he wrote a contact named Robert H. Gardner. He sold his ice cutting patent to Tudor for $2,500 and invested the money in arms, supplies, and equipment, including forty dozen five-pound beaver traps with double springs, jaws without teeth, and two-swivel chains six feet long. "Smith, Pilcher, Ashley, Soublette, Jackson of the western states are all said to have made money in this business," he wrote. He could think of no reason why he should not do so as well.[40]

So Kelley's Oregon expedition became Wyeth's. Kelley persisted all the same, tenacious of the fantasy that sooner or later he would dispatch large settler parties of men, women, and children to Oregon. "Probably two or three thousand emigrants will sail from different sea-ports in November, December and January next," he announced in the *New England Christian Herald;* "thence by carriages via the city of Mexico to Acapulco; and again take shipping. Fifty dollars meets the passage expense of a single grown person."[41] And he bitterly reproached Wyeth for deserting the Oregon Colonization Society.

Wyeth's company mustered on Long Island in Boston Harbor on March 1, 1832, for several days of toughening up under canvas. The expedition of twenty-four men sailed for Baltimore in the brig *Ida* on March 10. A rough passage of thirteen days allowed Wyeth time to reflect on the implications of his journey. An unquiet spirit, thirty years old in 1832, he had long battled ennui and self-doubt. He looked to the Oregon venture to quell his recurrent crises of purpose and resolve.

"My health is pretty good and hope and excitement has made another man of me," he wrote Leonard Wyeth. "I am determined to give up no more to melancholy feelings but to rouse myself up to exertions and enterprise and forget the things that have been and all but what is before me. If I am successful there will be some comfort in it if otherwise I will have some serious and present misfortunes to keep me from brooding over more distant and metaphysical ones."[42]

These last words were prophetic, for Wyeth would experience a lifetime's quota of mischance: dissension in the ranks, hunger and thirst, a murderous clash with Indians, shipwreck. The expedition reached Independence, Missouri, the jump-off point for the cross-country trip, in late April. There Wyeth made contact with the fur trader William Sublette, with whom his company of neophytes would travel. "He was bravely steering his way across the continent, undismayed by danger, difficulty or distance," Washington Irving would write of Wyeth, "in the same way that a New England coaster and his neighbors will coolly launch forth on a voyage to the Black Sea, or a whaling cruise to the Pacific." But already there were signs of mutiny. "Some of our company began to ask each other some serious questions; such as, Where are we going? And what are we going for," wrote John Wyeth. "But *Westward ho!* was our watchword, and checked all doubts." Not for long, though: two men dropped out in Independence, and three more deserted a few days into the journey, including Nathaniel Wyeth's kinsman Livermore, who absconded with three of the expedition's horses.[43]

The caravan followed the Platte, jogging along at a regular twenty miles a day. Passing the landmark of Chimney Rock on June 9, they crossed the Laramie River four days later and pushed into the sage barrens of Wyoming. "The country appears desolate and dreary in the extreme," Wyeth recorded in his journal. "One cannot conceive of the utter desolation of this region."[44] The people were surly; some spoke openly of turning back. But Wyeth worried more about the horses than the men. Several of the pack animals had given out already; others were failing for want of good grass.

Wyeth crossed the Continental Divide at South Pass in early July. The days were warm, the nights frosty, meat stocks so depleted in the days before they reached the Green River trapper fair that the men were forced to feed on the inner bark of balsam trees. They arrived at the rendezvous on July 6. A small city had grown up there: 120 lodges of Nez Perce and 80 lodges of Flatheads, trappers of the Rocky Mountain Fur Company and the rival American Fur Company, and independent mountain men. Within a day or so some of Wyeth's party, led by his brother Jacob, rose in rebellion. "We wished to have what we had been used to at home," John Wyeth wrote later, "a town meeting, or a parish meeting, where every freeman has an equal right to speak his sentiments, and to vote thereon."[45] Wyeth refused to convene a council of war, although he did gather everyone together and call the roll. Seven of the eighteen men, including his brother and his nephew, answered that they would return to St. Louis with Sublette.

"Thus ended all my fine prospects and flattering expectations of acquiring fortune, independence and ease," John Wyeth wrote bitterly, "and all my hopes that the time had now come in the order of Providence, when that uncultivated tract, denominated the *Oregon*

Territory, was to be changed into a fruitful field, and the haunt of savages and wild beasts made the happy abode of refined and dignified man."[46]

In the event, John Wyeth's travails had hardly begun. He reached St. Louis penniless and in tatters. He managed to work his passage to New Orleans as a fireman on a steamboat, but cholera broke out on board, taking the lives of 80 of the 240 passengers and crew. With severe outbreaks of cholera and yellow fever in New Orleans, Wyeth found work as a gravedigger for $2 a day. He dosed his own symptoms of the yellow jack with castor oil, a gill every eight hours as hot as he could stand it, and succeeded in throwing off the disease. He finally reached Boston on January 2, 1833, after an absence of ten months. His kinsman Jacob Wyeth turned up eventually in Galena, Illinois, where, his addiction to liquor notwithstanding, he attempted to settle down to the life of a small-town physician.

In retrospect, Nathaniel Wyeth doubtless wished he had exercised greater care in his choice of traveling companions. He might have predicted the idle and dissolute Jacob Wyeth's treachery; the nephew's vitriol caught him by surprise. Affixing a slightly larger share of blame to Hall Kelley than to his uncle, John Wyeth exacted his revenge in a book plaintively titled *Oregon; or a Short History of a Long Journey,* published later in 1833. Kelley's accounts of Oregon were "inflated and extravagant"—not surprising, as he had never approached nearer to the Columbia than Palmer, Massachusetts; Nathaniel Wyeth had been ill prepared to lead the expedition. "If the blind lead the blind we know what will be the consequence," Wyeth wrote. He concluded with a warning to young farmers and mechanics against the Oregon gamble:

> Oh happy—if he knew his happy state,
> The man, who, free from turmoil and debate,
> Receives his wholesome food from Nature's hand
> The just return of *cultivated* land.[47]

A violent encounter with a band of Gros Ventre Indians delayed resumption of Nathaniel Wyeth's westward march. A Canadian trapper's murder of a Gros Ventre chief touched off the Battle of Pierre's Hole on July 17. When rumors of Gros Ventre retaliation reached them, dozens of mountain men and their Flathead allies surrounded a small party of Gros Ventres in a makeshift redoubt and killed more than twenty in a short, sharp, and unequal fight. Wyeth with the rump of his company finally set out July 24, the trail leading past the scene of the battle. Vultures circled above a dozen or more Indian corpses decomposing in the sun.

Wyeth counted on trapping his way westward. But he found much of the country beyond the Green River denuded—the result of George Simpson's strategy to deny furs to the Americans—and he did not catch his first beaver ("a large one") until August 21. After a brief lay-over at the Hudson's Bay Company's Fort Walla Walla, he set out down the Columbia for Vancouver. John McLoughlin greeted him with "the utmost kindness" there on October 29. He could hardly believe the evidence of his eyes. After weeks in the wilderness, McLough-lin's wheatfields, orchards, livestock, trim white clapboard buildings, grist mills, and shipyard struck him as strange, dreamlike, and un-natural. They exceeded anything in Hall Kelley's feverish imperial imaginings.

Wyeth's business affairs, though, were a shambles. He learned at Vancouver that his seaborne goods had gone down in *Sultana* in a storm off the Society Islands. The people petitioned for their release. He assented to their going, having no choice; two of them drifted south to the Willamette Valley, the first Americans to settle there. "I am now afloat on the great sea of life without stay or support but in good hands, i.e. myself and providence and a few of the H.B. Co. who are perfect gentlemen," he wrote bravely. McLoughlin may have acted the gentleman, but he remained deeply suspicious of Wyeth. Had he come as trader or colonial agent? "Though it may be as he states," the doctor wrote warily, "still I would not be surprised to find that his views are in connection with a plan I see in a Boston paper of March 1831, to colonise the Willamette." While McLoughlin invited Wyeth to winter over at Vancouver, he bluntly warned him off trying to do business in Oregon.[48]

Wyeth's reconnaissances took him downriver to Fort George and into the Willamette Valley as far south as the embryonic community of eight or nine former Hudson's Bay Company *engagés* above the falls. Their material progress astonished him. "They have now been here one year have Hogs, Horses, Cows have built barns, Houses and raised wheat, barley, potatoes, turnips, cabbages, corn, punkins, mel-ons," he observed. Nothing he had seen in all his travels could sur-pass it.

"If this country is ever colonized this is the point to commence," Wyeth wrote.[49]

THE EVANGELS SOUGHT PROFIT of a higher kind in Oregon. As early as 1827 the Congregational-Presbyterian American Board of Commissioners for Foreign Missions proposed a new Plymouth colony along the northwest coast of America, a "planting of Christian institutions on the shores of the Pacific" that would strengthen and encourage the projected ministry among the Indians.[50] Hall Kelley's plea for missionaries to the Oregon Country stirred the Missionary Society of the Methodist Episcopal Church to issue its own call for a presence there. The appeal inspired the American Sunday School Union to donate a box of books for an envisioned Columbia River mission settlement.

Books notwithstanding, the colony remained notional. Then, providentially, the legend of the four benighted Flathead Indians infused the mission movement with energy and purpose. The Flatheads, so the story ran, had journeyed three thousand miles from the western flank of the Rockies to St. Louis in 1831 in search of "the book of Heaven"—the white man's Bible. A Wyandot Indian agent in Ohio heard the tale from a trader friend and passed it along, with embellishments and a drawing of natives with grotesquely misshapen heads, to the Methodist *Christian Advocate*, which published it on March 1, 1833. In the event, the Indians in question—one Flathead and three Nez Perces—had trudged all the way to the banks of the Mississippi out of wanderlust rather than a thirst for the Gospel. Nor yet were their heads flat. In *The Advocate*'s highly colored version of the legend, the four travelers from beyond the mountains were metamorphosed into the Wise Men of the West.

"The story has scarcely a parallel in history," wrote Missionary Society secretary G. P. Disosway. "Let the Church awake from her slumbers and go forth in her strength to the salvation of these wandering sons of our native forests."[51]

The Indians were alleged to have suffered neglect in St. Louis. Two were supposed to have died there, and nobody could say whether the others had survived to recross the mountains and deliver the soul-altering news to their people. But the quest for Christian truth took on a life of its own among the Methodists of New York and New England. Notes, letters, and donations of books, pamphlets, and cash flowed into the *Christian Advocate* offices. Willbur Fisk, the president of Wesleyan University in Connecticut, read the account and concluded that the Flatheads had come expressly in search of Methodists. He at once called for a mission to the natives on the far slopes of the Rockies. The Missionary Society formally approved the project in April, and Fisk set out to recruit volunteers for Flathead service.

"My heart rejoices in the prospect that the mission so near and dear to our hopes and prayers promises so soon to be established," Disosway wrote Fisk.[52]

American Methodists traced their origins to the charismatic English field preacher George Whitefield, whose evangelizing tour of the Middle Colonies and New England in 1739–1740 touched off the chain reaction of religious ecstasy that detonated the first Great Awakening. Whitefield was a friend and associate of John Wesley himself, the founder of the Methodist movement, although they would break in 1741 over Wesley's Arminianism—the anti-Calvinist notion that stressed the compatibility of divine sovereignty with the freedom of the human will. In Wesley's theology, free grace was within reach of all believers. The prospect of Christian Perfection formed the core of his thinking. Wesley built his doctrine on no less an authority than Scripture: "Be ye therefore perfect, even as your father which is in heaven is perfect" (Matthew 5:48). All the same, it was an elusive concept to define. Wrote Wesley in his journals, "Constant communion with God the Father and the Son fills [our] hearts with love. Now this is what I always did, and do now, mean by perfection."[53] Every Christian could strive for a state in which the love of God burned with so pure a flame that it consumed original sin, that instantaneous transfiguration, which could happen to any believer at any time, known as "the Great Salvation."

Wesley's emotionalism and his emphasis on a *personal* experience of God's love inspired a recurrent revivalism on the Methodist circuit, in camp meetings and in chapel. Wesleyanism experienced steady growth in the colonies, and in 1784 Wesley's American followers formally organized the Methodist Episcopal Church. They counted 43,000 members and 198 preachers in the United States at the time of Wesley's death in 1791, on the eve of the second Great Awakening. Distinct Wesleyan attributes of faith in universal salvation and human perfectibility animated this spiritual phenomenon. Missionary, education, and Bible and tract societies flourished as the Awakening burned a broad path through New England and New York. Wesley's doctrine that Christ died for everyone, not just the elect, and that anyone could achieve perfection had clear democratic implications. Wesleyan belief encouraged a social consciousness among Methodists that would eventually help propel the often contradictory reform movements of Jacksonian America: temperance, the abolition of slavery, women's rights, communitarianism, the salvation of natives, and westward conquest—what expansionists would come to call Manifest Destiny.

By the 1830s, the fires of the Great Awakening were banked and the Methodists had evolved from marginal and itinerant beginnings into the largest Protestant denomination in the United States. Churches flourished in settled communities, and a formal domestic missionary establishment reached westward as far as Shawnee Mission in Kansas. From Wesleyan in Middletown, Connecticut, Willbur Fisk led the Methodist free-response defense against a resurgence of neo-Calvinism in New England. One of a modest number of Methodist preachers with a college degree (from Brown University in Rhode Island), Fisk could hold his own intellectually with Yale's powerful conservative theologians.

Fisk emerged, too, as the leading champion of the Flathead venture. "No mission which has been undertaken in modern times seems to have excited such deep and general interest," he would write.[54] No thinking, feeling Christian, in Fisk's view, could deny the natives of the Columbia an opportunity to attain Christian Perfection. He settled in June 1833 on his choice to head the "Mission to the Flathead Indians of Oregon": a large, powerful, intense Vermonter named Jason Lee. He seemed to meet Fisk's exacting standard in every particular.

"God demands of the missionary his life, his all," Fisk once wrote. "The claim is met, the consecration is made, the life is laid upon the altar, and the covenant is ratified in heaven. The missionary goes forth now with a loftiness of purpose and a sublimity of feeling unknown to other minds. Talk no more about his sacrifices—*they are all made*—he is a consecrated man—the anointing of the Holy One is upon him. He now has nothing to fear."[55]

They had met in 1829, when Fisk taught Lee as a minister in training at Wilbraham Academy in Massachusetts. The orphaned son of a Revolutionary War veteran, Lee grew up on a kinsman's farm in Stanstead on the Vermont–Quebec border. He helped his uncle and cousins farm their north country hills; he worked for a while as a

Jason Lee (1803–1845) established the Methodist mission in the Willamette Valley that would form the core of American settlement in Oregon. Lee never successfully resolved the tension between mission work and colonization. (Library of Congress)

lumberjack. Lee had reached his early twenties when he experienced his life-altering epiphany, the flash of spiritual insight that led to his quest for perfection. He returned to Stanstead in 1830 to minister to the Methodists there. By 1833, at the age of thirty, he had risen to become an elder in the Methodist Episcopal Church.

Unencumbered with a family, eager to live among the natives, preach Christ to them, and introduce them to the arts of civilization, Lee struck Fisk as the ideal candidate for the Oregon mission superintendency. "He is the man on whom my mind rested when the subject of this mission was first agitated," Fisk wrote the *Christian Advocate*. "I know him well, and can most cordially recommend him to all the friends of the enterprise as one worthy of their confidence—and he certainly needs their prayers."[56] The tasks of raising money for the mission and arranging a passage to the Oregon Country could be entrusted to the industrious Lee. He quit Stanstead on August 19, 1833, on the first leg of the fifteen-month journey that would lead him to the valley of the Willamette.

Lee gleaned from the newspapers that Nathaniel Wyeth had recently returned to Cambridge from the Columbia with two Indian youths in tow; he and Fisk decided to approach him about the follow-ing summer's expedition. Wyeth remembered John McLoughlin's hospitality, but evidently the doctor's warning had slipped his mind, and he now hoped to further his trading scheme with the Hudson's Bay Company's cooperation. He had written George Simpson to that effect in March 1833, proposing a joint venture. The Little Emperor ignored him. Then, on the return trip East in the summer of 1833, he had fallen in with Benjamin Bonneville and, for a time anyway, con-templated joining forces with him.

Something of an equivocal figure, Captain Benjamin Louis Eulalie de Bonneville, a Paris-born U.S. Army officer on extended furlough, had been traveling in the West in the guise of a trapper-trader since the spring of 1832. Bernard DeVoto and others have speculated that he won the sabbatical in exchange for his services as a government spy. Obviously, writes William Goetzmann, Bonneville was "probing British strength and observing their operations" in the Northwest. War Department orders authorizing his leave called for a detailed report on the country beyond the Rockies lying "between our frontier and the Pacific." Whatever the formal arrangement, Bonneville con-tributed substantially to War Department knowledge of the geogra-phy, economic potential, and native inhabitants of the farther West. Bonneville's expedition took the first wagons over South Pass, blazing a practical route for wheeled vehicles. He established a trading fort near the Green River, a U.S. outpost on the marches of Hudson's Bay Company country. And his journeyings would yield excellent maps—the most accurate representations of the Rockies and the Great Basin of their time.[57]

Captain Bonneville planned two ambitious projects in mid-1833: the establishment of a trading fort in the Columbia basin, and a recon-naissance expedition southwest from the Great Salt Lake into Cali-fornia. Both evidently were meant to further U.S. imperial designs. In a report to the War Department in late July 1833 and based on sec-ondhand sources (including, doubtless, Nathaniel Wyeth), Bonneville described the Willamette as "one of the most beautiful, fertile and extensive vallies in the world, wheat, corn and tobacco country." It was, he suggested, time for action. "If our Government ever intend taking possession of Origon the sooner it shall be done the better," the report advised.[58]

Bonneville sought to draw Wyeth into his California scheme, possibly with the aim of deflecting the New Englander from his own Columbia River project. Wyeth may have considered leading the California expedition; at any rate, he wrote his patron Leonard Jarvis indicating he would stay on another year and trap his way south and west to San Francisco. But soon he changed his mind, and Bonneville turned to the veteran mountain man Joseph Walker to scout a route to California. Parting with Bonneville, Wyeth pushed on northeasterly toward the Missouri. His next venture fell into place suddenly when he met Milton Sublette on the Little Big Horn River in August and contracted with him to supply the Rocky Mountain Fur Company's brigades at the Green River rendezvous of 1834.

Wyeth reached Cambridge on November 6, 1833, and at once began to plan a second expedition to the mouth of the Columbia. He approached Henry Hall, a senior partner in the Boston merchant house of Tucker & Williams, about fronting the necessary capital to purchase the goods and charter a supply ship to send to the Columbia. "I am tired," he wrote Jarvis less than a week after arriving home. "I have nothing to do except make preparations to go and I begin to wish them done that I may be off."[59] By year's end Wyeth had raised $20,000 in capital for the start-up he denominated the Columbia River Fishing and Trading Company.

Jason Lee elected to establish contact with the peripatetic Wyeth in Massachusetts rather than try to join up with him in St. Louis in the spring. Lee had begun to raise money for the mission, raking down, for starters, a gratifying $700 from the Youth Missionary Society at Wesleyan. He, Fisk, and Wyeth met twice in early December at the Bromfield Street Methodist Episcopal Church in Boston, where Wyeth introduced the two Indian young men, one a Nez Perce, the other flat-headed, "though not immediately from the Flat Head tribe," and answered a set of six questions about life and labor on the far side of the Rockies.

What did Wyeth recommend for a mission site?
The enterprise should be not too far from a trading post, and not too high up in the mountains. Kettle Falls on the Columbia might answer. A good fishing spot, the falls drew large crowds of Indians during the annual salmon runs.

What could Wyeth tell the Methodists of the moral and religious character of the Flatheads and their neighbors?

They were Deists (!). "They have public prayers every day in the camp, the chief riding around on horseback and offering the public prayer, and blessing the people. Their morals are better than can be found in any other part of the world, probably, taking the whole population together. In a residence of several months among them, Capt. W never knew of an article being stolen, or a falsehood told, or a rough word spoken."

What is the condition of Flathead women?

The same as with the Dutch: women worked without cessation, although the harder tasks were reserved for men.

What are the prospects for agriculture?

The plains are treeless, the timbered sections steep and rocky. But many esculent roots and some grains were already in cultivation near the trading forts, and some livestock had been introduced.

What reception were the traders and Indians likely to give the missionaries?

The traders would be cordial so long as the missionaries made no attempt to interfere with their business or tried to regulate their dealings with the natives. The Indians were friendly unless provoked. "They receive all white men as friends, and look up to them as men of an order superior to themselves, and therefore capable of instructing them. Any white man gaining their confidence, therefore, will be able to mould and fashion them to almost any reasonable measures and principles."

What are the opportunities for keeping up contact with the United States and obtaining supplies?

Hudson's Bay Company expresses were the most reliable means of communication. A company ship from London called at the mouth of the Columbia once a year. Wyeth's own *May Dacre* would sail for the Columbia sometime before the autumn.[60]

Fisk and Lee collected $210 for the Oregon mission at a packed Sunday night meeting at the Bromfield Street church, then completed Lee's travel arrangements. "Our visit to Capt. Wyeth has been most providential," Fisk wrote his wife. "He is going out with a party in the spring & will take the missionaries under his protection. He is a fine man." Wyeth also offered to ship the mission's supplies in *May Dacre*.[61]

Lee now turned to the task of recruiting a mission staff: his nephew Daniel; schoolteacher Cyrus Shepard; a young Kentuckian named Philip L. Edwards; and Virginia-born handyman Courtney Walker, who—although not a Methodist—expressed, according to Lee, a desire to do good. By February 7, 1834, Wyeth was ready to depart Cambridge. He wrote from Pittsburgh at month's end to arrange for "some medicines for the clap and pox, [for] unless there are remedys the consequences are bad often inducing the men to desert in order to obtain relief." In a separate letter, he sent his wife, Elizabeth, left alone again with their three children, instructions about trimming the trees around the Cambridge house, along with an apology for his lack of warmth: "I have many [letters] to write and am unused to writing ladys anyway."[62]

Lee and the others set out separately for St. Louis in early March. Cyrus Shepard bade an emotional good-bye to his Sabbath classes in Lynn, Massachusetts. "During the recitation of the lesson the tears flowed freely," he confessed. "Could it be that I should behold their faces no more? Ponder with them no more the precious promises of the gospel?" A farmer's son, born in Acton, Massachusetts, in 1798, a meek, biddable, and contemplative lay brother, he taught Scripture to operatives in the shoe factories at Lynn. The African missions caught his fancy, and he had raised money—the substantial sum of $300 in 1833—for missions to the Indians of Canada. When he read of the four Flatheads in the *Christian Advocate*, he resolved at once to go himself to the heathen. "The Lord has opened the way before me," he wrote. "In him is my trust; I feel I can lay all at his feet—resign my friends, and every dear privilege enjoyed here in my native land, and go at his command, trusting in his righteous providence and grace to carry me through a long and wearisome journey in the wilderness." Shepard's name reached Jason Lee, and in November 1833 Lee recommended him to the board as a mission teacher.[63]

Taking leave of his aged mother, a brother and a sister, and the gentle hills of his native Middlesex County, Shepard boarded the mail stage for Springfield on March 4, 1834. The Vanderbilt steamer *Water Witch* carried him overnight from Hartford to New York. "All is alive—all hurry and bustle," Shepard found the workaday city. He compared the metropolis invidiously to orderly New England. "It appears as though most of the dirt and filth are thrown into the streets and the swine are ever ready to gather up the fragments (as they are here permitted to run at large and appear to be the sole scavengers of the City)," he wrote. He called on mission official Nathan Bangs at a Methodist bookstore and drew money for the onward journey, visited an asylum for the deaf and mute, gazed with a mixture of awe and distaste at the chaotic sight of a partially built railroad, and retired early to bed.[64]

The long stage trip from Philadelphia to Pittsburgh proved stimulating in spite of the dusty discomfort and the presence of a bawdy group of traders from Kentucky and Tennessee. They shared the coach with a hard-mannered bailiff escorting two horse thieves in chains. One of the convicts seemed penitent. "Talked with him and exhorted him to return to the path of virtue & rectitude, which he said he would do," Shepard wrote. The vehicle crept over the highest ridge of the Alleghenies; the passengers had to alight and walk three miles over a mountain road. As they descended, he noted with approval the fine stone or brick barns, their roofs thatched with straw, wooden trim painted more often than not. Pittsburgh, though, struck him as smoky, dirty, and foul-smelling. "Coal is universally used for fuel & is very cheap," he remarked. A dense, sooty residue settled on everything, even clothes and exposed skin.[65]

The river steamer *Planter* bore Shepard swiftly downriver. The boat called at Portsmouth, Ohio, to take on wood on March 16, a Sunday—"the second Sabbath that I have been obliged to spend in traveling, a circumstance which never before occurred in my life," Shepard observed with remorse. He went ashore and walked about in a lovely landscape—peach trees in early bloom, trees and shrubs in delicate leaf. But it was all disfigured by the miserable dwellings of the tumbledown town. *Planter* stopped later in the day at Marysville, Kentucky, and Shepard set foot for the first time on the soil of a slave state. "My feelings on this occasion may be more easily imagined than described," he confided in his journal. Someone told him that the steamboat tied up alongside *Planter* had been chartered to carry slaves.[66]

He overtook Jason Lee in Cincinnati. Brother H. B. Bascom delivered a sermon on I Corinthians 2:1–2 ("And I, brethren, when I came to you, came not with excellency of speech or of wisdom, declaring unto you the testimony of God") at the Wesley chapel on Fifth Street.

The congregation afterward contributed more than $80 to the Flathead mission. For some reason—possibly the cold rain that descended all through the day but more likely his own unruliness of spirit—Shepard found himself assailed by doubts and fears of the unknown.

"Soon I expect in the course of Divine Providence to leave civilization and all its comforts and go forth with a few Christian brethren to the benighted natives inhabiting west of the rocky mountains," he wrote in his journal that night. "Danger and death itself stair us in the face, our way is beset with difficulties innumerable. But our almighty Friend has promised 'to be with us always' & it is enough."[67]

The steamboat *Wyoming* delivered the missionaries to Louisville on March 21. Jason Lee preached an hour-long sermon to a joint Methodist-Presbyterian gathering at the Fourth Street Church. His purpose, as he explained it to the Louisvillians, was to preserve "one of the many remnants of tribes of the Indians in the distant west from utter extinction."[68] The collection plate yielded $90 for the mission. The party pushed on, reaching St. Louis on March 31. Both Lees spoke at the Methodist church there, raising another $83 for the cause. Jason Lee made contact with Wyeth; he and Shepard shopped for the traveling outfit. On April 4 Shepard pushed on alone for Independence.

Wyeth remained in St. Louis, attending to last-minute details. The expedition now took on a scientific as well as a mercantile and religious character with the arrival of the Harvard naturalist Thomas Nuttall and his ornithologist friend John Kirk Townsend. Wyeth and Nuttall had met through a mutual friend, James Brown, a publisher of Little, Brown. The Harvard Botanical Gardens, a Nuttall haunt, lay near Fresh Pond. By now Nuttall's fame rivaled his eccentricity. *Le fou* of Wilson Price Hunt's 1811 voyage had cofounded the Philadelphia Academy of Natural Sciences and risen to a lectureship at Harvard, where he won notoriety for his habit of entering his second-floor study by a rope ladder and trapdoor. There were substantive achievements, too: his *Genera of North American Plants* (1818) and *Manual of Ornithology of the United States and Canada* (1832, with an acknowledgment to Wyeth in the preface). Wyeth had tapped Nuttall's knowledge of the West before embarking on the 1832 expedition and sent him specimens from the Green River in 1833. He suggested then that Nuttall join the new venture. "The cost would be less than living at home," Wyeth promised.[69] Nuttall's young associate Townsend, the son of a Quaker watchmaker, had a reputation yet to make. Nuttall invited him along to study new bird species and collect specimens for the Philadelphia academy.

Wyeth assisted with their gear: "several pairs of leathern pantaloons," wrote the twenty-three-year-old Townsend, "enormous overcoats made of green blankets, and white wool hats, with round crowns, fitting tightly to the head, brims five inches wide, and almost thick enough to resist a rifle ball."[70] He and Nuttall decided to walk the three hundred miles to Independence while Wyeth wrapped up his affairs in St. Louis. They set out at noon on March 29, tramping northwest over a dry, heavily timbered plain. Nuttall refused to shoot, so it fell to the Quaker Townsend to supply game for meals as well as specimen birds: pileated woodpeckers, greater prairie chickens, varieties of waterfowl, sandhill cranes, passenger pigeons, Carolina parakeets. They observed mass flights of cranes, some cruising at extreme altitude. Townsend destroyed a quantity of golden plovers; they made good eating. The parakeets (Conuropsis carolinensis) were gaudy in their fine red and green plumage, and utterly innocent of humans and their weapons. (The species is extinct today, with the last confirmed sighting in Missouri in 1905, according to David Allen Sibley.) It grieved Townsend to slaughter them.

He wrote, "They seem entirely unsuspicious of danger, and after being fired at, only huddle closer together, as if to obtain protection from each other, and as their companions are falling around them, they curve down their necks, and look at them fluttering on the ground, as though perfectly at a loss to account for so unusual an occurance. It is a most inglorious sort of shooting; down right, cold-blooded murder."[71]

Weary of walking, Townsend flagged the upriver steamboat carrying Wyeth on April 9. Five days later the party came ashore at Independence. Situated on high ground commanding the surrounding country, the town consisted of some fifty log and clay houses, a half-dozen stores, and two taverns. Most of Wyeth's people lay encamped along the river awaiting the arrival of Jason Lee.

The steamboat Iowa, laboring against the spring current, carried Cyrus Shepard up the ale-colored Missouri, a tedious passage. Reaching Independence at last, he promptly fell ill. Sickly and depressed, he looked daily for Brother Lee's arrival. Easter on the Missouri frontier provided no balm to his troubled spirit. "How unlike this to a peaceful Sabbath morn in N.E. where the welcome sound of the

Church going bell calls to public worship and thousands, hearing, obey the joyful summons with willing feet," he wrote on Sunday the twentieth. "Here all is bustle & labor as on an ordinary day." Finally, on April 22, "to my unspeakable comfort," Lee arrived.[72]

Wyeth, meantime, had pushed on ahead of the missionaries. Perhaps it was the encounter with Jason Lee and company, or perhaps last-minute doubts akin to Shepard's, that led Wyeth to reflect on his larger purposes. What if the Columbia River Fishing and Trading Company should founder? In boom-and-bust 1830s America, sunny optimism warred perpetually with the bitter prospect of failure. Unburdening himself in a letter to his wife, Wyeth revealed uncertainties and ambiguities that he kept well-hidden in ordinary moods.

"I feel as much as you can do the lonesomeness of my way of life but you know the success of what I have undertaken is life itself to me and if I do fail in it they shall never say it was for want of perseverance," he wrote Elizabeth Wyeth. "But this is my last attempt and if I am not successfull I must come home and endeavor the best way I can to get a living and to pay my debts which will then be heavy. Still I am yet sanguine that I shall succeed. I will take good care of myself and perhaps the life which began in turmoil may yet end up in quiet and peace and our sun go down from a clear sky.

"I cannot but reproach myself," he went on, "that I have made you in some measure a widow when you ought to be enjoying yourself."[73]

Jason Lee arranged for the purchase of cows and extra horses and oversaw the loading of the pack animals on the morning of the twenty-sixth, a Saturday. The missionaries took the road for Wyeth's camp at noon, but with the late start covered only half the distance. Lee reluctantly violated his strictures against Sunday travel and continued on the next day, fearing Wyeth would leave him behind otherwise. As it happened, Lee read Wyeth accurately. The captain had sloughed off his melancholy and was in a tearing hurry to get under way.

"There are none of the Dignitaries with me as yet and if they 'preach' much longer in the States they will loose their passage for I will not wait a minute for them," Wyeth wrote his backers at Messrs. Tucker & Williams.[74]

SO CAPTAIN WYETH'S EXPEDITION commenced the journey westward, men with varying motives, instincts, and compulsions. Some, missionary and trader alike, sought escape from the vexations and anxieties of the competitive and tumultuous East. Life beyond the mountains, however trying physically, would be simpler anyhow. Wyeth went in search of the fortune that had eluded him up to now. For Nuttall and Townsend the trip promised adventure, and an opportunity to enlarge the nation's knowledge of the natural history of the West. At the conscious level, Jason Lee believed his advent in Oregon would better the natives' spiritual and temporal condition. He regarded himself as a minister, not a colonizer. In St. Louis he had met with representatives of an emigration group called the Western Colonization Society and judged their noble words as a cloak for a plan of conquest.

"The ostensible object of the society is the good of the Indians," he wrote the *Christian Advocate*. "But . . . their first object is to get a title to land, and hence circumscribe the boundary of the Indian. When they arrive they must, in the very nature of things, turn their attention to providing for themselves, and I am satisfied that such a colony will find enough to do for a long time, without looking after the welfare of the Indian. And it would have a tendency to collect the abandoned and disaffected traders and trappers; and, like every other colony that has been planted among the Indians, would ultimately scatter and cause to become extinct the very tribes which they designated to save."[75]

Still, Townsend discerned something of the pioneer in Jason Lee—a leader, a "tall and powerful man," he wrote, "who looks as though he were well-calculated to buffet difficulties in a wild country." He wondered whether Lee's natural executive abilities would deflect him from his vocation as a spiritual servant to the natives. Townsend detected a spirit kindred to his own in the younger missionaries, Daniel Lee, Edwards, and Walker. They had "arrayed themselves under the missionary banner chiefly for the gratification of seeing a new country, and participating in strange adventures," Townsend thought.[76] Shepard, older than the others, pietistic, ever anxious about the condition of his soul, stood a little apart. His journey led inward.

The Wyeth caravan, seventy men with two hundred horses and mules, struck tents and departed the riverside camp in the forenoon of April 28, 1834. A good road traversed rolling prairie. Each man rode a horse and led two pack animals. The missionaries with their horned cattle trailed a few miles behind. After the midday meal they picked up the pace, Lee wrote with a sense of the occasion, "and came into camp at dusk thankful that we were on our way to the farthest West."[77]

They had covered fifteen miles, crossing the Missouri line and penetrating a few miles into Kansas. Violent storms with heavy rain and hail the size of musket balls struck the train the next day. The missionaries gratefully passed the wet, muddy night of the twenty-ninth with the Methodists at four-year-old Shawnee Mission, near present Kansas City.

Wyeth's standing orders prescribed a nightly bivouac in a hollow square, with baggage piled up to provide cover against attack. The horses were staked out in the center of the square; a rotating duty roster detailed six men to stand watch through the night. The animals were turned out to graze at daybreak. The men broke camp at about seven-thirty, plodded westward until noon, rested for two hours, and continued on until just before sunset, Wyeth aiming for an average of twenty miles a day.

The stage of May 1 brought the first encounter with native people—a band of Kansa Indians (or Kaws, a branch of the Osage tribe). To Townsend, with his naturalist's attention to detail, they were picturesque: they used little or no paint; dressed in European pantaloons and, from the waist up, a blanket or a buffalo robe; and had their heads shaved except for a distinctive tuft gathered into a queue and plaited. The children ran about in the natural state. Long accustomed to Europeans (the Spanish and French began trading along the marches of their country in the seventeenth century), the Kansas were avid to deal, offering buffalo robes and hide halters in exchange for fat bacon and tobacco.

The missionaries regarded the Kansas with none of Townsend's scientific detachment. Here, gratifyingly if shockingly, were specimens of the human material they had come to remold. The Kansas were thievish, importunate, dirty, and hungry. Cholera had frightened most of the people away the year before, and their corn, beans, and pumpkins had rotted in the fields. "They appear in the most rude and uncivilized state of any human beings I have ever seen," Shepard thought. Some of the adults were so scantily clothed as to be virtually naked, and their nose, ear, and wrist ornaments struck him as grotesque. "Even their infants had large holes cut through various parts of their ears & ears & neck were set off in a gaudy manner with beads and other trinkets," he went on. All the same, he confided to Jason Lee that he had never been more certain of his calling to serve the Indians.[78]

"Never felt so much like making sacrifice of time, talent, strength and life for the amelioration of the condition of the red men as at present," Shepard wrote in his journal. "O how superlatively great are the blessings of Christianity and civilization and on the other hand how miserably wretched the condition of the poor savage."[79]

They crossed the Kansas River at midday on May 3, ferrying the baggage in a flat-bottomed boat and swimming the horses and cattle. Wyeth ordered a layover for the next day, Sunday. Rain fell in the morning. As before, the contrast of the past and the present moment oppressed Shepard. His mood veered abruptly: he felt morose, put upon, and resentful. "I am called to renounce the privileges and comforts of my own native land," he wrote, "& now while many Christian friends and brethren in New England are in the sanctuary of the Lord and about to celebrate the dying love of Christ, I with three Christian brethren am camped here on the bank of the Kanzas more than two thousand miles from home surrounded by a wicked profane & licentious company of white men and some scores of Indians whose minds are deep as night."[80] Lee complained, too, about Wyeth's infidel disregard of the Sabbath. Mounting guard, tending the animals, and mending harness—these duties and myriad camp chores had to be carried out every day, Sundays not excepted.

Hard marching through mixed prairie and woodland produced the expedition's first desertions (four men slipped away during the night of May 5) and casualty. Milton Sublette, Wyeth's Rocky Mountain Fur Brigade contact, experienced so much pain from a swollen and bruised leg—a fungal infection, according to Townsend—that he decided on May 8 to turn back for St. Louis. Food stocks already were running low. The Indians' half-starved dogs had broken into the provisions a night or two before and devoured fifty pounds of bacon, and a beef cow remained missing after wandering off during a thunderstorm. Lee began to doubt whether rations would hold out until they could gain buffalo country. The expedition of trapper William Sublette, also bound for the Green River rendezvous, caught up to and passed Wyeth on May 12.

The train traversed the disputed country between the Vermilion and the Platte. Several tribes here contested for primacy. By an 1833 treaty, the long-established Pawnees had ceded claims to hunting grounds south of the Platte, but Pawnee war parties were still apt to clash with Delaware and Shawnee bands the U.S. government had forcibly relocated from the Midwest. The Pawnees were quarrelsome and light-fingered, Wyeth told Townsend, explaining his decision to force the pace in hopes of clearing the country without incident. He managed to keep a day or two ahead of the main band, and offered presents to conciliate stray Pawnees who approached in twos and threes. They struck Townsend as noble-looking but mendacious. "Their persons were tall, straight and finely formed; their noses slightly aquiline; and the whole countenance expressive of high and daring intrepidity," he wrote. In their dealings with whites they were arbitrary and difficult, like the most disagreeable sort of merchant-huckster at home.[81]

The route followed the northward course of the Little Blue. Deer, prairie hens, and turkeys were abundant, but everyone kept a lookout for buffalo. Townsend sighted his first pronghorn antelope, "the most beautiful animals I ever saw." Agile and swift, they were nearly as large as a deer, with short, curved horns. "The ears are very delicate," he went on, "almost as thin as paper, and hooked at the tip like the horns."[82] The men judged the meat inferior to common venison and refused to eat it, although they gleefully carried out a great slaughter of antelope for love of "sport." A twenty-five-mile march on May 17 brought the expedition to the banks of the Platte. Courtney Walker caught a catfish to supplement the missionaries' meager diet of boiled corn and milk. Townsend observed great blue herons, sandhill cranes, and long-billed curlews stalking the shallows.

The Platte flowed thick, turbid, shallow, and nearly a mile wide through country as level, in Townsend's phrase, as a racecourse. But that was deceptive, for they were on a gradual, imperceptible, but steady uptilt. The horizons seemed boundless, the prairie like a dry tan and green sea. Rain fell on May 18, the first in nearly two weeks. Outriders shouted word of the first buffalo sighting on the twentieth. "Saw at least thousands of Buffaloe today," Lee wrote on the twenty-first. "The bottom lands along the river are literally black with them for miles."[83] Wyeth's hunters set off in pursuit, killing five buffalo that afternoon.

Within a day or so, the thick, dark animal mass had vanished as though the earth had opened and swallowed it. Townsend and Jason Lee joined the expedition hunters Richardson and Sandsbury, deployed to track down the herd. A cold wind whipped up clouds of gritty dust. After an hour's ride to the south, they spotted a number of animals rolling about in the sand. Hunting on his own, Townsend rounded the base of a low hill and encountered twenty buffalo lying on the ground thirty yards distant. He crept up from downwind, chose a large bull on the edge of the herd, took careful aim, and fired. The beasts rose and lumbered off indignantly. Just as he concluded he had missed, one of the animals came to a sudden halt.

"I rode towards him, and sure enough, there was my great bull trembling and swaying from side to side, and the clotted gore hanging like icicles from his nostrils," Townsend wrote. "In a few minutes after, he fell heavily upon his side, and I dismounted and surveyed the unwieldy brute, as he panted and struggled in the death agony."[84]

He tried to lift the creature's head so he could cut out the tongue, a delicacy, but it was too heavy. Richardson and Sandsbury teased him for destroying a bull; experienced hunters always marked out the cows, they reminded him, as superior eating. Plying long knives, they began "fleecing" the animal, skinning it along the back and down the sides to remove the choicer parts of the flesh.

Naturalist and missionary alike remarked on the hunters' appalling prodigality. A mature, healthy cow weighed 700 to 800 pounds on average, and yielded some 400 pounds of meat; bulls were considerably larger, averaging 1,800 pounds. Rib meat, the tongue and heart, and the marrowbones frequently were the only cuts the hunters bothered to carry away. Buffalo provided food, clothing, footwear, bedding, cookware, bowstrings, and fuel to the Plains Indians, but they could be wasteful, too. Anthropologist Shepard Krech III has estimated that the Plains tribes slaughtered 720,000 to 840,000 buffalo annually and that, like the whites, they often took only the most desirable parts in times of abundance, leaving the rest to rot and bleach in the sun.

Townsend estimated the waste of this hunt at a thousand pounds. Over the course of the journey, he would see dozens of buffalo slaughtered for their tongues alone, or for rifle practice. The wanton killing sickened Cyrus Shepard. "I consider it an abuse of the kind bounties of our heavenly father & lessening of the means of support to the poor *Indians*," he wrote.[85] On this hunting excursion, though, Richardson exploited even the animals' juices. As he slit open the paunch, a green, gelatinous liquid gushed out. The hunter strained the juice into a pan and offered a drain—cider, he called it—to Townsend and Lee. Both declined.

"It was too thick with excrement to please my fancy," said Lee, "though they affirmed with oaths that it was very good."[86]

The train forded the South Fork of the Platte on May 24 and struck out for the North Platte, twenty-five miles distant. Here the landscape began to change. High bluffs hemmed in a virtually treeless sandy plain. The men swaddled themselves in shirts, wore handkerchiefs over their faces, and pulled their coats over their heads for protection against buzzing throngs of gnats. Townsend reported sighting prairie dogs and rattlesnakes; Nuttall recorded dozens of new plant species every day. The solemn beauty of the country stirred Jason Lee emotionally, even though the constant "cursing and shooting etc." of Wyeth's rowdies drained away some of his pleasure in the journey. "I feel a lack in my own mind, a want [of] a closer walk with him whom my soul loveth, a more free and constant communication with the Author of all happiness," he wrote on Sunday the twenty-fifth. "O Lord my God make me spiritually minded which is life and peace."[87] The going was physically tougher now too: the roll and heave of the land; the disappearance of buffalo for several days (Wyeth ordered a steer killed); strong headwinds and driven sand thick as snow with the sting of a knife edge on bare skin.

The route crossed the indeterminate boundary between Pawnee and Sioux country and led past massive clay and sandstone outcrops that would guide thousands of travelers over the next thirty years: Courthouse Rock ("a dilapidated feudal castle," in Townsend's fanciful phrase), Chimney Rock, the layered clay and limestone formations of Scott's Bluff ("some of them extremely high and resembling different figures of buildings, fortifications & c," observed Shepard).[88] One of the men captured a young antelope; the missionaries helped tame the creature by giving her milk from a tin cup. After a while she responded to the name the men had chosen: Zip Coon; she rode part of the time in high style on one of the mules atop a pannier of willow branches. The caravan reached the Laramie River after several days' travel through a dramatically drab landscape. The snow peaks of the Black Hills (today's Laramie Mountains) loomed wild and romantic to the northwest. William Sublette's men were building a trading fort near the junction of the Laramie and the Platte. The neatly laid out rows of corn near the roughly built post, then dubbed Fort William, caught Lee's eye. He quoted:

> The sound of the church bell,
> These vallies and rocks never heard,
> Never sighed at the sound of a knell,
> Or smiled when a Sabbath appeared.[89]

Leaving the North Platte beyond the Red Buttes after three weeks along its course, the expedition entered a region of relentless sun, burned grass, and a ceaseless wind that coated food, equipment, and clothing with gritty layers of sand. Shepard had been unwell, afflicted with diarrhea; and despite regular sessions of hymn singing, praying, and Scripture reading with Daniel Lee, an intense spiritual desolation had again overtaken him. The corrupt side of his nature had regained ascendancy. Besides, he was tired and cold: wolves howled around the campsite all night, and when he arose before dawn he found a skim of ice in the half-full water pail.

The caravan advanced northwesterly through desiccated country toward the Sweetwater River. Wild sage and prickly pear grew profusely in the sandy plain, and buffalo were temporarily abundant again. They reached the humped granite monolith of Independence Rock, roughly a third of the distance to Fort Vancouver, on June 9. Wyeth etched his name into the bald brown stone. Nuttall discovered a nondescript whipporwill; Townsend collected a new specimen of mountain plover and sage thrasher. The Sweetwater here ran cool and limpid; for a change, the horses grazed on thick browse. Townsend sighted large flocks of brown, black, and white American avocets, elegant birds with long, upcurved bills. They pushed on slowly through wild and broken country, the jagged peaks of the Wind River Range soaring to the west. Buffalo had everywhere cropped the grass to the roots, and the horses were becoming so jaded from overwork and lack of nourishment that the men were obliged to walk most of the time. The cattle were exhausted, thirsty, and hungry; the cow column lagged farther behind every day. Mornings broke bitterly cold, but by midday the temperature had climbed into the eighties.

Wyeth cleared South Pass on Sunday, June 15, and followed the line of the Big Sandy south and west toward the valley of the Green River. He did not think to mention the landmark in his journal. Buffalo again were scarce. ("The life of our little favorite, 'Zip,' has several times been menaced," noted Townsend.) Then, too, the approaching rendezvous preoccupied Wyeth. He had sent an express ahead to announce his arrival but as yet had received no reply. The bitter blow landed on June 18: Thomas Fitzpatrick, representing the Rocky Mountain Fur Company, refused to accept Wyeth's cargo— $3,000 worth of pack saddles, hobbles and halters, shoes, saddle blankets, guns and ammunition, and provisions.

There was nothing to do but to plod on across the scorched hills. The expedition reached the junction of the Big Sandy and the Green on June 19, fifty-one days out of Independence—one of the fastest overland trips on record, according to William Goetzmann, but not fast enough. Outmarching Wyeth, William Sublette struck a wildcat deal to supply Fitzpatrick's brigades. Wyeth pitched camp near the site of the rendezvous, the tenth installment of the annual trapper-trader wilderness extravaganza. The legendary fur trader Billy Ashley had developed the system by which free trappers remained in the field all year, gathering in midsummer to deliver their pelts, trade, and indulge in a companionable excess of drinking, gambling, and other sinful pleasures. As Townsend remarked, they consumed vast quantities of diluted liquor sold at a profiteering $3 a pint and stumbled about the camp trailing wreaths of 10-cent-a-pound tobacco for which the traders demanded $2. Little or no specie changed hands at the rendezvous. The trappers paid in skins or charged their purchases against their wages; most returned to the beaver streams with only hangovers and debts to show for the previous year's exertions.

Wyeth had warned Jason Lee in advance about the rendezvous. "They threatened that when we came they would give 'them missionaries' Hell and Captain W. advised us to be on our guard and give no offense and if molested to show no symptoms of fear," wrote Lee. "I *feared* no man and apprehended no danger from them when sober and when drunk we would endeavor to [keep] out of their way." He decided to go into the trappers' camp and introduce himself. "Spent some time with them on the difficulties of the route, changes of habit and various topics," he wrote. As usual, Lee managed to charm people who in the nature of things would be expected to recoil in the presence of his overwhelming piety. He came away feeling assured there would be no trouble with the trappers.[90]

Townsend and Daniel Lee fell ill. Shepard dosed Lee with peppermint drops, bathed his feet, massaged his temples and legs, and pressed hot flannel onto his back and bowels, though without apparent effect. The ceaseless racket of roistering trappers grated on Townsend's nerves, adding fractiousness of spirit to physical ailment. He complained, "I am compelled all day to listen to the hiccoughing jargon of drunken traders, the *sacré* and *foutre* of Frenchmen run wild, and the swearing and screaming of our own men, who are scarcely less savage than the rest, being heated by the detestable liquor which circulates freely among them." Lee, in good health and spirits ("I am twelve pounds heavier than when I left the states," he noted with pleasure), engaged in some trading on his own, exchanging $55 worth of red cloth for a trapper's mule.[91]

Captain Wyeth was sunk in gloom, his mercantile plans deranged once again. The organizations, it seemed, had closed ranks against the solitary entrepreneur. The American fur brigades were evidently as exclusive a business fraternity as the Hudson's Bay Company. "So far this business looks black," Wyeth wrote Leonard Jarvis from the rendezvous. Thomas Fitzpatrick explained blithely that the partners had "dissolved" the Rocky Mountain Fur Company, rendering the contract null. In fact, the Rocky Mountain and American Fur Companies had decided to end their long rivalry and divide the country between them.[92] This would have the effect of squeezing out Wyeth, Bonneville, and other trappers new to the field. Wyeth suspected that William Sublette had simply bribed Fitzpatrick with a better offer. In any case he was without recourse, as he explained to Messrs. Tucker and Williams.

"There is no law here," he wrote.[93]

Lee enjoyed greater success in his dealing with the Flathead and Nez Perce contingents. Captain Bonneville had nothing but good to report of these tribes. "The Flatheads are said to be the only Indians here who have never killed a white man," he wrote; and the tribes together were "the most honest and religious people I ever saw, observing every festival of the Roman church, avoiding changing their camp on Sundays tho in distress for provisions."[94] A delegation welcomed Lee to "their country" on June 21. The next day, a Sunday, he invited a large group of Indians into his tent for a dissertation on the Ten Commandments. For now, anyway, they seemed more interested in the white men's practical skills, and in whether they planned to settle in the neighborhood and farm.

"They inquired if we could build houses and said that the Indians at Walla Wallah gave horses to a white man to build them a house and when he got the horses he went off and did not build it," Lee wrote in his journal. "We of course expressed our strong disapproval of his conduct. They said if we could build a house for them they would catch plenty of beaver for us which we take as a favorable indication showing their desire for improvement."[95]

The missionaries improved the time washing and mending clothing, saddles, and harness in preparation for the onward journey. Jason

Lee marked his thirty-first birthday on June 28. "Once I sincerely wished that I had never seen the light but bless the Lord it is otherwise with me now," he confided in his journal. "I thank God that I was ever born of the flesh that I might be born of the spirit."[96] On July 1 Lee sent off long letters to the editor of the *Christian Advocate,* Willbur Fisk, Nathan Bangs, and others. In the letter to the *Advocate,* Lee recommended Sublette's Fort William on the Laramie River as a suitable site for a mission to the Sioux, and suggested the Crows would welcome a band of missionaries. He also hinted for the first time that he had begun to revisit the original notion of settling in the interior along the western flank of the Rockies. Possibly the wild emptiness of the mountain country intimidated him; possibly Wyeth's descriptions of the soft and bountiful lower Columbia country subtly had begun to alter his thinking.

"We leave to-morrow, and shall probably reach the Pacific the last of August," Lee wrote the *Advocate.* "I think we shall experience some difficulty in choosing the place of our location. We shall pass speedily through the country, and shall not have time to examine it much; but I leave this with the Lord, who has pointed the way for us thus far, and who I trust will still guide us by his spirit."[97]

Making the best of difficult circumstances, Wyeth now resolved to push north into the Snake River country and halt to build a trading fort from which he could peddle the goods Fitzpatrick had refused to accept. On July 2 Lee parted company with the Indians with a feeling of regret, which only deepened when they asked when they would see him again. He equivocated, hinting that he might return after the second or third snow. "They all shook hands with me in the most cordial hearty and friendly manner," Lee wrote. "Lord direct us in our choice of a location." Wyeth broke out the liquor—too much liquor—on July 4 to celebrate the anniversary of U.S. independence. The indulgence had the effect of causing the men to reach for their firearms, and they discharged volley after volley into the mountain night. "We who were not 'happy' had to lie flat upon the ground to avoid the bullets which were careering through the camp," Townsend remarked. There were no casualties. They reached the Bear River without further incident on July 5, laagering up along its banks that evening.[98]

This was rough, volcanic country, the atmosphere suffused with the acrid exhalations of mineral hot springs. Little Zip, the tame antelope that had been the expedition's mascot since the first days along the Platte, stumbled on the march, shattered a leg, and had to be destroyed. Wyeth called on the tenth at Benjamin Bonneville's camp near Soda Springs. He doubtless talked over sites for his projected trading post with the traveler the natives called "the Bald Chief." The caravan reached the Snake River on July 14. The next day, Wyeth selected a broad plain at the junction of the Snake and the Portneuf and dispatched one party to fell cottonwoods for the stockade and another to collect meat for the next stages of the journey. Lee fell ill and retired to his tent, reading his Bible and the memoirs of Ann H. Judson, wife of the Burma missionary Adoniram Judson. The book had made the rounds among the Methodists, who regarded the Judsons' experiences along the Irrawaddy as a model for the salvation of the heathen.

From his sickbed, Lee considered the possibility of continuing westward with the Hudson's Bay Company trapper Thomas McKay, whose party lay in bivouac nearby. The Lees had dined with the affable McKay, the son of an Indian woman and Alexander McKay, the Astorian who had been blown up with *Tonquin* off Vancouver Island in 1811. "He appears quite friendly to us and our enterprise," Shepard remarked of McKay, "& promises us any assistance in his power."[99] McKay promised, too, to travel more deliberately than Wyeth, making life with the long-horned cattle easier.

Wyeth, meantime, christened the post Fort Hall, after his Boston patron Henry Hall. He seemed pleased with his craftsmanship, not least with the American flag he quilted from a rectangle of unbleached sheeting, red flannel, and patches of blue cloth. "I assure you the Fort looks quite as warlike as a pile of ice but not quite so profittable," Wyeth wrote his onetime partner Frederic Tudor. The hunters returned to camp on July 25 with twenty-four hundred pounds of meat baled in dried buffalo skins. On the evening of Sunday the twenty-seventh, Lee—still weak from fever—delivered what would go down in the annals as the first Protestant sermon west of the Rockies. A dozen or so Bannock Indians, most of Wyeth's men, and all of McKay's band gathered in a grove near the rudimentary fort. Shepard felt ill and depressed, a black reaction to the ecstatic joy he had experienced the night before, when his "soul caught new fire by a glimpse of the Divine glory."[100] Lee read from the Fiftieth Psalm:

A mid-nineteenth-century view of Fort Hall, Idaho. Massachusetts trader Nathaniel Wyeth built the original outpost at the junction of the Portneuf and Snake Rivers out of cottonwood logs. During the Hudson's Bay Company's occupancy, Fort Hall served as a resupply post for early travelers along the Oregon Trail. (Library of Congress)

> I will take no bullock out of thy house, nor he goats out of thy folds.
> For every beast of the forest is mine, and the cattle upon a thousand hills.
> I know all the fowls of the mountains: and the wild beasts of the field are mine.
> If I were hungry, I would not tell thee: for the world is mine, and the fulness thereof.
> Will I eat the flesh of bulls, or drink the blood of goats?
> Offer unto God thanksgiving; and pay thy vows unto the most High:
> And call upon me in the day of trouble: I will deliver thee, and thou shalt glorify me.

Townsend came away impressed. "The people were remarkably quiet and attentive, and the Indians sat upon the ground like statues," he wrote. None of the natives understood a word, although as Lee proceeded with the Methodist order of worship they kneeled when he kneeled, rose to their feet when he rose. "I really enjoyed the whole scene," Townsend went on; "it possessed the charm of novelty." After the service, McKay's free-spirited French Canadians purged themselves of high Methodist solemnity by organizing a horse race. One of the men was thrown and mortally injured. Lee officiated at the funeral the next morning, and all the Canadians turned out.

"Being Catholics they placed a black cross on his breast, made of cloth served upon his shroud," Shepard observed. They buried the body without a coffin, wrapped in a buffalo skin.[101]

The missionaries and the Scots gentleman-adventurer William Drummond Stewart, who had joined the expedition at the rendezvous, parted with Wyeth on July 30. Townsend, for one, felt sorry to see Lee and company go. The men, he thought, had liked Lee, too, in spite of his regular admonitions on drunkenness and profanity. "The reproof, although decided, clear and strong, is always characterized by the mildness and affectionate manner peculiar to the man," Townsend observed.[102] As the McKay caravan moved off, Wyeth's men fired a three-round salute. Lee and his people responded with three cheers.

With McKay in the van, the missionaries crossed the Portneuf and proceeded slowly through a region of round, sage-covered hills. Shepard accidentally discharged a rifle in the tent on the night of August 1, just missing Jason Lee's head. At least now, thought the pacifistic Shepard, he ought to be able to put away the rifle finally, for according to McKay they had cleared the country of the cantankerous Blackfeet. "My prayer to God has been that we might be kept from the sad necessity of conflicting with these untutored wild men who by nature are our brethren and whose salvation I most ardently desire," Shepard wrote. On August 7 McKay led the band through a long defile overspread with a forest canopy. A gradual climb to a summit revealed "a vast desert plain spreading out before us like the boundless ocean" to Shepard's weary gaze.[103]

Day after burning day the missionaries labored over brown hills scored with deep ravines. They were hungry most of the time, thirsty, sore, and pursued by clouds of stinging white gnats. Parties of Shoshone and Snake Indians turned up from time to time with offers of salmon for fishhooks, knives, and clothing. Shepard's mood swung from rapture to mortification and back again. "Suffered much last night and this morning from the risings of the carnal mind but on looking to Jesus I conquered through prayer," he confided to his journal.[104] McKay, who intended to remain in the mountains for another winter's trapping, parted from the missionaries on August 16, leaving them with twenty pounds of flour, tea, and a quantity of sugar. He also may have implanted a renewed vision of the lower Columbia in Jason Lee. McKay owned a farm in the *engagé* settlement in the

Willamette Valley and doubtless sang the region's praises to Lee—and perhaps mentioned, too, the need for a religious presence there. With the farewell to McKay, the missionaries continued westward in Stewart's company, making a steady fifteen to twenty hard, hot miles a day.

Leaving the Snake behind at last, they pushed into Oregon and savored a rare break from Sunday travel on August 24. "This holy Sabbath has been to us pilgrims little else for four months but a day of labor, toil and fatigue but far be it from me to murmur or complain," Lee wrote. "All is right. All is as it should be." A few days later the Lees and Shepard visited a Cayuse village. They tried to buy salmon and camas, but the Indians had none to spare. They were, however, offered a meal of boiled salmon and chokecherries in the chief's lodge; the Cayuse chief and a visiting Wallawalla Indian dignitary presented four horses to the missionaries. Lee played the natives a return at the missionary camp, making presents of knives, fishhooks, and awls to the headman and his entourage. "They called us friends, and seemed very anxious that we should return and live with them," he wrote. "Who would have thought that these Indians would have shown such kindness and generosity to strangers on account of their religion?" That explained, he decided, why the Indians took so much more interest in the missionaries than in others.[105]

A steep, hard climb through heavy timber brought the travelers on August 30 to the main ridge of the Blue Mountains. All the open country hereabouts had been charred black as a hat and smoke from grass fires hung so thick they could see only a few yards into the murk. After an abrupt descent, they pushed across sand and gravel hills toward the Hudson's Bay Company's Fort Walla Walla. Wrote Shepard, "Passed two small cornfields which gave us peculiar sensations of delight, being the first traces of cultivation we had seen for nearly four months."[106] The route rose to a summit, and in the late-afternoon light they caught their first distant glimpse of the fort's stockade and bastions.

Wyeth's party, short a dozen men the captain had left behind to garrison Fort Hall, arrived a day or two later. Wyeth had lingered in the Grande Ronde, where he had again fallen in with Bonneville, perhaps to discuss their independent challenges to Hudson's Bay Company dominance. Townsend expressed delight at his first view of "the white tent of our long-lost missionaries" pitched in the shadow of the drift-log fort. The post lay a hundred yards from the southern bank of the Columbia, in a sandy plain sparsely grown with worm-wood and thorn bushes. The company's agent, Pierre Pambrun, had laid out a kitchen garden along the river in a thin strip of rich alluvial soil in which he tended a subsistence crop of potatoes, turnips, carrots, and maize.

Provisions were scarce at Walla Walla, as Pambrun explained— only a little corn, flour, salt, fat, and a quantity of salmon. He could offer bread, though, the first the missionaries had eaten in months. "Capt. Stewart killed a horse for meat, being the only kind he could get here, as he could not eat fish," Jason Lee noted. "We concluded to live on fish." Shepard walked down to the edge of the Columbia. The river's banks, he thought, resembled "some of my favorite haunts on the shore of the Atlantic in the town of Lynn in New England." Shepard observed on September 4 that he had been away from home for six months to the day.[107]

The expedition divided again for the descent of the Columbia. The missionaries with Stewart set off by barge in the forenoon of September 4, leaving the long-horned cattle behind. The current carried them swiftly downstream, but soon they were forced to put to shore to caulk the leaky vessel. They resumed the journey the next day. Wyeth with Townsend and Nuttall followed on the tenth and overtook the missionaries at the Cascades on September 14, a Sunday. Lee and company had encountered rain and stiff headwinds for several days; Townsend found them wet and bedraggled in a make-shift camp. He helped them kindle a fire, and they made a supper of salmon bought from Indians. Showers of rain drifted across the river all through the night.

The missionaries pushed into the Columbia in an enveloping mist at about 7:30 A.M. on September 15 for the last stage of the overland trip. They reached "King George," as the natives dubbed Fort Van-couver, early in the afternoon. The Olympian, white-maned figure of John McLoughlin met them at the landing stage. As ever, he was cor-dial and open, despite his predatory appearance. Lee stared in frank wonder at groups of neat buildings (storehouses, gristmills, threshing mills, sawmills, and thirty or more log huts of the company servants); McLoughlin's dazzlingly white clapboard house dominating its quad-rangle; fine, open prospects to the south and southeast to snowcapped Mount Hood in the far distance; hundreds of acres planted to wheat, barley, peas, beans, corn, melons, pumpkins, and squash; peach and apple orchards ("I never before saw trees so heavily laden with fruit," marveled Lee); and arbors of grapes. Vancouver's herd of California cattle had grown to nearly seven hundred head. The munificent McLoughlin caused a sumptuous supper to be served and afterward showed the missionaries to their quarters.[108]

"This is the first time I have undressed and slept in a house for one hundred and fifty-two nights," Shepard noted gratefully in his journal.[109]

3

Arcadia

DR. MCLOUGHLIN COULD HARDLY have been more obliging to Jason Lee, offering advice, encouragement, and practical assistance in the form of guides and canoes for a missionary reconnaissance of the Willamette Valley. Far better, to the doctor's way of thinking, for Brother Lee to settle near the nascent Canadian communities of Champoeg or French Prairie above the falls of the Willamette than among the Indians of the Oregon interior, where they could prove meddlesome to Hudson's Bay Company traders. Imperial politics were involved, too. The Willamette flowed toward the Columbia from the south, through a region the British now virtually conceded as an American sphere of influence.

In the event, Lee needed scant persuading. He had contemplated the Willamette for the last thousand miles of the overland journey, and the appearance in the Columbia a day after his own arrival of Nathaniel Wyeth's *May Dacre* carrying the mission goods seemed to him a sign from Above that he had reached his final destination. "Is not the hand of Providence in this?" he asked himself. What seemed providential to Lee had been disastrous for the luckless Wyeth. Damage from a lightning strike at sea forced *May Dacre* into a Chilean port for emergency repairs, causing the brig to miss the entire spring salmon season and costing Wyeth a year's worth of trade.[1]

Lee and his nephew embarked in McLoughlin's vessels on the afternoon of September 18, camped on a sand beach overnight, and entered the Willamette the next morning. Advancing some sixty miles upriver to French Prairie, they met Joseph Gervais, other *engagés*, and two veterans of Wyeth's 1832 voyage and pitched their tent for the night in Gervais's melon patch. Ripe fruit was conveniently at hand for breakfast. In his critique of the Western Colonization Society only ten weeks earlier, Jason Lee had observed that, inexorably, newcomers would drive the natives off the land; they must have it, lots of it, for their own sustenance. The settlers of French Prairie already had many hundreds of acres in cultivation or enclosed for livestock. Lee seemed to have forgotten his own precept as he pursued his search for a mission site along the Willamette.

"Started early this morning and rode three or four miles up the river to examine the land," he wrote on September 23. "Found an excellent place for a farm above all the settlers."[2]

A plantation among the Canadians of French Prairie: this had not been Lee's original vision when he pushed out along what would become the Oregon Trail. True, there were scattered bands of Kalapuya Indians inhabiting the grasslands above the Willamette falls. At one time as many as 13,500 Native Americans dwelled in this part of the valley; as late as the 1780s the Indian population approached 3,500. By some calculations, the malaria epidemic in the early 1830s that devastated the Indian population of the lower Columbia swept away 75 percent of the Kalapuya nation. Some Indians blamed the outbreak on the arrival of an American trading vessel—the brig *Owyhee*, a "Boston ship"—in the Columbia in 1829. The captain, galled at being cheated in the beaver trade, "hung up a bad sail in a tree, and then opened, or uncorked, a small vial, and let out the ague and fever"—or so the story ran. McLoughlin inclined to a theory linking the epidemic to the first extensive plowing in the Vancouver area, postulating a connection between breaking up the soil and the fever.[3]

The contagion had burned itself out by the time the Methodists arrived, leaving perhaps a thousand Kalapuya survivors in the Willamette Valley. The remnants were culturally dazed, demoralized, and in poverty. The Canadians were putting the common lands into wheat, building permanent houses and barns, fencing off grazing areas. Once a Kalapuya winter gathering place, French Prairie now bore the expectant look of a frontier community. Early visitors to the Lee mission would be struck by the scarcity of Indians available for conversion.

Nathaniel Wyeth had advised Lee to settle near a trading post— Vancouver lay only two or three days' journey from French Prairie.

A.T. Agate's head and shoulders portrait of a Kalapuya man. An 1830s malaria epidemic decimated the Kalapuya nation. Methodist missionaries in the Willamette Valley encountered a declining population with little interest in Christian religious belief. (Library of Congress)

McLoughlin emphasized security; the Indians of the interior were unpredictable and not to be trusted. "My mind is yet much exercised on the subject of our location," Jason Lee wrote. "I know not what to do."[4] He came to a decision shortly after his return to Vancouver on September 27. The missionaries would settle in the country of the haunted Kalapuyas.

Meanwhile, Wyeth collected Thomas Nuttall and John Townsend and floated eight miles down the Columbia to Wapato (today's Sauvie) Island, where he set to work on a permanent post for the Columbia River Fishing and Trading Company. His arrival took McLoughlin by surprise. The doctor evidently had discounted Wyeth's 1833 vow to return to the Columbia. Wyeth now proposed a "live and let live" trade accommodation with the Hudson's Bay Company. He would salt salmon, provision American trappers in the Snake Country, and cede the fur trade north and east of the Columbia to McLoughlin. In return for a virtual beaver monopoly, the company would leave the salmon to Wyeth. McLoughlin thought over the proposal and—surprisingly, given his instructions from George Simpson—accepted it. "Finished an arrangement in regard to trade," Wyeth recorded in his journal in late September.[5]

With his base secure, Wyeth prepared to leave for the interior. Nuttall and Townsend explored the surrounding country while awaiting passage to the Sandwich Islands, where they planned to spend the rainy season. Cyrus Shepard settled in at Vancouver. Lee suggested that the lymphatic Shepard take charge of the company's school for a season, partly to recruit his health and to repay McLoughlin's hospitality but also, perhaps, to keep him out from underfoot during the building phase.

Lee preached morning and evening services to a mixed congregation in the refectory in McLoughlin's house on Sunday, September 28, taking Zechariah 6:12–13 as his text for the evening: "And speak unto him, saying, Thus speaketh the Lord of hosts, saying, Behold the man whose name is The Branch; and he shall grow up out of his place, and he shall build the temple of the Lord: Even he shall build the temple of the Lord; and he shall bear the glory, and shall sit and rule upon his throne; and he shall be a priest upon his throne: and the counsel of peace shall be between them both." Lee; his nephew, Philip Edwards; and Courtney Walker set out for the Willamette in the morning. Lee felt a twinge of conscience at the last about abandoning the Indians of the Snake Country. He ticked off the reasons: there were too few Flatheads to justify a mission, the Blackfeet were too close for comfort, a mission in the Willamette Valley would not only minister to white settlers but also produce supplies for the support of outlying stations in the future. Lee reminded himself, too, that he had made no promises at the Green River rendezvous.

"It being late in the season to go up the Columbia this year, we left Vancouver for the Willamette, having, for various reasons, concluded to make an establishment there," he recorded blandly in his journal.[6]

Isolated at Vancouver, Shepard lapsed into another deep depression of spirits. McLoughlin's *métis* wife Margaret sent him a present of a pair of "indian shoes" and two fine melons; her kindnesses failed to lighten his mood. "Feel a war within between the flesh and the spirit," he wrote, "the one being contrary to the other."[7] Word arrived during the second week of October that the missionaries had selected a site on the southern marches of French Prairie and commenced to build. Shepard began to suffer abjectly from homesickness for a place he knew only in his imagination.

McLoughlin loaned the missionaries eight oxen, eight cows, and eight calves, and they offloaded tools, building materials, and other supplies from *May Dacre*. They surveyed, split rails for a livestock corral, and laid out a farmstead at what would come to be known, prosaically, as Mission Bottom. Lee on October 6 raised the tent that would be the mission's home for the next four weeks. The site lay a few rods from the eastern bank of the Willamette River, in grasslands skirted with stands of cottonwood, ash, and white maple.

The twenty families settled in this part of the Willamette Valley were mostly French Canadians living with Indian women without benefit of the blessing. Lee preached at Gervais's homestead on Sunday, October 19, on the theme "Turn ye from your evil ways." As most of the crowd spoke only French, he could only guess at how much of his harangue they comprehended.

Curiously, Lee decided the language barrier precluded his preaching to the native people for now. He found the Kalapuyas destitute and miserable, ill-clad and subsisting mostly on roots. "They are emphatically Flat Heads," he wrote. "The children, when taken from the compressing machine, are strangely ridiculous looking creatures or rather I should say the most pitiable looking objects I have seen." One could hope at the least to turn the tribes from this savage custom, which seemed to validate phrenological theories coming into vogue in the 1830s. On a lecture tour of the United States in 1832, the German phrenologist Johann Spurzheim claimed to be able infallibly to assess a person's character and abilities by the size and shape of his skull. If, as Spurzheim taught, the civilized virtues were seated in the front of the head, then flattening might be both the cause and an outward symbol of barbarism.[8]

Lee aimed to improve the natives' standard of living, too. "There is a remedy; their land is good; teach them to cultivate it," Lee wrote. The Kalapuyas need only look to the Canadians for an example. The first settler had arrived in the valley only three years before, "yet he raised 500 bushels of wheat the past season," according to Lee. Gervais emerged as the most prosperous of the colonists, with 125 acres enclosed and 65 acres under the plow. Gervais would raise 1,000 bushels of wheat in 1836, the most bountiful harvest in the valley. Peas, barley, oats, beans, and potatoes flourished, too, in the local soil and mild, damp climate, Lee had been told, although Indian corn did not grow as well.[9]

The Canadians were gathering in their crops and planting for winter as the missionaries began to knock together their shelter. Lee discovered with pleasure that he retained the skills he had developed on his uncle's north country farm. "We have been engaged in preparing tools, fencing a pasture for calves, drying goods, &c.," he wrote. "Have for the first time been employed in making an ox yoke and succeeded beyond my expectation." Wielding a jackknife, Lee carved window sash and wooden hinges for the doors. The missionaries struck their rain-sodden tent on October 29 and moved into the unfinished dwelling measuring 32 by 18 feet and rising a story and a half high, with the logs hewn only on the inside. There were two rooms with four windows on the first floor and, at one end, "a good chimney, made of clay and sand, and probably as durable as brick," according to Lee. They cooked frugally there: unleavened flourcakes, peas, salted pork and barley boiled into a soup.[10]

Cyrus Shepard fretted away the weeks at Vancouver, alone with his obsessions. Awkward among the Hudson's Bay Company men of affairs and with too little to do, he worried that he was neglecting the duty that had carried him three thousand miles from Lynn. "Do not feel at home though everything is done and every attention paid here that I could wish," he wrote. "Have a longing desire to go to the Willammitt and be with those with whom my lot is cast."[11] He discovered, too, that his piety grated on his hosts. They were indifferent equally to his admonishments and to the power of his example; they challenged his authority to reorder their lives; they even questioned his conduct.

"Have felt much the importance of walking circumspectly towards those that are without and of letting my light shine before others," Shepard wrote one Sunday. "The importance of this has been more particularly impressed upon my mind from the circumstances of a certain individual who saw me writing in my journal and thereby excused himself for mending a watch and asked me if I thought there was any more hurt in mending a watch on the Sabbath than in writeing."[12]

He sought out the Fifty-first Psalm to tranquilize his nerves: "Restore unto me the joy of thy salvation; and uphold me with thy free spirit. Then I will teach transgressors thy ways; and sinners shall be converted unto thee. Deliver me from bloodguiltiness, O God, thou God of my salvation: and my tongue shall sing aloud of thy righteousness." King James's rolling cadences only briefly alleviated his distress. He resolved in early November to quit Vancouver at the first opportunity, and reached Mission Bottom on the thirteenth. There on the Willamette he enjoyed a respite, ministering to orphaned

Kalapuya siblings, rechristened John Mark and Lucy Hedding*—the missionaries' entire clientele, for they could not open a school for want of food and clothes for the scholars. Lee escorted Shepard back to Vancouver before Christmas. A harsh self-examination on New Year's Day 1835 summoned the blue devils once again, although as the first week of the New Year drew to a close he detected progress in his campaign to overcome the sensual desires of the flesh.

TOWNSEND AND NUTTALL EMBARKED in *May Dacre* in early December. The brig anchored off Fort George on December 8, Captain Lambert alert for an opportunity to dash cross the Columbia bar and make an offing for the Sandwich Islands. Townsend went ashore to explore the former Astoria, now reduced to a main house of hewn boards with a straggle of Indian huts nearby. The Hudson's Bay Company carried on a vestigial trade there now. Only a lone chimney of old Astoria still stood, "a melancholy monument," thought Townsend, "of American enterprise and domestic misrule." Lambert attempted the bar on the eleventh. After twenty minutes of terror, *May Dacre* and her cargo of Oregon timber swam easily on a placid sea under an escort of guillemots, pelicans, and other pelagic birds.[13]

Wyeth passed a profitless winter. He struck south in mid-November with four or five men into beaver country on the "American" side of the Columbia. Provisions ran short and beaver were scarce; Hudson's Bay Company trappers had done their work well. "Snow and rain all day a miserable Christmas," he wrote in his journal on December 25. His mood lifted a few days later when he removed the largest beaver he had yet seen from one of the traps. Caught in the heavy iron jaws, pulled underwater and drowned before it could gnaw off a leg and swim free, the sixty-five-pound creature settled the rations question for a day or so. Heavy snow fell during the second week of January, immobilizing the party. Idleness had the effect of turning Wyeth's attentions inward.

"The thoughts that have run through my brain while I have been lying here in the snow," he wrote on January 11, "would fill a volume

---

*The missionaries named the girl for Elijah Hedding, the Methodist bishop who had appointed Jason Lee.

and of such matter as was never put into one, my infancy, my youth, and its friends and faults, my manhood's troubled stream, its vagaries, its aloes mixed with the gall of bitterness and its results viz under a blankett hundreds perhaps thousands of miles from a friend, the Blast howling about, and smothered in snow, poor, in debt, doing nothing to get out of it, despised for a visionary, nearly naked but there is one good thing plenty to eat. Health and heart."[14]

So passed a dreary month. By now Wyeth surely had admitted to himself that he would have to cut ice for years to settle his mounting debts. Coming upon a camp of Wallawallas on January 29, he offered to trade for some of the deer haunch the Indians were drying. The transaction bucked him up for the moment. "This is my birthday," Wyeth noted, "but I've forgotten how old I am." (He was thirty-three.) Then, from one day to the next, Oregon winter gave way to spring. The sun shone, the snow melted away, and the frogs piped up in the bottoms. The Indians having informed him for perhaps the fiftieth time that British trappers had scoured all the country here-abouts, Wyeth reluctantly decided to withdraw to Vancouver.[15]

There, to his astonishment, he found Hall Jackson Kelley, the original Oregon projector. The encounter turned out to be the antithesis of cordial: criminations and recriminations. Kelley's dreams of leading a great migrant caravan had vanished into an abyss of misfortune. Fellow travelers robbed him of money and possessions in New Orleans; he suffered unendurably from seasickness on the passage to Veracruz; and he fell dangerously ill in the Sacramento Valley on the journey north with the Tennessee adventurer Ewing Young, a dozen or so drovers picked up in Monterey, and a herd of seventy or eighty California horses.

Kelley arrived in his Oregon paradise gaunt, malarial, and under suspicion of horse theft. The governor of California had written McLoughlin via the fast-sailing Hudson's Bay Company schooner *Cadboro* to accuse Kelley and Young of rustling the herd out of Mexican territory. The company wanted no part of trouble with the Mexicans, and anyway McLoughlin regarded Kelley as the advance agent for an American invasion of the Oregon Country. The doctor quietly instructed the Canadian farmers not to trade with Ewing and banished Kelley to the shabby outskirts of Vancouver. Young could look after himself (he would settle permanently in the Willamette Valley), but Kelley felt the doctor's animus keenly. "Kelley is not received at the Fort as a gentleman," Wyeth wrote. "A house is given him and food sent him from the Gov. Table but he is not suffered to mess here."[16] McLoughlin lodged him in a room in an *engagé* shack potent with the reek of fish. Kelley complained bitterly that the Lees and Wyeth refused to intervene, even though they knew him as a "man of character." Jason Lee, who may have regarded Kelley's settlement schemes as a threat to his ambition for a Methodist-dominated republic in the Willamette, visited surreptitiously, and Wyeth called on him but once.

"Well, Kelley, how did you get here?" he asked.

Then, according to Kelley, Wyeth let loose a volley of abusive remarks and walked out. Bereft, outcast, with enemies on all sides, Kelley prepared to return to the United States to wage a thirty years' pamphlet war against the imperious British; the duplicitous Lees; the faithless Wyeth; and even the unoffending Townsend and Nuttall, whom Kelley resented for failing to call on him as he lay burning with fever in his salmon-scented quarters. He might have consoled himself, had he come to think of it, with the notion that his Oregon vision had taken form in Lee's embryo colony at Mission Bottom.[17]

Wyeth pushed on downriver to his Wapato Island *pied-à-terre*, where he oversaw the planting of wheat and potatoes and awaited *May Dacre's* return from Hawaii with a cargo of cattle, sheep, goats, and hogs. The brig shot the bar at seven o'clock in the morning of April 16, 1835, cleared Baker Bay, and ghosted upstream. Captain Lambert discharged the returning passengers Townsend and Nuttall, the latter planning to work his way south to add California to his life list of exotic places before heading home to Cambridge. Field notebooks in hand, the naturalists combed the Vancouver hinterland. Nuttall collected the shells of twenty-three new species of freshwater mollusks, and Townsend worked away on his catalog of Oregon birds. He recorded his first sighting of the brown-headed titmouse, *a-ka-ke-tok* of the Chinooks, near the river in May.

"They hopped through the bushes, and hung from the twigs in the manner of other titmice," he wrote, "twittering all the time, with a rapid enunciation resembling the words, *tsisk-tsish-tsee-tsee.* Upon my return, I found that Mr. Nuttall had observed the same birds a few hours previously in another place. He said that they frequently flew to the ground from the bushes, where they appeared to institute a rapid search for insects, and quickly returned to the perch, emitting their weak, querulous note the whole time without intermission."[18]

The salmon run presented Townsend with an opportunity to observe the Chinooks' first-month rituals. He watched the Indians roast the heart and consume it "in silence, and with great gravity," a propitiation, he speculated, to the deity or spirit that presided over fish. Even though he knew it to be a sacrilege, he felt an overpowering temptation to visit the Indian ossuaries. He resisted for a long time until finally he crept out one midnight and abstracted an embalmed female corpse from a canoe in a tree. The flattened head especially might prove useful in phrenological studies, and he carefully packed away the skull and bones for shipment home. As it happened, the brother of the deceased found him out, tracking his footsteps to Wyeth's factory, where he complained of the theft. A Chinook elder managed to retrieve the relic. The kinfolk of the venerable old chief Concomly, who had died of measles in 1830, were not so fortunate a year or so later. A British physician dispatched to Vancouver to study Indian epidemics raided Concomly's grave in the night, decapitated the corpse, and shipped the severed head to England as specimen study for crackpot phrenological science.[19]

Daniel Lee and Philip Edwards called at Wyeth's establishment, now dubbed Fort William, in late May. The mission settlement on the Willamette evidently prospered. "They gave flattering accounts of their prospects," Townsend remarked; "they are surrounded by a considerable number of Indians who are friendly to the introduction of civilization and religious light, and who treat them with the greatest hospitality and kindness."[20] Shepard, now permanently in residence, kept the mission school, all of fourteen boarding scholars—three Kalapuya children and eleven of mixed French and Indian parentage.

The school grew steadily as the summer advanced. Baptiste Payette, Wyeth's *métis* charge, boarded there. A Tillamook named Hokallah responded well to Shepard's instruction, and the missionary argued hard with the boy's father when he came in mid-June to remove him. "He bid fair to make a fine scholar," Shepard lamented. Fever spread through the settlement in midsummer. Shepard passed his thirty-eighth birthday on August 14 in slow remission from a malarial attack, rising from his sickbed only to watch helplessly as an Indian youth named Kentotish died of pulmonary consumption. Kentotish's brother

The carved and painted raised burial platform of paramount Chinook chief Concomly. Around fifty in 1811, Concomly had welcomed the American explorers Lewis and Clark in 1805 and seemed eager to do business with the newly arrived fur traders of John Jacob Astor. (Library of Congress)

and three others came a few days later to open the boy's grave. "They put some shells a blanket & handkerchief on the coffin [and] sat down and wept bitterly," Shepard wrote. Joseph Gervais dropped off a girl he called Sophia Charponey—the daughter, it turned out, of the voyageur who had been killed in the horse race at Fort Hall a year earlier. By early autumn twenty-four children were in residence, half of them orphans, many of them ill. Lucy Hedding died of fever in November. Illness and the demands of farm work obliged Shepard to reduce the day school to half sessions.[21]

ALTHOUGH LEE AND THE METHODISTS were first in the Oregon field, the Flathead myth aroused rival mission societies, too. Congregationalist parson Samuel Parker had heard the story of the four wandering aboriginals at a missionary prayer meeting in Middlefield, Massachusetts, in 1832. A restless soul, Parker offered a lengthy résumé: home missionary work on the western New York frontier after graduation from Williams College in 1806; agent for the Auburn Theological Seminary; itinerant preaching; a Congregational pulpit in Middlefield; and a teaching post at a girls' school in Ithaca, New York. The Flatheads' plight inspired him to lobby the American Board of Commissioners for Foreign Missions, a joint venture of the Congregational, Presbyterian, and Dutch Reformed denominations, to underwrite a reconnaissance of the West. "My views are to take one or two others with me or go alone if best, and explore the field," Parker wrote the board in April 1833. The commissioners hesitated, citing Parker's age (he was born in 1779) and feeble health. He replied that he had gained the support, moral and financial, of his church in Ithaca.

He wrote, "Do you ask me when I would be ready to go?

"Tomorrow."[22]

Parker's persistence wore the commissioners down. They agreed in 1835 to send him cross-country to determine whether the Flatheads would accept a missionary presence and, if so, where to site an outpost. Traveling partway in Lucien Fontanelle's American Fur Company caravan with the would-be medical missionary Marcus Whitman, Parker followed the increasingly defined outline of the Oregon Trail, covering the last thousand miles on his own with an escort of Nez Perce Indians. He experienced an uneventful overland trip. In fact, Parker seemed to regard the voyage as something of a pleasure outing, even for a parson of advancing years. He expected many thousands of Americans to follow. Like Jason Lee's, Parker's vision shifted seamlessly from soul-saving to empire-building and back again.

"There would be no difficulty in constructing a railroad from the Atlantic to the Pacific ocean," he would write in 1838; "and probably the time may not be very far distant, when trips will be made across the continent, as they have been made to Niagara Falls, to see nature's wonders."[23]

Parker and Whitman parted at the Green River rendezvous, Whitman returning East with two Nez Perce boys he dubbed Richard and John, animate props for his campaign to recruit a mission staff. He and Parker agreed to meet at the 1836 mountain bazaar and establish a mission station along the western slopes of the Rockies. A Christian presence there would combat the influence of the trappers and traders who supplied the natives with liquor, debauched their women, and styled the packs of playing cards they sold them "bibles." Parker pushed on across the Snake River Plain, over the Blue Mountains, and down the Columbia, reaching Fort Vancouver in mid-October.

With Vancouver as a base (the hospitable McLoughlin put half a house at his disposal for the winter), he explored the surrounding country, industriously jotting down notes for his report to the mission board. Townsend tutored him in the avian life of the lower Columbia. He witnessed Halley's comet, its first appearance since 1759. The sophistication of the various Hudson's Bay Company subsidiaries—mills, farms, orchards, smithies—caught him by surprise. He had not expected to encounter workaday enterprise on such an extensive scale. Dropping downriver with Townsend in *May Dacre*, he landed on Wapato Island to inspect Wyeth's operation. The Cambridge trader's only too apparent difficulties could not mask the limitless potential of the region.

Parker wondered, "When will this immensely extended and fertile country be brought under cultivation and filled with an industrious population? From time immemorial the natives have not stretched forth a hand to till the ground, nor made an effort for the earth to yield a single article of produce, more than what springs up spontaneously; nor will they, until their minds are enlightened by divine truth."[24]

Striking out for the Willamette settlements on November 23, he stopped with Thomas McKay and Joseph Gervais before reaching Mission Bottom on the twenty-sixth. "For richness of soil and other local advantages, I should not know where to find a spot in the valley of the Mississippi superior to this," he remarked. Still, he could not help noticing how few Kalapuyas remained to be converted and civilized. Back in the States, the mission commissioners felt an urgency to Christianize the tribes before settlers from east of the Mississippi overwhelmed and destroyed them. Here, so far as he could judge, the process appeared to be well advanced. All the same, he judged it worthwhile to establish a Christian influence among the valley's beached sailors, superannuated hunters, lapsed trappers, and their Indian common-law wives.[25]

The Methodists at Mission Bottom viewed the matter differently. By year's end Shepard counted thirty-one scholars in the school. Jason Lee assigned some of the older boys to work parties to fell timber for an addition to the mission house to accommodate the growing numbers. In the spring they built a thirty-by-forty-foot log barn with a split-shingle roof. Lee replaced Courtney Walker, who had gone to work for Wyeth, with two of Ewing Young's Californians, but still experienced an acute shortage of labor. The mission board in New York responded with a resolution to send reinforcements in 1836: another missionary couple, a physician, a blacksmith, and two or three single female schoolteachers.

Lee thus could account the first year a success. With Indian help, the missionaries harvested 150 bushels of wheat; 250 bushels of potatoes; and lesser quantities of oats, barley, and peas. They sowed winter wheat in the autumn and enclosed more than twenty-five acres for grazing. True, the pace of heathen conversion was glacially slow. Even so, Shepard had launched the school on its task of saving the Indian youth from ignorance, superstition, and folly. Above all Lee had created the living core of an American settlement in the Oregon Country, a rival center to British Vancouver.

"You speak of building up a colony here," Lee would write the mission board secretary, Nathan Bangs. "I think we have made a fair commencement."[26]

The balance sheet for Nathaniel Wyeth's Columbia River Fishing and Trading Company, however, recorded a mercantile catastrophe. Desertions, canoe upsets, Indian killings of trappers, thefts of pelts, lightning strikes, and the Hudson's Bay Company's iron fist doomed his ventures. Taste and style played a part, too. McLoughlin had pronounced pickled or dried salmon a commercial nonstarter years before. Changing fashions—a sudden preference for silk over beaver felt for hats—would soon annihilate the market for beaver. Wyeth entered the fur trade just as it began its fatal decline. Washington Irving generously attributed his failure to a conjunction of accident, cross-purposes, and insufficient capital to offset early losses. Like the Astorians, Irving suggested, Wyeth suffered, too, from the neglect and lack of vision of an indifferent government.

"Had he been able to maintain the footing he had so gallantly effected," Irving would write in 1837, "he might have regained for his country the opulent trade of the Columbia." As long as the territorial issue remained unsettled, American traders would be too weak to compete with the British. The U.S. government should take the matter in hand, and sooner rather than later. "It is a question too serious to national pride, if not to national interest, to be slurred over," Irving concluded.[27]

Wyeth pushed up the Columbia for the last time in the autumn of 1835. Wintering at Fort Hall, he set out for the United States in

June 1836, detouring to the Green River rendezvous, then traveling southeast to Mexican Taos. Arriving home in the autumn, he turned at once to the melancholy business of winding up the affairs of the Columbia River Fishing and Trading Company. He sold Fort Hall to the Hudson's Bay Company but retained his claim to Fort William, holding out hope that he would someday acquire formal title to the place.

So the adventure ended for Wyeth, a man of inexhaustible energy and resourcefulness. He returned to the prosy business of mining Cambridge pond ice for shipment to the torrid latitudes. In his two cross-country voyages, Wyeth had clearly established the Oregon Trail; he was the first to make the through trip all the way to the Columbia. He escorted the first trained naturalists to the Pacific and, fatefully, the first permanent American settlers. Never again, though, would he glimpse black masses of fast-moving buffalo through the dust clouds, smoke and parley with Indians, pitch camp in the twilight with the pink flush of alpenglow on the snowpeaks, or descend rivers thick with fat salmon. Wyeth always had known he could make a living out of ice. He discharged his debts and prospered modestly in the twenty years that remained to him. Still, affluence for its own sake had never fired his imagination. In going West he had stretched out for more than a competence. He lived out his days knowing his reach had exceeded his grasp.

BRINGING TO A CLOSE an agreeable second interlude on the Columbia, Thomas Nuttall arranged a passage in a Hudson's Bay Company coaster bound for Monterey. Reaching the capital of the Mexican province of Upper California in March 1836, the naturalist indulged himself in a few weeks' exploring and collecting in the hill country in back of the village before resuming the southward journey in the hide-and-tallow brig *Pilgrim*. The vessel called at Santa Barbara, San Pedro, and San Juan Capistrano to collect hides, and Nuttall went ashore at each place, carrying out as detailed an examination of the plants, birds, and rocks of each locale as circumstance allowed. In mid-May *Pilgrim* negotiated the narrow opening of Mission Bay, San Diego, to land her cargo of hides in the Bryant & Sturgis depot on the sandy foreshore there.

Astonishingly, Nuttall encountered one of his former Harvard students in this unlikely place, Richard Henry Dana Jr., a twenty-one-

The Spanish established a presidio at the base of the Monterey Peninsula in California in 1770. The village that grew up around the military post served as the capital of Spanish, later Mexican, California from 1776 until the U.S. seizure of 1846. (Library of Congress)

year-old Bostonian who had sailed around Cape Horn as a foremast sailor in *Pilgrim*, a prescription for recovery from an attack of measles that left him with weakened eyes and jagged nerves. Dana had shifted from the brig to the homebound ship *Alert* by then, and when *Pilgrim*'s second mate, meeting him at Mission Bay, said they had "an old gentleman on board who knew me, and came from the college I had been in," Dana could not venture a guess as to the passenger's identity. He "spent all his time in the bush, and along the beach," the mate went on, "picking up flowers and shells and such truck, and had a dozen boxes and barrels full of them." The next day, the mysterious beachcomber wandered down to the strand just as Dana and his comrades were about to shove off for *Alert*. Nuttall wore an old sailor's pea jacket and a wide straw hat, his trousers were rolled up to the knees, and he carried his shoes. His pockets bulged with specimens.

"I should hardly have been more surprised to have seen the Old South steeple rise up from the hide-house," Dana wrote afterward.[28]

Pilgrim's people dubbed him "Old Curious." They thought him addled, and faulted his friends for being so unsolicitous of his welfare. "Why else should a rich man leave a Christian country and come to such a place as California to pick up shells and stones?" they asked Dana. Why, indeed? California had not yet developed its mystique as an arcadian paradise. Such English and American traders as had come in quest of sea otter skins, the hides of bullocks, or tallow described a poor and lawless country, misgoverned and inhospitable. Jedediah Smith was fortunate during his sojourns in 1826 and 1827 to avoid a Mexican *calabozo*, although the region's climate, richness of soil, and potential for exploitation had charmed him. Smith's travels, and the 1829 explorations of the trapper Ewing Young and the Hudson's Bay Company operative Peter Skene Ogden, piqued American interest in California. By Dana's time infiltration from the restless republic was well under way.

The British were alive to California possibilities, too, in part as a consequence of HMS *Blossom*'s 1826 cruise. A familiar sight along the Pacific Coast of North America (she had carried the American envoy Prevost to Astoria in 1818), *Blossom* arrived off northern California on the mist-veiled morning of November 6; after a while a light wind sprang up, revealing "cape after cape," reported her captain, Frederick William Beechey, "and exhibiting a luxuriant country apparently abounding in woods and rivers." An opening between two low promontories disclosed itself. The sloop glided through, passed under the guns of a fort flying the Mexican tricolor, and entered San Francisco Bay—"a broad sheet of water," Beechey wrote, "sufficiently extensive to contain all the British navy."[29]

Blossom lay for fifty-two days in the anchorage of Yerba Buena (soon to be rechristened San Francisco), a long break for rest and resupply at the midpoint of an expedition into Arctic waters in search of the western opening of the Northwest Passage. Beechey improved the time during his California layover with surveys of the harbor and landward excursions to the *presidio*, Mission San Francisco, and the hinterland. His narrative, published in 1831, portrayed a pastoral society in California on the eve of Mexico's secularization of the missions—the last years of an era that the historian Hubert Howe Bancroft apotheosized as a "Golden Age" of innocence and contentment.

"Never before or since," wrote Bancroft in 1888, "was there a spot in America where life was a long and happy holiday, where there was less labor, less care or trouble . . . the gathering of nature's fruits being the chief burden of life, and death coming without decay, like a gentle sleep."[30]

Casting a harder, cooler glance, Beechey found one of the great anchorages of the world innocent of shipping except for a flotilla of seaworn and disheveled American whalers moored in Sausalito, six miles distant across the bay. A soldier had hailed *Blossom's* arrival through a speaking trumpet, for there was no boat or barge to float a captain of the port out to inspect an incoming vessel. Beechey came ashore and struck out for the *presidio* a mile away. Only a single thin column of smoke rising from one of the buildings betrayed human habitation.

He entered a quadrangle with government houses and a chapel on one side; storehouses, shops, and a jail on two others; and a refuse heap on the fourth, on which ragged dogs and vultures grazed. The buildings were rough-made adobe with red tile roofs; only the governor's house and the chapel were whitewashed. The commandant, a Mexican army lieutenant named Ignacio Martinez, had not been paid in eleven years, although a brig had turned up not long before with a cargo of cigars to be issued to the garrison instead of dollars. "Fortunately for Martinez and the other veterans, both animal and vegetable food are uncommonly cheap, and there are no fashions to create any expense of dress," observed Beechey.[31] An air of waste and utter neglect hovered over this halcyon locale. Beechey observed that the soldiers lacked the energy even to grow their own food. Everything came from the mission, produced by the enforced labor of Indians.

The scarcity of supplies obliged Beechey to send a party overland to Monterey for medicines and other stores. As he would soon discover, tensions ran high between the mission and the *presidio*—in this case, jealously over how to divide the profits to be extorted from the sloop's hundred-man complement. Looking around, Beechey noted only this positive: the absence of the usual port amenities—pothouses and brothels—made for a healthier and more mannerly crew. He could only imagine what Anglo-Saxon energy and enterprise would make of such a place.

Relations between the *gente de razón*, as the Spanish Mexicans referred to themselves, and the *bestias,* as the overlords called the Indians, were essentially those of master and slave. Beginning in 1769 with the Majorcan priest Junipero Serra's founding of the first mission at San Diego, the Spanish practiced forcible conversion of the California natives as the key element in their colonization policy. Beechey judged that the Indians hereabouts—mostly Patwins, Wappos, and Miwoks—were better off in the mission "than in their forests, where they are in a state of nudity and are frequently obliged to depend solely upon wild acorns for their subsistence." The priests put their neophytes to trade as weavers, tanners, blacksmiths, and shoemakers; enforced chastity; solemnized marriages; and drafted them into the mission choir if they could sing. Recalcitrants were encouraged with goads and whips to attend Mass. Despite these blessings of civilization, the Indian population of Mission San Francisco had been falling precipitously, to about 260 souls in 1826, down from 1,000 a decade earlier.[32]

The blackrobes themselves, Beechey found, were generous, ill-informed, and bigoted. Serra lived on timelessly for the holy fathers, and the last half century had passed them by. "They had been so long excluded from the civilized world that their ideas and their politics, like the maps pinned against the walls, bore the date of 1772, as near as I could read it for the flyspots," wrote Beechey.[33] In his view, the Mexicans had done nothing to merit possession of the country.

Little in the next decade of California history would alter the perception Captain Beechey left with his readers. With secularization of the missions in 1833–1834, the surviving natives gained a nominal emancipation; the Mexican government parceled out the vast mission holdings as patronage to deserving *Californios*. The result: a system of great *ranchos*, some of many thousands of acres, that dominated California life. The power vacuum remained, along with the notion that this Pacific prize—temperate, rich, and virtually free of government control—somehow had been reserved for the eventual use of thousands of emigrants bound to follow the Anglo-American trappers, traders, and farmers who had been arriving in small numbers since the 1820s.

California prospects had fired the imagination of Pennsylvania-born Zenas Leonard, a clerk with the trapping/exploring/intelligence-gathering party of Bonneville lieutenant Joseph Reddeford Walker, the first American expedition to penetrate the Sierra Nevada and reach the Pacific. "What a theme to contemplate its settlement and civilization," Leonard wrote in his journal in November 1833. "Yes, here, even in the remote part of the great West before many years, will these hills and valleys be greeted with the enlivening sound of the workmen's hammer, and the merry whistle of the ploughboy." Thus a twenty-four-year-old novice fur trader produced an ex tempore articulation of America's Manifest Destiny a decade or more before an imperially minded journalist would coin the phrase.[34]

The Walker party left the Green River rendezvous on July 24, 1833, to scout a trail to Mexican California via the Great Salt Lake and the deserts of the Great Basin. Every man of Walker's sixty led four horses packed with arms and ammunition, blankets, buffalo robes, trapping equipment, and provisions. Friendly Bannocks advised Walker not to venture into the basin without ample stocks of meat, for he would find nothing there to sustain him. The Americans killed their last buffalo along the fringe of the brine sea in early September and struck west with sixty pounds of jerked meat per man. Just as the Indians had warned, the Salt Lake desert stretched barren from horizon to horizon, destitute of game except for a stray goat or jackrabbit.

They pushed on, following the Bannocks' directions: after a month's travel, the Indians told Walker, they would descry a high mountain, perpetually snow-covered, and the head of the river that descended into a sandy plain, formed innumerable small lakes, and eventually sank into the earth and disappeared. The country was bereft of vegetation—not "a stick large enough to make a walking cane," Leonard found—and many of the springs were salt. "The Indians say it never rains, only in the spring of the year," he noted in his journal. "Every thing here seems to declare that, here man shall not dwell."[35] They finally approached the snow mountain, nearly round, like an oversized burial mound: Pilot Peak rising abruptly from the level plain.

The Northern Paiute natives thereabouts were filthy, naked except for a grass shield draped around their loins, desperately poor, and thievish. The whites derisively called them Diggers, for they grubbed into the sandy earth for a subsistence of grass seed and roots. They ate frogs, too, and fish when they could catch them, and even a small fly, roughly the size of a grain of wheat, which they dried in the sun and laid in store for winter fare. Small bands of curious Paiutes trailed Walker's column, intending—so the Americans suspected—to isolate a man here and there and steal his traps and meat.

After a long descent, the Americans reached Humboldt Lake in present Nevada, the first good grazing in many days. They baited the horses in spite of signs of large parties of Indians nearby. Taking alarm finally, Walker ordered the horses picketed and breastworks of baggage thrown up. Before the men had settled into defensive positions, the weedy lake at their backs, a mass of Indians rose up out of the grass—as many as eight hundred, Leonard guessed—and advanced upon the Americans, "dancing and singing in the greatest glee."[36]

The Paiutes advanced to within 150 yards and halted while five of their chiefs went forward to propose a pipe. Walker refused to smoke, and the chiefs withdrew, plainly offended. The Indians, with their stashes of dried flies and sharpened bones for spearing fish, almost certainly had no experience of firearms. When the American marksmen demonstrated the destructive power of their rifles on a flight of ducks cruising above the lake, the natives again withdrew, clucking with astonishment, to a safe distance.

Walker resumed the march the next day, the Paiutes following discreetly. When a detachment of eighty or so pushed uncomfortably close, Walker issued the order to drive them off. At his command, the riflemen flashed out a volley; the panicked survivors retreated in all directions. Walking the battlefield, the Americans counted thirty-nine Indians dead or injured. Walker directed some of the men to finish off the wounded. Leonard supplied the standard rationale for the slaughter: the whites meant to strike a decisive blow with a view to preventing hostilities (and saving lives) later.

"The severity with which we dealt with these Indians may be revolting to the philanthropist," Leonard wrote, "but the circumstances of the case altogether atone for the cruelty."[37]

By mid-October the white-rimmed peaks of the Sierra Nevada were massed on the horizon. Walker mounted an assault on the range, already deep in snow, probably following a branch of the East Walker River to Mono Pass and then a westward-leading ridge dividing the headwaters of the Merced and Tuolomne Rivers.[38] It was an agonizing twenty-day ordeal, the van obliged to break a trail through several feet of snow. There was no game, although one of the hunters shot and killed two Indians he judged to be a threat. Only juniper berries, with their strong flavor of gin, were available for eating. The horses were starving, too. Some of the men began to plot a retrograde movement east as far as buffalo country. Yet the party staggered on, the horses following stupidly, using up the last of their strength to meet a last end in the drifts. Walker had two of the animals destroyed and butchered; the forbidden meat seemed to restore the men's morale, and—for the time being, anyhow—there were no more whispers of mutiny.

Shuffling along the top of the earth, the Americans advanced painfully in what is today Yosemite National Park, scouts alert for a seam down which the party could descend. At some point Walker's men became the first whites to view the spectacular falls of Yosemite. Then one of the hunters returned with a basket of acorns he had filched from a terrified Miwok Indian. Here was evidence of a temperate country, and soon they could *see* it, too—a vast plain stretching tantalizingly toward the setting sun. The men speculated on the distance to the Pacific, Walker guessing the ocean lay not far beyond what he could discern through his spyglass.

Twenty-four of the horses were dead by now, seventeen of them dispatched with a bullet to the head and consumed to keep the men alive. The seam appeared at last, and the Americans followed the plunging course of the Merced River down the mountain. The hunters turned up with fat haunches of black-tailed deer and bear. The snow thinned out, and the vegetation grew thicker. Here, suddenly, Arcadia opened out before them. Leonard marveled at "some trees of the red-wood species, incredibly large, some of which would measure sixteen to eighteen fathom round the trunk"—the regal *Sequoia gigantea.*

Walker's men followed the Merced into the San Joaquin Valley, trapping as they went. Leonard described a country of astonishing ripeness. Small streams lined with stands of timber coursed through the valley, and the plain extended on a level as far as the eye could see. The soil was rich, "so very strong and mellow that it requires but little labor to raise good crops."[39] Even the wild cattle and horses were large and fine-looking. Leonard attributed the unusual length of the cattles' horns to the softness of the California climate. Walker's course led north to Suisun Bay, then west over the Coast Range to the Pacific itself, which he reached at Año Nuevo Point, forty miles south of Yerba Buena. This time the Mexican authorities were as hospitable as the country. Governor José Figueroa granted the Americans permission to winter in the golden land, to hunt for the support of the company, and even to trade with the Mexicans.

Walker turned for home in mid-February 1834. Advancing through showers alternating with sun, the column approached the base of a gap in the southern reaches of the Sierra Nevada—today's Walker Pass, at 5,245 feet—and emerged on the eastern flank after four days of comparatively easy travel. Leonard, for one, exited California with the conviction that it must soon belong to the United States, even if the Americans had to seize it from their Mexican, British, or Russian rivals.

"Our government should be vigilant," he wrote. "She should assert her claim by taking possession of the whole territory as soon as possible."[40]

Like Leonard, the Harvard scholar turned hide trader Richard Henry Dana had concluded that California was wasted on the Californians. Dana spent eighteen months on the California coast in 1835 and 1836 collecting and curing hides for the Boston firm of Bryant & Sturgis. From beginnings in Monterey in 1822, the company had established a virtual monopoly on the hide and tallow trade, the hides (roughly one million of them between 1822 and 1848) bound mostly for New England tanneries and leather-goods factories. Bryant & Sturgis ships called regularly at Monterey, San Pedro, and San Juan Capistrano for the products of the *ranchos*. The work afforded Dana an intimate glimpse of California life in the last years before the American conquest. Like English and American observers before him, he extolled the country while ridiculing its inhabitants. His *Two Years before the Mast*, published in 1839, would become the most widely read and influential American narrative of the golden land of its time.[41]

After a 150-day voyage from Boston, *Pilgrim* made landfall at Point Conception on January 13, 1835, ghosted south for fifty miles, and came to anchor in the broad exposed crescent of the Santa Barbara roadstead, empty that day except for a Peruvian brig flying British colors. Dana watched that first evening as the Peruvians labored through the surf, carrying stiff hides on their heads one or two at a time or manhandling hide bags of tallow the size of sacks of ground meal. "Well, Dana," *Pilgrim*'s second mate called out to him, "this does not look much like Harvard College, does it? But it is what I call *head* work."[42] The town itself, a huddle of one-story mud-colored adobe houses and a *presidio*, lay half a mile inland. Beyond, on a low, treeless plain with mountains on three sides, stood Mission Santa Barbara, with its baroque belfry of five bells.

By Mexican law, foreign vessels were barred from trading in California without first clearing their cargo through customs at Monterey, the provincial capital. *Pilgrim* dutifully beat northward for Point Pinos, at the entrance to Monterey Bay. Dana found the country thereabouts greatly to his liking, green from the winter rains and richer in appearance than dismal Santa Barbara. The town was pretty, too, the red tiles on the roofs a pleasing contrast to the whitewashed adobe walls. "We felt," Dana remembered, "as though we had got into a Christian (which in the sailor's vocabulary means civilized) country."[43] Yet he and his mates could hardly approve of the way the *Californios* conducted their temporal affairs. Take, for instance, *Pilgrim*, which converted itself into a bazaar offering spirits by the cask, coffee, tea, sugar, spices, raisins, molasses, hardware, crockery, tinware, cutlery, clothing, boots and shoes from Lynn, cotton and calicoes from Lowell, jewelry, furniture, even Chinese fireworks. *Pilgrim*'s crowded decks suggested to Dana one of the ironies of life here.

"The Californians are an idle, thriftless people, and can make nothing for themselves," Dana wrote. Vineyards flourished, yet they bought wine shipped out from Boston. They bought "shoes (as like as not made from their own hides, which have been carried twice round Cape Horn) at three and four dollars."[44]

Expatriates dominated the California trade, such as it was. The authorities granted Protestants no political rights; they could not own property or stay in the country for more than a few weeks. So the merchants converted to Catholicism and married into California families, having left their consciences—so the saying went—at Cape Horn. The *alcaldes* at Santa Barbara and Monterey were Yankees by birth.

Exhausting the market at Monterey, *Pilgrim* weighed and stood south, calling at Santa Barbara, San Pedro (where the men, working double tides, landed fifty tons of trade goods and brought off two thousand hides in several days of backbreaking toil), and San Diego. The latter place, a settlement of forty dark-brown huts and three or four whitewashed adobes, dozed unambitiously under a mild sun. A ruined *presidio* overlooked the village, one of its two guns spiked, the other without a carriage. A dozen ragged soldiers formed the apathetic garrison. Except for the hide houses, Dana could detect no pulse of business in the town.

Put ashore with the hide-house crew, Dana in several months transformed himself, as he put it, from sailor to beachcomber and learned the art of curing along the way. Bullock hides arrived tough and filthy from the *ranchos*. The initial task was to stake them onto the beach at the low-water mark so the salt water could do its work with the incoming tide. Thus softened and cleansed, the hides were rolled up and plunged into vats of brine—seawater with salt added— and left in pickle for forty-eight hours. Then they were staked out again, Dana carefully trimming away any clinging meat and fat while they were still damp. As they dried, he scraped off the grease the sun

drew out. When fully dry, the hides were draped over a long horizon-
tal pole and beaten with flails. As a last step, they were stowed in the
hide house till they could be "carried to Boston, tanned, made into
shoes, and many of them, very probably, brought back again to California in the shape of shoes, and worn out in pursuit of other bullocks, or in the curing of their hides."[45]

The work, though demanding (it produced, too, "a stench which
would drive a donkey from its breakfast"), left Dana ample time to
comment on the *Californios*. Secularization made things worse both
for the missions and for the eighteen thousand Indians who remained
in a state of peonage. The natives were abused as before, but the
priests had lost all temporal authority, their possessions "given over to
be preyed upon by the harpies of the civil power." As a consequence,
the once-proud missions grew derelict. The Mexicans, "thriftless,
proud, extravagant," helped themselves to the riches of the country
but contributed nothing in return. Dana blamed this lack of development on laziness—"California fever," in the phrase of the Anglos.[46]

"In the hands of an enterprising people, what a country this
might be!"[47]

Eager to return home, Dana exchanged into *Alert*, scheduled to
fill her hold with hides and sail out of Mission Bay for Boston in mid-
1836. In preparation, the crew unloaded the ship, cleaned out everything but the ballast, shut her up tight and caulked her, and smoked
out the rats and other vermin. In six weeks of incessant labor, the
crew packed forty thousand hides into her hold. Every fourth day
four quarters of a fresh-killed bullock swung from the foretop, causing Dana to wonder what the vegetarian Dr. Sylvester Graham would
make of this all-flesh diet—fried beefsteak three times a day, great
gobbets of flesh and fat to fuel the exertions of lading.

Alert sailed for home on May 8, 1836. On July 22, as they coursed
along under the flying clouds of the austral winter, a shout of "Land
ho!" reverberated through the ship—Staten Island, east of Cape Horn.
Alert had rounded safely and entered the Atlantic. The lone passenger emerged from his cabin for the first time in a month. Thomas
Nuttall skipped onto the deck "bright as a bird" and asked for a boat
to put him ashore so he could examine the island's avian life.

Aware of the naturalist's eminence and of his eccentricities, the
captain mastered his mirth and politely declined to delay the voyage to

accommodate him. Nuttall would retire to a quiet life among his specimens, Staten Island a permanent lacuna in his collection. As for Dana,
he would set to work on the memoir that within a few years would
fire American imaginations with California's imperial possibilities.

NARCISSA PRENTISS AND MARCUS WHITMAN reached an understanding
over the course of a weekend in February 1835. They may have known
one another slightly before Whitman volunteered to march west with
Samuel Parker, or Parker may have introduced them as potential
recruits for mission service in the Flathead country. Whatever the
circumstances of their meeting, the young woman and her matter-of-
fact suitor were both ardent for the spiritual uplift of the heathen.
Were the American Board of Commissioners for Foreign Missions to
establish a station beyond the Rockies, Whitman would require a
helpmeet. Narcissa Prentiss longed for the heroic life of a missionary.
They agreed that if a woman could make the journey safely, and if
Oregon seemed habitable for women and children, Whitman would
return to Amity, New York, marry Narcissa, and take her over the
mountains.

So unfolded their courtship, a brief and businesslike affair. "We
had to make love somewhat abruptly," Narcissa Prentiss would say,[48]
each regarding the other as the means to an end. Her motives were
benevolent, her qualifications minimal: intermittent schooling; piety;
a rudimentary teaching background; and an encyclopedic ignorance of
Native American beliefs, ways of life, and languages. Wearing her
best black bombazine dress, she married Marcus Whitman on the
evening of February 18, 1836, in the candlelit sanctuary of the Presbyterian Church of Angelica, New York. They had spent no more
than a few hours together before their wedding day. Narcissa viewed
matrimony as convenience; she channeled all the romance within her
into the religious calling. Whitman made a scruffy bridegroom, but he
was an energetic Christian with a vocation to match her own.

Narcissa Prentiss was twenty-eight years old in 1836, a high-spirited
bride with a fresh complexion, light blue eyes, long blond hair, and
a round, full figure. No contemporary likeness of her survives. In a
sketch drawn from an acquaintance's description her features are
broad, flat, and rather coarse; a painting based on studies by the artist
Paul Kane, who lived at the Whitman mission for several weeks in

Narcissa Whitman (1808–1847). The Canadian artist Paul Kane sketched this likeness of Narcissa during a brief halt at the Presbyterian mission at Waiilatpu in the summer of 1847. There are no known photographs of her. After reaching Oregon with her husband in 1836 to bring Christianity to the native people, Narcissa became increasingly remote from Indian life. (With permission of the Royal Ontario Museum © ROM)

1847, represents her as a beauty. She was the third of nine children and the eldest daughter of farmer-builder Stephen Prentiss and his pietistic wife, Clarissa Ward of Prattsburg, Steuben County, in the religiously intense Burned-over District of western New York.

The Prentisses had pushed West into what was then the oak-clad wilderness of the Finger Lakes region in 1805. As Prattsburg evolved from a frontier settlement into a thriving market town with increasingly complex systems of production and exchange, Narcissa's surroundings became comfortably middle class. Her father prospered sufficiently in the 1820s to send her to the "female department" of Franklin Academy. Stephen Prentiss's acquisitory instincts were highly developed. He owned a considerable amount of land and at one time or another operated a distillery, a gristmill, and a sawmill. If not a member of the town's elite, he certainly graded as a leading citizen of Prattsburg, whose overwhelmingly white and native-born population approached twenty-seven hundred in the mid-1820s.[49]

By precept, Narcissa knew that a life-altering spiritual episode never could be an end in itself. Converts themselves were obligated to lead others to Christ. As a founder of the Prattsburg Female Home Missionary Society, Clarissa Prentiss proselytized among her husband, children, and acquaintances. Caught up in one of the periodic revivals that agitated the Burned-over District in the late years of the Second

Great Awakening, Narcissa joined the Prattsburg Presbyterian Church on Sunday, June 6, 1819, experiencing at the precocious age of eleven the full transformational cycle of all but unbearable anxiety, galvanic repentance, and exhausted affirmation. Two months before her sixteenth birthday, on the first Monday of January 1824 in her own exact recollection, she experienced the epiphany that revealed her missionary life's work.

She joined the Youth Missionary Society and sang in the church choir. With her sister Jane, she taught briefly at an infant school in Bath, the Steuben County seat. And she attracted a suitor, Henry Harmon Spalding, a Franklin Academy schoolmate six years her senior. Born to an unwed mother and reared in foster homes, Spalding survived a pinched childhood to become an awkward, uncertain, and charmless young man. All the same, he summoned the courage to propose marriage to Narcissa Prentiss. It was an unlucky choice. She turned him down.

Some years later, in mid-1834, Stephen Prentiss moved his family to Amity in Allegany County, fifty miles southwest of Prattsburg. Then as now Americans were compulsively mobile, but even so the uprooting seems a curious thing. Perhaps Prentiss had purchased success at too high a price, stirring envy or outright resentment among his neighbors. Perhaps economic anxiety (declining prospects in maturing Prattsburg) had driven him to a less settled place in search of new opportunity. Something alienated him from Prattsburg. For obscure reasons, Prentiss renounced the Presbyterian Church and allied with the Methodists. At about the same time, the town's temperance forces singled out the Prentiss distillery as a target for protest, an affront that may have sealed his decision to relocate.[50]

Samuel Parker traveled through the Southern Tier counties toward the end of 1834, narrating the legend of the four Flatheads to receptive crowds, raising money, and scouting for a man to accompany him to Oregon. Parker stopped at Wheeler, near Prattsburg, where Marcus Whitman heard him speak, and at Angelica, outside Amity, where his appeal moved Narcissa Prentiss, now twenty-six, to give tangible shape to her mission fantasies.

"I have found some missionaries," Parker wrote home to Ithaca. "Doctor Whitman has agreed to offer himself to the board to go beyond the mountains. He has no family. Two ladies offer themselves, one, a daughter of Judge Prentiss of Amity, Allegany Co."[51]

Born in 1802 in Rushville, New York, Marcus Whitman had known harder and more anxious times than his bride. His mother sent him away to live with his Whitman grandfather in southeastern Massachusetts after the death of his tanner father in 1809. When he journeyed home for the first time after an absence of four years, she failed to recognize him. Whether or not this display of maternal indifference inflicted a serious wound, Whitman dutifully returned to his grandfather, acquired the basics of a classical education, and experienced conversion at a revival in Plainfield, Massachusetts, in 1819. He returned not long afterward to Rushville, where his mother had married another tanner, this one named Loomis. Something of a termagant, she discouraged his ambition to become a minister and put him to work in his stepfather's shoe shop.

That would not do. Fleeing the tannery, Whitman apprenticed himself to a Rushville physician and obtained a medical license on the strength of a short course at a local college. He knocked around a bit, practicing medicine in Canada and earning a second medical degree before returning to western New York. The Congregational parson in Rushville recommended him to the mission board as a medical missionary. With Parker's support, he won the appointment in mid-January 1835. Within a month, he had negotiated marriage to Narcissa Prentiss.

Whatever the quality of his medical training, Whitman seems to have been a competent practitioner. Resenting the missionary presence, American Fur Company yahoos hurled rotten eggs at him when he and Parker turned up at the caravan assembly camp at Council Bluffs in June 1835. Then cholera invaded the camp. Three men died; Whitman sweated and double-dosed many others back to health. The chastened traders obeyed without protest when he ordered the camp shifted to higher ground with a purer water supply. The epidemic abated. If Whitman rose in the estimation of these hard men at Council Bluffs, their admiration knew no bounds after his surgical exploits at the Green River rendezvous, where he extracted a three-inch iron arrowhead from the back of the legendary mountain man Jim Bridger.[52]

Whitman returned to Rushville in late 1835, prepared to close the deal with Narcissa Prentiss and complete his search for an associate missionary for the Oregon station. For some reason no suitable candidate presented himself. Then someone—it may have been Narcissa—

Marcus Whitman (1802–1847). This Paul Kane sketch shows Marcus Whitman in the summer of 1847. Relations with the Cayuse inhabitants of the Walla Walla Valley were strained virtually from the founding of the Whitman mission at Waiilatpu in 1836. Tensions increased dramatically after Whitman returned from a trip east in 1843 with a migrant train of nine hundred settlers. (With permission of the Royal Ontario Museum © ROM)

suggested Henry Spalding. Whitman seized on the idea and wrote at once to invite him along.

By now Spalding had been ordained a Presbyterian minister; he had gained a measure of self-confidence as a temperance lecturer; he had married a slight, fragile, and determined Connecticut-born New Yorker named Eliza Hart; and he had been appointed missionary to the Osage Indians of Missouri. With Eliza pregnant, he deferred the Osage posting until the spring of 1836. Their child was stillborn in October 1835. He hesitated over Whitman's proposal, then spoke with what sounded like finality: "I will not go into the same mission with Narcissa for I question her judgment." The reaction sounds natural enough, as Narcissa's judgment had spurned him. Possibly, too, Spalding doubted her commitment, especially in contrast to the tranquilly devout Eliza's. But Whitman persisted. The Spaldings were two days into their journey to Missouri when he caught up to them at an inn in Howard, New York. According to Spalding, Whitman said he would be compelled to abandon the mission if the Spaldings declined to join it. After talking the matter over with his wife, Spalding agreed to push on with the Whitmans beyond the Rockies.[53]

Why? To save the Oregon project? Because he considered it his Christian duty? To put Whitman under his obligation? To abash Narcissa? As events would show, Spalding had not gotten over her—or anyway, her dismissal of him—and he would writhe in agonies of jealousy on the cross-country journey. The Spaldings and the Whitmans sometimes shared a tent, and at some point early in the trek, probably in June along the Platte, Narcissa conceived a child. Narcissa's very presence must have been a torment to Spalding. "The man who came with us never ought to have come," Narcissa wrote later. "My dear husband has suffered more from him in consequence of his wicked jealousy, and his great pique toward me, than can be known in this world."[54] In the event, Spalding's rancor and his rivalry with Whitman would nearly destroy the mission.

But that lay in the future. The Whitmans and the Spaldings joined forces in Cincinnati on March 17, 1836. Sister Whitman left no surviving record of her first encounter with Spalding as a missionary colleague. She doubtless carried it off with outward ease of manner. Yet she found herself making a continual series of interior adjustments as she embarked on her pilgrim's progress to the Oregon Country. She had abruptly left behind an ordered world where she might have sailed serenely into village spinsterhood, with the Sabbath school, hymn sings, prayer meetings, and revivals at the emotional center of her life. Although she could not know it, she would never see her parents, her brothers and sisters, or the Presbyterian church at Angelica again. Then, too, even as she tried to adapt to Marcus Whitman and to the complicated machinery of marriage, she had to confront Henry Spalding's emotional stresses and complexities.

"I think I should like to whisper in Mother's ear many things which I cannot write. If I could only see her in her room for one-half hour," Narcissa confided in a letter home as she prepared to leave St. Louis at the end of March.[55]

Still, she did not allow these undercurrents to affect her health or dull her observations. She felt fit and weighed a robust 136 pounds. The missionaries reached Liberty, Missouri, on April 7—a foreign country, so it seemed to her. The Missourians' peculiar argot had the charm of novelty. "Their language is so singular that I can barely understand them, yet it is very amusing," she wrote. "In speaking of quantity, they say 'heap of man, heap of water, she is heap sick,' etc. If you ask, 'How does your wife today?' 'Oh, she is smartly better, I reckon, but she is powerful weak; she has been mighty bad. What's the matter with your eye?'"[56] Whitman and Spalding, meantime, purchased outfit and livestock at extravagant frontier prices: a heavy farm wagon, twelve horses, six mules, fourteen cows, two bulls. The women stitched together a tent, conical in shape, out of bed ticking. They all shared it at night—the foursome; the Nez Perce boys; plus a new addition to the missionary party, William H. Gray.

Gray's arrival on April 18 caught Whitman and Spalding unawares. He presented his bona fides, an appointment letter from the Board of Commissioners, but the others remained skeptical even though with Gray the selection process could hardly have been more haphazard than their own. An artisan, a skilled fabricator of cabinets and chairs, Gray had hoped to study medicine or for the ministry but achieved neither ambition—perhaps because, as his pastor in Whitesboro, New York, explained, he was "a *slow scholar.*" Yet his lack of education had done nothing to blunt his self-esteem. "He evinces an unusual perseverance; and a confidence in his own abilities *to a fault,*" the Reverend Ira Pettibone went on, "yet this very confidence often gains him success in an enterprise where one of *greater* talents and less confidence might fail." The board's agent for upstate New York endorsed Pettibone's tepid recommendation by saying that Gray would be content to join the Oregon enterprise as a mechanic.[57]

His manual adroitness would be useful. "New work in new hands," Spalding remarked. "Neither Mr. Gray nor myself had ever seen a pack fastened on the back of a horse or mule."[58] Gray caught on quickly; Spalding limped for days after being kicked by a mule. The missionaries augmented the party with the hiring of two drifters: a man of all work called Dulin, and a nineteen-year-old Connecticut adventurer with some experience of wilderness travel named Miles Goodyear. They also arranged to take along a young Nez Perce, Samuel Temoni, to help Richard and John tend the cattle.

From the first, the missionaries lagged behind the main column. Spalding and Gray struck overland, while Whitman with the women waited at Liberty for the steamboat carrying the American Fur Company contingent upriver to the traders' assembly point. The boat chuffed past the Liberty landing without stopping, the captain calling to shore that he could take no more passengers. Thomas Fitzpatrick, the caravan leader, refused to delay his departure for the Whitmans. Forced marches were necessary, the anathema of Sunday travel, too. They overhauled Spalding after four or five days. With exhaustive effort, the combined party covered sixty miles in one day, gradually closed the range, and came up to the trading caravan at Loup Fork of the Platte.

The moving village—seventy or so men, two women, and four hundred animals—advanced at a steady fifteen miles a day. The missionaries traveled with, and sometimes in, two wagons, the heavy vehicle they had acquired in Liberty and a lightweight Dearborn wagon, a present from Eliza Spalding's family. Fitzpatrick rode up front ahead of the pack animals and seven heavily laden fur company wagons, each drawn by six mules. The missionaries formed the rear guard. The caravan reached buffalo country in early June, just as the store-bought provisions were running low. The open-air life and fatty fare roasted over a fire of—in the delicate phrase—*bois de vache* agreed with Narcissa.

"I never saw anything like buffalo meat to satisfy hunger," she wrote. "I have eaten three meals of it and it relishes well."

And a few weeks later:

"We have meat and tea in the morn, and tea and meat at noon. . . . So long as I have buffalo meat I do not wish anything else."[59]

Not so for Sister Spalding. By the end of June, as the expedition approached South Pass, the all-flesh diet had seriously deranged her insides. Never blooming, she now looked gaunt, her voice—surprisingly strong and rather coarse for so slight a figure—a scratchy whisper. "Only He who knows all things, knows whether this debilitated frame will survive the undertaking," she wrote in her diary. "His will, not mine, be done."[60] Her father's homely farm in Holland Patent had never seemed more distant.

Edgy and overwrought, Spalding could not fail to observe the contrast between his invalid wife and the lusty Narcissa. The daily routine exhausted him, and he found the travel tedious. The dry, antiseptic aroma of the high plains, camphor mingled with spirits of turpentine, left him light-headed. He resented Whitman's dominance. Command came naturally to the forceful Whitman, yet Spalding ranked him as the only ordained minister in the party. Then too, doubts about the undertaking assailed Spalding. He suspected the mission would prove an exercise in futility. "The Indian's love of revenge, the white man's avarice and the church's slow movements will annihilate the red man not many ages hence," he wrote gloomily.[61] And Eliza was withering before his eyes. She could keep nothing down. Even the smell of buffalo meat caused her stomach to heave.

The train reached the Green River rendezvous on July 6. The missionary women caused a sensation, the veteran trapper Osborne Russell reported, the Indians gazing on Mrs. Whitman and Mrs. Spalding with rapture and astonishment. They were perhaps the first European women the natives had ever seen, Russell thought, certainly "the first that had ever penetrated into these wild and rocky regions." The Indian women could not contain their curiosity. "As soon as I alighted from my horse, I was met by a company of native women, one after the other, shaking hands and salluting me with a most hearty kiss," Narcissa wrote.[62]

The comment is virtually the entire record of Sister Whitman's first impression of the heathen she designed to save from the eternal fire. The trappers and traders captured her fancy, uncouth men who summoned up long-forgotten gallantries in tribute to her. They buzzed around her like bees. Gray thought he detected something sportive in her response to the men's touching their hats when they passed her in camp. Certainly she liked the attention. "I wish Narcissa would not always have so much company," her mother once had remarked.[63] She had always been open to the world, eager for admiration.

Disquieting news awaited the mission men. They expected to meet Samuel Parker at the trapper fair; a native messenger arrived in his place with a bundle of unused white paper and a note expressing regrets. Even as Whitman and Spalding scanned the message, a westerly breeze propelled the Hudson's Bay Company vessel *Columbia*, with Parker aboard, toward Honolulu at a steady six or seven knots. In his *Journal*, published in 1838, Parker would say that he learned two things from his expedition: ordinary people could journey to and around the Oregon Country, and the natives embraced the notion of missionaries settling among them. For now, though, he had no particular advice or intelligence to offer about the Indians, Vancouver, traders, supplies, links to the United States, or the Methodist mission in the Willamette.

"Hope you will prosper," Parker wrote. "If you have brought out letters for me please send them on after me by way of the Sandwich Islands. . . . Don't forget to send my letters."[64]

Word that Parker had abandoned them filled Spalding with despair. He contemplated returning to St. Louis, and for a moment even the tough-minded Whitman's nerve failed him. Fortunately Nathaniel Wyeth, who had included the rendezvous on his homeward itinerary, turned up to provide a briefing, offering information on the route and enumerating the products of "civilization" available from Vancouver's fields, mills, workshops, and storehouses. Of more immediate interest, Wyeth suggested that the missionaries attach themselves to Thomas McKay's Oregon-bound Hudson's Bay Company caravan encamped nearby.[65]

For now, though, they kept mostly to themselves. Sister Whitman received calls from Joseph Meek and the more presentable of his mountain comrades; Meek and friends even may have accepted Bible tracts from her hand. Naturally she averted her gaze from the fair's signature pastimes: drunkenness, gambling, horse racing, and fornication. Eliza Spalding rarely left the tent. Her fever had broken finally, and she found herself able now to keep down small quantities of mashed dried apples and camas. She demonstrated a gift, too, for getting along with the natives. She had picked up a few words of Nez Perce and could carry on a halting conversation from the sickbed. "Feeble as she was, she seemed to be the favorite with the Indian women," thought Gray.[66] Sister Spalding had recovered sufficiently by July 13 to move with the others to the Hudson's Bay Company camp ten miles distant.

With an escort of two hundred Nez Perces, the McKay caravan got under way for Fort Hall on July 18. Whitman had triumphantly piloted the missionaries' wagons over South Pass, and he now conceived an ambition to take the Spaldings' Dearborn machine across the Snake River Plain, through the Blue Mountains, and all the way to the Columbia. Here, as the most taxing part of the journey stretched before her, Mrs. Whitman felt the full force of the deracinating effects of travel. Buffalo meat in all its protean forms finally began to cloy. "I thought of Mother's bread & butter many times as a hungry child would," she mused in her diary. The path wound along the steep sides of mountains and she found her vitality ebbing away in the stupefying heat. Her husband got into difficulties with the wagon. One morning it became lodged in a creekbed and Whitman manhandled it to shore; later it upset twice on narrow mountain tracks. "Did not wonder at this at all," Narcissa wrote. "It was a greater wonder that it was not turning a somerset continually." She came to loathe the vehicle. Possibly she was jealous of her husband's obsession with it; possibly she saw it as an outward and visible sign of his stubbornness. "All the most difficult part of the way he has walked in his laborious attempt to take the wagon over (Ma knows what my feelings are)," she reported. The exertions were wearing down Whitman, too. He looked jaded, he had come up lame with what he diagnosed as rheumatism, and he had lost a lot of weight.[67]

Narcissa dreamed of her mother's bake oven. "Girls, do not waste bread," she advised her sisters; "if you knew how well I should relish even the driest morsel, you would save every piece carefully." As they negotiated a dizzying mountain passage on July 28, the wagon's axletree snapped. Privately she and Eliza Spalding exulted, "for we were in hopes they would leave it, and have no more trouble with it." In the event, the men fashioned a cart of the wreck, using only the back wheels. Whitman, Narcissa decided, meant "to take it through in some shape or other," whatever the cost.[68]

They reached Fort Hall on August 3. Wyeth's lieutenant Joseph Thing remained in charge there, and he offered such hospitality as lay within his gift. There were a few vegetables, and Thing served up fried bread with a main course of dried buffalo. Mrs. Whitman found the post's starveacre kitchen-garden a sorry affair: thrifty turnips, mice-gnawed peas, and onions gone to seed. Thing explained that a hard frost in early June had damaged the garden beyond repair. Still, crude as it was, Fort Hall afforded the first habitation since Laramie two months before. "Thus you see we have a house of entertainment almost or quite as often as Christian of the Pilgrim's Progress did," Narcissa observed. She bade Thing and his ramshackle trading post a plaintive good-bye when the party pushed off for the Snake River Plain on August 5.[69]

The route followed the southern bank of the Snake, a region of greater travail, perhaps, than Christian's Slough of Despond. Travel now had become so arduous that Narcissa discerned something miraculous in their ability to surmount difficulties. After days of subsisting on flyblown dried buffalo, John McLeod supplied the missionary mess with fresh-killed antelope. "Thus the Lord provides and smooths all our way for us, giving us strength," she wrote home. Some days later, when they came upon a place with good browse for the spent animals, she asked in her diary: "Was there ever a journey like this, performed where the sustaining hand of God has been so manifest every moment?" Physically worn, her nerves stretched taut, she longed for a roof, a bed, and respite from mosquitoes, but knew she must not complain.[70]

Sister Spalding escaped serious injury when her horse stepped into a hornets' nest, threw her, and dragged her for some distance along rugged ground. "The hand of God has been conspicuous in preserving my life thus far," she wrote. To lighten the load, Whitman asked Narcissa to jettison the trunk she had carried west from Amity. He meant to get through with the cart, even if he arrived on the Columbia with nothing but a flatbed on a pair of wheels. She was past caring. "It would have been better for me not to have attempted to bring any baggage whatever, only what was necessary to use on the way," she decided. "The custom of the country is to possess nothing, and then you will lose nothing while traveling." The caravan reached Fort Boise on August 19. There Narcissa washed her clothes for the third time since leaving home in March. McKay would stop at Boise; Whitman arranged for McLeod to escort the missionaries on to Fort Walla Walla. Crossing the Snake on horseback and in a rush and willow canoe, they pressed on toward the Blue Mountains.[71]

"As for the wagon," Narcissa wrote, "it is left at the Fort, and I have nothing to say about crossing it at this time." With the animals breaking down and another mountain barrier ahead, Whitman finally, reluctantly, allowed himself to part with it.[72]

The missionaries labored through the broken, hilly Burnt River country. "In the afternoon we made 11 miles over hills I should have thought impossible to pass in N.Y.," Gray wrote. Then, on August 26, the party divided, the Whitmans and Gray taking the lead, and the Spaldings following at a more deliberate pace. With tensions among the missionaries rising to a shrill pitch, separation seemed advisable. Sister Spalding's debilities were an irritant. Her husband, whose ways would never have recommended him anywhere, increasingly exasperated Whitman. The men may have been engaged in a struggle for control, too. Whitman doubtless considered himself in charge by natural right. But Spalding could trump him with his status as an ordained minister.

So the Whitmans forged ahead to the Powder River, reaching the Lone Pine, a towering landmark for early travelers on the Oregon Trail, in mid-afternoon. Two more days saw them through the Grande Ronde—no time to linger in this enchanting valley—and into the foothills of the Blue Mountains. The hills and the thick stands of yellow pine reminded Narcissa of Steuben County. Then came the climb into the mountains proper, "the steepest ones I ever passed," Gray decided. "Mount Pleasant, in Prattsburg, would not compare with these Mount Terribles," thought Narcissa. The track, strewn with basalt shards, lacerated the unshod horses' feet. A last exertion just before sunset carried the party to a climactic ridge. From the crest a view of the valley of the Columbia opened out before them, with Mounts Hood and St. Helens distinct in the distance. Narcissa watched in awe as the sun dropped behind the 11,235-foot summit of Mount Hood, its rays throwing the whitened cone of the quiescent volcano into sharp relief against the twilight.[73]

Her weariness seemed to fall away, and the spectacular scenery— the visions of home it evoked—revived her. She rose at first light on September 1 to dress for the parade into Fort Walla Walla. The sun- struck outpost beckoned to the travelers like a mirage. "Both man and beast appeared alike propelled by the same force," Narcissa wrote. "The whole company galloped almost the whole way to the Fort."[74] Pierre Pambrun and John Kirk Townsend greeted the missionaries at the gate. Pambrun led them inside to a room with cushioned arm- chairs. He and Townsend were just finishing their breakfast and Pam- brun offered the guests fresh salmon, potatoes, butter, and tea. Chick- ens, turkeys, and pigeons pecked at the dirt in the dooryard.

The Spaldings straggled in two days later. The homely scenes charmed the missionaries—especially the women—beyond descrip- tion. "No one knows the feelings occasioned by seeing objects once familiar after a long deprivation," Narcissa observed. Pambrun lodged them in the west bastion, a stronghold with gunslits for windows, stands of firearms, and a cannon squatting on its breach. Grateful for shelter from the scorching sun, Narcissa hardly noticed the primitive- ness of the surroundings. The past few days had restored her ener- gies. Gray, for one, regarded her with frank admiration.

"Mrs. Whitman has indured the journey like a heroine," he wrote. "And shure I am from this experiment and the nature of the Moun- tain air and the exilirating influence of traveling through the romantic sceneries of the Mountains having an object worthy of a Christian, that if scores of the daughters of the church were to undertake the journey insted of remaining active on their soffas at home pale and ematiated and pining under sickness they would find health and vigor renovating their whole sistem."[75]

Gray rather cruelly overlooked the case of Eliza Spalding, who had been ill—sometimes dangerously so—for most of the march. But she rallied at Walla Walla and found the last stage down the Columbia restorative. Mrs. Whitman, on the other hand, faced yet one more test, perhaps the sternest yet. Seated on a rock at the base of an outcrop at The Dalles while her husband assaulted the summit, she felt something crawling along the nape of her neck, reached back, and captured two fleas. Glancing down, she saw that her skirts and the gathers around her waist were black with fleas. In following the Evangelist's way, Christian had been warned to expect to meet with "wearisomeness, painfulness, hunger, perils, nakedness, sword, lions, dragons, and, in a word, death, and what not!" Bunyan had not mentioned fleas, though perhaps they came under the heading of what-not. Frantic, speechless with mortification, Narcissa scrambled up the bluff in search of her husband. "I could not tell him," she wrote, "but showed him the cause of my distress. We brushed and shook, and shook and brushed, for an hour, not stopping to kill for that would have been impossible." She suffered silently in the crowded boat until they reached Vancouver, where she finally could bathe and get at a change of clothes.[76]

The decision to continue downriver had disappointed Narcissa, who favored selecting a mission site at once. The men decided, however, to confer with John McLoughlin; purchase additional supplies, seeds, and tools; and leave the women in the comfort of "the New York of the Pacific" (Narcissa's phrase) while they returned to the upper country to build. They also hoped—vainly—to make contact with Samuel Parker. When they reached Vancouver on September 13, Parker had been ashore on Oahu for nearly a month.

As it happened, the peripatetic Townsend met the missionaries at the river landing on September 13. He showed them around the place as though it were his own private estate, introducing them to McLoughlin, his second in command James Douglas, and their *métis* wives. The doctor escorted them around the garden, an Eden to the travelers' trail-weary eyes with its apple, peach, and pear trees; flowers; and—at one end—a summer house covered with grape vines. Sister Spalding could not help but notice the contrast between the imperial Hudson's Bay Company abundance and the squalor in which the natives lived. They "appeared destitute of the means of living comfortably in this life," she thought, "& ignorant of the rich provision made for that which is to come."[77] As at the rendezvous, Mrs. Spalding and Mrs. Whitman became objects of wonder to the Indian women, who noted with astonishment that they carried no burdens and dressed so differently from the men.

Whitman, Spalding, and Gray shoved off for the upper Columbia. Like Jason Lee and others, they departed with McLoughlin's good wishes as well as with such booty from Vancouver's ample storehouses as they could bear away. "Dr. McLoughlin promises to loan us enough to make a beginning and all the return he asks is that we supply other settlers in the same way," Narcissa wrote. "He appears desirous of affording us every facility for living in his power."[78] She offered no comment on the men's decision, evidently ratified at Vancouver, to establish two stations rather than pool their efforts at one. As Narcissa explained it, both the Nez Perces and the Cayuses wanted "teachers" among them, and the men were reluctant to disappoint one of the tribes. But there were personal considerations, too.

"Do you suppose I would have come off here all alone a hundred & twenty miles if I could have lived with him or Mrs. Whitman?" Spalding would ask Gray after he and Eliza had established themselves in the narrow valley of Lapwai Creek near present Lewiston, Idaho.[79]

Spalding returned to Vancouver on October 18 with word that each missionary had chosen a site and that, with Gray's assistance, Whitman had begun to throw up a shelter. So the Whitmans would settle among the Cayuses. We have only the missionaries' word for the Indians' enthusiasm for the mission. The Cayuses were a proud race, a tribe that sprang in time out of mind from the heart of a beaver, making them stronger and more favored than others. And it was true that they were rich in horses; some families owned hundreds. But the tribe had been under siege long before the missionaries arrived. Their numbers had declined (the population probably did not exceed four hundred in 1836), and they had so intermingled with the more numerous Nez Perces that they had adopted their neighbors' language. Still, the Cayuses retained a natural haughtiness. They had, for example, refused to collect furs for the North Westers or the Astorians. They practiced, too, a custom of putting to death *tewats*— medicine men—who failed to cure their patients.

What little Narcissa had observed of native life perceptibly cooled her missionary ardor. Indian customs and harsh codes of behavior appalled and sickened her. She cringed at the sight of an infant with its head in a pressing machine. She imagined a dull and heavy expression in the grown people's eyes. She met an Indian woman who had witnessed a chief shoot her husband to death; the ball exited the victim, passed through her arm, and grazed her breast. Then Spalding related the story of an Indian woman at Walla Walla who had died leaving a newborn. The father arranged for a woman to nurse the babe. The dead woman's father seized it presently, carried it to the mother's grave, opened it, and buried it alive.

"These things and others make me feel that I am on heathen ground," Narcissa wrote.[80]

Enthusiastic about her new home if not her vocation, she carried up from Vancouver apple, peach, and grape sprouts; strawberry vines; sheet metal for a stovepipe; a roll of bleached linen that would serve for bedsheets; tin milk pans; coffee pots; tea pots; candlesticks; and covered pails. Nearly six months with child, she caught a first glimpse of the mission on December 10 after a twenty-five-mile ride from Fort Walla Walla. The site lay in the bottoms on a peninsula formed by a U-bend of the Walla Walla River. The Cayuses called it Waiilatpu—place of the rye grass—and it had been a favorite camping site of Chief Umtippe until Whitman claimed it for himself. He and Gray raised a 1½-story saltbox dwelling on a 30-by-36-foot foundation, enclosed the mud-brick lean-to, built a straw and mud fireplace and chimney, and laid a floor of hand-sawed boards. Blankets covered the openings for windows and doors.

"The rivers are barely skirted with timber," Narcissa wrote home. "This is all the woodland we can see; beyond them, as far as the eye can reach, plains and mountains appear. On the east, a few rods from the house, is a range of small hills, covered with bunchgrass—a very excellent food for animals, and upon which they subsist during winter, even digging it from under the snow."[81]

Narcissa and her husband would be laid into an early grave on one of the "small hills" near the mission house. For now, though, she made a comfortable home for herself as she awaited the advent of the new life within her. Pambrun contributed a table and sash for the windows. As she primed the sash and set in some of the lights, she mused how handily her joiner father used to do such work. Narcissa had her own room, too—her insistence on middle-class standards of privacy would be a source of recurrent conflict with the Cayuses—and a woodstove to heat it. John McLeod supplied the mission with a dog and a cat.

The Whitmans' daughter emerged long and plump with a shock of light brown hair after an easy delivery at about 8:30 P.M. on March 14, 1837—by coincidence, Narcissa's twenty-ninth birthday. Catherine Pambrun acted as midwife, and Whitman helped her dress the babe. "On the second day I dressed her alone, sitting in the bed, and have ever since," she wrote. "She is a very quiet child, both night and day—sleeps all night without nursing more than once, sometimes not at all."[82] Within the month, Narcissa wrote home to Angelica to ask her father to record Alice Clarissa Whitman's name and date of birth in the family Bible.

Named for her grandmothers, Alice Clarissa from the beginning supplied a substitute vocation for Narcissa. She had delayed making her first visit to the nearest Cayuse village for nearly a month after her arrival. She was slow to learn the language, probably because she was unable to summon any enthusiasm for it. Her diary and letters for the winter of 1837 scarcely mention mission work, although she did make halting efforts to instruct the Indians in hymn singing. She took against Umtippe at once, a man full of deceit and guile in her view, for he had let it be known that he would charge the missionaries for tutoring in Nez Perce. And he broadcast an edict barring the Cayuses from the mission house till the Whitmans paid the tuition bill.[83]

IN FAMILY LEGEND, her father's tales of the Astorians excited Anna Maria Pittman's interest in the Oregon Country. George Washington Pittman's Lower Manhattan ropewalk had furnished the rigging for *Tonquin*, which sailed from New York for the Columbia in September 1810, the month of Maria's seventh birthday. Whether or not Astorian adventures were formative, this pious girl, quiet and contemplative among a rackety family of thirteen children, decided early on to pledge her life to the Oregon heathen. She joined the Allen Street Methodist Church in 1828 during her twenty-fifth year, and settled down to wait for an opportunity to reveal itself.

Chance favored her design when the Methodist Missionary Society solicited for single women to teach the Indians of the Willamette Valley. The board chose Maria Pittman, Elvira Johnson, and Susan Downing, offering a salary of $300 a year with all travel expenses paid and a $100 stipend for outfitting. Miss Johnson came to an understanding with the would-be missionary H. K. W. Perkins; Miss Downing, an unusually pretty girl, intended to marry Cyrus Shepard in Oregon. The sponsors hinted, gently at first, that Maria would make a worthy wife for Jason Lee, who had advertised his desire for a bride in mission circles. "I made the best shift I could without female assistance," Lee wrote of his first months at Mission Bottom, but "it is not good for a man to be alone."[84] Rising thirty-three, ambivalent about relinquishing the ideal of celibacy, Miss Pittman tried to ignore the insinuation. She and Lee had met once, in New York; neither had been impressed with the other. In any case she could think only of the benighted people of the Pacific Northwest.

"I shall labor and teach them the way of life and peace," Maria wrote. "They are ignorant of a Supreme Being. They know not who created them, they know not a Saviour died for them, neither do they know of a Heaven or Hell after death. When they die they take a leap in the dark. Ought not someone to go and open their eyes and teach them the way to salvation?"[85]

She made her way to Boston, where the first reinforcement for the Lee mission assembled in July 1836. Her New York provincialism bubbled up at once. "The houses are high, the streets narrow and crooked," she wrote home. Rather to her surprise, she found the churches overdone, veering toward the Roman in their appointments: "The curtains behind the pulpit are crimson and very full and rich and trimmed, the pulpits are mahogany—I do not approve of it." More to the point, she met a man who actually had been to Oregon. "He says it is a fine country, even better than this."[86]

Nathan Bangs of the Missionary Society appointed Dr. Elijah White of Ithaca, New York, to command the reinforcement. Just turned thirty, brash, and glib, with an ingratiating manner that charmed women and tended to repel men, White instructed the others to call him Father. Possibly under instruction from Bangs, his wife intensified the campaign to arrange a Lee-Pittman romance. "She says I must be ordained after we get to Oregon so they may call me Mother," Maria wrote home. "Do you know what that means?"[87] But she could hardly pretend to misconstrue a coarser hint from the missionary outfitter Rufus Spaulding.

"Mr. Spaulding purchased our matrases yesterday. He got me a double one. I would not have it and made him get me a single one. They seem determined to have me doubled. I will take care of number one and that is enough."[88]

Shopping with Mother White, Maria Pittman bought a sidesaddle for $16 and other kit. She collected French texts, too, for study at sea to prepare herself for a ministry among the Canadians of the Willamette Valley. For her private devotions she packed away the Burma missionary Ann Judson's memoirs and a parting gift from her parents, a copy of *The Experiences and Spiritual Letters of Hester Ann Rogers*, published in London in 1833.

Father White led the singing of the missionary anthem "From Greenland's Icy Mountains" as Captain Barker warped the brig *Hamilton* away from the wharf on August 10, 1836. Maria remained below-decks for the first days of the voyage—queasy, she admitted, although not technically seasick. She finished Mrs. Judson's book on September 9 and quietly celebrated her birthday on the twenty-third. In early October, as *Hamilton* sailed into the southern early spring, she broke out her cold-weather clothes. They sighted Staten Island on October 17, rounded Cape Horn on the twenty-fourth, and passed safely into the Pacific. The ship's cook died in early December. "He was sewed up in a hammock with bullets at his feet," Maria wrote.[89] White read the funeral service, and the cook's mates heaved the weighted corpse overside. The brig made landfall off Oahu two days before Christmas.

No vessel awaited the missionaries at Honolulu. Maria improved the time by writing to a Canton merchant for a set of tea and table spoons. In due course the Oregon-bound brig *Diana* arrived, took the party aboard, weighed anchor, and shaped a course for the Columbia. *Diana* experienced a boisterous passage, far more difficult than the voyage out from Boston. At first approach, on May 11, 1837, the dreadful bar looked impassable, and the brig stood out to sea. Returning the next day, the master judged sea and wind conditions tolerable and laid the vessel in toward the opening. "We prepared ourselves to be cast away," Maria wrote. "All the females were in the Cabin shut in. As soon as the worst was over we went on deck. The waves of the sea were boiling like water for a ½ mile."[90] As *Diana* came to anchor in placid Baker Bay, Maria could see that her missionary acquaintance in Boston had not deceived her.

"The scenery is good," she decided; "the birds are singing; the hills are covered with spruce pine and hemlock trees; we could see flowers growing on the sides of the rocks on the cape."[91]

From Fort George, the Hudson's Bay Company agent sent aboard fine specimens of fresh and pickled salmon, sturgeon, and venison. As the brig bumped its way upstream toward Fort Vancouver, twice scraping bottom, Maria observed the river Indians at work during the first days of the salmon run. They "caught 40 in one day," she noted, "some of them 4 feet long."[92] At Vancouver on the afternoon of May 17 the viceregal McLoughlin came aboard to extend an official welcome to the Oregon Country and invite the missionaries to dine.

"We were all seated around a long table, 18 of us, the table set with blue," Maria wrote her parents. "Our first course was Soup, the next boiled salmon, then roasted ducks, then such a roast turkey as I never saw or eat, it was a monster, it was like cutting off slices of pork, then wheat pan cakes, after that bread and butter and cheese, all of their own make, and excellent too.

"Travelling and high living agrees with me," she exulted. "I have gained 11 pounds since I left home."[93]

Jason Lee turned up a few days later to escort the party to Mission Bottom. Raillery and sly looks caused Maria Pittman agonies of embarrassment. Perhaps by design, McLoughlin left her introduction to Lee for the last. Neither made reference to their previous encounter. Lee had been told that she had come with the expectation that they would marry. Recalling his first impression of her, he decided—however much he longed for a companion—to proceed with caution. Maria's looks, he had to admit, had not improved with time.

"I had seen her before but was not at all favorably impressed with her personal appearance, and least of all, did I think she would ever become my wife, even when I was informed by letter that she was coming to Oregon," he wrote later, "and on my first interview with her there, my prejudices remained the same."[94]

Nevertheless, the others maneuvered Maria into Lee's canoe. They shoved off on May 25; portaged around the falls early on the second day; and pushed upstream to Champoeg, where they changed to horses. A fast ride over grasslands and through pine groves brought the party to the mission by late afternoon. Maria took in the settlement at a glance: a log house with two large rooms, a kitchen, and a schoolroom. "It is rough but good enough for the present," she decided. "It is a pleasant situation; a good farm in order, several horses and cows."[95] Cyrus Shepard bustled about the kitchen in a brown linen smock. An excellent cook, he served up a plentiful evening meal of venison, sausages, cheese, bread and butter, doughnuts, strawberries and cream, and tea.

Dr. White's services were required at once, for fever had laid the mission low. Fully half of the boarding children were too ill to rise from their rough-mat beds. Lee handed out the assignments: Mother White and Maria took over the housekeeping from Shepard. "We found things in old bachelor style," Maria reported. "We females soon made a different appearance in the house."[96] Lee at once signified his approval of the women's touch. Susan Downing assisted her fiancé with the children; Elvira Johnson became mistress of the schoolroom. Two of the newcomers, carpenter-joiner William Willson, a former New Bedford whaler with a sailor's gift for improvisation, and Alanson Beers, a Connecticut blacksmith, set to work putting up new shelter for the mission, whose population, now exceeding fifty, crowded tenementlike into the existing buildings. Maria saw that heavy work awaited her. There were no comforts for the boarders, fit or ill. She accompanied Lee on a visit to a dying Kalapuya woman, and they did what they could to quell her fear of the unknown with ecstatic visions of a Christian afterlife.

Lee, meantime, gained a measure of mastery over his feelings. He tried to see beyond Maria's unlovely features. "She was not a lady I would have fancied for a wife (there is no accounting for people's *fancies*)," he wrote; "but, perhaps, he who looketh not upon the outward appearance but upon the heart, has chosen her as far better calculated to increase the joys and lessen the sorrows of life, than one my *fancy* would have prompted me to choose." Two weeks after her arrival, Lee proposed marriage.

"You will be anxious to know if there is any prospect of my having a Protector," Maria wrote home. "Let me tell you there is. Mr. J. Lee has broached the subject. It remains for me to say whether I will be his helpmate in his important charge. It requires serious deliberation. I have thought much upon the subject, and my own mind is fixed. Relying on the grace of God, I expect to give my heart and hand to J. Lee."[97]

She replied to him in verse:

Yes, where thou goest I will go,
With thine my earthly lot be cast;
In pain or pleasure, joy or woe,
Will I attend thee to the last.[98]

Lee chose July 16, 1837, as the first Communion Sunday at Mission Bottom. Cyrus Shepard and Susan Downing were to be married during the service. A crowd assembled at eleven o'clock in a grove of firs near the mission house: missionaries and laymen, boarders, and Canadians with their common-law Indian wives. Jason Lee opened with a hymn, "When All Thy Mercies," then spoke briefly about the holy institution of marriage, partly to impress the adulterous Canadians, partly in anticipation of what was to come. "It is an old saying, and a true one, that example speaks louder than precept," he intoned, "and now I intend to give you unequivocal proof that I am willing to practice what I have so often recommended to you."[99] He turned to Maria Pittman and invited her to the altar.

Daniel Lee read the marriage service for his uncle and his bride. Jason Lee performed the office for Shepard and Susan Downing, and again for settler Charles Roe and a Kalapuya girl named Nancy McKay, whose brothers were enrolled in the mission school. The congregation sang "Watchman, Tell Us of the Night," Lee preached, and afterward his nephew administered communion to fourteen of their number. "We now held a kind of love-feast," Daniel Lee remembered, "and all the brethren and sisters brought in their offerings, and the Spirit of grace rested upon us."[100] Several in the crowd, taking sudden alarm over the black enormity of their sins, surged forward to repent.

If the Shepards felt the Jason Lees had upstaged them in the open-air triple wedding, they left no record of it. The two missionary couples, with Joseph Gervais as guide, set out in early August for a wedding trip to the lower Willamette Valley and on to the Pacific. They returned to work at the end of the month. Maria took charge of the mission kitchen, made clothes for the boarders, and conducted a class in the Sabbath school. The men and boys gathered in the harvest. Daniel Lee and Shepard journeyed to Vancouver in early September to meet the second reinforcement, the ship *Sumatra*, carrying mission goods; the Reverend David Leslie, his wife, and their three children; Perkins; and Miss Margaret J. Smith. Perkins and Elvira Johnson were married in November.

Maria Lee discovered at about this time that she was with child. She would face the latter stages of her pregnancy, the lying in, and childbirth itself without her husband, absent on mission business. Expansion preoccupied Lee during the winter of 1837–1838; Oregon political matters, too. He had run up a considerable surplus of missionaries, and the Mission Bottom station had far outgrown the Kalapuya population. Nor had the natives proved receptive to the Methodist dual message of salvation and material well-being. None had converted, and few responded to the mission's attempts to persuade them to live in little houses and take up settled farming. A few followed Christian forms of observance, but even those who accepted the faith remained Christian *Indians*. By the end of 1837 the Methodists had all but abandoned the direct effort to impose Christian order upon heathen chaos. The missionaries henceforth would lead by example. They would create a thriving settlement of farms, mills, shops, schools, churches, and hospitals—a replica of the communities they had left behind—and trust that the Indians would prosper by association.[101]

For colony-building Lee required artisans, mechanics, farmers, physicians, and others of a workaday bent. To preserve the *mission* franchise he detailed Daniel Lee and Perkins to open a substation at The Dalles, the great gathering place of the river tribes. As a group, the missionaries resolved to send an emissary to the States to plead the case for reinforcements for the developing colony, an enterprise that, while undeniably secular, would serve the ultimately sacred purpose of supporting and supplying the mission outposts. Jason Lee set out on a reconnaissance into the Umpqua country in mid-February to determine whether a second substation might be established there. He found the natives "savage as the bears," the country too perilous for whites. When he returned on about March 10, his colleagues had reached a consensus that he should make the trip to New York to explain the recast vision to the Missionary Society. Lee resisted, thinking the trip would damage his health. In the end, he decided that duty required him to go.

Maria Lee, six months pregnant, accepted the decision with outward equanimity. "To part with friends is trying—this I know from experience—when I left home and kindred I felt it to be a sacrifice," she confided to her mother, "but what is it in comparison with seperation from my *dearest half*, especially in my present situation." She had surprised herself by falling in love, if not with her actual husband as yet, then anyway with the *idea* of him. "I awoke very early in the morning; lay awake along time thinking about you," she wrote Lee three days after his departure. "Felt happy and wanted to sing, but was afraid of waking my neighbors. I find my affections twining closer and closer about you." And in mid-April: "I used to sing of the blessings of *Celibacy*. I have turned my song to: Oh, the happiness of *Matrimony*!"[102]

With Lee it is impossible to say. Increasingly a man of affairs, not only as head of the mission but also as the most influential citizen of the white settlements, he had scant energy to spare for the emotional development of his union with Maria Pittman. Along with the mission's request for assistance, he would carry East a frankly imperial plea—a petition to Congress proposing U.S. jurisdiction in Oregon. Written by Philip Edwards and dated March 16, 1838, it emphasized Oregon's "happy position for trade with China and India and the western coasts of America" and called for the United States "to take formal and speedy possession" of the country south of the Columbia. Thirty-six settlers, fully three-quarters of the adult white male population of the Willamette Valley, signed the petition: all ten members of the mission, seventeen Americans, and nine Canadians.[103]

So Lee parted with his dream of a theocracy on the Willamette. The American settlers of the valley were stirring politically, and neither the Methodists nor yet Dr. McLoughlin in Vancouver could dictate the course of events there. McLoughlin at least could keep the Canadians, accustomed to strict Hudson's Bay Company discipline, on a short political leash. The Americans brought their unruly politics and their insistence on running their own affairs with them to Oregon. There was no predicting what they might get up to.

WASHINGTON HAD TAKEN OFFICIAL notice of the Willamette colony in the earliest phase of its development. In November 1835, only a few weeks after the missionaries had stored away their first harvest, the administration of Andrew Jackson directed William A. Slacum to proceed to the Columbia to collect "specific and authentic information in regard to the inhabitants of the country and . . . to endeavor to obtain all such information, political, statistical, and geographical, as may prove useful or interesting to this government."[104] What piqued Jackson's interest is unclear. The nineteenth-century historian Frances Fuller Victor attributed it to a Hall Kelley broadside alleging settler abuse at the hands of the British.* Others have suggested that Captain Bonneville's report caught the president's attention. In the end,

---

* In Hubert H. Bancroft, *History of Oregon*, 2 vols. (1886–1888). Mrs. Victor, Bancroft's research associate, wrote the two Oregon volumes; Bancroft took credit for them.

the expansion-minded Jackson may have needed no prodding from any quarter to advance U.S. claims.

Slacum, a navy paymaster lieutenant, allowed neither storm nor shipwreck to deflect him from his mission. He made his way to Guayamas, Mexico, on the eastern coast of the Gulf of California and, finding no vessel available there to bear him away to Oregon, hired a twelve-ton longboat that once had belonged to the ship *James Monroe.* Gales forced the frail craft to put into Mazatlán after nineteen days at sea. Persistent and resourceful, Slacum eventually caught a ship at La Paz, Baja California, bound for the Sandwich Islands. There, in Oahu, paying out of his own pocket, he chartered with Captain Nye the American-owned *Loriot,* a hermaphrodite brig usually engaged in the California hide and tallow trade: "a lump of a thing," Richard Henry Dana would write, "what the sailors call a butter-box." *Loriot* carried Slacum safely to the mouth of the Columbia three days before Christmas 1836. A Chinook in a canoe inquired, "Is this a King George or Boston ship?"[105]

Slacum and McLoughlin were mutually wary. McLoughlin displayed his customary charm, but he plainly marked down Slacum as an American spy. As for Slacum, he justified the expense of chartering the brig by arguing that it allowed him to operate independently in the closely regulated domain of the Hudson's Bay Company, which he disparaged as a virtual police state. The company "had absolute authority over the inhabitants on either side of the river," controlled the distribution of all supplies, and held a monopoly on trade and livestock. *Loriot,* Slacum explained, conferred the shelter of the Stars and Stripes in his transactions with the natives and the white settlers.[106]

Slacum spent only twenty-three days in Oregon, but he witnessed and heard enough to draw up a detailed bill of particulars against the British. The Hudson's Bay Company introduced uncustomed British goods into the territorial limits of the United States via the Indian trade. Company servants were permitted to keep Indian slaves. The company undersold American traders, suffocated competition, taught the Indians that only British ships were allowed to trade in the Columbia, supplied arms and ammunition to the natives, and encouraged British agents south of the river to trap beaver out of season and ignore regulations against taking the beaver young. Dr. McLoughlin enforced settler dependence by controlling the market for the Willamette's main export, wheat. The doctor paid in cash or company scrip for only half the export crop, with the balance a discount on goods bought at company stores. McLoughlin requested authorization to offer extensive credit and other enticements to further bind the settlers. The company governors instructed him to choke off their development by supplying necessities only.

After a ten-day stay at Vancouver, Slacum headed up the Willamette, McLoughlin providing a complimentary canoe and crew. Touring with Jason Lee, Slacum called at the homestead of every white settler in the valley. Lee and the other missionaries duly impressed him. "No language of mine can convey an adequate idea of the great benefit these worthy and excellent men have conferred on this part of the country," he wrote in his report, noting with special approval the mission's efforts to suppress ex-trapper Ewing Young's latest venture, a distillery.

Young claimed that the Hudson's Bay Company, by refusing to trade with him, had forced him into the whiskey business as a matter of survival. He acquired pickling cauldrons and other equipment from the departed Nathaniel Wyeth and recruited a partner. With McLoughlin's quiet support the Methodists went over to the attack, petitioning Young to dismantle the apparatus and offering to reimburse him for his expenses so far. Young rejoined that he had to make a living somehow. Slacum offered to broker a settlement. Throwing himself into local affairs, he backed a scheme designed to part Young from his still and supply cattle to the colonists at the same time.

A settler could lease or even borrow cattle from the Hudson's Bay Company, but McLoughlin barred the outright sale of animals. He doubtless wanted, as a matter of business practice, to keep the settlers in liege to the British. That said, in his view there were too few cattle in Oregon to risk anything that might reduce the company's herd. The Americans felt just as strongly about gaining title to livestock of their own. "I found that nothing was wanting to insure comfort, wealth, and every happiness to the people of this most beautiful country, but the possession of neat-cattle," Slacum wrote. The settlers—Slacum, too—regarded the cattle monopoly as more than a question of property: it was an affront to American nationality. As it happened, McLoughlin's policy applied to everyone. The doctor refused as late as 1839 to supply fresh beef to a British surveying expedition on the northwestern coast.[107]

At a meeting at Champoeg in January, Slacum offered to convey a party of settlers in *Loriot* to California, where they could buy Mexican cattle and drive them overland six hundred miles north to Oregon. With Lee's connivance, he arranged for Young to be offered command of the cattle drive in return for exiting the whiskey business. Slacum loaned the mission $500 for shares in the Willamette Cattle Company. McLoughlin invested $900 of company funds in an enterprise expressly designed to break his hold on livestock, suggesting he really had enforced the monopoly on grounds of husbandry—and that he objected as strongly as the Methodists to the development of a whiskey industry in the Willamette.

So whiskey and livestock inaugurated the formal political history of the Pacific Northwest. Young's drovers returned to the valley with 630 head of cattle. Slacum left for the States convinced that the Jackson administration ought to exert itself on Oregon's behalf. The government's urgent duty lay in protecting the settlers not from Indians "but from a much more formidable enemy," the Hudson's Bay Company. Innumerable advantages would flow from U.S. rule. It would break settler dependence on the company. American jurisdiction would assure settlers of lucrative markets for their surplus wheat in Alaska and the Sandwich Islands, a civil society regulated on democratic principles, and a "surveyed and properly lighted" coast in the vicinity of the lethal Columbia bar. With such manifest benefits for the colonists and with a vast accession of territory and wealth available to the nation, Slacum regarded his expedition expenses—he stunned the State Department with a bill for $5,969.74, including the cost of chartering *Loriot*—as trifling.[108]

WITH SLACUM'S TOUR, settler opinion began to coalesce. Among the converts to American sovereignty was Jason Lee. From this point on, Frances Fuller Victor wrote, "we regard Jason Lee less as a missionary than as an American colonizer." Perhaps stretching the point, she went on to charge Lee with intentional deception of his Missionary Society sponsors in failing to disclose that he had written off the Indians and would now channel his formidable abilities into developing the white settlements. Still, Lee may not have found it necessary to mislead his supervisors, at least some of whom understood clearly the implications of the Oregon enterprise. "If the mission prospers, a colony will rise up," Nathan Bangs wrote H. K. W. Perkins more than a year before Lee set out for New York, "so we hope a foundation will be raised thus early for its future prosperity." Bangs and others were as ambivalent as Lee about conventional notions of Christianizing and civilizing the heathen.[109]

Carrying the settlers' petition "in a little trunk strapped to his horse's side," Lee left Mission Bottom on the morning of March 26, 1838, in company with Philip Edwards and two Chinook boys, William Brooks and Thomas Adams. His wife saw him off in verse:

> Farewell, husband, while you leave me,
> Tears of sorrow oft will flow.
> Day and night will I pray for thee,
> While through dangers you may go;
> Oh, remember,
> Her who loves you much: Adieu.

With her troublesome pregnancy, Maria Lee was at considerably greater risk than her husband on his transcontinental trek. From the fourth or fifth month she experienced virtually unrelieved distress. She wrote her husband on April 6 that she had left the house but once since his departure two weeks earlier. Dr. White told her he thought it likely she would go into labor before her time. She wrote Jason, "My being in so much pain he thinks will forward the business— what do you think?" She understood they were both approaching a threshold. "Oh my dear, if we never meet again on earth how pleasing it will be, even in eternity, to reflect on the pleasant life we have led since we became one," she wrote. They had been married for eight months.[110]

As illness tightened its grip, she sought solace in familiar things. "Your old chair is where it used to be when you sat in it to write," she wrote Lee after a sleepless night. "Your white hat hangs just where you left it and likely to remain there; even your old shoes remain on the shelf in silence waiting with patience the return of the wearer." Through veils of pain, she could discern the end. "I feel that I am now writing the last time," she went on. "Well it must be so, and I feel grateful for the privilege I have enjoyed. It has exceeded my expectations, and I have enjoyed it very much." The next day, April 16, she wrote her eleven-year-old sister Hester Ann with word that her new brother Jason would be visiting soon. "You must give him a kiss for me, and you may have one for yourself too."[111] It was her last surviving letter.

Maria Lee summoned Dr. White to her childbed on June 21. White needed forceps to extract the infant, a boy, on Saturday the twenty-third. The baby expired on Monday. Maria experienced "complications," in White's delicate term, and died in excruciating pain at about six o'clock on the morning of June 26, 1838. David Leslie preached the funeral sermon, and the missionaries buried her with her son in her arms in the grove of firs where she and Lee had been married less than a year before.

"Yes there I will go and tell the simple story of the cross," Maria Pittman had written her mother from Boston as she made final preparations to go West. "There will I toil, there would I live, there would I die, and there would I be buried."[112]

She made, in the idiom of the missionaries, a good death. She seems to have known intuitively that she would fulfill her prophecy prematurely; anyway, her friends spoke of there being an aura about her during the last months. "I think I never saw her in so happy a state of mind as for a season before I was called to leave for this station," Elvira Johnson wrote Maria's parents from The Dalles, where she had settled with Henry Perkins. "She seemed perfectly resigned to the will of God, and ripening for heaven."[113] From Vancouver, McLoughlin dispatched a special express to overtake Jason Lee with the news. It reached Henry Spalding at Lapwai on July 9; he forwarded it via six Indians to Fort Hall. There two trappers contracted to carry the message eastward over the Rockies.

4

The Missionary Impulse

THE ZULU LANDS OF SOUTHERN AFRICA were Elkanah and Mary Walker's original destination. Then William Gray turned up at the office of the American Board of Commissioners for Foreign Missions in New York City with Dr. Whitman's plea for Oregon reinforcements. The board acted at once to redirect the newlywed couple to the country of the setting sun. The need, so the commissioners agreed, seemed greater there. With Gray and his new wife, two other couples, and a bachelor, the Walkers struck out for the Oregon missions in March 1838.

Insistent that missionary candidate Walker acquire a wife, the board helpfully had proposed a candidate: Mary Richardson, a twenty-six-year-old schoolteacher from Baldwin, Maine. Walker dropped down from South Yarmouth one late-winter Sunday to preach in Baldwin, and Mary's father invited him home for tea after the meeting. Miss Richardson failed to catch Walker's drift at first, perhaps owing to a deficiency in his romantic technique. He managed to stammer out his intentions finally; she asked for a few hours to think matters over. Married on the morning of March 5, 1838, the Walkers left for New York that afternoon to rendezvous with the overland missionary party.

They were assigned to travel with Cushing and Myra Eels of Connecticut, also married on March 5, and Vermonter Asa Bowen Smith and his wife, Sarah. A thoughtful and studious youth, Smith had famously ignited his father's combustible temper by carrying a Latin textbook into sugar camp in the hills above their Williamstown farm. Smith experienced a religious epiphany in 1831, experimented with vegetarianism and Dr. Sylvester Graham's healthful gray-brown flour, and adopted the cause of temperance. He browbeat everyone in the family into taking the pledge except his irascible father, who doubtless saw him off to Middlebury College with relief. A subsequent two years at Andover Theological Seminary prepared Smith for the ministry. His search for a bride led him to West Brookfield, Massachusetts, the home of Sarah Gilbert White; he and the frail, vaporish, and pious Miss White soon reached an agreement. "The matter is settled about our going to the Indians beyond the Rocky Mountains & tomorrow we are to be married & set out for New York," Smith wrote his parents on March 14.[1] The Reverend and Mrs. Smith arrived in the metropolis four days later.

The New Englanders arranged to meet the party's bachelor, Cornelius P. Rogers, in Cincinnati and their leader and guide Gray, with his wife Mary Augusta, at the trailhead in Independence, Missouri. The mission board allocated $1,000 for the passage to Independence and another $2,000 for the onward journey. From his home in East Windsor, Connecticut, Eels posted Walker advice on essentials for the trip: a change of clothes; a buckskin ensemble of coat, pantaloons, and drawers; boots or shoes; five or six striped cotton or linen shirts; a change of pillowcases; shaving tackle; and pencils and a box of "water paints"—the entire outfit not to exceed twenty-five pounds per person. His wife should pack a good-quality riding dress, and he should obtain a rifle and learn to use it. The missionaries would travel to Pittsburgh by stage, then by steamboat via the Ohio, the Mississippi, and the Missouri to Independence.

"From that place one must be prepared to start on horseback by the 28th of April if the spring be forward," Eels advised.[2]

Walker drew up a list of questions: What were the dangers? Would Sunday travel be necessary? Should they take a bed? Would he not need a considerable library? Schoolbooks? Farming tools? Why did the trip cost so much? The commissioners evidently replied to Walker's satisfaction, for he and his stranger-wife arrived in New York City on March 17, met with David Greene, the board secretary, the next day, and set out for Pittsburgh in company with the Eelses and the Smiths on the twentieth.

The vast country that opened out beyond the Appalachians alternately fascinated, disoriented, and repelled the New Englanders. Myra Eels recorded her first encounter with the Peculiar Institution in the person of a chambermaid assigned to her stateroom on the boat from St. Louis to Independence. "She is owned by the captain of the steamboat," Mrs. Eels wrote with manifest distaste. "She can neither read nor write. She says her master treated her kindly. We saw nothing to the contrary." Her New England conscience began to pulse and throb. "Today have my feelings moved almost to indignation on account of the wretchedness of slavery," she wrote. "Our hearts are made to bleed for the poor slave." For Asa Smith, too, the actual experience of slavery carried a more intense emotional impact than he had imagined. "Slaveholders are afraid to have anything said to their slaves or have them instructed at all, lest they should learn to value their liberty and take measures to obtain their freedom," he wrote. "This is one of the horrors of slavery." In other ways, though, Smith concluded that his informants had exaggerated the sinfulness of the country. "I find some wickedness at the west, but not so much as expected," he wrote his sisters. "There has been some gambling & drinking on the boat, but less than I anticipated." That said, the women were showy and fond of trumpery, not so "solid" as the Yankee ladies of his acquaintance.[3]

The missionaries cleared Westport, Missouri, with one wagon, ten mules, and twelve horned cattle at noon on April 23, 1838. There were difficulties with horses, mules, and cattle unaccustomed to the rigors of the trail. Myra Eels averted her gaze from naked Indians and shivered at the sound of wolves prowling just beyond the glow of the fire at night. Three horses bolted. Covering a hundred miles in five days, they overtook the American Fur Company caravan, Captain Drips commanding, on the forenoon of April 28. Asa Smith brooded on Drips's insistence—Rule 1 of western travel—that the missionaries carry arms.

"The fur company will not afford us aid unless we do this," Smith wrote home. "This you know is painful to me, for I am a peace man. O how does it look for a missionary of the Prince of Peace to go forth to preach the gospel, carrying with him weapons of war? I shudder at the thought. I should feel more safe to go without any weapons."[4]

Day succeeded monotonous day of the cross-country odyssey. Myra Eels, Mary Walker, and Mary Gray improved the time on the first half day of travel by kindling a large fire on stones in the shallows of a creek for an open-air laundry. "We would have got on well had the water been soft," Mrs. Eels lamented, "but that being so hard, it took all our strength and a great deal of our soap—but we found that we could heat water, wash, boil and rince our clothes in the same kettle."[5] She recorded routine pratfalls and illnesses along the way: Smith accidentally ignited a grass fire, wild horses threatened to stampede though the camp, Mary Gray came down sick, then Eels. They reached Fort William (later Laramie) on May 30 and rested there for three days. Grateful for the respite, Myra Eels found the post a hangdog sort of refuge all the same.

"It is a large hewed log building with an opening in the center. It compares very well with the walls of the Conn. State Prison," she wrote dryly.[6]

The exertions of travel began to exact a toll. Mary Walker, fairly certain by early June that she was pregnant, underwent a profound physical and spiritual trial. "If I were to yield to inclination," she wrote in camp along the North Platte on a rare Sunday layover day, "I should cry half my time without knowing what for. So much danger attends me on either hand; a long journey yet before me, going I know not whither. Without mother or sister to attend me, can I survive it all?" She had no complaints about Walker, though, except perhaps his addiction to chewing tobacco. "He treats me very kindly, and I can but believe he loves me," she wrote.[7] The others, however, with their personality quirks, readiness to take offense, and penchant for quarreling, were a heavy burden.

Mrs. Walker found her tentmates' solecisms all but intolerable. Asa Smith loved to find fault; Sarah Smith had a fretful, unquiet disposition and a maddening habit of incessant whispering. Besides, "Her husband is very much of a hog at table; and he frequently treats me with what I deem rudeness. There is that about them which looks a good deal like pure selfishness." Although fractious, coarse-spoken, and something of a martinet, William Gray at least treated the Walkers with consideration. For his part, Smith thoroughly detested the bumptious carpenter and judged him unfit for his place. "Br. Gray is so anxious to get along cheap that he subjects us to more hard labor than we have really been able to bear," he complained. Their relations went from bad to worse. Gray had a tendency to lose self-control, snapping, scolding, riding roughshod over the others' feelings. "This much I can say in truth," Smith wrote home, "I never rec'd so much personal abuse in all my life as I have from this man. He has treated us like servants. His conduct is such that he is hated by all who have been with us." All the same, Smith developed a hyena's appetite as the summer advanced, and boasted in letters home of his growing stamina and strength.[8]

"I eat as well as I sleep & eat meat too, for I must eat it or go without," he wrote. "I get lame and sore some, but my health is good & I get so hungry sometimes that I feel as tho' I could eat a millstone."[9]

Adding to Mary Walker's general debility, the high-fat diet of the trail touched off acute attacks of diarrhea that made an embarrassing misery of the daily stages. Sarah Smith entered the tent one evening to find her in tears. A High Plains storm howled outside, and water flowed in cascades under the edges of the tarpaulin. "I cried to think how comfortable father's hogs were," she explained to Sarah.[10] Then, from one moment to the next, the sky cleared to reveal the distant snowy brows of the Wind River Mountains. The spectacle greatly cheered Mary.

"I wish Mr. Walker would seem to feel as much interest in viewing the works of nature as I do," she wrote. "I think the journey would be much less wearisome to him."[11]

Captain Drips's trading caravan reached journey's end near the junction of the Popo Agie and Wind Rivers during the third week in June. The trappers convened there for the 1838 mountain fair—one of the last of the annual gatherings, as it turned out, given the emergence of silk. Asa Smith preached to forty men and women from the Indian camp on Sunday, July 1. Mary Walker thought the natives rather enjoyed the singing, even if they comprehended scarcely a word of Smith's sermon. The whites, even some of the trapper leaders, were stupefied with drink most of the time. Jim Bridger's brigade arrived on Wednesday the fourth and touched off a licentious salute to the national day that kept the missionaries awake and on edge all night. "The musick consisted of tin horns accompanied by an inarticulate sound of the voice," Mary Walker reported. "They hallooed, danced, fired and acted as strangely as they could." Revelers burst into the Gray-Eels tent looking, thought Myra Eels, "like the emissaries of the devil worshipping their own master."[12] One man carried a Blackfoot scalp and sang a hymn to an outbreak of smallpox in the tribe.

There were no messages from Whitman or Spalding, though, and no sign of an Indian escort for the remaining eight hundred miles to the Columbia. An express finally arrived from Whitman with instructions for the onward journey. Henry Spalding had forwarded provisions to Fort Hall, and a Cayuse guide with fresh horses would deliver the travelers to Waiilatpu. Jason Lee, eastbound on his errand for the Methodist mission, turned up with a Hudson's Bay Company party under the command of Francis Ermatinger. Lee told Gray that Ermatinger approached the Green River expecting to find the rendezvous at the usual place. The valley was deserted, but someone had left a hastily scrawled message: "Come to Popeasia, plenty of whiskey and white women." Lee staged through Waiilatpu, where Narcissa Whitman saw him off with the present of a small keg of butter; he reported that the Whitman and Spalding missions were prospering in their work, although greatly in need of help. Lee rested for two or three days, left letters for Ermatinger to carry back to Vancouver for his wife, now ten days in her grave, and resumed the eastward trek.[13]

The Gray party pushed on to Fort Hall. There on July 26 they learned from Hudson's Bay Company runners of the death of Maria Lee. Smith pursued his language studies with a band of six Nez Perces who turned up at the fort to meet the missionaries. "I have already learned several words so that by these and signs I can make them understand very well," he wrote. All the same, he felt the first stirrings of the disgust for the natives that later would virtually incapacitate him. The Bannocks he reported as filthy in appearance and habits. "One squaw caught lice & eat them most of the time," he wrote. "This is common among the Indians, to eat them."[14] Mary Walker arrived with a streaming cold and a toothache. She had the tooth extracted that evening, rested the next day, and felt a little better when the party resumed the march on Tuesday, July 31. The days were hot, the nights chilly, the traveling monotonous through a desolate landscape of basalt and sedge. At Fort Boise on August 16 the missionaries savored milk and butter with their dinner of salmon, boiled pudding, and turnip sauce. Mrs. Walker recorded the ornamental detail that a cow at the fort yielded twenty-four quarts of milk a day.

The Grays ranged ahead, while the main party struggled through the Burnt River country and the foothills of the Blue Mountains. "They told us we were done with the mountains long ago; but if these are not hills I know not what they are," wrote the bulbous Mary Walker, who found sitting on a horse a torment. Reaching the Lone Pine landmark on August 24, the missionaries met two Cayuse Indians awaiting them there with letters from Whitman. In the Grande Ronde the next day, Mrs. Walker reported the confinement of the Indian wife of James Connor, one of the guides: "At noon she gathered fuel, and prepared dinner: gave birth to a daughter before sunset." Mother and babe rejoined the party the following morning.

"The squaw came into camp about ten with her child in her arms, smart as could be," Mrs. Walker wrote.[15]

The band reached Waiilatpu at about two o'clock in the afternoon of August 29 after 129 days on the trail. The Spaldings trekked down from Lapwai to join the Whitmans and the Grays in the reception party. The travelers could not have been more relieved to reach journey's end than the Whitmans were to embrace their dust-encrusted persons. Year-old letters from David Greene reaching the station earlier in the summer had indicated there would be no reinforcements anytime soon, causing Narcissa Whitman to all but give up hope of white female companionship. "But the Lord was better to us than our fear," she wrote, "and we feel to admire and adore his great kindness and love to us and these interesting heathen, that he has disposed to send us helpers in this glorious work so soon." Walker and Eels would establish a new mission station, Gray and Cornelius Rogers were assigned to Lapwai, and the Smiths would stay on to assist the Whitmans at Waiilatpu. Narcissa decided on impulse that she would make an intimate of Sarah Smith. She called her sister Clarissa to mind, only Sarah was not quite so tall.[16]

"They all appear friendly and treat us with great hospitality," Myra Eels wrote of her missionary colleagues. Yet despite the experience of the preceding four months the reality of Waiilatpu under its immense canopy of blue sky left her in a state of mild shock. She had imagined something along the lines of a Connecticut hamlet—say, Broad Brook or Windsorville. She hardly knew what to think of the outlandish adobe mission house. "I cannot compare it with anything I ever saw," she wrote—and she had slept in the rude snuggeries of Fort William and Fort Hall. "There are doors and windows but they are of the roughest kind, the boards being sawed by hand and put together by no carpenter but by one who knows nothing about the work as is evident from the appearance." The furnishings were rudimentary: wobbly chairs, crude tables, wooden bedsteads nailed to bare walls still reeking of sap, with husks and blankets for bedding.[17]

With other matters to preoccupy her, Mary Walker graded the accommodations adequate. "I am glad to find so comfortable a house prepared for me, and find it very gratifying to meet mothers who know how to sympathize with me," she wrote. Smith expressed admiration, too, for what the Whitmans had claimed from the wilderness. With seventeen acres under the plow, Whitman had harvested—although not yet threshed—a fine wheat crop. As a Vermonter, Smith could not help marveling at the fact that, with grass available for the livestock through the winter, there would be no need to cut and stack hay. The mission farm produced three hundred bushels of corn and a thousand bushels of potatoes; the two-acre kitchen garden yielded quantities of root and garden vegetables and an abundance of melons.[18]

The men met in conclave on Saturday, September 1, to ratify the mission assignments. The decision to send Walker and Eels on an exploring expedition into the Spokan Country vexed Mary Walker; her husband, eager to get started, felt a tug from opposite directions. "Still it was hard to leave my wife, leaving her alone when she demanded more than ever my presence and attention," he wrote in his diary.[19] He decided to go anyway. Walker preached the Sunday sermon to a mostly Indian congregation from the text "Herein is my father glorified." Smith followed him, translating in pidgin Nez Perce, fractured English, and with hand gestures the arcana of Presbyterian worship. The whites then celebrated the Lord's Supper. For now, anyway, the upheaval of the overland journey could be forgotten.

"We had an interesting, and I think, a happy season, notwithstanding all the hardness that has existed among us," Mary Walker wrote. "We feel that we have great cause of gratitude, and much encouragement to go forward in the work."[20]

THE MESSAGE FROM THE WILLAMETTE overtook Jason Lee at Shawnee Mission, Kansas, at midnight on September 8–9, 1838. He doubtless regretted the loss of his wife; there is nothing to suggest that Maria's death grieved him deeply. In any event he pressed on for New York, breaking the journey to promote the Oregon venture in Peoria, Chicago, Detroit, and Buffalo. Lee's lectures, together with the colorful asides of the Chinook Thomas Adams, drew large crowds and, in Peoria, anyhow, touched off an intense interest in emigration. A hyperactive

Vermont-born Peorian named Thomas Farnham organized an all-male company of "Oregon Dragoons" over the winter with plans to set out for the Columbia in the spring. A lawyer, Farnham omitted no detail in his preparations. His quasi-military fifteen-man expedition would even march with its own flag. Farnham's wife created it herself, stitching the company's motto—"Oregon or the Grave"—into the cloth.

Lee reached New York City in late October. His report to the Missionary Society carried conviction, and he managed to override the objections of the board's doubters in arguing that the society should send laymen to Oregon in substantial numbers in a bid to "establish the institution of Christianity before the natives become yet more defiled by the proximity and intermingling of unprincipled white men." Possibly the loom of competition—reinforcements for the Whitman-Spalding missions, and two Roman Catholic priests rumored to be heading for the Willamette Valley (where Canadian settlers had built a chapel, St. Paul's, in anticipation of their arrival)—influenced the sponsors. "I think I shall succeed in getting forty men and women," Lee wrote David Leslie at Mission Bottom, and he directed his second-in-command to gather supplies for the reinforcement.[21]

"Do not be afraid of purchasing too much," Lee advised Leslie, "for I would not like to have our people starve the first year."[22]

Lee and his associates presented a persuasive case for expansion. To achieve independence from the Hudson's Bay Company, Lee proposed a merchant-partnership with Joseph Thing, Nathaniel Wyeth's former lieutenant. Thing planned to return to the Columbia with a shipload of trade goods and set up in competition with the company; he needed the assurance of steady mission business to minimize the risk for his investors. "I have no doubt you will avail yourself of the opportunity," Lee wrote Nathan Bangs, the Mission Board secretary. "In my next I shall send you a long list of necessaries." Lee promised, too, to pay closer attention to the Mission accounts (he admitted having overdrawn by some $600 to meet salary and other expenses), increasingly a point of contention with Bangs and the board.[23]

As his uncle plodded slowly eastward, Daniel Lee dispatched a plea of his own for reinforcements. "Oregon is ripe for the sickle, and [the sponsors] cannot be too soon in employing a sufficient number of laborers to secure the harvest," he wrote Bangs. This was no time for the board to stint the mission. "Whether ten, or fifty, or one hundred thousand dollars are sufficient to defray its expenses, it is enough that the work must *be done*," he insisted. Fifty "effective men" were needed for religious work, along with a hundred or more laymen—carpenters, coopers, cobblers, blacksmiths, millwrights—and their families. The natives of the Willamette had raised their voices as one in crying out for the dual blessings of Christianity and civilization *and* for protection from main-chancers, whiskey-makers, and other sinful characters drifting in from the States.[24]

"It is not the time to sit in cold debate, while the eternal interests of dying hundreds are calling us to hasten to their relief," Daniel Lee wrote. "What we do we must do quickly, that our work [be] in advance of the ingress of designing men, who may introduce intemperance, and thus finish the work of death already so far advanced by disease."[25]

Via Jason Lee, David Leslie petitioned Willbur Fisk to use his influence with the board to secure a female teacher for his three sprightly daughters and the other six children of the missionaries. He anticipated the board's objection: Why couldn't the girls attend the mission school with the Indian and mixed-blood children? That certainly had been Brother Lee's expectation—at first, anyway. Closer examination revealed that the "vulgar stile" and "mongrel dialect" of half-taught Indians would corrupt the schoolroom. And worse: "Any person unacquainted with the moral and physical contamination of the heathen of every sex and age as it is found throughout this country cannot at all appreciate the reasons why our children may not associate with the natives," Leslie wrote, adding that he had found the Indian children to be adepts of the most "revolting" vices. "I could say more."[26]

The Missionary Society on December 5 voted $40,000* to expand the Oregon venture and recruit five missionaries, six artisans, four farmers, and the female teacher. At the same time, the board approved the purchase of milling equipment and authorized development of a gristmill at the Willamette Falls, where the Hudson's Bay Company had long since pegged out a claim. Curiously, the board overruled Lee on one point: he had requested only two missionaries. Possibly

---

* Frances Fuller Victor asserted that the society came up short of money for the venture and that the U.S. government provided $50 per passenger from a "secret-service fund" to promote Oregon settlement.

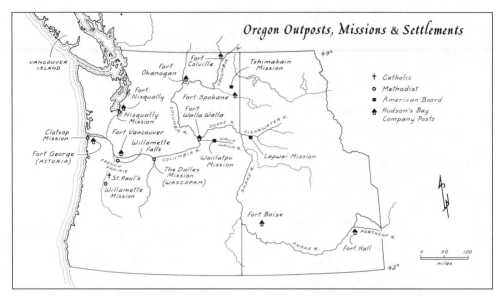

Oregon outposts, missions, and settlements, 1811–1840. (© 2003 by Jackie Aher)

Daniel Lee's memorial had influenced the members. In any case the board evidently continued to view Oregon as a *mission*, with Nathan Bangs emphasizing that the society would send out farmers and mechanics to cultivate crops and build houses "only so far as these things are necessary to realize the primary object of the enterprise, which is, the salvation of the souls of the people in that region." Finally, the board instructed Lee to embark on a fund-raising tour that would carry him south as far as Virginia, north to Quebec, and west into the Burned-over Country of upstate New York.[27]

Lee took to the road in early December. He shared a platform in Philadelphia with the State Department agent William Slacum; the Chinook youth William Brooks spoke, too. The three together managed to extract $512.26 from the crowd, the largest collection of any stop on the tour. Tall, prophetically bearded, with the romance of Oregon clinging to him, Lee cut an impressive figure wherever he went. "I think I never saw a nobler specimen and example of what a Missionary should be," the *Zion Herald*'s correspondent wrote.[28] Lee moved on to Washington, D.C., where he spent a week in mid-December on political as well as mission business.

He pressed Oregon's claims through Representative Caleb Cushing of Massachusetts and Senator Lewis Linn, a Missouri colleague of expansionist Thomas Hart Benton; the settlers' petition emphasized the economic exploitability of the fertile, well-watered, mild, and snow-free Willamette Valley. "We flatter ourselves that we are the germ of a great state," the petition ran. In a letter to Cushing of January 17, 1839, Lee proposed an American guarantee of title for the whites' land and improvements and for the extension of U.S. government authority to regulate colonist relations among themselves and with the Indians. "You are well aware, sir, that there is no law in that country to protect or control American citizens," Lee wrote. "And to whom shall we look, to whom can we look, for the establishment of wholesome laws to regulate our infant but rising settlements, but to the congress of our beloved country." Linn introduced a Senate bill in late 1838 authorizing U.S. military and territorial occupation of Oregon and presented the petition of the Willamette settlers early in the new year.[29]

Reaching Middletown, Connecticut, in mid-January 1839, Lee met with his mentor Willbur Fisk to discuss strategy for deploying mission reinforcements. Fisk advised him to invest as heavily as possible in the milling business. While the mission's exclusive object remained the benefit of the Indian tribes, Fisk asserted that "it is necessary to cultivate the soil, erect dwelling houses, and school houses, build mills and in fact, introduce all the necessaries and helps of a civilized colony."[30] Fisk identified a more immediate advantage as well: the milling enterprise could challenge Hudson's Bay Company commercial dominance and relieve the mission of debt.

Fisk rose from his sickbed on the evening of January 16 to accompany Lee to his lecture, Fisk's last public appearance before his death in early February. Lee pushed on for evening meetings in a succession of icy churches in New England places large and small: Norwich and West Thompson, Connecticut; and Foxborough, Walpole, Lowell, Newton Upper Falls, Boston, and Lynn, Massachusetts, this latter place the home of Cyrus and Susan Shepard and, by coincidence, of the *Oregonian and Indian's Advocate*, a short-lived journal that promoted American settlement on the Columbia. He spoke in Newburyport, Massachusetts, the hometown of Caleb Cushing (and the implacable abolitionist editor William Lloyd Garrison), on February 1 and concluded the northern tour with stops in Portland, Maine, and Portsmouth and Concord, New Hampshire. Altogether, he raised $2,500 on his swing through New England.[31]

Fisk also advised Lee to remarry. As Lee told one of his audiences, he had done duty as "nurse, cook and farmer" at Mission Bottom before Maria Pittman's arrival and did not wish to go it alone again. A call upon a Wilbraham Academy classmate in Newbury, Vermont, yielded a potential bride: Lucy Thomson, twenty-eight years old, a recent graduate—valedictorian of her class, in fact—of the Methodist seminary at Newbury. Lee arranged to meet Miss Thomson at a church gathering in Montpelier in mid-March, where she expressed a keen interest in mission work. Lee visited her people in Barre, Vermont; he and the ecstatic Lucy were married on July 28, 1839, thirteen months after Maria's death in childbed.

"My further acquaintance with Mr. Lee proves him to be worthy of the confidence I reposed in him," she wrote her family from New York City. "In a word, he is all to me that an earthly friend could be."[32]

Word of Lee's impetuous remarriage mortally affronted his late wife's people. At the least, Mary Pittman told him coldly, he might have bidden his time till he had visited her daughter's grave. His failure to inform the Pittmans beforehand compounded the offense. Bewildered, perhaps unused to such blunt criticism of his conduct, Lee tried to explain: he withheld mention of the matter when he called on the family in New York because Mary Pittman was hard of hearing; he judged it best to keep his courtship of Miss Thomson a secret; it never occurred to him to announce such momentous news in a letter. Besides, he had only acted after consultation with Fisk and Bangs and in the best interests of the mission.

"More than a score, probably, of my most judicious and intelligent friends not only *advised* but *urged* the measure; and begged me not to return to Oregon alone, but to choose a suitable companion to accompany me," he wrote Mrs. Pittman. "If there are any doubts still on your mind I would ask are you not satisfied that the measure will be conducive to my comfort, and happiness, and usefulness among the Indian? To promote my comfort was the grand object to which your Maria, and my Maria had devoted herself; and ought they to be sacrificed to meet the views of propriety of a single individual against whose views there is such a fearful odds!"[33]

In the meantime, Lee attended to the details of "the great reinforcement," reviewing applications for mission openings, laying in supplies, purchasing milling equipment, and chartering a vessel, the ship *Lausanne,* Josiah Spaulding, master, to transport the migrants and their cargo to Oregon. Qualifications were minimal: candidates were asked to commit to a ten-year stay and were expected to be financially solvent. (The board showed itself willing to waive this latter stipulation; Elijah White's creditors in Havana, New York, claimed he decamped to Oregon with the first reinforcement to escape his debts.[34]) Unattached women were turned away. When the board rejected Adelia Judson, the sister of a missionary, she plotted the courtship of James Olley, a forty-nine-year-old carpenter accepted for *Lausanne*, marrying him a mere twenty-four hours before the ship's scheduled sailing time.

Thirty-six settlers with sixteen children boarded the vessel on the morning of October 9. The passenger manifest included Thomas Adams, who had made his way east from Peoria to rejoin Lee, but not William Brooks, who had sickened and died during Lee's tour of western New York. Lucy Lee groped her way below through the half-light to the tiny stateroom she would share with her husband on the twenty-two-thousand-mile voyage and nerved herself for the ordeal.

"I can only say my trust is in the living God," she wrote home to Vermont. "I am calm and resigned. I look forward upon my future life expecting it will be one of unremitting toil and anxiety. I expect to be subject to many privations and hardships, but none of these things move me. Neither count I my life dear unto myself, if I but win Christ."[35]

Lausanne slipped her moorings off Sandy Hook on October 10, 1839, sank the land, and stood to the southeast under easy sail. The Lees suffered terribly from seasickness. The ceaseless heaving of the ship so debilitated Lucy Lee that she could not rise, dress, or walk the deck unsupported during the first seven weeks of the voyage. Here, Mary Pittman might have suggested, was divine punishment for Lee's impiety in taking a second wife with such unseemly haste.

AS JASON LEE GATHERED reinforcements in New York and Boston, the Whitman-Spalding enterprise moved into an expansionist phase of its own along the eastern marches of Oregon. From the Willamette Valley, the Methodists maintained personal and professional contacts with the American Board missionaries. Elvira Perkins at The Dalles struck up a correspondence with her Kent's Hill Seminary classmate Mary Walker. They had traveled a long way from their time as schoolgirls together in Maine. "This is a changing world is it not: or people change about in it," Mrs. Perkins wrote. "Now we are both in Oregon.

I little thought when I left, I should so soon be permitted to hail friends and acquaintance in this distant land, but the Lord has dealt kindly with me."[36] The reminder of home doubtless cheered Mrs. Walker, who experienced only a brief respite from the "hardness" she had found so wearing on the overland trip. She had barely learned to find her way around Waiilatpu before discord erupted again with volcanic force.

The missionaries, so it seemed, could stand virtually anything but one another. So acrid was the atmosphere at the Whitman station that Mary Walker would rather have kept to her husk-filled palliasse some mornings. "Mrs. Eels is in a great worry because she expects to be obliged to winter here; and Mrs. Smith is worried for fear her husband will not get along so well if Messrs. Walker and Eels are here," Mrs. Walker observed. Myra Eels annoyed the others with her habit of snuffing. "I wish someone would tell her about it," Mrs. Walker wrote. Walker's favorite mule kicked him. With the Cayuses preparing to move off to their winter encampments, the missionaries came to question their vocation. Heavy, slow, drained of energy much of the time, Mary Walker could barely keep up with the sewing, let alone help minister to such natives as remained in the neighborhood. Asa Smith, sharp-set as always, went to the pantry one forenoon, found nothing but milk and melons, and noisily expressed his displeasure to the household management.[37]

Walker and Eels set out on their search for a mission site in the Spokan Country in the late afternoon of September 10, 1838. Mary Walker, six months pregnant, saw her husband off with misgivings. "After crying a little picked up and found myself somewhat tired," she wrote in her diary that evening. "Oh! Dear how I would like to be at home about this time, and see brothers, hear from all the good folks. I wish I could have a letter from some of them."[38] Instead, she negotiated Waiilatpu's daily ordeal of contrariety, whims, and moody absorption.

Walker and Eels struck north on horseback over rolling, sage-covered prairie. Making good time, they reached a Palouse Indian encampment late in the afternoon of the twelfth and bought a quantity of fresh salmon to satisfy their wolfish appetites. "How many ladies at a boarding school would it take to eat as much as we did?" Eels asked him. He thought for a moment, then answered, "About three score and ten."[39] They slept in the open air, rose in the twilight of dawn, and covered another fifty miles in nine hours. A stretch of volcanic country opened out onto tableland, and the horses practically flew—another fifty miles for the day—to the banks of the Spokane River.

A substantial band of Indians, probably an entire village, converged on the camp the next morning. Brother Eels read to them in English from the New Testament. "Tears came into their eyes," Walker wrote. "I never so much desired the gift of languages. To see immortal souls around you, perishing for lack of knowledge, and not able even to say Christ died for them, is a trial indeed." Small parties of Spokan Indians drifted into camp the next day—Sunday the sixteenth. When a sufficient number had assembled, Walker and Eels commenced a "New England–style" worship service, speaking through an interpreter. "Twice I attempted to say something about the death of Christ, but could not make them understand anything about it," Walker wrote. "It seems that they had no language to express the atonement." The audience was raptly attentive, though, leaving Walker to wonder how faithfully his words were being translated. In the afternoon he narrated the story of the Flood, explaining that, next time, fire would destroy the world.[40]

They set out for Fort Colville on the upper Columbia on the foggy morning of September 17 in company with a Spokan chief called Big Head. The track dropped down into a long valley, the finest country Walker had yet seen, then rose to a summit with views of the distant Hudson's Bay Company outpost. "Beyond Colville meets your eye far beneath you, looking like a city under a hill," he wrote: fenced fields, dwellings, stables and barns grouped together, stacks of hay and grain, cattle and hogs foraging on the plain. Walker and Eels hoped to enlist the Hudson's Bay Company agent in charge, McDonald, in their mission scheme. But he seemed indifferent and, far from welcoming a religious presence, neglected even to ask the missionaries to give thanks at table or lead family prayers in the evening. Questioning whether they could proceed at all without the company's patronage, Walker turned to II Corinthians, chapter 4, for solace:[41]

> We are troubled on every side, yet not distressed; we are perplexed, but not in despair; persecuted, but not forsaken; cast down, but not destroyed.

After two days of company hospitality, Walker again scouted the mission idea. The Spirit had evidently worked on McDonald in the interval, for he now volunteered with a good grace to help Walker and Eels establish a station and farm. The agent introduced them to an Indian guide who led them east over a substantial mountain and down into a narrow valley to an Indian village of sixteen lodges along the shore of a lake. Packs of half-starved dogs roamed the paths leading from lodge to lodge, but the people anyway seemed to welcome strangers. "Long and hard were the grasps on my hand, and many were the thanks uttered that I had come into their country," Walker wrote. "I sat on my horse shaking hands until my arm ached."[42] He dismounted, sang a hymn, and offered up a short prayer. The Indians led them to a campsite, cut wood, and kindled a fire. After a while Walker heard the sound of a bell. To his astonishment, a large lodge in the center of the village turned out to be a sort of chapel. The Jesuits had traveled this way.

"We heard singing, then a voice in prayer, and again singing," Walker wrote. "I would not believe it if my own eyes had not seen that such things exist in a heathen land."[43]

The barking and scuffling of the village dogs kept Walker awake most of the night. He finally lapsed into a fitful sleep. Then, before dawn, "Brother E. was awakened by a dog eating near his head; and, lo, a poor, half starved to death dog had eaten a large hole through the tent and about half of our meat."[44] The sun heaved up finally and the men roused the village and again shook hands with everyone, a hundred or more men, women, and children. Big Head marched them into the lightly wooded valley of a stream leading to the Spokane River. With the help of a sagacious-looking Spokan Indian they dubbed Solomon, they chose a site for the mission near a spring of good water. The promised provisions and tools arrived from Fort Colville, seventy miles to the north: two axes, ten pounds of Indian meal, thirty pounds of flour, and quantities of buffalo meat and bacon. Big Head supplied potatoes.

Walker marked trees for felling; Spokan laborers under Big Head's direction cut them down. Within a day or so he and Eels gauged they had sufficient timber—green pine a foot in diameter cut in fifteen-foot lengths—for two houses. They christened the place Tshimakain (place of the spring) on September 28. Some linguists translate Spokan as "children of the sun," but the tribe had been ill-favored in recent decades. There were probably fewer than a thousand Spokan

Indians in 1838, numbers that would decline further with epidemics in 1846 and 1852. As they worked, Walker filed away words and phrases of the tribal language, a variant of Salish. By October 1 the rudiments of the station were in place. Vowing to return with their wives in the spring, the missionaries set out for the Spalding mission on Lapwai Creek. A 120-mile march to the southeast brought them to Lapwai on October 5.

They found the Spaldings settled comfortably among the Nez Perces. The air of the valley of Lapwai Creek agreed with the fragile Eliza, who had survived several weeks in a buffalo-skin lodge with no ill effects until Spalding, William Gray, and their Indian volunteers had the mission house ready for occupancy in the early winter of 1837. Spalding planted potatoes and peas and set out apple trees in the spring. Eliza successfully delivered a daughter in November 1837 and now approached the eighth month of a second pregnancy. (She would give birth to a son, Henry Hart, in late November.) Her school flourished, too, with upward of a hundred Nez Perces regularly enrolled. She taught them Scripture with the aid of crude paintings depicting such scenes as the parting of the Red Sea and the crucifixion.

The Spaldings occupied a third of the building, the school and chapel the rest. Rough but serviceable, the mission even ran to an approximation of a library. Walker attacked it at once. "I was truly delighted to see Mr. S's books, having been so long without them," he wrote. "I was soon at his Hebrew and Greek."[45] Still, Henry Spalding's rough manners offered no great inducement to linger. Walker and Eels departed Lapwai on October 9 and reached Waiilatpu at midday on the thirteenth, after an easy journey.

"Was glad enough once more to see my husband, and he seemed to be glad to see me," Mary Walker wrote. "I suppose he really was, for he has no faculty for making believe." Tensions mounted now that they all were together again, mewed up inside the adobe walls of the mission. With her lying-in approaching, Mary sought to withdraw into herself. Thinking of home, leafing through old journals, only made her sadder. There was no privacy anywhere, no place of refuge from Sarah Smith's whispering, Myra Eels's snuffing, Narcissa Whitman's jagged flashes of temper. October gave way to November and a spell of bitter cold. One hardly dared venture more than a few feet from the fire. And there was no pleasing Narcissa.

"Mrs. W. appears to feel cross at everybody," Mrs. Walker recorded in mid-November. "She seems in a worry about something; went out and blustered around and succeeded in melting over her tallow."

And in early December, "Monthly Concert in the evening, after which Dr., his wife, Mr. E & wife, husband and self sit up till midnight talking about Mrs. S. &c. Mrs. W. gets to feeling very bad, goes to bed crying."[46]

The new arrivals were but a temporary antidote for Narcissa Whitman's loneliness amid the piercing silences and inhuman scale of the country. With Marcus Whitman absent from the mission for long periods, she filled her letters home with appeals for comfort. "It is nearly two years and five months since I left, and have not heard a lisp from you," she wrote to her sister Jane.[47] She had not seen any papers from the United States except for scattered 1836 copies of the *New York Observer*. She urged her sisters and parents to keep her abreast of the news, even though a full three years would elapse from the dispatch of a letter to the receipt of a reply.

"Do, all of you, write often, and send to Boston, for opportunities frequently occur of sending to the Sandwich Islands, and we can always get them from there once or twice a year."[48]

Sarah Smith turned out be no comfort to Narcissa after all. She checked Mrs. Smith on numerous occasions, even countermanding her orders to one of the Indian servants to fetch a bait for her ravenous husband. For their part, the Smiths recorded little but grievance. Smith took on the task of supervising the construction of a second adobe house. But resources were scarce and labor hard to find. "There is no good building timber nearer than 20 miles," he wrote home. "We are in great want of tools of almost every kind."[49] The conflict between spiritual and temporal concerns agitated him from the start. Like the Lees, he found himself preoccupied, even obsessed, with making a living: tending crops and grazing animals and putting up shelter for the winter.

"You may think that I think more about farming than I do of anything else," he wrote home. "It is true that I am under the necessity of thinking much about such things, but I hope I shall not forget the spiritual good of these perishing souls around us. If we are faithful I have no doubt but that we may see many of them brought into the fold of Christ."[50]

The realities of existence in a primitive land became uncompromisingly clear as autumn advanced, all but dissolving the romance of the missionary spirit in Smith. When he had dreamed of mission work at home, he imagined himself surrounded by "thousands & millions" in Asia. Here at any one time there were hardly more than a few dozen indifferent Cayuses. Solitude tended to cool his ardor of piety, to give him "the feeling of a worldling." The vocation had not transfigured him, nor any of his associates, for that matter. The New Yorkers Whitman and Spalding were ordinary "western men," partaking "of the peculiarities of western men"; they were sadly lacking in scholarly and spiritual attributes. Their immersion in everyday affairs seemed to Smith to account for what he characterized as the coarseness of life at Waiilatpu. Nor was Smith himself immune to the rasp of circumstance.[51]

"I often heard it said in the States that missionaries were but men & I believed it, & now I find it fully true," Smith wrote his brother. "I find myself but a man, & 'subject to like passions' with others & I find my associates the same. When we hear from a missionary from a distant land, it comes to us like the voice of an angel, but come to the spot where he is we find him nothing but a man & perhaps an ordinary one too."[52]

The Cayuses, too, failed to rise to the occasion. Their manners appalled Smith. They approached the mission at inconvenient times. They peered rudely into the windows. They were self-centered and thoughtless. They followed some external forms of Christianity—they would not eat without asking a blessing—but they were at all times strangers to what Smith called vital piety. "There is much of the Pharisee among them & they need searching truth to show them their true condition," he wrote home. They were immodest, vulgar, promiscuous.

"So much for the goodness of the people," Smith would conclude after a year in Oregon. "The more I see of this people, the more I see of their wickedness, their deep rooted selfishness, their hatred of the gospel."[53]

Smith had his suspicions about the Walkers, too. When their newborn arrived in early December, Smith counted back and calculated that they had been precipitous. "Mr. Walker has a son born the 7th of this month which was just *2 days* over nine months from the time they were married, the 5th day of March," he wrote home. "What I think of such things you know already. I feel thankful that I am not in such an embarrassed situation and at present there is no prospect of it." With Dr. Whitman attending, Mary Walker delivered a healthy babe, in due course christened Cyrus Hamlin, after a difficult ("felt as if I almost wished I had never been married") but mercifully brief labor.[54]

She had hoped for succor from the other women; she reproached her husband for his lack of feeling for her plight. "Like Job's comforters," she complained, "he only referred the cause of my troubles to my own imprudence." Walker placed mission business ahead of her well-being, busying himself with fabricating whips and harness, for example, rather than preparing a comfortable room for her lying-in. Besides, she went on, "Mr. W. has not bathed for some weeks."[55] She found Waiilatpu's winter fare unappetizing, too—boiled wheat, potatoes, horsemeat, and salt fish. Cushing Eels raised objections to the late hours she kept; her stirring about disrupted his slumbers.

More troubles ensued: the milk fever and painful difficulties nursing the babe. "Very nervous," Mary Walker wrote. "Milk gets caked in my breast, have it steamed and drawn alternately, till it seems better, then cover it with sticking plaster. Husband sleeps, but I get very little." Her breasts ached, her bowels griped, she caught a cold. Whitman dosed her with morphine and calomel. She tried but failed to invent a set of artificial nipples. "Feel very much unreconciled to the idea of being unable to nurse my babe," she wrote in late December.[56] She got ahold of a mare's tit and hoped to try it on the infant. As the New Year approached, even thoughts of home caused her pain. It seemed incredible to reflect that a mere twelve months ago she had not yet heard the name of Elkanah Walker, had no inkling of his existence.

"A year ago tonight I sat with my sisters by the fire at the side of my father, and watched to see the old year go out," she wrote on the thirty-first. "Now I find myself on the other side of the continent, a wife and mother. Surely this is a changing world."[57]

The New Year of 1839 brought no relief to the miserable band at Waiilatpu. The Walkers anyway could look ahead to resettling at Tshimakain. Asa Smith, confined to Waiilatpu, knew despair. "I lament the day that connected me with this mission," he would write Walker in the spring. "Why it is that I am here I know not."[58] Mary Walker worked on a Nez Perce grammar and awaited the arrival of a printing press, shipped from the Sandwich Islands in the care of Edwin O. Hall. When he finally reached Waiilatpu, Hall could hardly believe the evidence of his senses.

"The state of things is truly lamentable," he wrote David Greene, the American Board mission secretary in New York, "and I have been exceedingly grieved to find such a want of confidence and brotherly love (in fact, common politeness) among those who bear the name of missionaries."[59]

The Walkers escaped to the twelve-foot-square log pen at Tshimakain in early March. Smith wrote at once to report the volley of "severe remarks" the Whitmans had loosed upon them after their departure. "Nothing but the arm of God can save this mission from being a failure," he wrote Walker. Hall pushed on with the printing press to the Spalding mission. "I have a great anxiety to see the Indians in possession of the first rudiments of knowledge, as the prospects and success of your mission so much depend on enlightening the mind, as well as reforming the heart," Hall wrote Walker and Eels.[60] In due course Walker sent the sixteen-page manuscript of his Nez Perce primer to Lapwai, where Spalding struck off copies of what Mary Walker proudly called "the first book in Flathead."

THE ACTUAL EXPERIENCE seemed to undermine Thomas Farnham's faith in the West. His Oregon Dragoons set out from Independence on May 1, 1839, and proceeded for week after dreary week toward Bent's Fort on the Arkansas River. Historian David Lavender calls the Peorians the first "avowed" settler party, but they proved a quarrelsome band of brothers and voted themselves out of existence at the Bent brothers' post, squabbling to the end over how to divide the common property. Farnham pushed on to the Green River with a remnant of four men. There a mountain man named Paul Richardson sketched out the bleakest imaginable prospect of the Oregon Country. Richardson claimed to have spent two years there, so he spoke with what sounded like authority. Farnham transcribed his account gloomily:

"It was not so productive as [stony, intemperate] New England; fifteen bushels of wheat to the acre was an extraordinary crop; corn and potatoes did not yield the seed planted; rain fell incessantly five months of the year; the Indians and whites residing there had the fever and ague, or bilious fever, the year through; what little of human life was left by these causes of destruction, was consumed by mosquitoes and fleas; that the Columbia River was unfit for navigation—fit only for an Indian fish-pond."[61]

Richardson wanted extra hands for his return trip to Independence; his hair-raising profile of Oregon inspired two of Farnham's remaining Dragoons to fall in with him. Farnham with the last of the loyalists soldiered on for the Willamette. Nothing he saw along the sinuous course of the Snake, through the wilderness of the Blue Mountains, or on a late September detour to the Whitman homestead restored his shattered dream. "The plains far and near were dry and brown," Farnham wrote of the approach to Waiilatpu. "Every form of vegetation was dead save the forest trees." He met Marcus Whitman at the gate of the mission fields. Shouting at the top of his voice, the missionary was exhorting a party of sullen Cayuse Indians to drive their cattle out of his garden.[62]

Farnham's glance registered the crude mission buildings, the glint of the river just beyond, and some two hundred ripening acres planted in wheat, corn, onions, turnips, rutabaga, melons, squash, and tomatoes. So far as he could judge, the harvest would be bountiful. A corral held a yoke of oxen and an American bull. Hogs rooted about. A waterwheel powered a primitive gristmill. Beyond, though, stretched a sunburned plain covered with dry bunchgrass and smoking with breeze-stirred dust. The absence of rains and dews and the difficulty of irrigation, he concluded, suggested the region would be unsuitable for large-scale farming or grazing.

Dr. Whitman introduced Farnham to his wife and resumed his rounds. Narcissa Whitman spoke at once of her grief. It had been a Sabbath afternoon, the twenty-third of June. She and Whitman were in the parlor, reading. Little Alice Clarissa, age two years and three months, slid down from her father's lap, murmuring something about fetching water for the dinner table. A few moments later Narcissa detailed a servant to retrieve her. After a while an Indian named Mungo appeared at the door to say he had observed two tin cups floating in the river. Narcissa rushed down to the bank, "searching down the river, and up and down again in wild dismay."[63] An old Cayuse plunged into the stream, slid underwater, and emerged cradling the girl's still form. The current had lifted her sodden dress like a veil to cover her face.

Narcissa's heart died within her. Whitman seized the child and worked furiously to revive her, but the stream had extinguished her life. "Mysterious event!" Narcissa wrote. "We could in no way account for the circumstances connected with it, otherwise than that the Lord meant it should be so." Whitman sent a messenger to Henry Spalding at Lapwai. Narcissa, meantime, executed the numbing ritual of preparing the corpse for burial and arranging the shroud and cerements. She returned to the body time and again, whispering endearments, her hands caressing the tiny inanimate form. "She did not begin to change for the first three days and I could not bear to have her out of my sight," Narcissa wrote in a whisper. "But when she began to melt away like wax and her visage changed I wished then to put her in so safe, quiet and desirable a resting place as the grave." The Spaldings and Pierre Pambrun arrived from Fort Walla Walla at midday on Thursday and they buried Alice Clarissa in the afternoon.[64] Henry Spalding chose II Kings 4:26 for his text:

"Run now, I pray thee, to meet her, and say unto her, Is it well with thee? Is it well with thy husband? Is it well with the child? And she answered, It is well."

She told and retold the story of the child's last days, re-creating (or perhaps inventing) details that now seemed to her to achieve a mystic significance. She had never known Alice Clarissa to go near the river "or to appear at all venturesome" until, a day or two before that fateful Sunday, she dashed out of the garden with a radish in her hands—into the kitchen ell, her parents supposed. When Whitman went down to the river to wash the soil and manure off his hands he found her there, kneeling on the bank and industriously scrubbing the radish. "We told her that if she should fall in the river she would die, and then father and mother would have no little Alice," Narcissa wrote. But the curving, silvery stream now seemed to hold an irresistible attraction for her.[65]

As her parents sometimes allowed her to do, Alice had selected the hymn for the worship service that twenty-third of June, "Rock of Ages":

> While I draw this fleeting breath
> When my eyelids close in death;
> When I rise to worlds unknown,
> And behold thee on thy throne,
> Rock of Ages, cleft for me,
> Let me hide myself in Thee.

Whitman set out for Tshimakain in mid-July (Myra Eels had fallen ill), leaving Narcissa alone with the sorrows of her turbulent heart. She found that first Sabbath after his departure almost unbearable. Alice haunted her: "I seemed to hear her voice—her footsteps near me all day long." That night dysentery carried off two Indian boys in the Cayuse lodges. The Indians blamed the suddenness of their deaths on the small and ineffectual doses of salts Narcissa had administered earlier in the day. It fell to her to bury the boys and to meet "with all the superstitious feelings and notions in regard to sickness and dying among the natives." It was too much.

"What I underwent at this time I cannot describe," she wrote her mother.[66]

Thomas Farnham found Narcissa fragile and remote but determined to do her duty. He observed her closely as she gathered the school one afternoon, summoning forty or so Indian children with a handbell and working from the Walker-Spalding "Flathead" primer in the cool of the shady side of the mission house. At the end of the lesson, mostly monosyllabic iteration, she led the children in hymns Asa Smith had composed in Nez Perce. Whitman conducted services at ten o'clock on the last Sunday in September, following the Presbyterian order of worship: invocation, hymn, prayer, hymn, sermon, prayer, hymn, and blessing. When Farnham set out next day for The Dalles, Narcissa roused herself to send him off with a traveler's due—a rucksack stuffed with bread, meat, and other provisions.

He paused for a night at Fort Walla Walla in its "ugly desert." He and Pambrun discovered a common interest in Napoleon, although it was unlikely that Farnham chronicled to the Hudson's Bay Company functionary his Napoleonic scheme of single-handedly attaching Oregon to the United States. They parted friends, Pambrun planting presents of sugar, tea, and bread on him before he struck westward.

Thus fortified, Farnham proceeded down the southern bank of the Columbia to the Methodist outpost below The Dalles. He spent a week at the mission, established only eighteen months before a mile south of the river and three miles from the great native trading place. Henry Perkins and Daniel Lee were hospitable, and he passed the days in comfort, "eating salmon and growing fat." The walls of the log mission house were covered with beautiful native rush mats. A shingle roof and plank floors were other marks of civilization. Lee had sited the mission on rising ground near a spring of sweet water issuing from a ledge of rock. Timber fringed large open tracts around the site.

The Methodists' ambitions were large: a chapel, a school, a workshop, a sawmill, and a gristmill. Perkins calculated that acorn mast collected from the oak copses would sustain a thousand hogs; the grasslands would support "at trifling expense, immense numbers of sheep, horses and cattle." A modest five acres in 1839 yielded twenty-five bushels of small grains, seventy-five bushels of potatoes, and ample quantities of garden vegetables.[67]

Farnham drifted downriver below Vancouver as far as the ruins of Nathaniel Wyeth's trading factory on Wapato Island, then pushed up the Willamette Valley. The route led through champaign country, eminently suitable for grazing and crops, the midautumn weather mild and damp. At the falls of the Willamette, he noted, the company had begun to construct a mill raceway; a short ride southward brought him to the homesteads of Thomas McKay and his neighbors. Each of the five farms in the neighborhood had fifty to a hundred acres in cultivation, and there were other artifacts of colonization: a blacksmith's forge and shop; a Yankee tinker's cabin; St. Paul's, the Roman Catholic chapel, a low wooden building thirty-five or forty feet in length; and the parsonage, a comfortable log cabin.[68]

The long-rumored Papists had arrived, hoof and horns, the year before, two priests with instructions to convert the Oregon Indians and minister to white and *métis* Roman Catholics. The Protestant missionaries on the Willamette and in the Cayuse and Nez Perce country regarded the blackrobes as a challenge and a threat. The Nez Perces especially were susceptible, Asa Smith believed, but the missionaries had an ally in one persuasive convert, a young man dubbed Lawyer. "He heard that the priests said we were bad because we had wives, they had none," Smith wrote. "Week ago last Sabbath [Lawyer] talked to the people on the subject & told how Abraham & the people of old had wives. Peter had a wife etc. & wanted to know how there would be any children if there were no wives. One shrewdly asked me a few days ago if the Catholic priests were not eunuchs."[69] Smith did not record his reply.

Beyond Thomas McKay's neighborhood lay another fifteen or twenty farmsteads, a few Americans, and the company *engagés* Father Francis Blanchet had come to serve. Blanchet accused the Methodists of expending more effort on colonization than on conversion of the Indians, and he annoyed his rivals with his insistence on remarrying the Canadian couples the Methodists had joined previously. Farnham took the Protestants' part. He spent four or five days at Mission Bottom and found himself impressed, as others had been before him, with what the Methodists had created. They seemed equally interested, he thought, in civilizing and Christianizing the Indians *and* in establishing permanent religious and cultural institutions for the white settlers.

"Their religious feelings are warm, and accompanied with a strong faith and great activity," he wrote. "In energy and fervent zeal, they reminded me of the Plymouth pilgrims."[70]

The lawyerly Farnham detected—and perhaps helped to foment—dissatisfaction in the settlements. Refusing to truckle to the Hudson's Bay Company, the missionaries rose to challenge McLoughlin for political control, appointing judges and magistrates to rule on disputes in the Willamette settlements. The colonists were uneasy with this, and with what they perceived to be a general descent into lawlessness, complaining to Farnham that "crimes of theft, murder, infanticide, etc.," were on the rise in the absence of formal government. But if they balked at the Methodists, they were more skeptical yet of company rule.[71]

According to Farnham, a number of Americans—men *not* connected with the mission, he took care to emphasize—appealed to him to press for the extension of U.S. authority into Oregon. "Why are we left without protection in our country's domain? Why are foreigners permitted to domineer over American citizens, drive their traders from the country, and make us as dependent on them for the clothes we wear, as are their own apprenticed slaves?" Farnham extended his sympathies to Ewing Young, who dressed himself all in skins because, Young complained, the Hudson's Bay Company refused to sell him a stitch of clothing. Farnham could offer no explanation for what he had come to regard as the "unpardonable negligence" of the American government in failing to look out for such stalwarts as Young.[72]

Farnham did, however, offer to carry a settlers' petition home to the U.S. Congress. The colonists in due course presented him with a memorial "signed by sixty-seven citizens of the United States, and persons desirous of becoming such ... and, in conclusion, a prayer that the federal Government would extend over them the protection and institutions of the Republic." The American naval officer Charles Wilkes would report in 1841 that Farnham and Dr. William Bailey together drew up and circulated the petition. David Leslie and Elijah White of the Methodist mission evidently were implicated in the matter, too. Whoever had launched the campaign, settler or missionary, grievance centered on the imperial and authoritarian Hudson's

Bay Company and its Canadian vassals, some of whom—perhaps out of confusion—actually signed Farnham's paper. But Father Blanchet's scrawl was conspicuous by its absence.[73]

Farnham pocketed the petition and bade the Willamette colony farewell. He had been six weeks or so in Oregon and, like Napoleon in Egypt, had seen enough. He descended the Willamette with Daniel Lee, availed himself of Dr. McLoughlin's hospitality for a few days, and sailed for the Sandwich Islands in the company ship *Vancouver*. Farnham forwarded the colonists' plea from Honolulu, and it reached Lewis Linn in time for the Missouri senator to present it to his colleagues on June 4, 1840.[74]

Farnham's book, published in London in 1843, would add its mort to the swelling U.S. demand for sovereignty in Oregon on behalf of the Willamette pioneers. "The reader will find it difficult to learn any sufficient reasons for their being left by the Government without the institutions of civilized society," he wrote. "Their condition is truly deplorable. They are liable to be arrested for debt or crime, and conveyed to the jails of Canada!"[75]

AT SOME LEVEL, the Methodist revivals of the winter of 1839–1840 were a response to the blackrobes' presence. Father Blanchet's stately self-assurance, his easy ways with the Indians and his Canadian parishioners, unnerved the Protestants. The nightly revival meetings beginning in late December sought to ignite a spiritual fire in the Willamette colony. They provided plenty of heat, if not light. "Campbell and Edmunds were deeply wrought upon, and cried aloud, almost in an agony of despair," Daniel Lee wrote. "Poor C. felt as if he was just falling into hell, and with the greatest earnestness besought the prayer of all present."[76] James O'Neil, who had come to Oregon with Nathaniel Wyeth in 1834, accepted Jesus Christ as his savior. And two children were baptized, among them the Shepards' little girl, named for Anna Maria Lee.

Cyrus Shepard experienced the thrill of the revivals from his sickbed. The trouble, an infection and inflammation of the knee that Dr. White diagnosed as scrofula, had afflicted him since the spring of 1838. Arrested for a time, the infection and swelling returned with redoubled virulence in the autumn of 1839. White amputated Shepard's right leg without anesthetic on December 11. By then the insignia of death had fastened itself upon him. Shepard lingered on, in racking pain at times, until New Year's Day 1840. He scratched his last words on the margins of a letter from his wife to Daniel Lee. "I cannot say I shall get up from this bed," he wrote, signing himself "A part of Cyrus."[77]

Shepard had never shown much interest in the secular development of the mission, in settler petitions, cattle companies, or trials of strength with the Hudson's Bay Company. His school could not be accounted a great success but he persevered anyway, faithful to the last to the Methodists' founding vision. *Lausanne*, the symbol of a new vision, dropped anchor in Baker Bay on May 21, 1840, after a touch-and-go call at Honolulu where Jason Lee negotiated an informal trade treaty with King Kamehameha II. *Lausanne's* river pilot, a one-eyed Chinook, offered a curious link with the region's secular and commercial history: he answered to the name of Ramsay, after the Astorian Ramsay Crooks, and he was the sole survivor of the *Tonquin* explosion, the interpreter who escaped—and lived long—to bear the tale. The arrival of the newlywed Lees with the Great Reinforcement marked an end and a beginning in the Oregon Country: the transformation of the Methodists' errand among the Indians into the colonial venture Americans had envisioned since *Columbia* cruised the Northwest coast in 1792.

Lee and his bride encountered a double vexation at Mission Bottom, now crowded with some four dozen new arrivals. Some of his colleagues, male and female, looked askance at his rather abrupt remarriage. Lucy Lee felt the chill of their disapproval. And the insufferable Dr. White, grown accustomed to the loose reins of David Leslie, renewed his criticism of Lee's management of the mission. Lee's critics evidently regarded him as too much under the influence of the Mission Board in New York and, perhaps, too dependent on McLoughlin as well. The dispute dated to at least the first months of 1838, when White with Leslie and others addressed a "memorial" to Lee that advised him to return home "in the hope that commingling once more in polished society would result advantageously" to himself and the mission. That memorial, as White reminded him, "caused you to walk the floor, wring your hands and cry so much." White now stepped up his attacks, pressuring Lee to resign the mission superintendency.[78]

Lee hardly knew how to meet the charge. He had brooded on the Leslie-White memorial all through the long journey over the mountains in 1838, and offered up his resignation when he met with the board in November. "You would not hear a word of it," he wrote the commissioners later, "and heavy as the cross was I took it up." Still, doubts about his fitness assailed him. He faulted himself for his preoccupation with temporal activities and his inability to make conversions among the dwindling numbers of Indians in the Willamette Valley, although in the end he did pronounce himself satisfied with the "general outlines of the picture" of the mission, its purpose, and its direction.

"I know full well the main object I have kept in view has been the glory of God in the salvation of souls," he wrote, even as he acknowledged his shortcomings. "The *filling* up, the FILLING UP [of the outline], there is the difficulty."[79]

All the same, his powers were considerable, certainly adequate in the summer of 1840 to dispatch such a nuisance as Elijah White. Lee challenged White's business dealings in his absence, especially a number of unauthorized overdrafts on the mission tab at Fort Vancouver. White claimed he needed supplies for the mission hospital then in the process of being built; Lee refused to approve White's accounts as "settled." He questioned, too, White's behavior with certain mission women—details unspecified, insinuation damaging—and revived his New York neighbors' charge that he had fled to Oregon ahead of a posse of his creditors.[80]

White counterpunched, but weakly. He asked Lee to return the 1838 memorial; Lee responded that he did not have it. He also demanded particulars of Lee's charges. "What evidence [do] you have of my being 'a bag of wind with more gab than substance.' In what way have I manifested a deadly opposition to you ever since I first saw *you*. Please answer this last question explicitly."[81] Plaintively, he reminded Lee that he had named an Oregon-born son Jason Lee White. Then he went on to deny Lee's charges about his financial dealings and to issue a not-so-veiled threat.

"Here allow me to say as you refuse to sign a paper giving me a good character I beg you will take no offense if I should not give as good a character to you as the board might be happy to see of their Superintendent in Oregon," White wrote.[82]

Lee responded with a reckless mix of metaphors:

"You have raised the hatchet . . . you have thrown the gantlet, you have passed the Rubicon—you have if I understand it waged a war of *extermination.* There is to be no *quarter,* you or I 'must fall.' No sir having no preparation whatever for *war,* offensive or defensive, it is fortunate for me, that you are a random shooter.

"I hereby notify you that I consider you as having virtually abandoned your work, and forfeited your standing among us as a missionary; and unless you report yourself ready to do your duty, within two days, I shall consider that you have really deserted your post and broken [your] engagement."[83]

White issued a retaliatory call for Lee's resignation as superintendent, although it must have been clear to him by then that he had overplayed his hand. In any case, a trial at Mission Bottom in September swiftly resolved the issue. In the Methodist equivalent of a drumhead court, White's colleagues voted to expel him from the mission. He left Oregon in *Lausanne* trailing clouds of recrimination and with a vow to return betimes and cause as much pain for Jason Lee as lay within his power.

THE *VINCENNES* SLOOP-OF-WAR, leading the gunbrig *Porpoise,* felt its way cautiously around Cape Flattery and into the Strait of Juan de Fuca on the thick, rainy early morning of May 1, 1841. Variable and baffling during the night, the wind died away altogether after daybreak. Lieutenant Charles Wilkes, commanding *Vincennes,* ordered the boats lowered and the vessels towed, more to exercise the men than with any expectation of gaining steerageway. The sun pierced the overcast at about four o'clock in the afternoon, and soon festoons of sodden clothes and bedding were dangling from the spars and rigging. Two Indians came aboard wearing red frock coats—"I suppose," Wilkes remarked in his diary, "the livery of the H.B.C." The sloop rocked in the swell. Finally a breeze sprang up out of the west, pushing the Americans along the strait at an exhilarating seven knots. Navigating by George Vancouver's charts and his narrative account, *Vincennes* and *Porpoise* glided to anchor in the evening in the "perfect harbor" of Port Discovery, a haven Vancouver had surveyed with Britannic meticulousness in 1792.[84]

Wilkes, forty-three years old in 1841, commanded the U.S. South Seas Exploring Expedition—the most extensive and far-ranging reconnaissance the American government had ever attempted. He had won the coveted appointment over officers of greater seniority owing to his expertise as a hydrographer and, as the *North American Review* remarked,

Charles Wilkes (1798–1877). Wilkes commanded the four-year U.S. Navy scientific expedition to the Pacific, 1838–1842. His 1841 surveys of the Pacific Northwest coast left him unimpressed with the American missionary-colonizers in the Willamette Valley. (Library of Congress)

"his proficiency in the manipulation of magnetic instruments."[85] As official keeper of the national charts and instruments he was, in historian William Goetzmann's phrase, the leading U.S. naval scientist. For all his technical skills, though, even his most ardent admirers would have been hard pressed to make his case as a leader or a diplomat. He claimed to be a grandnephew of the troublemaking eighteenth-century English radical John Wilkes, an ancestral connection that perhaps explains what the *Dictionary of American Biography* tactfully styled his "limitations of temperament"—in plain language, a chronic inability to get along with just about everyone.

Authorized in 1836 to extend U.S. naval reach and to search out new whaling and sealing grounds for the New England fisheries, the Wilkes expedition sailed from Norfolk, Virginia, in August 1838. By the time *Vincennes* and her consort appeared off Cape Flattery, the squadron had logged some 70,000 miles and surveyed 280 Pacific islands, including the Society, Samoan, and Fijian groups; charted 1,500 miles of Antarctic coast; and established Antarctica as a continental landmass. The Pacific Northwest would be the final stop on the expedition's four-year itinerary. Wilkes prepared to survey this putative

The USS *Vincennes*, flagship of the Wilkes Exploring Expedition to the Pacific and the Northwest Coast, 1838–1842. The sketch was published in 1844 in Charles Wilkes's *Narrative* of the expedition. (Library of Congress)

American domain and concurrently investigate missionary and settler allegations of Hudson's Bay Company maltreatment.

Variously characterized as self-assured, disputatious, peremptory, a hard horse, easily flustered, conceited, capable, splenetic, and indecisive in a crisis, Wilkes ruled the exploring expedition with punctilio. In a long assessment of Wilkes's *Narrative* of the expedition, the anonymous *North American Review* essayist conceded his skills as a practical observer, then went on to puncture his "pretensions to the character of a theoretical philosopher," as, for example, when he scrupled to "cast a doubt upon the universal application of Dr. Wells's theory of dew." The *Review* also faulted the commodore for "a want of true dignity" in working off his humors, at one time or another, on virtually every one of the squadron's officers.[86]

At the outset, Wilkes ordered the officers to keep detailed diaries of the cruise for the permanent record—and to submit them to him on demand for his inspection. Midshipman George Sinclair's entries so vexed him that he summarily removed Sinclair from command of the schooner *Flying Fish*. Expedition logbooks recorded innumerable instances of Wilkes ordering officers in arrest for minor derelictions.

He filled his own diary with vituperations against his superiors and the squadron's officers and men. He was, by all reckoning, a tiresome and litigious man; and besides, in the private judgment of his officers, only averagely competent as a seaman.

Wilkes set to work in early May organizing surveys of Puget Sound and overland expeditions east toward Fort Walla Walla and south to the Columbia. He sent a messenger to the Hudson's Bay Company post at Fort Nisqually with a request for a pilot familiar with local waters. In the meantime, he studied the contours of the country. Admiralty Inlet reminded him of the Hudson River above Poughkeepsie. To landward, dense stands of pine alternated with lush meadows. Wild strawberries were in profuse blossom. Wilkes found the natives squalid and reeking of fish, but well disposed to his shore parties. Some turned out to be Papists, evidence of the work of Father Modest Demers, who had traveled west with Norbert Blanchet in 1838. The pilot, probably the company retainer and sheep rancher I. H. Heath, boarded *Vincennes* as she lay at anchor off Whidby Island. With Heath's expert navigation the vessels pushed slowly up the sound, clearing the Narrows near the site of Tacoma with "splendid views of Mount Rainier" on May 10 and anchoring off Nisqually before sunset the next evening.[87]

As ever, the company's factors were hospitable. "They appear desirous of affording us all the assistance in their power. At least such was their offer," Wilkes wrote cautiously. "A few days will show the extent of it." Captain William McNeill led him around the celebrated *Beaver*, said to be the first steam vessel in Pacific waters. Built in England in 1835, the 120-ton *Beaver* had a clumsy appearance; her paddlewheels, placed well forward, suggested "the forepaws of a land terrapin" to one observer. She had, too, a voracious appetite for fuel, consuming some forty cords of wood a day. But Wilkes found much to adore in the flagship of the company's fleet, especially the gleaming good order of her seventy-horsepower double engine.[88]

He also concluded almost at once that the Americans had to possess these northern precincts of the Oregon Country. In no circumstances should the United States settle for an international boundary along the Columbia. Puget Sound and its parklike interior were strategically important ("All the navies of the world might be furnished with spars here," he observed of one pine-fringed anchorage); rich in appearance; easily traversed; and, from what he gathered, lightly peopled. "Nothing can be more striking than the beauty of these waters without a shoal or rock or any danger whatever for the whole length of this Internal Navigation the finest in the world," he wrote.[89]

The Americans already in residence impressed Wilkes far less favorably than the land- and seascape. He found the Methodist missionaries at Nisqually impercipient and uninformed about the country and its inhabitants. John P. Richmond and William Willson, members of the 1840 reinforcement, had labored with slight success to establish an influence among the scattered natives of lower Puget Sound. "I have now been among them for a year, and if any good has been done it is not perceptible. . . . No earthly power can rescue them," Richmond came to believe, "and their habits are such that I am fearful they will never be reached by the voice of the Gospel." He eventually decided there were too few Indians thereabouts to make the work worthwhile. (Jason Lee, who had trekked north to Nisqually not long after the founding of the station, expressed skepticism from the start. "Instead of hundreds or thousands" of natives, he wrote, "I only saw a few score.") For his part, Wilkes regarded with imperial approval the missionaries' claim to the country, a sturdy log homestead set in a skirted plain with views all around of snow-crested "Alps on Alps" and a delightful freshwater lake 150 yards from the dooryard.[90]

In the missionaries' "four fine rosy and fat children" Wilkes read evidence of the suitability of the country for American settlement. The little missionaries may have charmed him; he did not, however, warm to the grown people—especially Richmond, who warmly returned the sentiment. Wilkes "thinks himself too important and *dignified* to give attention and consequently to impart any additional influence that he might to American settlers and American missionaries as I believe they are entitled to," he wrote to the board in New York. "I care no more for Lieutenant Wilkes than I do for the humblest citizen of the U States." In a word, Richmond thought, Wilkes looked down upon the Americans and fawned on the British.[91]

Wilkes on May 17 dispatched boats and crews to survey the southern inlets of Puget Sound, made ready for his overland voyage to Forts Vancouver and George, and cast Lieutenant Robert Johnson ashore to complete his preparations for the march across the Cascades to Fort Colville. Impatient to be off and in a fret about the overdue *Peacock* and *Flying Fish*, which he had sent on independently from the Sandwich Islands to the Columbia, he berated Johnson for his "fussing and figeting" about cruppers, girths, and other details. The bluejackets were out of their element on horses and the unyielding earth, but the martinet in Wilkes cut them no slack. Johnson finally shoved off for the mountains. Awkwardly straddling a borrowed Hudson's Bay Company mount, Wilkes set out for the Columbia on the nineteenth with three men and a Canadian guide.[92]

"It was a strange cavalcade," he admitted. The travelers covered twenty-two miles the first day, following a trace that led through a broad belt of cedars rising two hundred feet above the spongy ground. City-born and bred to the sea, Wilkes was awestruck. Only development was lacking, the "go-ahead principle so in vogue at home" that would conjure townlets with mills, smithys, stores, schools, and churches out of this incomparable wilderness. The soil appeared suited to grains; fields thick with ripening wild strawberries suggested that vines and orchards would flourish here, too.[93]

He confirmed these impressions when the party reached the Hudson's Bay Company farm on the Cowlitz River on May 21. The agent there, one Forrest, oversaw six hundred acres planted in luxuriant wheat and yielding twenty bushels to the acre. With Forrest as guide, Wilkes toured the gristmill, the sawmill, the granaries, and the cowsheds and observed an artisan efficiently and rapidly curing "the cloth of the country"—buckskin. "He stated to me that he had put a suit on twenty-four hours after the animal had been running in the forest," Wilkes marveled.[94] He could see as well that the natives were unlikely to disturb the peace and good order of the Cowlitz farm. They were too few and too demoralized to cause any trouble. Already the Indians were utterly dependent on the company for staple foods and clothing. In a few years, Wilkes thought, they likely would pass from the scene entirely.

Taking to company-supplied canoes, the party careered down the twisting Cowlitz for twenty-four miles to its junction with the Columbia, then descended the great river to Fort George, reaching there to a lantern-lit welcome from company agent James Birnie at about midnight of May 22. Wilkes found the "somewhat famous" Astoria primitive in contrast to Nisqually and the Cowlitz farm. "Perhaps as it is avowedly on the American side of the River it is thought unnecessary to continue operations that would not be permanent," he speculated. Over the following days he toured the disintegrating remains of Lewis and Clark's Fort Clatsop, examined Alexander Ross's famously girthy pine tree, and paid his respects to the burial canoe of the celebrated (and, since 1835, headless) Chinook chief Concomly.[95]

Wilkes had an affinity for this landscape with its fields of white clover and stands of familiar if oversized trees—and he took a proprietary interest in it. "I felt that the land belonged to my country, that we were not strangers on the soil, and could not but take great interest in relation to its destiny, in the prospect of its one day becoming the abode of our relatives and friends," he wrote. As at Nisqually, though, he felt a twinge of embarrassment about the American colonists. He could detect "little of the missionary spirit" in the Wesleyans, nor yet any missionary work for them to do among the remnant of the coastal Indian bands. Joseph H. Frost and his wife manned the Clatsop mission station, established in a narrow valley south of Point Adams the year before as a rival center to Fort George. A shoemaker by trade, Frost was a timorous man with phobias about canoes, bears, and Indians. The notion of an artisan-class missionary struck Wilkes as indecent somehow, and Mrs. Frost's efforts to show him hospitality elicited only ridicule. Bustling and cheerful, she prepared dinner and served it on crockery shipped out in *Lausanne*, trying—in Wilkes's haughty phrase—to come off the lady "but with ill success." Quantity, too, may have been lacking at the Clatsop board, for Wilkes later stigmatized Frost as close, miserly, and idle.[96]

Wilkes allowed himself to be somewhat more pleased with Asa and Sarah Smith; possibly, in his calculus, Presbyterians were more stylish or could claim a better pedigree than Methodists. He met the disaffected Vermonter and his now consumptive wife at Vancouver where, having finally abandoned the Whitman mission, they awaited a passage to Hawaii. To the end, Smith filled his letters home with laments about the vulgar, immodest, and sinful predilections of the Indians. "All the young people have come together without any regard for marriage," he wrote from his station in Idaho among the Nez Perces. "So much for the goodness of this people." He doubted whether any missionary could make a difference in Oregon, then went on to treat Wilkes to a lurid account of the "dissipation and morals" of the white trappers and traders of the Idaho country.[97]

Wilkes and Jason Lee met quite by accident and only briefly on Wapato Island, where Lee halted for the night on the way to the Clatsop station. They exchanged pleasantries and may or may not have ventured a talk about politics; Lee recorded their encounter in his diary without comment. Wilkes had a bit more to say, though he observed there had not been much substance to the conversation. "We were going one way, they the opposite," he wrote. "We told all the news we had on both sides & separated." Plagues of mosquitoes and sandflies bedeviled the sailors in camp that evening. Lee and company did not seem to notice, an immunity Wilkes found irksome.

"Being Methodists," he remarked waspishly, "they were used to such accommodations before they left the U States."[98]

Courtesy of McLoughlin, Wilkes toured the Willamette settlements in a mat-lined bateau with nine Hudson's Bay Company *engagés* at the oars. The fastidious commodore found the settlers not quite the thing, "an uncombed, unshaven and a dirty clothed set," though with some pretensions to importance: one had marched across the Rockies with Lewis and Clark, and another had served in the USS *Constitution* during her encounter with the British frigate *Guerrière* in the War of 1812. They were alarmingly fired with political enthusiasms, too, "all agog about laws and legislatures, with governors, judges & all the minor officers in embryo." Complaining bitterly about the lordly McLoughlin and British abuses of liberty, they pined for a civil apparatus of their own.[99]

Rudimentary institutions had sprung up when the need arose, as, for instance, in 1835, after a notorious murder on Wapato Island. Hubbard, gunsmith, and Thornburg, tailor, had been feuding for weeks, although the court never learned to its satisfaction why a plyer of needle and thread would be foolhardy enough to try conclusions with a gunmaker. In any event, Hubbard claimed he slew the tailor in self-defense. Drink may have fueled Thornburg's rage. John Townsend reported that not long before the regrettable incident Thornburg had drained a two-gallon whiskey jug filled with spirits in which Townsend had preserved reptile specimens. In due course the hastily assembled court returned a verdict of justifiable homicide.

In particular, the Methodist mission groaned under the company's trade dominance. Lee's agent at Willamette Falls supplied Wilkes with the details of a continuing dispute with McLoughlin over the mill site there; characteristically, the commodore took the company's part. "I cannot help feeling it is quite unsuited to the life of a missionary, to be entering into trade of any kind," he offered. Reliant on McLoughlin for all manner of necessities, Jason Lee found himself entangled in a credit dispute with the company: the Mission Board insisted he draw on New York for funds to meet obligations to Vancouver, while McLoughlin refused to accept drafts on any but the company's London bankers. When the doctor suspected Lee of scheming to evade company trade and credit restrictions, he retaliated.

"We cannot *depend* on Vancouver at all," Lee wrote the board secretary, David Greene. "Dr. McLoughlin took a freak that we had done something by way of trade that did not suit their interest and consequently refused to let me have a pair of Blankets; alleging as the reason, that Blankets were scarce. But when I learned the real cause, I conversed with him on the subject, and he was convinced that he has been misinformed. This, however, shows how little dependence is to be put on the Com. for our supplies."[100]

The 150 or so American colonists in the Willamette circulated petitions (Jason Lee's, Farnham's) and prevailed on visitors (Slacum, Spaulding of *Lausanne*) to carry their grievances home to the States. They gathered informally, town meeting–style, to regulate their affairs. The Methodist mission moved slowly toward adopting forms of law and local self-government independent of Dr. McLoughlin. Settlers appointed missionary David Leslie justice of the peace in 1839. Veteran trapper Ewing Young's death early in 1841 exposed the inadequacy of existing informal civil institutions. Two late-winter meetings, one under Lee's direction, the other under Leslie's, led to the establishment of a probate court to settle such matters as the disposition of Young's holdings. A third meeting, in June, appointed a committee to discuss a government for the Willamette with McLoughlin and Wilkes.[101]

Whether by accident or design, Lee left serious political discussion to others. The settlers' "committee" soon discovered that Wilkes had scant sympathy for their cause. Crime was anyhow virtually nonexistent in the valley, though the commodore did report the case of "a settler who had been detected stealing his neighbor's pigs, by enticing them into his cellar, where they were slaughtered and afterwards eaten." Piles of bones outside his farmstead gave the thief away; the power of public opinion forced him to make restitution for the value of the stolen swine. In Wilkes's view, a law code and formal courts would accomplish nothing beyond antagonizing the company and the Canadians. He urged the colonists to wait "until the government of the United States should throw its mantle over them"—an event the commodore evidently expected any day now.[102]

Wilkes pushed south through the Canadian settlement at Champoeg and on to Mission Bottom, dining there "*à la* Methodist" with David Leslie and his associate brothers and sisters. What he observed there confirmed his initial unfavorable impression of Lee's abilities. Buildings and grounds were untidy and in disrepair. A patent threshing machine lay abandoned in the dusty track and exposed to the elements. By Wilkes's estimate, the equivalent of a thousand bushels of wheat had been left to rot in the fields. Lee "did well enough when he had the management of a small set," he decided. "But his mind is not sufficiently comprehensive neither has he the ability to manage as large a mission as it is at present." If Lee and his associates were incapable of operating a mission efficiently, how could they expect to govern the Oregon Country? Wilkes advised the missionaries, too, to lie low until the U.S. government decided to act.[103]

Still without news of *Peacock* and anxious on that account (the sloop had been expected in the Columbia on about May 1), Wilkes on June 17 set out on the return to Fort Nisqually. He reached the post in time for an Independence Day celebration with gun salutes, a dress parade, three cheers, dancing, "foot ball," an ox roasting on a windlass, and, to conclude, a special holiday issue of "old Rye." As *Vincennes*'s people celebrated, the much-delayed *Peacock* clove the water on a northeasterly course. One of the officers experienced a premonition that they would meet "disaster & distress or death" on the Columbia tide race. *Peacock*'s captain, William Hudson, uneasily consulted Henry Broughton's 1792 chart as well as up-to-date directions for crossing the bar from *Lausanne*'s master. The sloop reached soundings in the forenoon of July 17, and soon the masthead caught glimpses of Cape Adams through veils of rain. The fog rolled up in late afternoon, revealing the bolder profile of Cape Disappointment to the north. With the weather closing in again in the evening, Hudson decided to stand off for the night.

Adumbrations of disaster proved only too accurate. *Peacock* approached the shoaling bar in thick mist at about noon on the eighteenth. An opening appeared in what a moment before had been a continuous line of foam. Hudson steered for it, *Flying Fish* following close. *Peacock* struck hard sand bottom at a few minutes past one o'clock. A heavy swell smashed into the vessel before Hudson could bawl out the order to shorten sail. The helm refused to answer; the sloop no longer swam. Hanging by the keel, *Peacock* endured a ferocious pounding through the afternoon and evening. Hudson sent the men to the pumps, but the sea gained rapidly through the night. A log entry at 4:00 A.M. on the nineteenth read: "Water above the chain lockers . . . we have no hope but of saving the crew."[104]

At daybreak, Hudson ordered six boats lowered and saw the sick, the scientists, most of the crew, and the official logs and papers out of the doomed sloop and safely ashore. The remaining officers and men slashed away at the rigging and cut down the masts. This steadied the battered hull, but by afternoon the sea had reached the berth deck. Hudson and the others abandoned the hulk at last. It soon sank beneath the swell with much of the cargo, including priceless expedition collections and supplies from the Sandwich Islands for the Methodist mission. *Flying Fish* cleared the bar and anchored in Baker Bay. Frost at Clatsop and Birnie at Fort George distributed tents, blankets, and rations to the shipwrecked sailors, and Indians soon turned up with salmon and fresh venison for sale.[105]

Word of *Peacock*'s fate reached Wilkes via a survey party at Gray's Harbor. Natives there told the bluejackets that a Boston ship had "got broke" on the bar. Wilkes himself arrived off the Columbia entrance on August 7, where he impulsively adjudged Hudson "wanting in prudence and caution" in neglecting to send the nimble *Flying Fish* over the sandspit first. Choosing not to risk *Vincennes*, Wilkes shifted his flag to *Porpoise*, sending the heavier vessel on ahead to San Francisco, the expedition's last port of call before sailing for home. At Vancouver he negotiated the purchase of a whiskey-laden Baltimore brig to replace *Peacock*. McLoughlin bought up the entire cargo to keep it from the natives and settlers; Wilkes rechristened the brig *Oregon*. In the meantime, the commodore's crews, working double tides, completed the surveying task Hudson's men had begun, charting the river as far as the Cascades.[106]

Wilkes maintained easy relations with Dr. McLoughlin, although Wilkes made it clear that he granted the Hudson's Bay Company no authority whatsoever over his movements. This second tour on the Columbia only strengthened his conviction that the Pacific Northwest soon would be "full part and parcel of our country." Still, loss of

The USS *Peacock* of the Wilkes Exploring Expedition hard upon the treacherous Columbia River bar in July 1841. Pacific breakers pounded the sloop into a total wreck; the crew escaped without loss of life. (Yale Collection of Western Americana, Beinecke Rare Book and Manuscript Library)

Peacock forced him to abandon the original plan of exploring east as far as the headwaters of the Yellowstone River. He contented himself with sending an expedition overland through the country of the fierce Umpquas to explore the marches of the Oregon-California border.[107]

As this party gathered itself for the southward march, the Methodists at Mission Bottom, desperately overcrowded since the arrival of the 1840 reinforcement, carried on with the initial stages of a relocation a dozen miles south to a place called Chemeketa, a broad, fertile plain (the site of today's Salem) along the eastern bank of the Willamette. Lee's motivations were both practical and imperial. An infestation of bedbugs provided the immediate impetus. "After having suffered indescribable annoyance for nearly a year, they have finally driven us from the premises and taken entire possession," he wrote glumly. "I left my things with the bugs, and have no home where to lay my head."[108] In the long term, the move would extend mission and American presence into a desirable new territory. Lee laid claim to some two thousand prime acres, began building, and shifted supplies and equipment to the new settlement by the canoeload.

Soon two trim log houses were ready for occupancy. Seven years in Oregon, however, had not made Lee a complete master of frontier life. He and his associates found the task of assembling the gristmill beyond their capacity: "The stones were set the wrong way," wrote Frances Fuller Victor, "and when at work threw out all the wheat." On his early autumn visit to the new mission Wilkes would ask to inspect the manual labor school; the teachers told him the pupils were unavailable. As it happened, the missionaries were too busy to instruct them. Wilkes observed groups of ragged native boys idling in the shade of the oaks.[109]

Perhaps in connection with the move to the new station he dubbed "The Mill," Lee changed his mind about returning some of Anna Maria Pittman's effects to her parents. He packed a box with his late wife's collection of shells from the Sandwich Islands, a lock of her hair, a gold locket she bought in Boston before sailing in 1836, and a valuable beaver and otter pelt that George Pittman could sell should he find himself in low water. Lee left the box with Wilkes's purser for shipment to New York in *Vincennes*. Wilkes overruled the purser and refused to carry Lee's personal cargo in a naval vessel. Maria's relics lay in storage at Fort George, awaiting a passage home.[110]

AMERICANS CONVERGED ON CALIFORNIA from the north and east in the summer of 1841. Lieutenant George Emmons, late of *Peacock*, led a joint expedition of sailors and settlers south from Oregon. The vessels of Commodore Wilkes's exploring squadron arranged a rendezvous in San Francisco Bay. And a wagon train with Roman Catholic missionaries and settlers from the Missouri frontier slogged up the Platte toward the Wind River snowpeaks.

Emmons marched from the Columbia through the Umpqua wilderness of southern Oregon with eight sailors and marines and half a dozen migrating families, a total of thirty-nine men, women, and children with eighty horses. The Joel Walkers, "the first family of declared emigrants for Oregon," according to historian John Unruh, found the climate of the Columbia region too damp and chill for their liking and, after only a year, decided to migrate south to the perpetual spring of California. The party cleared the marches of the unpredictable Umpquas, crossed the Rogue River on September 25, and penetrated the country of the "Shasty" Indians. It was a pitiful progress, the Americans racked with fever, their horses slowly starving. They skirted Mount Shasta; crossed the Destruction River; and, on October 19, reached the safety of the vast Sacramento Valley domain, eleven Spanish leagues (roughly fifty thousand acres), of the German-Swiss land baron John August Sutter.

Stout, florid, cordial, and bedizened with a small arsenal of side-arms, the self-styled Captain Sutter showed Emmons over his New Helvetia estate with its adobe stronghold, granaries, smithy, distillery, wheatfields, and seven thousand head of longhorn cattle. A draper and dry-goods shopkeeper with grand ideas, he had fled Basel for New York City in 1834, leaving a wife, five children, and an abyss of debt behind. Sutter pressed on for St. Louis, where he engaged in the Santa Fe trade and extended his reputation for equivocal business behavior. In 1838 he struck west for Mexican California ahead of a new outbreak of scandal—more debt, with the frisson this time of a murder accusation.

A charming, large-hearted rogue, Sutter made useful friends in Monterey, among them Governor Juan Alvarado, who—on the condition that he become a Mexican citizen and nominal Roman Catholic to conform to California law—granted him his vast tract in the unspoiled Sacramento Valley. Alvarado evidently regarded Sutter as flank protection for the San Francisco Bay settlements; in the event, he would act as an advance agent of American penetration of the country. With Indian assistance he put up the adobe fort and manned it with a cutthroat garrison of mountain men, beached sailors, kanakas, and malleable Indians. From the start, Sutter set up as a friend to Americans trickling into the Mexican province. As generous in his way as Dr. McLoughlin on the Columbia, Sutter supplied Emmons and his bluejackets with food, lodging, comforts, amusements—even a boat to carry them in comparative comfort 115 miles downriver and across San Francisco Bay for their appointment with *Vincennes* at Sausalito.

The Missouri overlanders—for the record, the Bidwell-Bartleson Party—diverged in late August from the now familiar Oregon route at Soda Springs beyond South Pass and advanced west and a little south toward the Great Salt Lake. Up to then the journey had been more or less routine, except for the marriage of Mr. Kelsey and Miss Williams below Grand Island, and for the misfortune that befell a member of the party named Shotwell, who accidentally shot himself along the Platte. Joseph Reddeford Walker of Bonneville's expedition had ventured west to California across desert and basin in 1835, but John Bidwell and the others knew nothing of Walker's experience. Guide Thomas Fitzpatrick and friendly Indians supplied vague directions: Don't push too far north, where broken canyon country would bar the way, nor yet too far south, where water and grass were scarce. So this augur of the Mexican dispossession groped its way along the northern edge of the Great Salt Lake toward a river said to flow somewhere over the horizon.

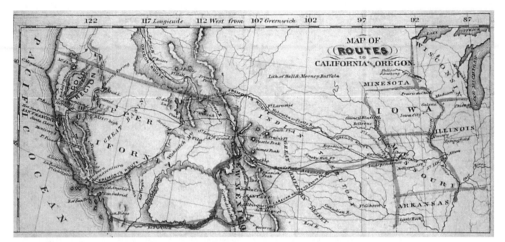

The emigrant routes to Oregon and California. Trappers roughed out the earliest overland routes; formal surveys by John Charles Frémont and others assisted thousands of migrants pushing out from the Missouri frontier to Utah, Oregon, and California. (Library of Congress)

Twenty-two years old in 1841, Bidwell had walked away from his family's western Ohio farm two years before, cadged a ride on a produce wagon headed for market at Cincinnati ninety miles distant, and traveled by river steamer to Burlington, Iowa, via Louisville and St. Louis. Carrying $75, the clothes he wore, a change of clothes in a knapsack, and a pocketknife, he sought work as a laborer and contemplated homesteading in eastern Iowa. Finding the Mississippi Valley a sickly locale ("all the people in the neighborhood became ill with fever and ague," he would recall), he drifted south and west to the Missouri frontier. He taught school for a year in Weston, on the northern bank of the Missouri near Fort Leavenworth, laid out a claim near the village, and summoned his father from Ohio. Taking a sabbatical in the summer of 1840, he journeyed downriver to St. Louis for schoolbooks, supplies, and a taste of settled life. He returned to Weston to find that a man had jumped his claim. As Bidwell soon discovered, the interloper had what passed for the law on his side: Bidwell was unmarried, and he hadn't actually *lived* on the claim. He decided to push on to California in the spring.[111]

With other restless, dispossessed, or fever-haunted Missourians, Bidwell established the Western Emigration Society over the winter of 1840–1841. Eventually five hundred men and women enrolled. A local newspaper reprinted a rapturous letter from the California settler John Marsh; and a veteran trapper passing through Weston, one Robidoux by name, delivered live firsthand accounts of Arcadia. He spoke at Bidwell's invitation to a gathering of the emigration society, describing California as a balmy paradise of orange and lemon groves and grasslands thick with wild horses and cattle available for the rounding up. The lecturer's repertory was limited, so Bidwell soon opened the meeting to the audience.

Crowd: Were there fever and ague?

Robidoux: "There was but one man in California that had ever had a chill there, and it was a matter of so much wonderment to the people of Monterey that they went 18 miles into the country to see him shake."[112]

As matters fell out, only sixty-some members of the emigration society actually set out from the rendezvous in May 1841. From the Bear River, Fitzpatrick veered north to Fort Hall with the Roman Catholic missionary Pierre de Smet and thirty Oregon-bound settlers. Bidwell and more than thirty fellow travelers embarked headlong on a march into the unknown. They had studied a map that represented the Great Salt Lake as three hundred or four hundred miles long, with two outlets, each emptying into the Pacific; Bidwell's landlord advised him to pack tools so he could build a canoe and float down to California. The caravan wandered over the Salt Plain for several days, then decided—it was September, toward the end of the traveling season—to abandon the wagons and advance at a faster pace with oxen, mules, and horses. In fits and starts they approached the yet-to-be-named Humboldt River (Ogden had traced its course in 1828), following the stream to its marshy Sinks, a journey of many days.

Then along the Carson River to the Walker River and the abrupt granite vault of the Sierra Nevada: October now, the nights bitter, snow lying deep in the passes. The Americans ascended along the northern bank of the Walker toward Sonora Pass, butchering the last ox on October 22 and subsisting afterward on juniper berries, crows, and a wildcat. Hurrying one morning to catch up to the head of the caravan, Bidwell found that one of the hunters had killed a fat coyote. Those in the van had fallen upon it ravenously. Only the lights and windpipe remained; he breakfasted on them with relish.

Down, down: in the foothills along the main branch of the Stanislaus River, game and wild fruit were abundant. Marksmen harvested thirteen deer and antelope and jerked the meat. Bidwell admired the

Sequoiadendron giganteum; he would later boast (without foundation) that he had been the first white man to see them. The migrants struck the Stanislaus River on November 1 and three days later reached the Marsh ranch in the eastern foothills of the Coast Range in present-day Contra Costa County. Dr. Marsh turned out to be something less than the paragon they had envisioned after reading his California letter. They found him querulous, stingy, and resentful of the cost of feeding and lodging the Americans. (He calculated it at $100 and despaired of seeing a *real* in return.) The caravan disbanded there, Bidwell pushing on for Sutter's Sacramento Valley principality to find work as his factotum and eventually—after taking Mexican citizenship and (fingers crossed) converting to Catholicism—obtain a land grant of his own. Of the thirty who reached the San Joaquin Valley with him, a dozen would return to the United States in 1842.[113]

John Sutter's reckless extravagance would ruin him in time. For now, though, he received the Americans "with open arms and in a princely fashion," Bidwell wrote. "Everybody was welcome, one man or a hundred, it was all the same." Arriving at Yerba Buena (later San Francisco) by sea at the end of 1841 to scout the country, particularly the Russian lodgment at Fort Ross, for the Hudson's Bay Company, George Simpson saw at once that Sutter would play a crucial role in expanding American influence in California, well placed as he was for furthering "Brother Jonathan's" ambitions. Sutter's New Helvetia domain, the Little Emperor observed, "excludes the Californians from all the best parts of their own country"—the San Joaquin and Sacramento Valleys—and once the Americans asserted dominion over the interior, they would demand a maritime outlet. Yerba Buena, not much of a prize yet but potentially a dominant trading center, sooner or later would fall into their hands. As for the Mexicans, the nominal rulers, they were swiftly becoming irrelevant. Simpson, the Hudson's Bay Company, and, by extension, the British Empire, had decisions to make about California—about whether they would challenge the Americans for primacy there.[114]

"Either Great Britain will introduce her well-regulated freedom of all classes and colors," Simpson predicted, "or the people of the United States will inundate the country with their own peculiar mixture of helpless bondage and lawless insubordination."[115]

5

The Great Migration

Destiny was calling. Even the self-absorbed Henry Thoreau responded to its insistent voice. "Eastward I go only by force," he would write; "but westward I go free."[1] From Hall J. Kelley's lonely cry of the early 1830s, the summons to the Pacific rose to a full-throated shout. Jason Lee's fund-raising lectures, Washington Irving's popular accounts of the Astorians and of Captain Bonneville, artist Alfred Jacob Miller's sepia sketches and watercolors depicting picturesque Rocky Mountain scenes: all conspired to beckon Americans to claim what they regarded as the next installment of their western inheritance.

In an extended essay in its January 1840 number, the influential *North American Review* took notice of the stirring of Americans' interest in the Pacific Northwest, surveying the long, gradual revelation of the country from Jonathan Carver's speculations about *"the river Oregan, or the River of the West"* through Astor's traders, mountain men, the entrepreneurs Wyeth, Lee, and Bonneville, and the government agent Slacum to the recently published narrative accounts of missionary Samuel Parker (1838) and naturalist John Kirk Townsend (1839). Carver's journey in the late 1770s carried him only as far as the Minnesota country; his reports came secondhand, from Sioux Indian informants; and anyway he probably confused the Columbia with the Missouri or its sources. All the same, the *Review* credited Carver with being the first to implant in the American consciousness the notion of an outpost on the western river that would serve both as a collection point for goods of the interior and a gateway to the riches of China and the East Indies.[2]

The *North American Review* presented the hapless Kelley as an untimely prophet, a visionary. After all, Kelley had caught the zeitgeist a decade earlier, recognizing "the intrinsic value of the country" sight unseen. His imagination at once comprehended Oregon's salubrious climate, strategic and military importance, and boundless economic potential. "But he suffered the too common fate of those who conceive a great idea, and dedicate themselves to a great object, in anticipation of the progress of knowledge and opinion around them," the magazine lamented. Now, too late for poor loopy Kelley, alas, American opinion had matured.[3]

With his book and lectures, Parker introduced the West to a still wider audience, even if the *Review* found the published account "somewhat deficient in method and literary execution." The anonymous essayist concluded, too, that Parker had uncritically accepted a legitimate British claim to the country, probably as a consequence of Hudson's Bay Company propaganda. Like so many travelers before him, he succumbed to the powerful waves of John McLoughlin charm during his stay at Fort Vancouver. In spite of these flaws, the magazine greeted Parker's *Journal of an Exploring Tour* as well as Townsend's *Narrative of a Journey across the Rocky Mountains* as important and influential additions to the literature of the West. Taken together, they were "a new indication of the growing interest of the community in regard to that important portion of the territory of the United States."[4]

The bitter reality of social and economic circumstance contributed substantially to the buildup of that interest. The Panic of 1837 touched off a general economic slump that would linger into the mid-1840s. Unemployment, deranged banking and credit systems, and falling prices and saturated markets for agricultural products burnished distant Oregon's appeal. Americans anyway accepted as their destiny that they eventually would people the entire continent, Atlantic to Pacific; the early development of railroads in the East—twenty-eight hundred miles of track had been laid by 1840—made the western ocean seem closer and more accessible. "We can go to Oregon with safety, the most perfect safety, and be sure of a reception from Englishmen, every way worthy of the hospitable name of that ancient beef-eating people," the Methodist-inspired *Oregonian and Indian*

Advocate announced in a late 1830s call for Christian settlers of the Pacific Northwest.[5] Soon hundreds, then thousands of Indiana, Illinois, and Missouri farmers, devout and otherwise, would push west to escape hard times and fever in the malaria-racked Mississippi River Valley. Missourian Daniel Waldo, who would trek to Oregon with Marcus Whitman in 1843, combined both motives. Ill and in debt, his Missouri farm producing surpluses nobody wanted to buy, he looked to Oregon as an escape and a new start.

"I left everything I had, a big tract of land there and left that," Waldo would recall in an acerbic memoir appropriately titled *Critiques*. "There was no market anywhere on the Mississippi River. They used bacon for steamboat firing that year. (But) I did not come to make money. I just came for my health. I had my health after I come here."[6]

In the rudimentary communities of the Willamette Valley, settlers were calling for an end to the Anglo-American joint occupation, the security of American legal and political institutions, and eventual absorption into the United States. "Man, we fear, might, among the other definitions, be not inaptly described as a stealing animal," observed an anonymous reviewer of Irving's *Astoria*. Not to put too fine a point upon it, a country that belonged to two powers belonged to neither. Although the 1818 boundary convention nominally placed the United States and Britain on an equal footing, the reviewer went on, "the country is rapidly passing, in reality, into British hands." McLoughlin and the British-Canadian Hudson's Bay Company were the law of the land. It was time for destiny to take a hand, to demolish the British claim with its flimsy rationale of Henry Broughton's low-comedy flag-raising six months *after* Robert Gray's discovery of the Columbia. As ever, the Indian nations could be dismissed as irrelevant. The United States should move at once to finish what Captain Gray and J. J. Astor had started.[7]

So Oregon insinuated itself into the collective imagination of Americans, blazing the way for the arrival of a celebrity, a national darling, a personification of westward expansion. For a brief historical moment, John Charles Frémont would sustain that role to perfection. In three cross-country exploring expeditions of the 1840s, the charismatic "pathfinder of empire" would bring the West symbolically and practically closer to the older America. Reports of his first two expeditions, struck off government printing presses in 1843 and 1845, would pass from hand to hand in city precincts of the crowded East and from farmstead to farmstead in the Mississippi Valley, helping to touch off a folk movement that would set thousands of people in westward motion within a decade. From 1840 to 1842 a total of 196 migrants trekked overland to Oregon and California. From 1843 to 1848, 20,800 men, women, and children would cross the mountains to Utah, Oregon, and California. As a boy on an Ohio farm, future overlander and California poet Joaquin Miller devoured the report of Frémont's 1842 expedition.[8]

"I fancied I could see Frémont's men, hauling the cannon up the savage battlements of the Rocky Mountains, flags in the air, Frémont at the head, waving his sword, his horse neighing wildly in the mountain wind, with unknown and unnamed empires at every hand," Miller recalled long afterward. "I began to be inflamed with a love for action, adventure, glory, and great deeds away out yonder under the path of the setting sun."[9]

Man and boy, Miller doubtless had only the haziest notion that the intrepid Lieutenant Frémont followed a trail the Whitman missionaries had broken in 1836 and 1837—the doctor and Henry Spalding, Narcissa Whitman and Eliza Spalding, the Walkers, the Eelses, the Smiths, and William Gray. That dreamy parson Samuel Parker, paunched and hardly robust, had successfully completed the trek, too. Parker's son would later charge that, through the caprice of fame, Frémont wore the crown that rightfully belonged to his father and other earlier travelers. "This is a common fault with all 'great men,'" Samuel J. Parker complained, "and especially all War Department men." Historian Frederick Merk regards Frémont a promoter mainly— "the popularizer of the achievements of the mountain men rather than an explorer in his own right." To dismiss Frémont as an explorer *manqué* is perhaps too harsh an assessment; after all, in his great circuit of the West, he would traverse more of the unknown regions than anyone, man or woman, who came before him, and his reports and maps—while they certainly were designed to appeal to a popular audience—revealed much new data about western basin and range country. He would play, too, a vital part as symbol and standard-bearer of national and imperial ambitions.[10]

FRÉMONT'S PARENTS were a romantic, even lurid couple. Ann Beverly Whiting, descended from an established Virginia family that claimed kinship with George Washington, married the elderly Richmonder John Pryor, a well-to-do livery stable and amusement park owner, in 1796. She was seventeen years old; Pryor was in his sixties, gouty and probably impotent. The old man took in boarders from time to time, an enterprise that would prove subversive of his domestic tranquillity. In June 1810 a French émigré who styled himself Fremon rented a cottage on the Pryor property. Jean Charles Fremon seems to have been a native of Lyons or its thereabouts; it is unclear why or how he came to the United States. In any case, he earned a sustenance with itinerant work as a French teacher and dancing master, as an instructor in a girls' academy, as the proprietor of a night school, and as a tutor in private homes.

Within a year, Pryor found himself obliged to confront Fremon about the émigré's intimacy with his comely wife. Fremon and Ann Pryor answered the charge by eloping, fleeing first to Williamsburg, then to Norfolk, then to Charleston, and eventually to Savannah. Pryor at once inserted a notice in a Richmond newspaper announcing the scandal and repudiating his wife's debts. He would charge in a divorce petition that Mrs. Pryor had abandoned him; she would assert that the old man turned her out of doors during a storm.

Whatever the truth of the matter, Charles Fremon and Ann Pryor settled in as common-law man and wife. So far as is known, they were faithful to one another—a love match. Fremon gave French lessons, worked in a dancing academy, opened a livery stable, and—heedless of Pryor's fate—admitted boarders into his house. Their first child, John Charles, was born in the Georgia city on January 21, 1813. Conditions were precarious, although for a time the ménage owned a slave, a nurse named Hannah. "We can be content with little," Ann remarked primly, "for I have found that happiness consists not in riches." For reasons that remain obscure but that doubtless involved the absence of riches, Fremon found it expedient to move about a lot. Their second child, a daughter, was born in Nashville in 1814. She lived only a few weeks. Ann Pryor delivered another daughter and a second son in Norfolk in 1815 and 1817. Fremon died of unknown causes there in 1818. By 1823 his widow had returned to Charleston, where she tried to keep up genteel appearances on such leavings as had survived him.[11]

Charley, as his mother called her firstborn, went to work at age thirteen in the law office of John W. Mitchell, the first in a series of

John C. Frémont (1813–1890).
This image, published after
1850, shows "J. C. Frémont, The
Explorer of the Rocky Mountains."
The Pathfinder's first two exploring expeditions, to South Pass in
1842 and to Oregon and California
in 1843–1844, made him a national
celebrity. (Library of Congress)

influential men who would take a decisive interest in his future. His
biographers characterize young Frémont (at some point he added the
accent and the *t* to his surname) as an outsider, a loner resentful of
authority and contemptuous of the rules. That may have been so, and
yet at critical points in his life he usually contrived to connect himself
to a powerful patron. Possibly he had a sort of homing instinct for men
who liked to live dangerously. In any case, lawyer Mitchell sent Frémont to the preparatory school of John Roberton, where he learned
Greek and Latin—Greek especially held "a mysterious charm" for him,
he would later say—and, so it appeared, excelled in mathematics.[12]

He won over Roberton at once. The master recalled Charley as
"graceful in manners, rather slender, but well formed, and upon the
whole, what I would call handsome; of a keen, piercing eye and a
noble forehead seemingly the very seat of genius." On the strength of
Roberton's recommendation, Frémont entered the College of Charleston in May 1829, evidently with an idea of studying for the Episcopal
ministry. But the disciplines of academic life bored him, and anyhow

he had no vocation for the priesthood. The college authorities expelled him for "incorrigible negligence" in February 1831, just three months before graduation. Charley would claim afterward it was love that made him neglect his studies and cut his classes, sometimes for days together.[13]

Frémont does not explain in his lengthy and in places unbearably tedious *Memoirs* how he managed to escape a permanent connection with the charming Creole girl he courted so relentlessly. In fact, the *Memoirs* explain little or nothing of Frémont's early life. There were "few things worthy of note" in his childhood and youth, he would write; he omits or conceals nearly everything of interest, making no mention of the ambiguous circumstances of his unwed parents, and little of his mother's struggles as a grass widow. Charley did cite two books as seminal in forming his youthful character, though typically he neglected to supply author or title for either: a boys' chronicle of heroes and villains, and a treatise on practical astronomy by which he taught himself to navigate by the stars.[14]

Frémont's sister Elizabeth died in 1832, and his adventurous younger brother Frank struck out for a career on the boards. The dissolution of the family seems to have concentrated Charley's mind. As though on cue, another powerful patron now turned up, the South Carolina political grandee Joel Poinsett. A former U.S. minister to Mexico (he returned home with the showy scarlet flowering plant he would introduce to Americans as the poinsettia) and a leader of Union political forces in South Carolina during the Nullification Crisis, Poinsett arranged for Frémont's appointment as mathematics instructor in the USS *Natchez*. The Jackson administration dispatched the sloop to Charleston to compel collection of the tariffs the state had declared null and void. Frémont remained aboard after the crisis abated and sailed in *Natchez* in 1833 on a two-year cruise to South America.

Frémont left a sketchy record of this interlude, although he did dilate on his role in managing a harmless duel between two of his charges. Doubtless he perfected his dead reckoning skills as he tutored the midshipmen. The navy thought highly enough of his work to offer, in 1835, an appointment as instructor of mathematics at a salary of $1,200 a year. For some reason Frémont felt sufficiently secure to decline the sinecure; perhaps he simply disliked shipboard life and, with the conceit of the young, figured something better would turn up. In the event, Poinsett engineered his appointment as a civilian adjunct to a U.S. Corps of Topographical Engineers expedition to survey a route for the proposed Charleston and Cincinnati Railroad.

The assignment turned out to be "a kind of picnic." For weeks he tramped the upcountry of the Carolinas and eastern Tennessee, often alone except for a guide. The railroad survey evolved into a military reconnaissance of Cherokee country during the winter of 1836–1837 in service of Andrew Jackson's policy of Indian removal. On this mission into the rugged, beautiful mountain and hollow country where Georgia, the Carolinas, and Tennessee meet, Frémont showed another, less callow side of his personality, perhaps a result of his own precarious status. Adopting white ways, the Cherokees were indistinguishable for the most part from their neighbors. "In their villages and in their ordinary farming life they lived peaceably and comfortably," he recalled. "Many of their farms were much the same as those that are to be met everywhere on our remote frontier. The depreciating and hurtful influence was that of the whites."[15] All the same, Jackson and his successor, Martin Van Buren, moved aggressively to resettle the Cherokees beyond the Mississippi. The reconnaissance set the stage for the army to carry out the eviction in 1838 along what would be known infamously as the Trail of Tears.

The expeditions had a galvanic impact on Frémont. The interlude in the Cherokee wilderness revealed to him his true calling. "Here," he would write, "I found the path which I was 'destined to walk.' Through many of the years to come the occupation of my prime of life was to be among the Indians and in waste places."[16] Once again, the hand of Joel Poinsett reached out to direct Frémont's destiny. Joining Van Buren's cabinet as secretary of war, Poinsett obtained for Frémont a second lieutenant's commission in the Topographical Corps. Something of an elite branch, the corps consisted mostly of West Point–trained officers who formed a sort of surveyors' clique. Entering via political influence, Frémont always would stand a little apart, an interloper in the eyes of his comrades.

The commission bore the date of July 7, 1838. By then Frémont had joined the French scientist Joseph Nicollet's survey of the Plains country lying between the Mississippi and Missouri Rivers, another appointment courtesy of Poinsett. With Nicollet's expeditions to Minnesota in 1838 and the Dakotas in 1839, Frémont would complete his apprenticeship as an explorer, gaining a wealth of experience to supplement his subaltern's salary of $4 a day, with 10 cents a mile for travel expenses.

Nicollet had arrived in the United States in 1832 to conduct a private "scientific tour" to expand the geographical understanding of North America. His work so impressed Poinsett that he obtained U.S. government sponsorship for the 1838–1839 expedition. Nicollet would be a model of the scientific explorer for the flighty Frémont, who observed him attentively during the months they traveled and worked together. "I feel myself sensibly advancing in professional knowledge & the confused ideas of Science & Philosophy wh my mind has been occupied are momently arranging themselves into order & clearness," he wrote Poinsett after a few weeks in Nicollet's company.[17] The protégé deeply admired Nicollet's cultivated, urbane persona; his scientific exactitude; his air of quiet command; and his careful, painstaking administration of the survey party.

"I could not dwell too much upon his superb management of the expedition," he wrote breathlessly to Poinsett in September 1838 "—not an article lost or broken throughout our long journey, not a horse injured or stolen, a set of the most ungovernable men in the world reduced in less than a week to perfect order & obedience, the whole party cheerful and contented & all conducted with the strictest regard to economy, superintending in person the most trifling details— giving, himself, the Reveille at 4 in the morning, traveling all day pencil in hand sketching & noting everything—nothing but the most extraordinary devotion to the cause of science could have supported him under such unremitted labor."[18]

Frémont returned to Washington late in 1839 to help Nicollet prepare the report and the detailed map that would be the yield of the two expeditions to the northern prairies. The lieutenant did not find the city congenial. "That first impression of flattened lonesomeness" Washington had given him on his first visit early in 1838 remained with him always. There was little to the city beyond Pennsylvania Avenue, few places for a young man to find companionship or amusement. Nicollet set up shop first in the Capitol Hill home of his German-born colleague Ferdinand R. Hassler, chief of the U.S. Coastal Survey, then later in the Coast Survey building itself.[19]

There they bent to the task of mapmaking, reducing the meticulously recorded field observations to longitude and latitude, projecting the fixed positions onto the manuscript map, tracing the lines of rivers, the forms of lakes, and the contours of hills from the expedition sketchbook. Here, too, in the crowded spaces of Hassler's spare rooms, Frémont met Senator Thomas Hart Benton, the next—and most important—in the succession of powerful men who would shape his life and career.

Frémont's use of the phrase "waste places" in the epiphany that revealed his vocation suggests he regarded the wilderness that so captured his fancy as valueless, latent, passively awaiting its destiny until someone—soldier, scientist, miner, settler—came along to develop it. Certainly Senator Benton came away from his first visit to Nicollet's rooms impressed with the expedition's evidence of the "farming value," the highest and best use, of the Minnesota and Dakota country. These wastes only awaited the settlers' plow to be transformed.

Benton called on Nicollet expecting a finished map that would show his restless Missouri constituents the way to the new lands. He was disappointed at first, until he saw the masses of data strewn on the benches and tables and learned something of the elaborate cartographic process from Nicollet and his acolyte. The project fired Benton's imagination with visions of a broader work, a survey of the entire western half of the continent from the Mississippi to the Rocky Mountains and on to the Pacific. Frémont listened with rapt attention as the senator elaborated on his expansionist themes.

"The interview left on me a profound impression," Frémont wrote. "The thought of penetrating into the recesses of that wilderness region filled me with enthusiasm. In this interview with Mr. Benton my mind had been quick to see a larger field and differing and greater results. It would be travel over a part of the world which remained the new—the opening up of unknown lands; the making of unknown countries known; and the study without books—the learning at first hand from nature herself; the drinking first at her unknown springs—became a source of never-ending delight to me."[20]

In company with Nicollet, Frémont paid Benton a return and opened a campaign to ingratiate himself with the Missourian. He visited the Bentons' C Street home near Capitol Hill often during the following months, meeting the senator's colleagues and political friends, mostly Westerners who shared the Bentonian view of America's Pacific destiny. As Nicollet's health began to fail, Frémont took on greater responsibility for the preparation of the Minnesota map and enjoyed a corresponding rise in Benton's esteem.

He seems to have fallen in love with the Benton household—a warm place, intimate, informal, and above all, *intact*—long before he fell in love with one of the Benton girls, Jessie Ann. They met at a concert at Miss English's Female Seminary, Jessie's Georgetown school, to which the dashing lieutenant escorted the Bentons' eldest daughter. There matters stood for several months. When Jessie returned home for the school vacation they saw each other often, for Frémont by now had become a habitué of the Benton place. She was sixteen years old, dark-haired, passionate, strong-willed, unrestrained—and heedless of the consequences of casting her lot with an obscure twenty-seven-year-old soldier of marginal background and doubtful prospects. The Bentons, naturally, were appalled.

The Frémonts' daughter destroyed stacks of her parents' correspondence after their deaths, so there is little on record about the progress of the courtship. In the *Memoirs*, Frémont remarked that he and Jessie fell in love, and he left it at that. He at least attempted an apology for omitting the best parts: "The very details, which for various reasons are forced from the page, are just what might prove interesting as making up our human life."[21] The Bentons were vigilant, the senator doubtless cursing the day he invited Frémont into the family circle. A glance, whispered confidences, a squeeze of the hand doubtless told Frémont all he needed to know about Jessie's impulsive heart. With a touch of the macabre, he arranged for the climax to occur in Nicollet's workrooms, to which he had invited the Benton family to observe the funeral procession of the ninth president, William Henry Harrison, who died in April 1841, thirty days after taking office. Frémont removed the worktables; decked the rooms with spring flowers; and, wearing his best uniform, served tea and cakes to the guests. At some point he and Jessie Benton came to an understanding.

"The funeral occasion proved, as I had hoped, to be my red-letter day," he wrote.[22]

Next day, Frémont sent the flowers to Jessie's mother. Immune to flattery, Elizabeth Benton brought her considerable powers to bear in an effort to extinguish the romance. She cited Jessie's age; privately, she felt qualms about Frémont's antecedents, and she certainly had no wish to see her daughter follow the drum. She herself had refused to marry Benton until he agreed to give up soldiering. Jessie accused her parents of conspiring to remove Frémont from her presence by arranging for him to be assigned to tie up a minor loose end of the Nicollet project, a survey of the lower reaches of the Des Moines River in the Iowa country. This work occupied Frémont for several weeks in the summer of 1841. He returned to Washington in August. Arranging to meet in secret, he and Jessie reaffirmed their pledge. She went through with her society debut on schedule in early October, at a presidential ball given in honor of a son of King Louis Philippe of France. They eloped shortly thereafter. Two Protestant ministers refused to perform a secret marriage ceremony. A Roman Catholic priest attached to St. Peter's Church in the capital read the couple the marriage sacrament on October 19, 1841. Even years later, the Frémonts instinctively concealed the details, Jessie withholding the location (a hotel room or, possibly, a confederate's home) and the fact that a Roman Catholic priest had officiated.

"Civil contract only, I should say," she would write a friend during Frémont's brief incarnation as a presidential contender, when any Catholic connection would have been harmful. "It was a drawing room—no altar lights or any such thing—I was asked nothing but my age—& the whole thing was very short."[23]

Jessie returned to C Street after the ceremony, for she and Frémont had agreed to keep quiet about the marriage for a year. An impossibility: the news spread rather quickly, a Coast Survey acquaintance writing Frémont with congratulations—and advice—within ten days of the elopement. Ferdinand H. Gerdes urged him to make the event public sooner rather than later, for "the possibility of an accidental discovery is very strong!"

Gerdes went on, syntax betraying his German origins: "Why don't you go, manly and open as you are, forward and put things by a single step to right—never mind in what this step consists—only act now and you will *soon* get over little disturbances wich might arise at first. Nothing very serious *can* happen now more to you—the prize is secured and the rest will soon be smoothed by help of time and mutual affection and love."[24]

Word soon reached Elizabeth Benton, and she expertly winkled the particulars out of Jessie. She sent for her husband, en route to St. Louis, to turn about for Washington at once. There was, of course, little the Bentons could do. The senator did evict Jessie from the house ("The marriage was published & Frémont took his wife to his lodgings," a Washington gossip reported), and he refused to permit a second, Protestant exchange of vows. Still, Benton apportioned the blame equitably. "John C. Frémont did not marry my daughter," the exasperated senator confided to a friend; "she married him." After a brief banishment, he found it in his heart to forgive the couple, for he loved Jessie and, as a matter of policy, concluded that he could find uses for a young soldier whose loyalty and biddability he could take for granted. Benton initially sought Joseph Nicollet to command the great western survey he had in mind. When Nicollet declined the appointment, pleading poor health, the senator turned to his new son-in-law.[25]

THE FRÉMONTS PRESENTED a bold and attractive facade to the fusty society of the nation's capital. Although not quite a beauty, the lively, animated Jessie was a vivid presence. As for Lieutenant Frémont, a Capitol Hill hostess would recall him as "quite simply the handsomest man in Washington."[26]

Bright, springlike weather attracted larger-than-usual crowds to President Tyler's 1842 New Year's Day reception. In consequence, there were rows of witnesses to remark the ostentatious arrival of Frémont and bride at the gates of the Executive Mansion. Their emergence from the notorious "ark," Coast Survey chief Ferdinand Hassler's clumsy, oversized carriage, set the gossips humming again—the elopement only two months earlier, the Bentons' outrage, the lieutenant's murky background and indeterminate prospects.

"It took some nerve to drive up in the ark among the holiday crowd," Frémont wrote modestly.[27]

Clearly, by arranging an entrance in state in Hassler's outlandish machine, the Frémonts had settled on a policy of brazening things out. This would become a defining feature of their partnership. Reading the expedition journals, Ralph Waldo Emerson would be struck by what he characterized as Frémont's "passion for seeming." Frémont "is continually remarking on 'the group,' on 'the picture,'" Emerson wrote. Hunger, thirst, peril, the thrill of the unknown: nothing, he went on, "could repress the eternal vanity of *how we must look.*" Then and later, the Frémonts would present a brash, unabashed, even impudent front to the world.[28]

The president's lackeys threw the doors open at noon. A marine band played, and Washingtonians high and low queued up in the Blue Room to grasp the president's hand. Here the capital's leading figures were gathered—cabinet officers, Secretary of State Webster towering and dominant among them; senior diplomats; the splendid General Winfield Scott; and senatorial powers such as John C. Calhoun and Benton himself. Tyler pursued a cautious western policy; as for Webster, he might be characterized as the anti-Benton. "What can we do with the Western Coast?" Webster, more concerned with expanding trade than adding territory or settlement, once asked the Senate, "What use have we of such a country? I will never vote one cent from the public treasury to place the Pacific Ocean one inch nearer Boston than it is now."[29] In the glitter and swirl of finery, Benton doubtless caught a glimpse of his daughter, conspicuous in an elegant blue velvet gown and bonnet with three yellow ostrich feathers. By now he had forgiven her, and Frémont, too. Benton's plans for his son-in-law had matured. The invitation to New Year's dinner at the C Street House might be taken as a sign, if not of the senator's blessing, then at least as an acknowledgment that active hostilities had ceased.

There Benton again bruited the project he had mentioned in Nicollet's workrooms months before—a series of exploration and mapping expeditions to the West, paid for (anti-Webster) out of the public treasury, with a view to asserting American sovereignty in Oregon, securing a window on Asia, and opening the region to mass settlement. These were familiar subjects to Jessie Frémont. She had heard the phrases "Oregon occupation" and "India trade" for as long as she could remember. "They connected themselves with big English lawbooks in my father's library, whose Hogarth-like pictures were a delight to my childhood when there were no picture-books made for children," she would write.[30] Tonight, though, her father had something more substantive than phrases to offer. Benton told Frémont that, as chairman of the Senate Committee on Military Affairs, he had arranged funding in the Topographical Corps budget for a four-month journey into the Rocky Mountains, and that he, Frémont, would command the expedition.

As Frémont understood it, the foray would be "auxiliary and in aid to the emigration to the lower Columbia." Benton wanted him to mark, map, describe, and publicize the Oregon route as far as the sources of the Sweetwater River at South Pass and to reconnoiter sites for military posts—all more or less without the knowledge of the Tyler administration. The Frémonts later would play up the conspiratorial element of the assignment. Wrote Frémont, "I felt I was being drawn into the current of important political events: the object of this expedition was not merely a survey; beyond that was its bearing on the holding of our territory on the Pacific; and the contingencies it involved were large."[31] Benton counted on Frémont's work to open the floodgates of migration to the Willamette Valley, where several hundred Americans were now settled, and to California, where the first overland train, John Bidwell and company, had arrived after a precarious crossing of the Sierra Nevada only two months earlier. Of benefit in itself, the westward movement also served imperial purposes. Intermittent negotiations on the British–U.S. boundary disputes in Maine and Oregon were to resume in 1842. The Wilkes exploring expedition had emphasized the importance to the United States of Puget Sound's safe deepwater anchorages—after all, Commodore Wilkes had lost a sloop on the Columbia bar.

"Emigration," Benton declared, "is the only thing which can save the country from the British."[32]

So the reconciliation was complete. The Frémonts moved into a back room of the Benton house, and in the early spring Jessie discovered she was pregnant. She expected to give birth in November, at about the time of Frémont's anticipated return from South Pass. Orders from John J. Abert, the chief of the Topographical Corps in Washington, reached him before the end of April:

> You will repair as soon as practicable to Fort Leavenworth in order to make a Survey of the Platte or Nebraska river, up to the head of the Sweetwater. Having been already employed on such duties, and being well acquainted with the kind of Survey required, it is not necessary to enumerate the objects to which your attention will be directed. These duties being completed, you will return to this place in order to prepare the drawings & report.[33]

A week later, Frémont bade farewell to Jessie and set out for St. Louis.

LIKE SAILORS, LIEUTENANT FRÉMONT'S *voyageurs* recoiled from a Friday embarkation as inauspicious, unlucky. They invariably would recall the day of departure in times of danger, hardship, and vexation. But heavy rains had delayed Frémont for several days, and he was anxious to make a start. The party of twenty-one consisted of the French-speaking rank and file, mostly recruited in St. Louis; the guide

Kit Carson, whom Frémont had met on the steamboat that carried him up the Missouri; the cartographer Charles Preuss; and two "gentleman travelers," Henry Brant, nineteen years old, and Jessie Frémont's twelve-year-old brother, Randolph Benton. The skies cleared finally, and on June 10 the expedition marched west from Cyprian Chouteau's trading post on the right bank of the Kansas River on what Frémont called his "campaign in the wilderness."[34]

The route traversed territory familiar to a generation of traders and mountain men. Within a week, news reached Frémont of the emigrant party of Elijah White—Jason Lee's nemesis at the Methodist mission on the Willamette, now returning to Oregon with a federal commission as Indian agent—traveling three weeks ahead. The expedition trailed in the wake of this caravan of eighteen heavy Pennsylvania wagons and more than a hundred men, women, and children: for now, anyway, Frémont would neither pathfind nor explore. All the same, he would encounter all manner of novel experiences and sensations along the Oregon road. For example, one of the men shot a prairie snake that had insinuated itself into a colony of swallows' nests. When they opened it up, they found eighteen living swallows inside.

Recalling Nicollet's precision in such matters, Frémont established a strict trail routine early in the voyage. He usually signaled a halt thirty minutes or so before sunset, laagering the wagons for defense, pitching the tents, hobbling the animals, and turning them loose to graze. Horses, mules, and oxen were driven into camp at nightfall. Three men mounted the first guard at eight o'clock. Reveille sounded at daydawn, the animals again were allowed to browse, and the march resumed between six and seven o'clock. The noon halt allowed the people and livestock an hour or two of rest.

The trail led through the broken country of the Big Blue River, the hills colorful with the blooms of wild roses. Frémont pitched camp beside the cold ashes of the White party on June 21—traces, he observed, that relieved "a little of the loneliness of the road." Amenities were not lacking—not yet, anyway; one of the men found a pack of cards the emigrants had discarded, and the cow, milked that night, yielded cream for their morning coffee.[35]

Charles Preuss found meager comfort in such treats. Dour, querulous, depressive (he would hang himself in 1854), he regretted from the start having signed on with Frémont. A gentleman of urban tastes, he had been an associate of Hassler's in the Coast Survey, an easy billet he now looked back on with desperate longing. His attitude toward the commander veered from grudging admiration to contempt. Frémont was "foolish," a "simpleton"; he indulged in "childish" fits; he showed no aptitude for managing the traveling enterprise. Preuss grumbled about the food, the weather, and about long, racking hours on horseback. He fantasized about what he could do with a bottle of good wine. The laconic complaints of his journals—"Nothing but prairie. Made twenty miles. Very hot"—provide a bracing antidote to Frémont's sunny romanticism. "Eternal prairie and grass," Preuss observed. "Frémont prefers this to every other landscape. To me it is as if someone would prefer a book with blank pages to a good story." On the second night out the men slaughtered an ox, roasted the choicer parts, and vied for tidbits of raw liver. The scene robbed Preuss of his appetite.

"I was satisfied with bread and coffee," he wrote sourly; "I am not yet so hungry that I would gulp down very fresh meat, which is repulsive to me. Tomorrow, to be sure, it will taste excellent.

"June 13 (Monday)

"It did not taste excellent."[36]

The expedition reached the Platte River, 326 miles from the mouth of the Kansas, on June 26. Two days later Frémont met with a trapper party that included the Connecticut adventurer Rufus B. Sage, whose memoir of wilderness travel would be published in 1846 as *Rocky Mountain Life*. The trappers had suffered much from hunger and privation—they "looked like the last remnant of hard times," Sage wrote—and their appearance in the distance alarmed Frémont's sentinels.[37] The camp cleared for action; a patrol of armed horsemen returned within a few minutes to report that the strangers were harmless. Frémont distributed tobacco and the latest news before seeing Sage and his companions off downstream. Sighting buffalo for the first time on the twenty-eighth, the messes soon were warming their evening meals over fires of *bois de vache*. Fifteen miles below present North Platte, Nebraska, Frémont measured the breadth of the Platte, here flowing in two channels, at 5,350 feet. Great packs of wolves surrounded the camp at night, circling and howling.

Perhaps longing for untrodden country, Frémont on July 4 divided the party, sending the main detachment under Clément Lambert direct to Fort Laramie, while he struck southwest with six men along the line of the South Platte River toward Vrain's Fort. All were armed to the teeth with rifles or double-barreled shotguns for this trek through the country of the Arapahos. The men loaded a spare horse and a pack mule with provisions and the survey instruments: compass, sextant, barometer, artificial horizon, spyglass. Frémont himself carried the precious chronometer. He ordered Preuss along for topographical expertise, a move he shortly regretted.

They covered thirty-six miles that first day, exertions that left Preuss so worn he could barely keep his feet. To add insult, the cook forgot to pack coffee, sugar, and salt. The hunters shot an old bull, and in the evening the people squatted dejectedly to a meal of bread and tough buffalo meat. Preuss made no effort to suppress his feelings. Perhaps tiring of his litany of complaint, Frémont sent him back to the main party the next day. Preuss was overjoyed.

"I feel better because of Frémont's absence," he wrote.[38]

The South Platte detachment trudged on under a high, hollow sky through barren country—a "naked waste" of alternating clay and sand, in Frémont's phrase. The mercury climbed to 103 degrees Fahrenheit on July 7. The next day, they encountered evidence of the presence of Indians in the neighborhood: the fresh tracks of horses; a buffalo carcass; and, a bit farther on, the bones and festering waste parts of many buffalo, "which showed that Indians had made a surround here, and were in considerable force." They glimpsed a dark mass that soon enough resolved itself into a band of mounted Indians bearing down on them. The men deployed and prepared to open fire; Frémont stayed them at the last moment, when Lucien Maxwell called out that he recognized one of the warriors. They were Arapahos on the hunt.[39]

After a parley, Frémont watched the hunt from a distance, too far away to hear anything. Animal and human figures moved dreamily through great clouds of dust, as though choreographed. Later, one of the chiefs invited him to the village. More than a hundred lodges, mostly Arapaho, a few Cheyenne, were disposed along a broad avenue that ran parallel to the South Platte. A sort of tripod frame had been erected outside the host's lodge with a spear and shield affixed, evidently the weapons of a chief. Inside, the host chief spread a buffalo robe for Frémont to sit upon, gestured for a large bowl of buffalo meat, and lit a pipe. In due course five or six other Arapaho chiefs entered the lodge and silently took their seats.

In this recreation of an overland scene, hunters pursue buffalo crossing the Oregon Trail near the Platte River in Nebraska. A wagon train and Fort Kearny are in the background. As early as the mid-1840s Frémont and others reported buffalo as increasingly scarce. (Library of Congress)

With grave courtesy, the paramount chief opened the questioning. What brought Frémont to the Arapaho country? What was the object of his journey? The lieutenant replied with candor: "I had made a visit to see the country, preparatory to the establishment of military posts on the way to the mountains." Though the chiefs had no cause to be pleased with this news, they showed no sign of resentment, according to Frémont. They smoked placidly for a while; finally the head man offered Frémont a bundle of dried meat—most welcome, as his party had none—and saw him off to his camp.[40]

Next day, July 9, the Rockies loomed behind a gauze of thin mist, a first view of the snow-covered summit of Long's Peak "showing like a small cloud near the horizon" sixty miles distant. This country, too, proved well traveled. Within a few hours Frémont encountered, first, the party of Jim Beckwourth, an African American trader/trapper then working the upper Arkansas and South Platte country, and a little later a camp of four or five whites, "New Englanders," the lieutenant wrote, "who had accompanied Captain Wyeth to the Columbia River" and now were trapping independently. They traveled with their women and a surprising number of "fat little buffalo-fed boys."

Two miles beyond lay the camp of Jean Baptiste Charbonneau, a son of Sacajawea, the Indian woman who had guided Lewis and Clark forty years earlier. Charbonneau's retainers, mostly Mexicans from Taos, gathered mint, mixed a tolerable julep, and supplied a light meal of boiled buffalo tongue.[41]

The expedition reached Vrain's Fort late in the evening of the tenth. The fort lay forty feet above the South Platte in a broad swatch of upland prairie. Smoke from a fire that had been burning for several months among the pine forests to the south obscured Pike's Peak, visible on a clear day a hundred miles away. Frémont hired a Taos man and purchased a couple of horses, three stout mules, and a few pounds of coffee from Marcellin St. Vrain before resuming the journey on July 12.

The route led north and west through rough hill country broken by numerous streams, some of them salty and intermittent. Cacti flourished; little else. Toward the end of the third day of hard travel along a succession of bleak ridges they approached the American Fur Company's whitewashed and picketed outpost on the Laramie River for a reunion with Clément Lambert and the main detachment, which had arrived two days earlier. A party of Sioux had pitched a cluster of lodges under one of the walls of the quadrangular stockade.

The camp vibrated in a state of high alarm. Pushing on direct for Fort Laramie, Frémont's main group on July 8 had encountered mountain man Jim Bridger, who bore tales of a bloody battle the previous summer and more recent near-escapes from Sioux war parties. The Sioux were said to be sweeping through the country in force and, seeking revenge for their losses in the 1841 fight, making war on every living thing. At the moment Sioux outriders were in the vicinity of the Red Buttes directly athwart the expedition's line of march. To Charles Preuss's surprise, the news seriously affrighted the *voyageurs*. "All night, scattered groups were assembled around the fires, smoking their pipes, and listening with the greatest eagerness to exaggerated details of Indian hostilities," he wrote.[42] In the morning a majority argued for turning back; with much difficulty Lambert managed to persuade them to continue on as far as Laramie, where Lieutenant Frémont would make the ultimate decision.

The expedition picked up fresh intelligence, too, of the White-Hastings party. The trek had not gone well; the traders at Laramie reported dissension and weariness in the emigrant ranks. Quarreling

A view of the emigrant way station of Fort Laramie, Wyoming. Built originally as Fort William, it was a ramshackle fur trader outpost in its early days. "It is a large hewed log building with an opening in the center. It compares very well with the walls of the Conn. State Prison," missionary Myra Eels wrote in 1837. (Library of Congress)

broke out early, a few days into the journey. "All appeared to be determined to govern, but not to be governed," wrote Lansford W. Hastings. Then White, in his capacity as representative of the national government in Washington, issued a bizarre order: All the caravan dogs were to be destroyed before hydrophobia drove them mad in the desert. "King Herod's edict anent the slaughter of the innocents could scarcely have called forth a louder wail of lamentation," Francis Fuller Victor observed. So the party divided into two hostile factions, White's and that of Hastings.[43]

The Fort Laramie traders told the overlanders that their cattle were too footsore to travel; besides, in a drought year, there were few or no buffalo and no grass to support the trains. Falling for this sharp practice, they exchanged their heavy wagons and cattle for "miserable worn out horses," paid out $1 a pint for flour and $1 a pound for coffee and sugar, and continued west with frontiersman Thomas Fitzpatrick as a guide. Almost at once, a Sioux war party set upon their trail.[44]

Frémont learned later that Fitzpatrick, who commanded wide influence among the Sioux, had negotiated safe passage for the emigrants, but that the Sioux chiefs vowed to destroy the next party of whites to pass through the country—his. Kit Carson expected trouble and said so; he rather ostentatiously made his will at Fort Laramie, with damaging effect on company morale. (Preuss later would accuse Carson of exaggerating Indian dangers "in order to make himself important.") A cooler head, the trader Joseph Bissonette, advised Frémont that there would be little danger if he traveled with an interpreter and two or three old Sioux from the Laramie lodges who could explain their purposes to the war parties. Bissonette, who spoke the Sioux language, offered to accompany the expedition as far as the Red Buttes, 135 miles down the trail.[45]

As it happened, only one man asked for a discharge at Laramie, although Frémont, doubtless imagining Senator Benton's reaction should misadventure befall his son, ordered both young gentlemen to stay behind. The expedition struck tents, saddled the horses, geared up the pack mules, and resumed the westward march on July 21. With Indian alarms fresh in his mind, Frémont contemplated matters of high strategy as the column advanced along the valley of the North Platte beyond present Guernsey, Wyoming, the most beautiful country he had yet seen. As early as 1840, his mentor Poinsett, as war secretary, had recommended three forts at intervals along the Oregon Trail. Frémont judged that frequent shows of military force would be necessary, with Fort Laramie an ideal base of operations for U.S. mounted patrols that could prevent aggressive alliances among the Sioux, Gros Ventre, and Cheyenne and "keep the Oregon road through the valley of the Sweetwater and South Pass of the mountains constantly open."[46]

The parched and burned landscape of yellow grass and withered artemisia confirmed reports of severe drought. Springs had dried up, and the horses began to suffer from thirst. A party of Sioux—friendly, as it happened—warned that there would be no water, not a blade of grass, no buffalo, and plagues of grasshoppers in the country ahead. Despite this bleak forecast, Frémont jotted down a set of optimistic notes for travelers. He found the road running west from Laramie, generally regarded as the most difficult stretch east of the mountains, better than he expected, "without any difficult ascents to overcome." It was poorly marked, though, and in places could only be inferred from the absence of artemisia bushes. The expedition made steady progress and, contrary to Sioux report, met with plenty of buffalo.[47]

The Frémont party reached the Red Buttes on July 29 without incident. ("One cannot count on these windbags," the saturnine Preuss complained. "One day they talk as if there were little or no danger; the next they talk as if we should expect nothing but killing and murder.") Here the Pathfinder decided to leave the trail where it crossed over to the Sweetwater and continue along the Platte valley in search of better grass. He soon encountered evidence of famine after all: the poles of discarded Sioux lodges and the sun-bleached skeletons of horses, evidently destroyed for food. With Carson as guide, the party struck overland for the Sweetwater and encamped on the night of August 1 below Independence Rock. There they found the wooden racks the White-Hastings party had used for jerking buffalo meat, as well as a bullet-pierced pair of bloody trousers, suggesting the Sioux had exacted at least partial revenge after all.[48]

The snowpeaks of the Wind River Range showed themselves intermittently during a succession of overcast, showery days. A long, gradual ascent carried Frémont to the Continental Divide on August 8. "We were obliged to watch very carefully to find the place at which we had reached the culminating point," he wrote.[49] Here, then, 950 miles from the mouth of the Kansas River, was the South Pass of Robert Stuart and Jedediah Smith. The much-quoted description in Frémont's report would salve the anxieties of a generation of overland travelers:

"From the impression on my mind at this time, and subsequently on our return, I should compare the elevation which we surmounted at the pass, to the ascent of the capitol hill from the avenue, at Washington. It will be seen that it in no way resembles the places to which the term is commonly applied—nothing of the gorge-like character and winding ascents of the Allegany passes in America, nothing of the Great St. Bernard and Simplon passes in Europe."[50]

Perhaps it was a sense of anticlimax that led Frémont to plot his excursion to the high peaks. Certainly the timing seemed inauspicious; the spirits of the people were low and stocks of provisions lower still for a party that on standard rations consumed two buffalo every twenty-four hours—only two or three pounds of coffee, a little macaroni, barklike slabs of jerked meat. The dawn of August 10 broke clear, pure, and cold, with a sunrise temperature of 33 degrees Fahrenheit. ("The cook's washrags are frozen stiff," Preuss reported.) A short climb led to "a most beautiful lake, set like a gem in the mountains," three miles long, of irregular width and evidently quite deep. Frémont decided to leave ten men encamped on the shore of today's

Fremont Lake and strike out for the summits with the remainder and fifteen of the best mules.[51]

He had reached that "newer world" of his imagination at last, a region that mountain men, hunters, traders, and certainly missionaries had never penetrated. He packed the barometer, thermometer, sextant, compasses, and spyglass and set out through steeply sloping country thickly grown with balsam pine. The course led up a narrow valley that ended at another tarn. Leaving the mules, provisions, and all but three or four of the men behind, he pushed on toward what he perceived to be the highest summit of the range. Reaching the tree line, with patches of snow in the lee of the rocks, they came to a third lake late in the afternoon, and Frémont pitched camp there. (Frémont dubbed it Island Lake; it lies eighteen miles in an air line from present-day Pinedale, Wyoming.) Calculating the altitude at ten thousand feet above the Gulf of Mexico, Frémont set about observing and taking notes: alpine flowers abloom but animal life sparse, only a nondescript bird the size of a sparrow, and a tiny furred animal with short ears and no tail.

The hunters returned empty-handed. Frémont blamed lack of food, fatigue, and possibly the altitude for the severe headaches and vomiting that now afflicted him. These debilities left him short-tempered and he quarreled with Carson, whom he accused of setting too brisk a pace. Preuss complained bitterly of the roughness of the track, his aging legs, the cold, and gnawing hunger. "No supper, no breakfast, little or no sleep—who can enjoy climbing a mountain under these circumstances?" he wrote, with understatement for a change. Wandering off from the others, Preuss lost his footing and tumbled two hundred feet down the icy crust of the mountainside. He escaped the ordeal with nothing worse than two light bruises, "one on my right arm and one on my arse."[52] Frémont, meantime, launched an assault on the summit, but headache and altitude sickness forced him to suspend it. He sent one of the men back to the base camp for blankets and provisions and, after another cold night in camp along the edge of the snowfields, resolved to try again in the morning.

"Well, Mr. Preuss," he said, "I hope we shall, after all, empty a glass on top of the mountain."[53]

At daybreak, Frémont asked for volunteers. A couple of men agreed reluctantly to accompany him. Preuss had to go, of course, to take the instrument readings. So, too, did Johnny Auguste Janisse, "who," according to Preuss, "as a mulatto, had no privilege to choose." Frémont led them along a rough, slippery defile that rose to three small, brilliantly green lakes. They turned the mules loose in a patch of good grass nearby and pushed on toward the summit on foot. "This time," wrote Frémont, alluding to his rather hysterical climb of the day before, "like experienced travelers, we did not press ourselves, but climbed leisurely, sitting down so soon as we found breath beginning to fail." The more deliberate method seemed to answer, and after a hard climb he approached the crest, a three-foot-wide slab of granite canted at a slope of twenty degrees. One at a time, he allowed each man to squat on this perch, then mounted the barometer in the snow, drove a ramrod into a crevice of rock, and unfurled a home-made flag, alternating red and white stripes with a hand-drawn eagle and stars on a white background, "to wave in the breeze where never flag waved before."[54] From Preuss's measurements, Frémont reported an altitude of 13,570 feet above the gulf and concluded—quite wrongly—that he had scaled the highest peak of the Rocky Mountains.

At this moment of triumph a bumblebee flew in from the east and landed on the knee of one of the men. Frémont invested the incident with enormous symbolic importance. In the arrogant way of his human kind, he had imagined himself to have passed beyond the farthest frontier of animated life. "It was a strange place," he wrote in the expedition *Report,* "the icy rock and the highest peak of the Rocky Mountains, for a lover of warm sunshine and flowers, and we pleased ourselves with the idea that he was the first of his species to cross the mountain barrier, a solitary pioneer to foretell the advance of civilization." Frémont had the creature seized, pressed into a large book of botanical collections, and carried down the mountain as a souvenir. Two days later, on August 17, he issued the order to turn homeward.[55]

THE FRÉMONT EXPEDITION reached the junction of the Platte and the Missouri on the last day of September. The camp awakened the next morning to the tinkling of cowbells, confirmation of a return to "civilization." Four weeks' easy travel brought Frémont to Washington, where he reported to Colonel Abert on October 29, 1842, and settled in again with Jessie as she neared term with their first child. She had been anxious, fearful that he would be unable to return in time for her lying in. Altogether it had been a difficult summer, with her mother gravely ill and only now beginning a slow recovery from the effects of a paralytic stroke, and her father depressed and in near-despair about his wife's prognosis. Frémont evidently expunged these trials from his memory. Anyhow, he made no mention of them in the *Memoirs*.

"I found the family well," he wrote.[56]

Jessie Frémont safely delivered a daughter, Elizabeth, to be called Lily, on November 15. Jessie recovered from the rigors of childbirth in time to rescue her husband from a severe case of writer's block. Overwrought, in a state bordering panic, he suffered again from the old mountain debilities: headaches, nosebleeds. "The horseback life, the sleep in the open air, had unfitted Mr. Frémont for the indoor work of writing," Jessie recalled tactfully. She finally offered to help him get started on the expedition report. "I was let to try," she wrote, "and thus slid into my most happy life work." Her intervention proved decisive. Frémont called her his "amanuensis," but she seems to have been far more than that. Frémont partisans portray Jessie as a mere stenographer; to Jessie's champions, she is a coauthor at the least. Her admirers have a point. Nothing in Frémont's surviving correspondence hints at more than modest literary skills.[57]

With a Benton servant detailed to look after the child, the Frémonts began work each morning at nine o'clock, Jessie seated at a writing table, her husband, notes in hand, pacing the room restlessly. He delivered a narrative monologue, consulting the notes from time to time, often lost in a sort of haze of recent but kaleidoscopic memory. Jessie shaped the contours of the story, exploited the dramatic elements of the experience, played up the color and exoticism of a country known to a comparative few. Sometimes Frémont studied his wife's face as he dictated, "the slightest dissent confirming my own doubt," he recalled, "or the pleased expression which represents the popular impression of a mind new to the subject." In fact, as Benton's daughter, Jessie knew a great deal about the subject, and her father's expansionist attitude found its way prominently into the report.[58]

While the Frémonts pegged away at the text, Preuss prepared the maps. At Benton's suggestion he worked up a separate series for the overlanders' use, "a guidebook in atlas form," according to Frémont, breaking down the daily stages on the Oregon Trail and clearly marking campsites with grass and firewood. The botanist John Torrey assembled a catalogue of plant specimens, and Frémont collated astronomical and meteorological observations. With these appendices he delivered the manuscript to Abert on March 1, 1843. Benton's Senate colleague Lewis Linn arranged for a government printing with a thousand extra copies, launching Frémont's famous first expedition report on its influential journey.[59] Newspapers excerpted it widely, translators rendered it into foreign languages, scientists welcomed its data, and influential periodicals praised it to the skies.

"Few books have been recently read (in this reading age) with more avidity than Frémont's reports," observed the enthusiastically imperialistic *United States Magazine and Democratic Review*. "There is in them a singular mixture of science, and wild and romantic adventure, equally captivating to all classes of society."[60]

The Frémonts' lively prose captivated the epic poet Henry Wadsworth Longfellow along with the rest. "Well, another week gone. It has given me no literary results, but much material," the author of *Evangeline* wrote in his quiet Cambridge study. "Frémont has particularly touched my imagination. What a wild life, and what a fresh kind of existence! But, ah, the discomforts!"[61]

DEBT, DESERTION, AND UNREMITTING PRESSURE from the Mission Board in New York conspired to cast a shadow over the Methodist colony in Oregon. Jason Lee had expanded at too brisk a pace. Dwelling-houses and the Oregon Institute for white children at the new mission at Chemeketa, the Island Milling Company and associated mercantile operations at Willamette Falls in competition with Dr. McLoughlin, and the outlying stations at Clatsop, The Dalles, and Nisqually on Puget Sound were more than the enterprise could afford. Lee's obligations to the Hudson's Bay Company, compounded at 5 percent, and the board's reluctance or inability to discharge the debt and increase the subsidy left the mission in a precarious position. And with the steady influx of whites into the Willamette Valley, the Indian population, the mission's supposed *raison d'etre*, had declined to near-insignificance.

"Unless the board send us some goods, or letters of credit, on London the mission will be Bankrupt next year, and then we shall be forced to do, what we have been accused of doing in a paper published at Oahoo, *viz*, all turn *Farmers*," Lee wrote the new Mission Board secretary, Charles Pitman, in the spring of 1842.[62]

Instead of aid, Secretary Pitman delivered a scathing critique of Lee's superintendency. Passing along the board's message, he accused

Jason Lee's Methodist mission house on the Willamette River is shown in this Henry Eld drawing. It formed the rallying point for a growing American presence in the Oregon Country. (Yale Collection of Western Americana, Beinecke Rare Book and Manuscript Library)

Lee of financial mismanagement, of failing to file complete and accurate reports of mission operations; and, perhaps most seriously, of neglecting spiritual work for colony-building. The board, he wrote, lacked the resources to bail out Lee; overall debt approached $50,000 and fund-raising operations were moribund, in part because of the lingering effects of the Panic of 1837 but also because the Oregon mission could not supply or anyway had not supplied the anticipated stream of spiritually uplifting stories about leading the natives out of eternal darkness of the sort that inspired Methodist constituencies to pony up.

"Only let us hear from you frequently, and especially let us hear that the good work of evangelizing the heathen is going on, and we have a text from which we can, in our begging operations, preach successfully," Pitman wrote.[63]

He went on to lay down the law: Lee must "undertake no business or enterprise which will in the least interfere with your appropriate work"; he should submit detailed reports of mission activities and finances at least once a year; and he must in no circumstances exceed the budget the board would set for him—in other words, Lee must no longer pursue the independent economic and political policies that had fostered the development of a substantial American colony in Oregon.[64]

The Lee-Pitman correspondence was curiously one-sided. A letter took many months to reach Lee via the Hudson's Bay Company overland express or by sea. Letters crossed in transit, were delayed in passage, or vanished altogether. Lee complained of the board's haphazard ways of dispatching its correspondence; bags or boxes of mail lay moldering in Oahu storehouses or the holds of company ships for months at a stretch. He complained, too, of the absence of specific guidelines: How many hogs to feed, how many cows to milk were too many for a missionary? How did the board define "appropriate work"? Lee knew that unfavorable reports of his stewardship had reached Pitman and the board, if only through Elijah White. Lee had a fairly thorough grasp of the particulars long before Pitman's letter came into his hands. Somewhat disingenuously, he continued to assert that, despite vicissitudes, prospects for the Oregon mission remained bright.

Wrote Lee, "Your exertions Beloved Brethren have not been misdirected as some have judged and though your expectations may not have been fully met, yet the day of eternity will reveal the good effected here in Oregon will ten thousand times repay the labors and expense of this mission."[65]

To add insult, Pitman tipped Lee to the impending arrival of his old enemy Dr. White. Traveling in advance of the emigrant train, White reached the Whitman mission at Waiilatpu on September 9. Elements of the divided caravan straggled into Waiilatpu over the next ten days. With provisions scarce on the concluding stages of the journey, the overlanders had reached the end of their endurance. "Mr. Smith & family Mr. Lovejoy and several other Americans arrived today," Mary Gray recorded in her diary. "Mr. S said they were starving, wanted to buy food." The mission sold Smith a quantity of flour, accepting a dollar and the promise of another later; Mrs. Gray gave him butter and cheese before seeing his lean and hungry party off for the Willamette. Her husband returned from the Methodist mission two days later to inform her that they, too, would soon be on the wing for the Willamette colony. After six years of quarreling with the Whitmans and Spaldings, the splenetic Gray finally gave up his evangelical calling. He accepted an offer from Jason Lee to build and superintend the Oregon Institute.[66]

White pushed on down the Columbia to Vancouver. Bearing his U.S. warrant as Indian subagent, White nourished an ambition to become de facto governor of the American colony. While welcoming White as a representative of the United States, the settlers were not, however, inclined to grant him an expanded role—mainly, suggests Frances Fuller Victor, because of Lee's enmity toward him. The mission superintendent "still controlled the majority of American minds in the Willamette Valley," she asserted, and he quietly directed the mission's "determined and often underhanded opposition" to White's efforts to assert control.[67]

"Dr. White has arrived," Lee wrote Pitman bleakly in mid-October. The symptoms of ague were upon him, he had no fire in the room (an economy perhaps meant to impress the board with his frugal management of mission resources), and his fingers were so cold he could barely steer his pen across the foolscap. Somehow Lee found the strength to report that White, to his surprise, had been fulsome in his efforts at reconciliation. Lee responded coolly, insisting that White withdraw the accusations and insinuations against him. This White readily agreed to do, perhaps because he sensed he had mortally wounded Lee and that his removal would be only a matter of time, or possibly because he sought to neutralize Lee's opposition to his, White's, political aims. Lee agreed that they would "agitate the subject no more" in Oregon. He also informed Pitman that he intended to arrange a passage home to chase away the "dark cloud" on his character.[68]

The tide set strongly against Jason Lee in the year 1842. Lucy Thomson Lee died in March three weeks after delivering their daughter, leaving him a widower for a second time. "You wished me to see the grave of my Dear Maria before I married again," he wrote his first wife's mother. "I can now look upon two graves, and reflect that I have lived in perfect peace and harmony with the inmates of both, and that I am now standing *alone,* having no one to share my sorrows or participate in my griefs."[69] Bereaved, despondent, his health beginning to fail, he had to confront, too, the reality that missionary colleagues, one after another, were proving to be men of little faith.

David Leslie and John Richmond, among others, concluded finally that there were too few Indians about to justify their presence in Oregon; they charged, too, that Lee's secular efforts ill became a missionary. Leslie and Richmond applied for a discharge and passage home—another financial burden on Lee. Skeptical of the mission's purpose from the outset, Richmond simply abandoned the Nisqually post. (Not long after he departed, the mission house burned to the ground; Indians were suspected of setting the fire.) Richmond also hinted broadly that he harbored complaints he could make against Lee when he reached New York, if anyone troubled to ask him for his views. Leslie pleaded the cause of his three motherless little girls, but in the end he, too, decided that such scattered bands of hapless natives as remained in the Willamette Valley were not worth his trouble.

Perhaps only Henry K. W. Perkins at Wascopam station at The Dalles continued fully to share Lee's faith and vision. There, at the trading seasons, Indians still assembled in large numbers to offer a field for his labors. Perkins regarded the defectors as little better than agents of the Dark One. "'To save is next to create,' and if it be so, to neglect to save is next to destroy, and who of us are willing to take upon us the guilt of destroying the heathen?" he wrote Pitman. Richmond and others were only too plainly willing to run that risk. Richmond put the natives of Nisqually out of his mind and served out his last days as a missionary at the Clatsop station, waiting for a homebound ship to emerge from the mists off the Columbia bar.[70]

The arrival of the White-Hastings caravan in the autumn of 1842 presented Lee with both an opportunity and a threat. More than a hundred new citizens would require provisions, shelter, and supplies—custom for the mission's mercantile operation at the Willamette Falls. Lee's vision of making the mission self-sustaining—and freeing it from the fetters of the Hudson's Bay Company *and* the Mission Board—now seemed possible of realization. At the same time, the overlanders were not missionaries. There were free white men among them, some fifty men age eighteen or older, who would demand a say in the colony's affairs, and they were unlikely to be as deferential to the Methodist mission as the longer-term settlers had been. The influx both intensified the Methodists' rivalry with McLoughlin at the Willamette Falls and accelerated the move toward more permanent forms of government in the settlements.

Turning up late in the year with little more than the clothes on their backs, the emigrants naturally looked to the Hudson's Bay Company for assistance. The White-Hastings party formed the core of what would become the Willamette Falls settlement of Oregon City. McLoughlin supplied provisions on credit out of Fort Vancouver stocks and hired the new arrivals as laborers to improve his Oregon City claim. Under his direction a substantial community sprang up during the winter of 1842–1843. By the spring, Oregon City had become a busy townlet of thirty or more sturdy structures, among them a McLoughlin gristmill that presumably would drive the Methodists' Island Milling Company from the field.

These developments intensified the land dispute between Lee and McLoughlin. McLoughlin assiduously protected his commercial monopoly and decreed that no one could settle at Oregon City without his permission. Lee and the agent in charge of the mission store and mill, George Abernethy, strove to break McLoughlin's grip on the colony. The mission operations were intended, Lee said, to "bring in other vessels besides the H.B. Co.'s" to the landing just downstream of the falls. Methodist Alvan Waller believed that the mission and allied American farms could supply the Sandwich Islands and other export markets with grain, salmon, and timber—a lucrative business for individuals and the institution. The falls site seemed "destined to be the great emporium of the interior of the country," wrote Waller.[71]

Using White's rival Lansford Hastings as his agent, McLoughlin now industriously began to market building lots in Oregon City to the newcomers. Lee vigorously protested this encroachment—political *and* real-estate claim-jumping, in his view. "I made enquiries as to the *kind* of deed he gave, and told him very pleasantly, that I thought it assuming rather high grounds for a private individual to give deeds to land in neutral Territory to which the Indian title had not yet been extinguished," Lee wrote White in April 1843. "In short to do what no Government could do. I could not conceive that his deeds would be of the least use to anyone." All the same, Indian title or no, Lee authorized Waller to go ahead with construction of a Methodist chapel in Oregon City. The 1842 emigrants carried word of Missouri senator Linn's pending Oregon land bill with its promise of 640 acres to each settler, giving Lee a reasonable certainty that government—and he meant the U.S. government—eventually would confirm the Methodist claim.

"Let the Church build a Chapel upon the ground, and it shall have it—without money and without Deed," Lee wrote Waller. "[The mission] should not pay Dr. McLoughlin Ten Dollars for a quit claim

deed to every few feet square we needed at the Falls for our Missionary purposes, as I considered his Deeds good for nothing and especially as we were the first residents at the Falls."[72]

The campaign for a provisional government raised delicate issues.
Mission and lay settlers sought secure titles to their land and improvements, sureties only a sovereign authority could grant. At the
same time, Lee and his mission colleagues intended to keep the
ambitious apostate Elijah White out of political power—in Mrs. Victor's phrase, they "quietly used their influence to snub his pretensions without openly working against him." McLoughlin, too, seemed
doubtful about White, regarding him as "active, forward and very pre-
sumptuous." This may partly explain the doctor's listless response to
the Americans' political schemes. However tenuously, White represented the United States. McLoughlin preferred an independent
colonial government to a formal U.S. role—and believed most of the
settlers did, too.[73]

The Americans initiated the preliminaries of their coup in the
winter of 1843 at two "wolf meetings," so called because they ostensibly dealt with wild animal attacks on livestock, an issue on which
U.S. and British nationals could unite. The recently arrived William
Gray took a leading part in these sessions. The first met at the newly
opened Oregon Institute (Gray had taken up residence there) in Chemeketa in early February. The settlers fixed a bounty for the killing
of wolves and other predators, then arranged a second session, for
March 6, at the farm of Joseph Gervais, a long-time ally of the Methodists. Taking up the real business of the "Wolf Organization," this
meeting issued a call for a mass gathering to "consider the propriety
of taking measures for the civil and military protection of this colony."
Gray, for one, loathed and mistrusted the Hudson's Bay Company
and Roman Catholic priests and communicants with roughly equal
intensity; an American settler government would form a bulwark
against foreign and papish domination. The session adjourned after
appointing a twelve-man committee, dominated by Americans and
with a strong mission influence, to pursue the larger issue.[74]

Within a week or so, a third meeting convened at the Willamette
Falls. Lansford Hastings, probably acting on McLoughlin's behalf,
introduced a motion for Oregon independence. A majority evidently
favored the resolution, but reconsidered under Methodist pressure
and went on to set the agenda for a meeting of all the settlers at

Champoeg on May 2. In the meantime, mission interests quietly backed what came to be known as the Shortess petition, the latest expression of settler grievances and a renewed plea for U.S. sovereignty. Robert Shortess, who had arrived in Oregon with Thomas Farnham in 1840, and George Abernethy evidently collaborated in drawing up the petition, which claimed that the Hudson's Bay Company had "driven Americans from their homes" and that "a Doctor McLoughlin, an English subject, was in the habit of making and selling deeds for land which belonged to the United States alone." Shortess collected some sixty-five signatures, though not those of Lee and Abernethy, who refused to sign out of fear it would damage their relations with the company.[75]

White openly opposed the Shortess diatribe, probably because he recognized the mission influence behind it and figured it would advance the mission cause. "The gentlemen of this company have been fathers and fosterers of the colony, ever encouraging peace, industry and good order; and have sustained a character for hospitality and integrity too well established to be easily shaken," White wrote the U.S. commissioner of Indian affairs in defense of McLoughlin and associates. Characteristically, McLoughlin responded by simply refusing to have any dealings with his critics.[76]

By some reports, a head count showed 102 men present at Champoeg on May 2, about equally divided between Americans and French Canadians. The Wolf Organization committee recommended provisional rule until the United States should establish a territorial government for Oregon. The Americans overcame the opposition of Canadians loyal to McLoughlin by the narrowest of margins, after a confused vote in which a division of the house revealed that a bare majority of those present approved the motion. The meeting went on to elect a supreme judge, a treasurer, magistrates, constables, and a legislative committee charged with drafting a code of laws for the colony.[77]

The code-writing committee convened in May and June at the granary of the old Methodist mission. It divided the colony into four districts, established a system for making and recording land claims, limited the maximum claim to 640 acres, and introduced a novel form of taxation by volunteer subscription. The Methodists certainly were responsible for the provision that barred settlers from holding claims on town properties or other potential mercantile or manufacturing sites—a thrust at McLoughlin's Oregon City venture—but exempted "any claim of any mission of a religious character" from the general prohibition.[78]

The final version contained two key components: Based as it was on the Northwest Ordinance of 1787, the law code banned slavery in Oregon; it also claimed for the provisional government jurisdiction of the whole of Oregon until the United States should come into possession of the country—ignoring British claims to any part of the territory. Taken together, the components were a sharp check to McLoughlin. The mission and its allies smote the doctor hip and thigh. They evidently did not pause to reflect on the fact that their colony almost certainly would not have survived without McLoughlin, whose generosity and sense of fair play they repaid with the assault on his own interests. As Mrs. Victor suggests, McLoughlin consistently underestimated the cunning and determination of the Americans, "who though sometimes dressed in skins possessed the faculty of making themselves masters of whatsoever destiny fortune laid upon them."[79]

Most observers detect Jason Lee's influence behind the coup that brought the Oregon provisional government into being on July 5, 1843. The evidence is circumstantial, for so far as is known, Lee hardly appeared in the matter. He did not cast a vote at the Champoeg meeting. True, Robert Shortess and William Gray, aggressive promoters of the new government, might be regarded as representing mission views. Lee's longtime ally Gervais, however, voted against the scheme. Possibly Lee held himself aloof because he suspected that a settler-dominated government would meddle in mission affairs, even though its advocates had gone out of their way to write a promission clause into the land claim section of the law code.

Lee's troubles with the Mission Board, and perhaps with his conscience, preoccupied him all through the spring. Where, in all the bustle over land claims, commercial monopolies, and law codes, did the poor benighted Indians figure in? And just as the political battle lines began to form, John Frost became the latest of the missionaries to ask for a discharge, partly owing to a breakdown of his health but mostly because he, too, had concluded that his "services as a minister of the gospel were not needed in this country."[80] Even so, Lee continued to profess his belief in the enterprise, even as his actions suggested he had long since abandoned hope of any great harvest of souls.

"Some dark clouds seemed to hang over the prosperity of this mission for two or three years past," Lee wrote Charles Pitman in the early spring of 1843. "Our afflictions have been many, and *severe*. . . . I have been looking for better days, and I firmly believe they are not far distant. I never *have* despaired of the *ultimate success* of the Oregon Mission, and I trust I never shall. The fire that has been kindled here may be *small*, but that spark which lighted that fire was of *heavenly* origin, and will not be easily extinguished.

"Oregon is still of infinite importance as a field for Missionary operations among the Indians," Lee went on. "All that is wanting is a proper system of operation and the right sort of duly qualified Missionaries."[81]

The Mission Board remained dubious. Everything Pitman had seen and heard suggested a severe cost-benefit imbalance, and to such a degree that he now threatened to send out an auditor to examine Lee's accounts, spiritual and secular. The mission sustained twenty-six white clergy and lay members, nineteen white children, and four Hawaiian laborers. Two dozen Indians—thirteen boys and eleven girls—boarded at the mission manual labor school (as distinct from the whites-only institute)—"native Elishas," Lee rather grandly dubbed them; he counted upon them to go out someday to do his work for him, elevating "their degraded countrymen to the rank of *civilized* and *christianized* men." Fewer than two hundred natives remained in the vicinity, taking salmon in season and digging roots in the cruel months after their immemorial fashion, and even Lee conceded that "we have no evidence that one soul has been converted." The Mission Board's investment in Oregon exceeded $100,000. Seven years after Lee's arrival on the Willamette, Pitman demanded a reckoning.[82]

"How many Missionary stations have you in Oregon? What are their names, locations, distances from each other, and the distances of each from the Willamette Station? What portion of the year at home? How many schools? How many Indian children in our schools? What are the spiritual prospects of the Oregon Mission generally, and of each station particularly? Do the Indians connected with your various stations hold their numbers, or are they gradually wasting away?"[83]

Pitman probably knew the answers already, or anyway could guess at them. Elijah White, David Leslie, and other disaffected ex-missionaries had done their work. Charles Wilkes's scalding accounts of missionary indifference to the "miserable remnants" of the coastal tribes had been widely circulated. Still, Pitman wanted a candid appraisal from Jason Lee. Dr. Whitman of the rival Presbyterian mission had recently returned to the United States and—much to Pitman's chagrin—carried no dispatches from the Willamette addressed to him or to the board.

MARCUS WHITMAN HAD DECIDED ABRUPTLY in September 1842 to assay a difficult late-autumn crossing of the Rockies. He "has about concluded to start next Monday to go to the United States," Mrs. Whitman wrote her sister offhandedly, as though he were merely dropping down to Vancouver for supplies. Narcissa made something of a mystery of the reason, too, explaining only that "the missionary cause in this country calls him home." In fact Whitman had just received orders from his sponsors, the American Board of Commissioners for Foreign Missions in Boston, to close up the station at Waiilatpu, join the Walkers and the Eelses at Tshimakain in the remote Spokan country, and send the Spaldings and William Gray home. Six years of discord and disaffection among the Presbyterians in Oregon—the Mission Board characterized the situation there as "painful & humiliating" for the mission cause—had finally worked their dolorous result.[84]

Whitman summoned Walker, Eels, and Spalding to an urgent meeting at Waiilatpu on September 26. They agreed after two days of parsing the board's letter that Whitman would journey overland to Boston and appeal for a reversal of the decision; he would ask the board, too, to reinforce the mission and promote the migration of Christian settlers to Oregon. Five days later, Whitman set out on horseback with 1842 migrant A. J. Lovejoy, bound for Fort Hall and South Pass. He hoped to reach St. Louis by about the first of December, "if he is not detained by the cold, or hostile Indians," Narcissa wrote her parents, and then push on to Washington, D.C., and Boston.[85]

His departure left Mrs. Whitman alone and anxious. Tensions with the Cayuses had been on the rise for more than a year, a compound of cultural misunderstanding, conflict over resources, and the increasing pressure of white settlement. Some two dozen migrants, the Oregon offshoot of the Bidwell-Bartleson caravan, had stopped at Waiilatpu to refit and reprovision in the autumn of 1841. Elijah White's much larger party passed through in 1842. "There is every reason to suppose that there will be at no distant day a numerous white population," Elkanah Walker wrote the Mission Board secretary,

David Greene, shortly after the White party moved on to the Willamette.[86] Large-scale stock-raising, farming, and timber enterprises would further disrupt the Cayuse social and economic order. What Walker saw from backcountry Tshimakain the Cayuses could certainly see from the Waiilatpu mission, which by the autumn of 1842 had become a way station for Oregon-bound emigrants.

"Doubtless every year will bring more and more into this country," Narcissa Whitman predicted. "We have probably seen our most quiet time."[87]

Members of the Wilkes exploring party had commented on testy missionary-Indian relations after their call at Waiilatpu in the summer of 1841. The Cayuses turned their horses loose to graze in the Whitman grainfields. They demanded payment for timber Whitman felled and rent for mission plowlands. Whitman debated the point with a Cayuse named Tilokaikt. "He said that this was his land and that he grew up here and that his horses were only eating the growth of the soil, and demanded of me what had I ever given him for the land," Whitman wrote Greene. The tribe resented Whitman's rules barring free entry to the mission house. Cayuses threatened to kill mission livestock and burn the Waiilatpu mill, Whitman's pride. On at least two occasions an angry Cayuse struck Whitman; he turned the other cheek, a gesture the Indians probably misinterpreted. Matters came to a head when several Cayuses—"a horde of lawless savages," in Whitman's words—broke into the house brandishing hammers and war clubs. The leader insisted as the price of peace "that we would not shut any of our doors against them." Whitman replied that he wrote the rules and expected the Indians to obey them. The next day, the Sabbath, as it happened, roving Cayuses broke mission windows and scattered the livestock.[88]

The Whitmans attributed the troubles to a few disaffected younger Indians, meddlesome Roman Catholic priests, and the increasing availability of ardent spirits. Whatever the cause, they appealed for aid to Archibald McKinlay, who had succeeded Pierre Pambrun as the Hudson's Bay Company agent at Fort Walla Walla. McKinlay delivered the patented company harangue, and the Cayuse leaders vowed to restore order in the tribe. "I then told them that I was very willing to blot from my memory their dogly conduct and that I was sure you would do likewise," he wrote Whitman. This restored calm, but Narcissa's apprehensions returned in full force during her husband's fre-

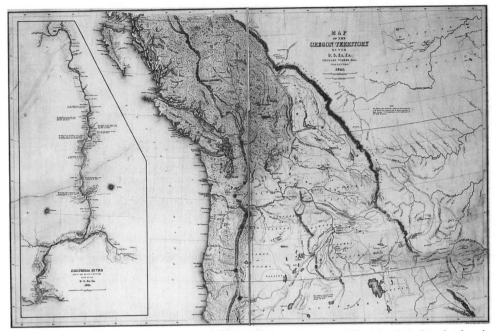

The Wilkes Exploring Expedition produced this map of the Oregon Territory based on land and Columbia River surveys of 1841. (Library of Congress)

quent absences from the mission. "Jane, I wish you were here to sleep with me, I am such a timid creature about sleeping alone that sometimes I suffer considerably," she wrote her sister during one of Whitman's tours abroad, a visit to Tshimakain to attend Mary Walker in childbirth. Apprehension about the Cayuses doubtless contributed to Narcissa's growing obsession with her physical health. Something of a *malade imaginaire*, she complained regularly of headaches; of stomach troubles; and of having to use spectacles to read, write, or sew.[89]

Events of the night of October 6–7, four days after Whitman's departure for Fort Hall, upset a tenuous equilibrium at Waiilatpu. The sound of someone fumbling with the latch to her room awakened Narcissa at about midnight. She lay tense, listening. The door opened slightly. She sprang out of the bed, crossed the room, and threw her full weight against the batten. The intruder pushed hard from the other side; she screamed frantically for the servants. Suddenly the pressure on the door ceased. "Had the ruffian persisted I do not know what I should have done," she wrote her husband the next day. "I did not think of the war club, but I thought of the poker." With trembling, cold hands she lit a candle, returned to the warmth of the bed, and thanked her Heavenly Father for deliverance. When sleep would not come, she insisted that one of the servants bring his bedding into the kitchen and pass the remainder of the night within call.[90]

Narcissa's language hints strongly that she regarded the incident as an attempted rape. It is difficult to assess this. Narcissa's biographer suggests that she may have invented the break-in.[91] Certainly McKinlay at Fort Walla Walla took her at her word, insisting she leave Waiilatpu as soon as practicable. He came himself with the wagon and escorted her to the safety of the company post, which they reached on October 12. In the aftermath, all her physical complaints returned. She dosed herself with powder of quinine and calomel and kept to her bed. For some reason her relations with McKinlay and his wife were stilted ("they know not how to make one as easy and comfortable as Mr. Pambrun used to"), so she accepted gratefully when an invitation arrived from Henry and Elvira Perkins to spend the winter at the Methodist mission at The Dalles.[92]

Settling in comfortably at Wascopam despite evil associations with The Dalles, where (as she reminded her parents) she had fought her epic battle with fleas in 1836, Narcissa soon formed a warm feminine circle with Mrs. Perkins; Daniel Lee's wife, Maria; and Laura Brewer, the wife of the mission farmer. More disturbing news soon reached her there: the Cayuses had fired the mill at Waiilatpu, whether by carelessness or design no one seemed to know. Along with the building and machinery, more than two hundred bushels of wheat, corn, and flour were incinerated. "The sensible part of the Cayuses feel the loss deeply," Mrs. Whitman wrote, "and they will feel it more when they want their wheat ground next fall." She saw in the arson, if that is what it was, not a protest of white incursion or a warning to the missionaries, but a lesson for the Indians. In the fall, the return to the old ways of grinding corn would remind them of what they had lost, and make them a better people.[93]

Reports of the Indian troubles brought Elijah White, the federal Indian agent, to Wascopam to hear the details of the Waiilatpu incidents firsthand from Narcissa. Rumors reached him, too, of difficulties with the Nez Perces at the Spalding mission at Lapwai. He resolved to journey to the upper country and lay down the law to the tribes. With the Whitman mission abandoned for now and the Cayuses scattered to their wintering quarters, he decided to call at Lapwai first, after insisting that Narcissa accompany him to Waiilatpu when the Indians returned in the spring. He also conscripted Cornelius Rogers, a former member of the Presbyterian mission who had resettled in Oregon City, to travel with him as guide and interpreter.

Nearly everyone liked Rogers, and he had done rather well for himself since leaving the Presbyterians out of uncertainty about whether the mission would continue to support him now that he had married one of David Leslie's older daughters and become a family man. With the arrival of the 1842 caravan and the boom at the Willamette Falls, Rogers's services as a builder were in great demand. "It was only by almost main force that I was brought on this trip," he wrote Walker, with whom he remained on cordial terms. "I have more than two thousand dollars worth of work lying nearly or quite idle because I am absent." But White insisted, and the affable Rogers could not disappoint him.[94]

They left Oregon City on November 15, paused at Waiilatpu to meet with the few Cayuses who remained in the area, and reached Lapwai in early December after a difficult journey—intense cold, and the Columbia choked with ice in places. White called a mass meeting of the Nez Perces; delivered a scolding; and, John McLoughlin reported dryly, "spoke to them of religion and advised them to become farmers." He also instructed the tribes to select a head chief who would be responsible for policing a new code of laws that would protect the whites and their property. The Indians resisted at first, assuming he had come to regulate the price of beaver. "We soon undeceived them," Rogers wrote. "We hope good will come out of our visit." By December 13 the business was done. The Nez Perces agreed to White's reforms and installed a princeling named Ellis as head chief.[95]

White and Rogers returned to The Dalles in the last week of December. Mrs. Whitman at once launched into a campaign to persuade Rogers to escort her to White's meeting with the Cayuses in the spring and perhaps to stay on at the mission as a teacher. Noncommittal, eager to return to his lucrative building contracts, Rogers left after a few days for Oregon City with White, his wife, and several others. On the way, one of those sudden, unaccountable calamities that were such a feature of life in a new country stilled his cheerful voice forever. As Rogers and his companions cleared the portage just above the main cascade at the Willamette Falls, the current grabbed the canoe, slewed it around, and shot it into the suction of the falls. Vessel and passengers plunged over the precipice into the swirling river below. Rogers, his wife, her younger sister, and two others were drowned.

The news struck Narcissa a heavy blow. She felt as though she had lost a brother. Soon, too, ominous intelligence reached her from the upper country. The Indians had heard that Whitman would return in the autumn with a large party of American settlers. White's embassy, as it happened, had irritated rather than soothed the tribes. Never much of a diplomat, White managed to leave the Indians with the impression that the whites meant to send a punitive expedition into their country. "All decisive measures and language used to them they construe into threats, and say war is declared and they intend to be prepared," she wrote. Narcissa tended to blame the Cayuses for the mischief. Their wealth, especially in horses, made them haughty and insolent, she thought.[96]

Anticipating a possible return to Waiilatpu for the summer, Mrs. Whitman came up to Fort Walla Walla in April with the Hudson's Bay Company's spring flotilla. Friction with the Cayuses seemed to have abated, she thought, with Dr. McLoughlin's promise that the British had no intention of making war on the tribes. "This relieves them considerably," she observed. "Now their fear is the Americans. They have been led to believe that deceitful measures are being taken to rob them of their land, to kill them off."[97] The more percipient among the Cayuses recognized the truth of this. As Narcissa wrote the lines, her husband was in Westport, Kansas, preparing to cross the Plains with an Oregon-bound caravan of nearly a thousand emigrants—what would be dubbed the Great Migration. Within days, John Frémont would strike out on the second of his great reconnaissances, this one taking him all the way to the Columbia. Within a decade, the scattered remnant of the Cayuses would find themselves utterly dispossessed.

"The signs of the times seem to indicate change in Oregon," Elvira Perkins wrote her friend Mary Walker at Tshimakain. "I hope nothing serious will grow out of the difficulties with the Kaiuse, but I have many fears and apprehensions, there is so much talk about war at present. My nerves are not very firm, and the longer I live among the savages, the more timid I grow."[98]

FRÉMONT REACHED WESTPORT in mid-May with thirty-nine men and the twelve-pounder mountain howitzer that would fire the imagination of young Joaquin Miller. Accompanying him were the saturnine Charles Preuss; a young Washingtonian named Theodore Talbot; the gentleman-traveler Frederick Dwight, bound for China via the Oregon Trail; and eighteen-year-old Jacob Dodson, a freeborn African American former servant of the Bentons. Frémont hired the veteran Thomas Fitzpatrick, who had safely piloted the White-Hastings emigrant caravan through turbulent Sioux country in 1842, as guide for this second reconnaissance. As ever, the vexations of preparing for a long voyage delayed the departure. The expedition set out at last in twelve mule carts and a light wagon on the cold, rainy morning of May 29, spent the thirtieth in camp, and passed the last night of the month in bivouac near the California-bound overland party of Joseph B. Chiles.

This time, to avoid traffic on the well-traveled Oregon Trail, Frémont planned to vary the route, following the valleys of the Kansas, Republican, and South Platte rivers to the headwaters of the Arkansas, where he hoped to freelance his way to an opening through the central Rockies. He sought, as he put it, to break a new road to Oregon and California, a southerly route in a more genial climate. Frémont surely realized by now what experienced western travelers had known for some time: the Oregon Trail offered the shortest and most direct route to the Pacific, with the easiest grades and ample water, grass, and buffalo. For the Pathfinder, the chief advantage would consist in cutting loose from the westbound traffic stream with its trains of white-topped wagons almost constantly in view.

Not even the influential *New York Weekly Tribune*, with its blunt warnings of calamity, could deflect this folk movement. "Starvation and the bullets of successive tribes of savages are dangers which the adventurer dares with almost every mile of his progress from Missouri to Oregon," the *Tribune* asserted.[99] The alarm, accompanied by the *Tribune*'s publication of Thomas Farnham's *Travels*, with their account of virtually nonstop dissension, hardship, and peril, sounded too late. Momentum was building even before the introduction of Senator Linn's land bill and the circulation of Frémont's first report, with its description of the easy-as-kiss-my-hand road to the gentle swell of South Pass. Linn's homestead measure had *not* passed (and never would); all the same, the emigrants interpreted it as a guarantee of government protection. The Ashburton Treaty of 1842 settled Anglo-American differences along the Maine boundary but left the Oregon question in abeyance; even so, the American march to the Pacific now seemed unstoppable.

"Hundreds are prepared to start thither with the spring, while hundreds of others are anxiously awaiting the action of Congress in reference to that country, as the signal of their departure," wrote a *Tribune* correspondent from the Iowa territory. "Some have already been to view the country and have returned with a flattering tale of the inducement it holds out. They have painted it to their neighbors in the highest colors. These have told it to others. The Oregon fever has broken out and is now raging like any other contagion."[100]

The Frémont expedition encamped on the night of June 1 near the Kansas ford. Marcus Whitman and his nephew Perrin lay nearby, preparing to attach themselves to the Great Migration, the largest emigrant caravan yet—a thousand men, women, and children; two hundred wagons, and a drove of two thousand cattle. The Presbyterian Mission Board, displeased with Whitman for leaving his post, refused to cover his return expenses. So Whitman and his nephew traveled light, dependent on handouts from travelers for their sustenance, the doctor offering medical aid and his services as a trail guide in return for their daily bread.

"He had nothing to start with but a boiled ham," recalled overlander Daniel Waldo, who sometimes fed Whitman out of his own stocks. "I reckon he expected that ham to last him all the way across. He expected the emigrants to feed him and they did."[101]

Like Frémont, Whitman had been delayed—he had been waiting to start for three weeks while the caravan massed. On the road at last, he expressed satisfaction with his traveling companions—they augured well, he believed, for the future of Oregon. "They appear very willing, and I have no doubt are generally of an enterprising character," he wrote his brother-in-law Edward Prentiss. "My expectations are high for that country. I believe it must become one of the best of countries very soon."[102] He believed, too, that his trip East had secured the future of the Presbyterian mission, though its character would evolve gradually from an outpost among the barbarians into a way station for the right sort of settlers and a stabilizing and civilizing influence on the natives.

Meeting with the board in Boston, Whitman had dealt rather easily with the question of dissension in the mission, persuading the members that "the difficulty between Mr. Spalding and the others was apparently healed," and that relations would improve with the departures of Asa Smith and William Gray. Following Jason Lee's example, Whitman went on to lobby for funding for schools and other institutions that would attract and serve *settlers* primarily. "It is now decided in my mind that Oregon will be occupied by American citizens," he wrote another of his wife's brothers, Galusha Prentiss. "Those who go only open the way for more another year." In winning the reprieve for Waiilatpu he emphasized the combined Catholic/British threat to U.S. interests in Oregon, reinforcing Elkanah Walker's view that without the mission "the whole country would be thrown open to [the papists] & the first influence the settlers to this country would meet would be that of Romanism." In effect, Whitman asked board members to shape the character of the emigration. He requested an additional preacher and five to ten "Christian men" to work the Waiilatpu fields and mills. By precept, the new arrivals would help the Indians become homesteaders; beyond that, they would release the missionaries from the tedium of manual labor. Whitman articulated his vision for the mission's future in a letter to the board sent from Shawnee Mission, Kansas, a couple of days' march along the westward trail.[103]

"We do not ask that you become patrons of emigration to Oregon, but we desire you to use your influence that in connection with all the influx into this country, there may be a good proportion of good men from our own denomination who shall avail themselves of the advantages of the country," he wrote. "We cannot feel it at all just that we are doing nothing while worldly men and papists are doing so much. You will see . . . that the papal effort is designed to convey over the country to the English. I think our greatest hope for having Oregon at least part protestant now lies in encouraging a proper attention of good men to go there while the country is still open."[104]

Beyond agreeing to extend the life of the mission, the board made no promises. Nor did Whitman's discreet lobbying with the government achieve any discernible result. His movements are not traceable in detail, but the evidence suggests that he spent some time in Washington during the winter of 1843; if so, he probably discussed Oregon with senior War Department officials. Whitman endorsed the proposals of Senator Benton and War Secretaries Poinsett and John C. Spencer for the establishment of a chain of government posts along the Oregon Trail to offer travelers aid and protection from Indian attack. He also alerted the War Department to the transcendent significance of sheep, recommending that the government supply the Indians with ovine livestock rather than money for title to their lands.

"I intend to impress the Secretary of War that sheep are more important to Oregon's interest than soldiers," he wrote Galusha Prentiss. "I have written him on the main interests of the Indian country; but I mean still to write a private letter touching some particular interests."[105]

The paths of Whitman and Frémont diverged on the second or third day out. Frémont followed the Kansas River due west in search of the hoped-for new road south of the Oregon Trail. Reaching Vrain's Fort on July 4, he turned south for the Arkansas River; fell in with his 1842 companion Kit Carson, whom he rehired at once as hunter and guide; and doubled back toward Vrain's. The route led over rough, dry ground with the promise of a mineral spring of high local repute along the way. "I believe seltzer water with Rhine wine would taste better to me," Charles Preuss remarked. Young Talbot, meantime, meditated upon the etymology of "Arapaho." "The word means 'side ribs,' or the ribs over the heart," he concluded, "and if an indian would signify to you that he belonged to that nation, he lays his hand upon his left side." (Modern scholarship suggests that Arapaho derives either from a Pawnee word for "trader" or a Kiowa and Spanish word for "ragged and dirty clothing.") Halting only briefly at Vrain's Fort, Frémont ascended what he took to be the Cache la Poudre River in search of an opening through the Front Range. He concluded that "an excellent road may be made with a little trouble" up the narrow valley, then shaped a northwesterly course for the emigrant trace near today's Laramie, Wyoming. A day or two later the party encountered a large red ox, clear evidence he had come upon the overlanders' trail.[106]

Frémont reached the Sweetwater, "our familiar river," east of Devil's Gate on August 9, where more evidence of the Great Migration presented itself: the overlands' heavy wagons had beaten down the artemisia over a broad swath and so pulverized the soil that the slightest breath of breeze stirred up a storm of fine white dust. Whether for amusement or for killing efficiency, Frémont ordered the howitzer into action to slaughter buffalo. Just beyond South Pass, a cow and her calf wandered into camp with further tidings of the migration; she also obliged the mess with an abundance of milk. As the expedition approached the Bear River Valley, the van came upon the fresh grave of one of the emigrants, a victim of the bilious fever.

Horace Greeley's skeptical *Tribune* had foretold this. "This migration of a thousand persons in one body to Oregon wears an aspect of insanity," the newspaper declared. "What seek they?" Good soil, fair climate, schools, churches: all were available in the United States. "For what, then, do they brave the desert, the wilderness, the savage, the snowy precipices of the Rocky Mountains, the weary summer march, the storm-drenched bivouac, and the gnawings of famine? Only to fulfill their destiny.

"We do not believe nine-tenths of them will ever reach Oregon alive."[107]

The evidence of the artemisia suggested that most of the overlanders were still very much alive indeed. For administrative convenience and to quell dissension, the train had divided into two main components: a stripped-down light column, organized for speed and, trailing, the "cow column" with the impedimenta of livestock. Frémont camped the night of August 21 with a party of stragglers—two men, their women, and several children. He could not help but admire the sturdiness of their cattle: they "really looked as well as if they had been all the summer at work on some good farm," he thought.[108] The expedition overtook the main caravan the next day, late in the afternoon. Frémont described a homely pastoral:

"The edge of the wood, for several miles along the river, was dotted with the white covers of emigrant wagons, collected in groups at different camps, where the smokes were rising lazily from the fires, around which the women were occupied in preparing the evening meal, and the children playing in the grass; and herds of cattle, grazing about in the bottom, had an air of quiet security, and civilized comfort, that made a rare sight for a traveler in such a remote wilderness."[109]

One of the migrants confirmed the essence of Frémont's pastoral in a dispatch sent East from "this wild world of hills, antelope and buffalo" that would find its way into the *Tribune* by year's end. "We have come this far with great ease and safety," wrote Peter H. Burnett, "the difficulties of the way not coming up to our anticipations." It was Burnett who reported the death by bilious fever and a second fatality, a five-year-old boy who drowned. Indians had given no trouble. There had been, however, a good deal of argument and one full-blown fight, "fist and scull, on the road—and neither party hurt." As for the roads, they were better, Burnett judged, than any turnpike in the United States.[110]

The caravan councils called for a pause of several days in the Bear River Valley to rest and refit for the most arduous stage of the journey, the crossing of the Snake River Plain and the Blue Mountains of eastern Oregon. Here again it devolved upon Daniel Waldo's turn to feed Marcus Whitman. "I did not like it much, but he was a very energetic man and I liked him for his perseverance," Waldo wrote. Whitman anyhow could earn his passage now. Most experts warned the emigrants against taking wagons beyond Fort Hall. Former missionary turned Oregon Trail consultant P. L. Edwards, for instance, graded parts of the last third of the journey beyond category of difficulty for even an empty wagon. "I should always prefer horses and mules to any other mode of conveyance," Edwards advised in a May 1843 letter in the *St. Louis New Era*. Whitman, however, assured the overlanders that he and the Cayuse guides who would meet them at Fort Hall would lead their vehicles and teams safely through to the Columbia.[111]

"If we would trust him he would see that we reached The Dalles with our wagons," Texas overlander John Zachary recalled.[112]

All this company began to grate on Frémont and his people. "What exploration!" Preuss grumbled. "What monkey business!"[113] Rather than trail along in the emigrants' dust, Frémont here decided to detour south along the Bear River Valley to the Great Salt Lake, an inland sea around which a generation of trappers' tales had formed a legend encrusted with mystery and obscurity. By report, a terrible whirlpool swirled somewhere on the surface, drawing the lake's briny waters to the Pacific through a system of subterranean rivers. Frémont planned to skirt the lake, investigate its possibilities, and rejoin the emigrant road at Fort Hall. By then, late September, he reckoned the trail would be clear of covered wagons, pregnant women, children, drovers, and cattle.

The route traversed a volcanic plain. Provisions were short; Frémont reported that a camas root supplement purchased from a band of Snake Indians produced a mournful effect on the *voyageurs'* digestion. The landscape, here some five thousand feet above sea level, took on the appearance of autumn, with "crisped and yellow plants and dried-up grasses." A rare bleached buffalo skull heightened the effect of barrenness. Preuss observed that most of the game appeared to have taken alarm. In the expedition report Frémont would digress for a discussion of the extraordinary rapidity of the disappearance of buffalo on the western slopes of the Rockies. According to Thomas Fitzpatrick, the once-abundant herds had begun to thin in the mid-1830s; by 1840 they had virtually disappeared from the Green and Bear River Valleys. Like the Indians, buffalo were everywhere visibly diminishing by 1843. Frémont attributed this to the American appetite for buffalo robes and the absolute reliance on buffalo of some Indian tribes.* White and native alike "slaughter them with a thoughtless and abominable extravagance," he remarked.[114]

Water birds rising into the air with the sound of distant thunder alerted the expedition to the proximity of the Great Salt Lake. Frémont caught sight of its broad sheet from the summit of a butte (today's Little Mountain) on September 6. "It was one of the great points of the exploration," Frémont wrote, "and as we looked over the lake in the first emotions of excited pleasure, I am doubtful if the followers of Balboa felt more enthusiasm, when, from the heights of the Andes, they saw for the first time the great western ocean."[115] They descended to the shoreline and camped in a grove near the outlet of the Weber River. The briny waters were nearly transparent, and in color a beautiful bright green.

Frémont left the lake on September 12 and retraced the route north, with a final observation that would inspire the embattled Mormon community of Nauvoo, Illinois, to seek out Utah as the Promised Land. "The bottoms . . . form a natural resting and recruiting station for travelers, now, and in all time to come," Frémont wrote. "Water excellent; timber sufficient; the soil good and well adapted to the grains and grasses suitable to such an elevated region." He proposed a U.S. military post and settlement for the valley of the Great Salt Lake; the Mormon chieftain Brigham Young moved first, however, leading a vanguard of Latter-Day Saints into the valley in 1847. By 1860, forty thousand of Young's followers would be established there.[116]

---

* Modern scholarship endorses Frémont's speculation but extends it, adding that climate change, competition for food, and cattle disease played a significant role in the destruction of the bison. Some historians emphasize, too, that by the 1840s the Plains Indians had begun taking large numbers of bison for their value as a commodity marketable to whites. See the *New York Times*, Nov. 16, 1999, D3.

With the approach of winter Frémont decided to strip down the expedition, sending ten men home from Fort Hall. McLoughlin's agent there, Talbot remarked, spoke of "the country as British, the Indians in it, as serfs of the Hudson Bay Compy," and had refused to sell supplies to Chiles's California caravan. *Noblesse oblige*, Richard Grant unbent for Frémont, trafficking in provisions along with several indifferent horses and five good oxen. The Americans resumed the westward march in a fall of heavy, wet snow on September 19. Snow and rain descended intermittently as they advanced along the Snake River Plain. In camp below Salmon Falls, Frémont purchased a quantity of dried fish from a band of Shoshones and marveled at their description of the springtime runs. "The Indians made us comprehend that they are so abundant that they merely throw in their spears at random, certain of bringing out a fish," he wrote. A spell of fine autumn weather set in, allowing Preuss to resume sleeping in the open air and escape the snoring of his tentmate Dodson. Reaching Three Island Crossing (present-day Glenns Ferry, Idaho) on October 3, they forded the Snake, swimming the animals, and moved overland toward Fort Boise.[117]

As advertised, these stages were the most trying of the entire voyage. The expedition struck into the foothills of the Blue Mountains via the Burnt River on October 13, following a rough track with steep ascents and frequent crossings and recrossings of the stream. "I have never seen a wagon road equally bad in the same space, as this of yesterday and today," the usually sunny Frémont complained. "Still, there is no mud; and the road has one advantage, in being perfectly firm." The track climbed to a summit, and Frémont stared into the distance in search of the landmark known as *l'arbre seul*—the lone tree. Descending, "we found a fine tall pine stretched on the ground," the victim of some migrant vandal's ax. "It had been a beacon on the road for many years past," he noted mournfully.[118]

The trace led through thick balsam forests to a dividing ridge from which the expedition could peer down into the nearly perfect circle of the Grande Ronde, then up, up again through thick woods to a last high ridge with views of Mount Hood far to the west and, toward the horizon to the north, the glint of the Walla Walla River. "Occasional spots along its banks, which resembled clearings, were supposed to be the mission or Indian settlements; but the weather was smoky and unfavorable to far views with the glass," wrote Frémont. As they dropped down to the river they caught sight of bands of Cayuses driving hundreds of horses to pasture. Pushing on past unfinished houses and patches of corn and potatoes, they reached Waiilatpu on the afternoon of October 23. Frémont found a family of emigrants in residence, wolfing mission potatoes and to all appearances in robust health. The Whitmans were away downriver and, the mill having burned, there was no flour to be had. Laying in a quantity of potatoes, the expedition continued west, reaching the Columbia—"the great river on which the course of events for the last half-century has been directing attention and conferring historical fame"—on the twenty-fifth.[119]

Frémont followed a poor track downriver toward The Dalles, contrasting his hard slog through loose sand salted with sharp fragments of black rock to the swift, smooth, waterborne progress of Jesse Applegate's emigrant company, which shot past "fast as arrows." Land parties, Frémont learned a few days later, had not fared so well. Indians had plundered one band of fourteen in camp near the Deschutes River. Just below the Deschutes, on November 4, the expedition approached two houses, a schoolhouse, stables, a barn, a kitchen garden, and extensive cleared fields—the Methodist mission station at Wascopam. Here Frémont learned that Applegate had met with misadventure, too. One of his barges overset and three passengers were drowned, among them Applegate's son and nephew. The Willamette still lay sixty miles distant. Some overlanders asserted in after years that these last miles were the most difficult and dangerous of all.[120]

This would be the second expedition's farthest westward penetration. Frémont paid the obligatory call on John McLoughlin courtesy of Henry Perkins, who arranged an Indian canoe and crew to bear him down to Vancouver. He had completed his assignment, joining his survey to that of Charles Wilkes, and the season was well advanced. He took a final leave of the emigrants at Vancouver, indulged in a moment's regret that he would not reach the Pacific after all, and embarked in McLoughlin's canoes for the upriver trip on November 10 in company with Peter Burnett, the *Tribune* correspondent who had left his family and goods at The Dalles while he arranged for winter shelter and supplies. With McLoughlin's aid—Vancouver provided three months' stock of flour, dried peas, and tallow—Frémont made ready for the next stage of the voyage, a winter circuit south and southeast through the bleak, dry, and forbidding unexplored region between the Sierra Nevada and the Rockies that he designated the Great Basin.

THE LAST OF THE GREAT MIGRATION trickled into the Willamette Valley in October and November 1843. The stragglers left The Dalles just before the Frémont expedition reached there, some moving painfully overland, others floating downriver on "ark-like rafts," in Frémont's words, "on which they had embarked their families and household, with their large wagons and other furniture." Most had to be supplied for the winter out of Hudson's Bay Company stores at Vancouver—on credit, of course—and in some cases sheltered from the cold autumn rains in company shacks, too. Some found work with Dr. McLoughlin. Daniel Waldo led his cattle into the hills southeast of Chemeketa and established a homestead there. Peter Burnett and another man staked a claim on the Willamette and platted a town they named Linnton, after the Missouri senator.[121]

In the meantime, the peripatetic Narcissa Whitman impatiently awaited the return of her husband, shuttling with her foster daughter Helen between the Methodist mission at Wascopam, McLoughlin and company at Vancouver, and Jason Lee's establishment at Chemeketa. She felt Whitman's absence keenly. Ailing again, her nervous system "impaired," she remained at Vancouver for two months under the care of the company's doctor. He diagnosed an enlarged right ovary and treated it with iodine. But 1840s medical science could not reach the deepest of Narcissa's hurts. At least she passed the months away from Waiilatpu in what she regarded as civilized surroundings. Feelings of loneliness washed over her in waves. Letters from her sister Jane dated March and April 1842 reached her in the midsummer of 1843—the first word from home she had received since 1840.[122]

She dropped down to Fort George in August "to enjoy the benefit of a sea breeze" for her health and to see off Daniel Lee and John Frost, who now followed Richmond, Leslie, and others out of the mission. "Thus one after another of our Methodist brethren leave the country," she wrote, a sad discouragement to those who remained. Daniel Lee's decision caught everyone unawares, including his Uncle Jason. "They are pious, devoted missionaries," Mrs. Whitman observed, "but Mrs. Lee's health has failed, and they feel it their duty to go home."[123] She still had no news of her husband, no idea when he would return.

The Hudson's Bay Company's Fort Vancouver, built 1825–1826, soon became a thriving center of trade and settlement on the lower Columbia. "The buildings already completed are a Dwelling House, two good Stores, an Indian Hall and temporary quarters for the people," Sir George Simpson wrote in March 1826. "It will in Two Years hence be the finest place in North America, indeed I have rarely seen a Gentleman's Seat in England possessing so many natural advantages." (Yale Collection of Western Americana, Beinecke Rare Book and Manuscript Library)

Reaching Waiilatpu in September, Whitman at once set to work repaying the overlanders for looking after him on the cross-country trek. Strongly advising the travelers to push on to the Willamette, he arranged for Indian guides to pilot them as far as The Dalles and, according to John Zachary, "cheerfully furnished his beef and what grain was raised that season." By now Whitman embraced the migration with all the zeal of a brand-new convert. "I have no doubt our greatest work is to aid the white settlement of this Country," he wrote his wife's parents; as for the Indians, the mere offer of the Christian way would have to suffice. The tribes could either accept it, and all it implied about settled patterns of living, or be plowed under.[124]

Medical responsibilities—Eliza Spalding's illness at Lapwai and Myra Eels's lying in at Tshimakain—claimed Whitman's attention and delayed his reunion with Narcissa. They met finally at The Dalles in October after a separation of more than a year. Narcissa dreaded the return to Waiilatpu, which from the vantage of the American settlements in the Willamette Valley now seemed to her a "place of mortal darkness." She fell ill on the journey home, remained bedfast for six weeks after her arrival, and had as little as possible to do with the Cayuses. An "inflammation of the bowels" nearly carried her off around Christmastime, and early in the New Year she developed a new illness, an "organic affection of the main artery below the heart, a beating tumour which is liable to burst and extinguish life at any moment." These frailties, together with the daily demands of running a household now expanded to include six foster children, excused her from mission work altogether.[125]

Whitman and Jason Lee met at The Dalles—the pioneers of the Oregon missions holding counsel together, in Narcissa's phrase. There Whitman dashed the superintendent's hope that he had provided a satisfactory accounting of the Willamette enterprise. Lee had suffered the death of two wives; Dr. White's attempted coup; the desertions and subsequent complaints of his missionary colleagues; and the doubts, questions, and accusations of the Mission Board. Now Whitman, whom he barely knew, let it fall that he had learned from a Methodist mission agent in New York that Lee would be recalled and the Oregon mission drastically scaled back. The news must have rocked Lee back on his heels. He took it stoically.

"Be it so," Lee wrote Charles Pitman. "You sent me here and I dispute not your right to call me away. I frankly confess that I do not wish to linger in the service of a Board who have so far lost their confidence in me as to talk of recalling me, and yet have me to learn this from strangers."[126]

Lee left Oregon for New York in February 1844 with the object of saving the Methodist mission—and himself. The board heard his plea and absolved him of financial wrongdoing, but refused to reappoint him as mission superintendent. Lee returned to his native Vermont in the autumn, caught a chill over the winter, and died in March 1845. His remains lay undisturbed under the north country snows until 1906, when they were disinterred and removed to Chemeketa, which from rough mission beginnings had become Salem, the capital of the state of Oregon.

6

Manifest Destiny

THE FRÉMONT EXPEDITION trudged south from the Columbia through a wintry landscape, following the valley of the Deschutes River over stony ground thickly grown with cedar and pine. Water froze in the tents late on November 26, the second day of the march, and the mercury dropped to −2.5 degrees Fahrenheit at daybreak. The rising sun cast a tinge the color of deep rose on the snowmass of Mount Hood bearing south 85 degrees west. Trees and bushes glittered with snow newly fallen in the narrow valley, and a swift current bore great chunks of ice down the stream.

A journey of fourteen days brought Frémont to his first objective, the Klamath country along the marches of the California border. Here the Indian guides from the Methodist mission turned back for The Dalles, and the *voyageurs* entered uncharted territory. Dr. Whitman had advised Frémont to travel home via the Mexican port of Veracruz. Thomas Fitzpatrick recommended a southeasterly course for Santa Fe. Frémont's commanding officer, Colonel Abert, had issued explicit instructions to "return by the Oregon road."[1] Frémont ignored the experts' advice as well as Abert's direct orders. For the record, he planned to turn east at Klamath Lake, advance to the Humboldt River, explore the Great Basin to the southern reaches of the Great Salt Lake, execute a winter crossing of the Rockies, and locate the headwaters of the Arkansas River before steering for St. Louis and home.

The Klamaths were a shy and mysterious people, unused to whites and suspicious of them. Mindful of Jedediah Smith's disaster in the Umpqua country in 1828, Frémont mounted a vigilant guard. But nothing moved in the gelid silence of these snowbound uplands. The early-morning temperature regularly dipped toward zero. Snow descended all day on December 16 as the Americans climbed painfully through a dense pine forest. Toward midday the country opened up. Reaching a snow-covered summit, Frémont looked down from the rim of a nearly vertical wall of rock onto a transformed scene: a green prairie a thousand feet below and an ice-free lake washed with sunlight, the shoreline fresh and green with springlike vegetation. Beyond, the vast, arid plain of the Great Basin stretched away to the east. The pale-green alkaline water beckoned. Frémont christened the place Summer Lake.

Befouled with salts, the lake water proved undrinkable. The caravan pushed on over rough ground, still moving mostly eastward, reaching another, larger lake, salty and bitter, too, on the twentieth. Frémont named it for his Topographical Corps chief, Colonel Abert—an honor not particularly flattering to the colonel's self-esteem. (Abert routinely belabored Frémont, a casual bookkeeper to say the least, with demands for clarifications on requisitions and disbursements large and small. Here, perhaps, was the Pathfinder's revenge.) With a series of seemingly impassable rocky ridges barring the way, Frémont bore off to the south over broad sagebrush tableland bereft of water or grass.

Christmas came in sunny and warm. The people celebrated with small-arms fire and the discharge of the howitzer. Frémont treated every man to a tint; he doled out rations of coffee and sugar, too. Otherwise the day passed like any other, the line of march mostly south skirting the lavabeds and alkali flats of the Black Rock Desert in present-day northwestern Nevada. A series of volcanic ridges towered on the left hand. On the twenty-seventh a gap opened in the mountain wall and they again turned east toward home. A bewildering fog persisted into the first days of 1844. Water and grass remained scarce, available fodder barely sufficient to sustain the pack animals. The crusted snow and broken ground sliced up the horses' feet. Eight or nine animals gave out entirely on this stage of the journey. Frémont here noticed that when a mule was about to die, it left the band, crept into camp, and dropped down by the fire. To ease the strain on the surviving animals, he ordered everyone to walk. Anxiety grew on him with the prospect of famine and thirst. Frankly in dread of the winter desert, he turned south again in search of the elusive Buenaventura River, which by persistent if unconfirmed reports cut a path through the Sierra Nevada to the Pacific.

Frémont would explain later that the trend of the land dictated his southward course. For whatever reason, he made little or no easting during these early January stages. The route on January 10 led along a hollow gradually up to a crest from which another expanse of water, this one far grander than Summer or Abert Lakes, "broke upon our eyes like the ocean."[2] The waters were dark green, suggesting great depth. A singular island, shaped like a great pyramid (Frémont would liken it to Cheops, probably his wife's fanciful touch), thrust up along the near shore. He named it Pyramid Lake.

The Americans descended to the shore and followed an Indian trace to a village of straw huts at the mouth of a river (today's Truckee) flowing into the southern end of the lake. "These Indians were very fat," Frémont observed, "and appeared to live an easy and happy life." Prosperity evidently rendered them friendly and unafraid of strangers. One of the inhabitants proffered a large fish to trade—a cutthroat trout *(Salmo clarkii)*. It so delighted the *voyageurs* that the Indians were persuaded to supply a sufficient quantity to feed the entire hungry camp. They also provided travel directions. Using signs and scratching in the dirt, the villagers explained that another large lake lay three or four days' march to the southwest, with two rivers beyond, along one of which "people like ourselves traveled." Frémont asked for one of the Indians to guide the expedition, but they only exchanged knowing glances and laughed.[3]

Guideless, he followed the course of the cottonwood-fringed Truckee southeast, the Sierra Nevada rising on the right hand. The caravan left the river at its westward bend on the seventeenth, following another Indian trail that traversed level country for some twenty miles south to another substantial stream. Frémont allowed himself to speculate that this might be a branch of the fabled Buenaventura. (In fact it was the Carson River.) Here was wishful thinking of a high order, or perhaps a ruse by Frémont to prepare the people for what he must have known would be a treacherous winter crossing of the Sierra Nevada. The notion that Frémont actually believed in the existence of the eighteenth-century Spanish explorer Escalante's mythical river

The Frémont Expedition at Pyramid Lake, Nevada, in January 1844. In his expedition narrative, Frémont would liken the lake to the Egyptian pyramid of Cheops, probably Jessie Frémont's fanciful touch. (Library of Congress)

strains credulity. He may have calculated that a search for it—and the path through the mountains to the Sacramento Valley it supposedly offered—would ease the men's anxieties.

At any rate, Frémont here formally announced his decision to abandon the eastern course, conquer the mountains, and winter over in Mexican California at John Sutter's New Helvetia domain. The Pathfinder wrote in retrospect that the people responded with enthusiasm. If that were so, they presumably shared his terror of the desert and anticipated an easy march along the Buenaventura into the perpetual spring of the Sacramento Valley. The suspicion persists that the idea of a reconnaissance into California as much as jaded animals or fear of the unknown led Frémont to alter his plans. Charles Preuss had remarked in October, more than a month before the expedition set out from The Dalles, that he almost certainly would not reach home that winter. ("I am making plans in my spare time of how to spend all the money I shall have earned by next spring," he noted in his diary.)[4] As an alternative to California, the Frémont expedition could have passed the hard months encamped quite comfortably along the Truckee, fattening on cutthroat trout as the animals browsed contentedly on the floodplain. But Frémont pushed on, continuing south, camping the night of January 20 on the Walker River near the site of Yerington, Nevada, southeast of today's Carson City.

Naturally, Jessie Frémont knew nothing of his plans. Certainly no clause in his orders as she understood them granted him discretionary power for a detour to New Helvetia. Jessie had stayed on in St. Louis in anticipation of his return no later than year's end. Christmas, New Year's, and Twelfth Night came and went with no word from Frémont. By the first of February she admitted to herself that the expedition was overdue. She suffered from "sick headaches occasioned by the sickness of the heart," she wrote Adelaide Talbot, who carried her own weight of worry over her son Theodore's well-being. Jessie struck a bracing note in letters to the older woman.

"Mr. Frémont may come in any conveyance but a steam car & from the moment I open my eyes in the morning until I am asleep again I look for him," she wrote. "I hurry home from a visit and from church & the first question is 'Has he come?'"[5]

A family friend with experience of the mountains spread a map before Jessie, traced Frémont's presumed route, and assured her that he would be home by the end of February. But she would be disappointed for many months yet, for even as she stood sentinel expectantly day after day, the second expedition limped west at a painfully deliberate pace into the snowy and broken high country. The days were mild, the nights piercingly cold. Snow depths increased as they climbed: to six inches, a foot, three feet. The half-starved animals dragged the talisman howitzer though encrusted snow and over glittering and treacherous surfaces of ice. Frémont caught glimpses of small groups of Washoe Indians "circling around us on snowshoes and skimming along like birds." The Washoes, with slight experience of whites, were bashful and refused to approach to within speaking range. Struggling through deep banks of snow, climbing steeply, men and beasts approached exhaustion. The strain finally forced Frémont to concede defeat and abandon the gun in the drifts.[6]

The Americans coaxed a band of Washoes off the mountainside and into the camp on the evening of January 29. Despite the language barrier, the Indians made it instantly clear that an impenetrable road lay ahead. Frémont had been traveling along the edge of the Great Basin since mid-December, moving crabwise though nearly always in a mostly southerly direction, "and still had the great ridge on the left to cross before we could reach the Pacific waters." Pointing to the snow on the summit, the Indians raised their hands over their heads to indicate depth, and they categorically refused to lead Frémont across to the western slopes. The thing could not be done in winter.[7]

The people had gone without meat for several days, and stocks of peas, flour, coffee, and sugar were dwindling. The Washoes offered pine nuts, one of their staples and in sufficient quantity an adequate substitute for meat. Frémont mourned the loss of his howitzer, a clever weapon the French had designed for their colonial wars in the mountains of North Africa. "The distance it had come with us proved how well it was adapted to its purpose," he wrote, adding—for the record, for surely even Frémont did not believe this—that entire party regretted its absence.[8]

They reached a pass, executed a precarious descent into a narrow valley, and saw before them at last "a great continuous range, the lower parts steep, and dark with pines, while above it was hidden in clouds of snow"—what Frémont identified as the central ridge of the Sierra Nevada. Indian informants again warned him off the attempt. Communicating by signs, they explained that a summer journey of six sleeps would bring him to the settlements of the whites. But it was winter now and the snows would swallow him, they said; they offered to conduct him to the ice-free shores of a fish-rich lake (today's Tahoe, the source of the Truckee River), where he could pass the winter in comfort. When Frémont declined, the Washoes reluctantly produced a young man who had "seen the whites with his own eyes" to join the caravan as guide.[9]

The Pathfinder called the people together the next morning to deliver a morale-building harangue on the necessity and desirability of conquering this last forbidding ridge, dilating on the sensual delights of Sutter's principality only seventy miles distant. "I assured them that, from the heights of the mountain before us, we should doubtless see the valley of the Sacramento River, and with one effort place ourselves again in the midst of plenty," he wrote later.[10] He might have added, though probably he did not, that they had reached and probably passed the point of no return and that provisions were all but depleted. Even pine nuts were in short supply. With famine looming, one of the messes sacrificed to the pot a camp dog, an amiable creature that had attached itself to the expedition in the Bear River Valley the previous summer.

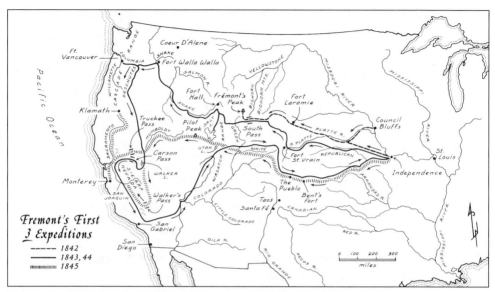

Frémont's expeditions, 1842, 1843–1844, and 1845. (© 2003 by Jackie Aher)

"No longer any salt in camp," wrote Charles Preuss. "This is awful."[11]

The final ascent commenced on February 2. Frémont reported the men as unusually quiet, as though out of respect for the sullen power of the snow, ice, and granite that threatened to destroy them. Ten men in the van broke a trail through the snow. One man and a horse would slog ahead, then fall to the rear when exhausted, the next pair in line taking over the task. In this way the expedition covered sixteen miles before halting for the night around great log fires along the banks of the frozen East Carson River. Frémont calculated the elevation of the camp at 6,720 feet above sea level.

Slow travel over the next two days: the summit now appeared as a range of bare peaks the eternal winds had scoured of vegetation and even of snow. Weak and demoralized, the horses finally refused to go on. Frémont sent them back under escort to the previous night's halt, pushed on with a small advance party, and made an early camp, the men cutting pine boughs to fashion beds on the snow. A strong wind flayed the mountain and the mercury fell to 10 degrees Fahrenheit, making this one of the bitterest nights of the entire journey. An ancient Indian visited the camp to repeat the prophecy that they all would founder in the snow and die. Seating himself by the fire, the old druid expressed his meaning through gestures and with a loud, singsong repetition of phrases. The night, Frémont would recall, was too cold for sleep.

At sunrise he and Fitzpatrick ranged ahead on snowshoes, marching ten miles to the crest of one of the peaks. They were rewarded with a view of a broad, snowless valley and, beyond, a low line of mountains—the Coast Range. Frémont traced a dark line through the prairie that he took to be the course of a substantial river. Ahead, between the summit and the valley, lay "miles of snowy fields and broken ridges of pine-covered mountains."[12] On the return trip to camp, he measured snow depths along the route at an average of five feet, with drifts and banks twenty feet deep.

Wind-hurled snow obliterated the trail the men and horses had broken with such terrible exertions the day before. The animals sank up to their ears. They were too weak now to pull the sleds; the *voyageurs*, themselves nearing the end of their endurance, took turns hauling the baggage. Necessity abraded the edges of even the finicky Preuss's inhibitions. "It is certain that we shall have to eat horsemeat," he wrote. "I should not mind if we only had salt." But when they killed his own mule Jack, the fattest creature still standing, Preuss refused to eat any of the cuts. All the same, he stood guard at the "kitchen hole"—a snow-free circle created by setting the trunk of a fir alight—and managed the campfire and two pots, one with peas stewing with pieces of Jack, the other with half of Klamath, the last of the camp dogs. He alternated cook's chores with interludes reading Byron's *Don Juan*.[13]

Frémont, with Preuss in tow, veered off course on February 14 to scale the highest peak on their right hand, the summit offering views of a shimmering mountain-ringed inland sea to the northeast. Frémont called it Mountain Lake in the early editions of the expedition report, then renamed it Bonpland Lake in honor of a French naturalist who had traveled with Humboldt. From the time of the Civil War (though not officially until 1945) it would be known as Tahoe, its Washoe Indian name transliterated. Frémont and Preuss were almost certainly the first whites to behold it.[14]

Two days later, as Frémont carefully observed, the advance party "encamped on the headwater of a little creek, where at last the water found its way to the Pacific." He persuaded himself that they had "struck the stream on which Mr. Sutter lived." By February 20 all the people and the 57 surviving horses and mules (they had left The Dalles with 104 pack animals) were assembled on the summit of the pass. Though the precise point of the crossing has not been determined, it lay somewhere in the vicinity of 8,573-foot Carson Pass southwest of Lake Tahoe. The boiling temperature of water gave Frémont an elevation of 9,338 feet. From the pass, he could trace the line of the Sacramento all the way to a silvery sheath that he identified as the bay of San Francisco.

"We now considered ourselves victorious over the mountain," he wrote.[15]

There were no provisions at 9,338 feet, so the victory remained incomplete. The animals were now their only recourse from starvation, and they killed and consumed two mules in two days. Deep snow in the timber forced them off the ridgelines and onto the mountainsides; they painstakingly hacked a way through ice and calcified snow with axes and mauls. Even as they descended to the verges of the snow line, the going continued hard; on the twenty-fourth, they advanced only three miles in nine muscle-tearing hours. Then suddenly they struck an Indian footpath. Green patches of grass appeared here and there. Rain began to fall—an unalloyed pleasure after weeks of wind-driven snow. Frémont measured the elevation at 3,864 feet. The next day he pushed on ahead with eight of the sturdiest men along the southern branch of the American River, determined to force the pace to Sutter's ranch, then return with provisions for the half-starved main band. The advance party executed another mule on the twenty-seventh and boiled its head into a soup.

"When cooked all night," Preuss observed, "a mule head is a delicacy."[16]

Preuss, for one, meticulously analyzed his obsessions. "I should like to know if a scholarly philosophical mind would think so much about eating in a similar situation, or whether this is only the case with us human animals," he wrote on February 29. He examined his conscience and passed the test. "To my credit," he went on, "I must say that I think more of my wife and children than of my meals. A close second, to be sure, are bread, butter and potatoes."[17] Within a couple of days of recording this entry, he found himself dining off an anthill, licking the insects off the palm of his hand.

Drifting away from the caravan, Preuss wandered lost, alone, and hungry. Frémont managed to pick up his trail and came upon one of his camps, but his shouts and discharges of firearms failed to produce the missing traveler. "This is beginning to get serious," Preuss finally admitted to himself. He proceeded deliberately along the line of the river, figuring that sooner or later he would come across evidence of his comrades. "Oh, my old sweetheart," he called out to his wife, giving voice to his thoughts, "if you knew how badly off I am at the moment!" Nearly delirious with hunger and fatigue, he fell to his knees before pools of rainwater, caught small frogs, tore off their legs, and gnawed at them for what little sustenance they could supply.

"Everything will be all right if I only keep a stiff upper lip," he assured himself. "I am not afraid of the Indians. Unlike Kit [Carson], I don't see a murderer in every miserable human being."[18]

He wandered on, following mule tracks, and eventually came to a hut in front of which five or six Indians squatted on their hunkers. They proved friendly, fueling him for a few more hours' exertion with a gift of roasted acorns. In the meantime, Frémont advanced on a broad path along a ridge angling to the river, camping on the evening of March 4 in a lovely glade of live oaks with a rich carpet of grass running to the water's edge. Toward evening he heard a weak shout, and a moment later Preuss stumbled into camp. He had missed tobacco most of all, he told Frémont; the dried oak leaves he smoked as a substitute simply would not answer. The ants, though, were all right. They possessed, he said, an agreeably acidic flavor.

With the horses now strong enough to bear their weight, the men again were able to ride. The route led through surpassingly beautiful country. Reaching what they took to be the Sacramento River, they advanced down the right bank, drifts of California poppy in vivid blossom along the river's edge. Following cattle tracks, they came upon a large Indian village whose inhabitants were neat and clean and wore cotton shirts. A well-dressed native with good Spanish corrected their geographical misapprehension—they were on the main stream of the *American* River, a few miles above its meeting with the Sacramento. Waxed Frémont, "Never did a name sound more sweetly! We felt ourselves among our countrymen."[19] The Indian introduced himself as a *vaquero* in Sutter's employ. He led the Americans into New Helvetia, on the opposite bank of the river, on the evening of March 6.

The hospitable Sutter provided horses and provisions, and Frémont set off the next day to rejoin Fitzpatrick and the main caravan, encountering them on the second day just below the forks of the American. The people were on foot, ragged and emaciated. The descent had claimed a number of pack animals, several losing their purchase on icy surfaces and falling to their deaths; one tumbled down a mountainside with all the plants Frémont had collected since leaving Fort Hall. Only thirty-three animals reached the valley, none in a condition for work.

The reunited party pitched a comfortable camp at the junction of the American and Sacramento Rivers. "For fourteen days we lived in luxury," Preuss reported, and in truth the Americans provided a powerful spur to the New Helvetia economy. The famished people fed heartily on excellent beef, salmon, and bread. The expedition needed everything: mules and horses, horseshoes, bits, bridles and ropes, packsaddles, beef cattle, flour. Sutter liberally provisioned Frémont from California's bounty; Frémont just as liberally pledged U.S. War Department credit. He cast a soldier's eye, too, on Sutter's stronghold: a quadrangular adobe structure mounting twelve guns and capable of accommodating a garrison of a thousand men. Forty Indians and thirty whites comprised Sutter's present strength. Barracks, a smithy and other workshops, and a distillery extended from the inner walls of the quadrangle. A schooner lay just off the landing stage in the Sacramento two miles distant, preparing to sail for Vancouver to collect a cargo for Sutter.[20]

As *alcalde* of the settlement, Sutter dutifully reported Frémont's arrival. The Mexican authorities were, after all, rather sensitive about U.S. military incursions into the province. Eighteen months earlier, an overzealous American naval commander, Thomas ap Catesby Jones, acting on a rumor that the United States and Mexico were about to go to war, had sailed into Monterey Bay, landed marines, and occupied the defenseless California capital. Dispatches arrived the next day, apprising Jones of the geopolitical status quo. He made such amends as he could for the outrage, lowering the U.S. colors, withdrawing the marines, and laying on a shipboard banquet for the Mexicans before sailing away in a state of acute embarrassment.

Sutter alerted the U.S. consul in Monterey, the merchant Thomas Oliver Larkin, to the arrival of the exploring expedition, providing Larkin with a cover story—true as far as it went—to explain Frémont's presence. Quoting Sutter, Larkin reported to the State Department that deep snow, loss of animals, and short rations had forced Frémont off course and into the California settlements. "The visit of the exploring expedition I attribute entirely to accident," Sutter wrote Larkin. "The starvation and fatigue they had endured rendered them truly deplorable objects." In any event, Frémont gave the Mexican authorities no opportunity to overhaul and interrogate him. He broke camp on March 24, heading south with a trailing column of 130 horses and mules and 30 head of cattle. Three days later, a patrol of 25 Mexican dragoons arrived at Sutter's ranch in search of the Americans.[21]

Shaping a course for Tehachapi Pass, Joseph Walker's crossing point in 1835, Frémont advanced down the San Joaquin Valley, the river on his right hand and the loom of the Sierra Nevada on his left, fording a succession of streams with their origins in the massif: the Cosumnes, the Mokelumne, the Calaveras, the Stanislaus. He judged the country "admirably suited for cultivation," though he did observe fields of young wheat tinged yellow from lack of rainfall. The livestock were wild as buffalo, he reported, forcing the column along at a lively pace of five miles an hour. The route passed through thickets of aromatic lupine, some of it growing twelve feet high, open groves of live oak, and patches of gaudy California poppies. For several days at the end of March a warm, pleasant rain fell—a benison for Sutter's wheat fields.[22]

"It is true," thought the normally restrained Preuss, "this valley is a paradise."

John Muir (born in 1838) would describe the great California valley one day as a vast bee-garden. Preuss in 1844 marveled at El Dorado's embarrassment of riches: thick, lush grass; a riot of wildflowers; and thousands of deer, elk, and wild horses. "One can kill a fat oxen without asking permission; all one has to do is give the hide and tallow to the owner," Preuss remarked. "The lazy Spaniards just scratch the surface with a spike instead of plowing the ground, yet everything grows wonderfully. Plenty of grapes and figs." He proposed Sutter as the model for intelligent exploitation and began to think seriously of taking up Sutter's offer of as much land as he could use. Even the local Indians were companionable and eager to please. At a dance arranged to entertain the Americans, one of the natives charmed Preuss by painting his penis in the Prussian national colors—black and white.[23]

"One thing is certain," he recorded in his journal, "if I cannot make a living in the United States without much soliciting and long rigmarole in the future, I will move on. After this job is finished, I shall go via Vera Cruz, Mexico, and Acapulco to the San Francisco Bay district and settle there."[24]

The country gradually changed as the expedition pushed south, flattening out and appearing less fertile, but thick with bands of elk and wild horses. Large willows replaced live oaks. The San Joaquin flowed through a lacustrine landscape and "nearly on a level with the surrounding country, its banks raised like a levee, and fringed with willows."[25] The river and all its sloughs were full.

By mid-April the expedition had cleared the bulrush country and entered a region of rolling hills and unusual vegetation, with many plants new to Frémont. Gooseberries were abundant and almost ripe. Fields of yellow flowers covered the hillsides. The route ascended gently to a pass, not Walker's Tehachapi after all, but more likely Oak Creek Pass five or six miles farther south. From the summit Frémont's gaze again encompassed the vast horizons of the dry and barren intermountain country. They descended rapidly into a forest of yucca—the Joshua tree, "to the traveler the most repulsive tree in the vegetable kingdom," thought Frémont, suggesting as it did the petrified landscape of the desert.[26]

"One might travel the world over, without finding a valley more fresh and verdant—more floral and sylvan—more alive with birds and animals—more bounteously watered—than we had left in the San Joaquin; here, within a few miles ride, a vast desert plain spread before us, from which the boldest traveler turned away in despair," he wrote.[27]

All the same, the expedition struck into the sun-seared wilds of the Mojave, with its prospect of thirst, exposure, and outbreak among the animals of a disease that desert veterans dubbed "the foot evil." (In his report, Frémont strongly advised travelers against venturing onto the Old Spanish Trail with unshod horses and mules.) Frémont paid off his Spanish-speaking guide with presents of knives and scarlet cloth and watched him bear away to the southwest. A few days' ride, he noted, would bring the Indian to San Fernando, "one of several missions in this part of California, where the country is so beautiful that it is considered a paradise, and the name of the principal town (*Puebla de Los Angeles*) would make it angelic."[28]

THE ASHBURTON NEGOTIATIONS evaded the matter of the Oregon boundary. To the *New York Tribune*, skeptical of the Oregon excitement all along and doubtful whether such a distant outpost ever could or should participate fully in the American republic, the claims of both sides were murky. The British put forward the voyages of Cook, Meares, and Vancouver, along with the maps of the Pacific coast their explorations yielded. The Americans sought to trump the British with Robert Gray's lucky venture into the Columbia, Lewis and Clark, and the Astorians. The case for U.S. sovereignty south of the Columbia seemed secure enough; that to the north, and especially to 54°40′ beyond the northern tip of the Queen Charlotte Islands, fragile to say the least. "The honest truth is that neither of us have a very good title—except by possession," the *Tribune* argued. In the end, though, the flag—Union Jack or Stars and Stripes—would hardly signify.

"No matter who owns or governs Oregon, our people will subdue and possess it," the newspaper added with resignation.[29]

The *Tribune*'s solution: independence for Oregon, with British protection until the colony matured. This, in fact, sounds like a rough approximation of Tyler administration policy, though Tyler, for all his interest in improving relations with Britain, could hardly run the political risk of mentioning a British protectorate. "Under the influence of our free system of government, new republics are destined to spring up, at no distant day, on the shores of the Pacific, similar in policy and feeling to those existing on this side of the Rocky Mountains," Tyler predicted in his annual message for 1843. (In a nod to political reality, he also ritually asserted the U.S. claim to 54°40′.)[30] The *Tribune*'s prescription for an (at least temporarily) independent Oregon found no favor with expansionist Democrats—it was one thing to live with the ambiguity of joint occupation for a while, another to actually cede territory to a rival, actual or potential; but even the most ardent expansionist would concede that American settlers, with their rough-and-ready genius for self-aggrandizement, would have the final say.

The brazenly imperial *Niles' National Register* conceded that the steady pressure of "silent emigration"—the American population would approach 6,000 by the mid-1840s—eventually would resolve the Oregon dispute. No need, or so the journal implied, for diplomatic ultimata or military shows of force to secure "the glory or welfare of this republic."[31] Essayist Peter A. Brown, LL.D., of Philadelphia, presented the case in the *Register*'s editorial columns.

"Our best hopes of present public prosperity, and our most devout expectations of future public renown, are intimately connected with

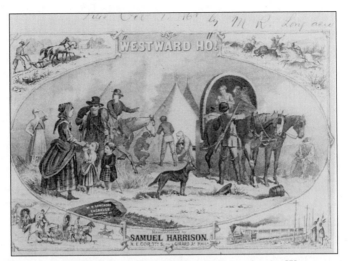

In this idealized view, American settlers set out for the West.
Between 1840 and 1860, the overland trails would carry some
quarter of a million emigrants to Oregon, California, and Utah.
(Library of Congress)

one word—'OREGON,'" wrote Brown, "and the American citizen
who would refuse to listen to the voice of truth in regard to the
momentous national questions connected with that territory, must be
either too supine to be a good or valuable member of this community,
or too subservient to the inordinate ambition and avarice of a rival
nation, who would rob our children of a noble inheritance.

"The true mother," Brown concluded with Solomonic wisdom,
"never consents to divide the child."[32]

The states of the Old Northwest and the transmississippi frontier
brought the strongest political pressure to bear on the Oregon question. State legislatures in Ohio, Illinois, Iowa, and Missouri prodded
Congress to annex Oregon and establish territorial government there.
"Resolved," the Indiana House and Senate voted in January 1844,
"That our Senators in Congress be instructed, and our representatives
be requested, to provide for the immediate occupation, organization
and defense of the Oregon Territory—peaceably if we can; forcibly if
we must." Tyler, an apostate Democrat serving out the final year of
his anomalous presidency (his own adoptive Whigs had read him out
of the party 1841) and preoccupied with the issue of Texas annexation, had no desire to provoke the British over the Oregon matter.
"The United States would be at all times indisposed to aggrandize

themselves at the expense of any other nation," Tyler said mildly in his annual message. Privately, Tyler also seemed willing to settle for a compromise line at 49°, with Britain retaining all of Vancouver Island (the parallel bisected it) and rights of navigation on the Columbia. In public he advised patience; a solution eventually would present itself, and time favored the Americans. After all, Tyler's own war secretary, John Spencer, had been a firm believer in the power of silent emigration—protected, it was true, by a line of military outposts to the Rockies and, if necessary, long-range patrols of U.S. dragoons.[33]

In Oregon itself, the overlanders of 1843 were anything but silent. Westerners mostly, men accustomed to seizing the initiative and unimpressed with their own daring in completing the twenty-five-hundred-mile cross-country trek, they moved with dazzling speed to seize land and political control. They were prospering, too, many of them. Writing from "our new town, which we have named in respect for Dr. Linn's services to this territory," Peter Burnett portrayed Oregon as peaceful, rich, and fairly bursting with opportunity. Burnett and his business partner were selling lots in Linnton for $50 apiece, and selling them fast. He lived on fat salmon, he reported, traded with Indians for game at great advantage to himself, and consumed substantially less firewood, corn, fodder, and pork than he had in Missouri.[34]

"A first rate market can be had here for any and everything, and you have never seen business more brisk," Burnett wrote. "You can move here with less expense than you could to Tennessee or Kentucky. It is my deliberate opinion that no country in the world affords so fair an opportunity to acquire a living as this. I can see no objection to it, except it be by a man who loves liquor, for he can get none here."[35]

From Waiilatpu, Marcus Whitman acknowledged that the raw determination and power of Burnett and his kind foreshadowed swift and permanent change for the colony. "It cannot be hoped that time will be allowed to mature either the work of Christianization or civilization before the white settlers will demand the soil and seek the removal of both the Indians and the Mission," he wrote. "What Americans desire of this kind they can always effect, and it is equally useless to oppose or desire it otherwise."[36] His words were prescient, applicable alike to the natives, the Hudson's Bay Company, and the American religious colonies.

With the arrival of the 1843 overlanders, the future met the past in the Willamette Valley. Years later, incoming Missourian Daniel Waldo recalled a brief encounter with outgoing Jason Lee. Waldo liked Lee well enough, so he said, but he comprehended at once that the settlers and the Methodist mission would clash.

"He played the devil up here in The Dalles," Waldo remembered. "He said the mission had always ruled the country, and if any person in the emigration that did not like to be ruled by the missions they might find a country elsewhere to go to.

"It got all over the country of course very quick," he went on. "That made war with the missionaries at once. We came here pretty independent fellows and did not ask many favors."[37]

In this war, the emigrants mobilized the big battalions—with nearly three hundred white males sixteen or older in the Great Migration, they commanded the votes. In May 1844 the settlers launched what amounted to a democratic coup, toppling the year-old provisional government. The Canadians participated fully this time. They sought protection and security for their homesteads, they wanted a voice in Oregon's affairs, and they favored a simple government, "as the more laws there are the more opportunity for trickery for those who make the law a profession." The Canadians also demanded assurances that the Americans would respect their customs, especially their language and their living arrangements with Indian women.[38]

The newcomers rallied Canadian support, both to overthrow mission power and to neutralize Hudson's Bay Company influence. Together, they elected six of the eight members of the new legislative board. The Champoeg district chose Daniel Waldo; Peter Burnett represented Tualatin. Only David Hill of the 1843 provisional government retained his seat. Of the three members of the new executive committee, W. J. Bailey (1835) and ex-trapper Osborne Russell (1842) predated the Great Migration; P. G. Stewart represented the class of '43. Bailey and Russell were not, however, particularly close to the Methodists and their allies—the political and social grouping that would become known, derisively, as the Mission Party.[39]

The new government went to work at once on alterations to the provisional law code of 1843. Meeting at a settler's home in Oregon City in mid-June, the legislators drew up a scheme for a governor and a thirteen-member assembly to be chosen at the next annual election, established a supreme court with a judge and two justices of the peace, and introduced a system of taxation with a penalty of loss of franchise for those who refused to pay. And in a direct attack on the Methodists, they repealed the 1843 land law that allowed Lee's mission to claim an entire township of twenty-three thousand acres, placing religious groups on the same footing on land matters as ordinary settlers. The committee also struck out the clause that bilked John McLoughlin of his Oregon City land claim.[40]

Initially, in deference to Dr. McLoughlin and the Hudson's Bay Company, the new leaders restricted their claim of jurisdiction to the region south of the Columbia River. (Fewer than 750 British subjects were settled north of the river in 1844.) Then news of the U.S. presidential campaign reached Oregon, emboldening the Americans. With a strong push from southern and western Democrats, territorial expansion—the annexation of Texas, the acquisition of Oregon— emerged as the leading issue of the 1844 presidential season.

The Democratic national platform went so far as to demand a permanent Oregon boundary at 54°40'. Following the Democrats' lead, the Oregon legislative committee in December extended its claim, asserting that Oregon encompassed all the territory from the Rockies to the Pacific and from the frontier of Mexican California to the boundary of Russian America—the present states of Oregon, Washington, and Idaho, and the Canadian province of British Columbia. That put Oregon in company with the improbable Democratic nominee, James Knox Polk, who had emerged as a compromise candidate on the convention's eighth ballot when it became evident that former president Van Buren's inexpedient views on Texas annexation—he opposed it on grounds it would lead to war with Mexico—cost Van Buren a third chance for the prize.

By December Polk, an austere and humorless North Carolina–born Tennessean and (like Thomas Hart Benton) a graduate of the university at Chapel Hill, was president-elect. Another emigration had reached Oregon by then—1,475 men, women, and children by one estimate, nearly a third again as large as the Great Migration. Among the arrivals was a babe born to the Snooks family along the trail, a boy Mrs. Snooks christened Oregon.

"This," noted *Niles' National Register*, "is the right way to settle the Oregon question."[41]

The 1844 caravans encountered difficulties from the start. Heavy rains filled the streams and turned the early stages of the Oregon

Trail into rivers of mud. The lead column struggled for two weeks to cover the first hundred miles. Continued wet weather bred dysentery and rheumatism. Delays mounted, and winter caught substantial numbers on the difficult mountain stretch between Fort Boise and the Columbia. Stragglers wintered over at the Waiilatpu mission, where Narcissa Whitman reluctantly agreed to take permanent charge of seven orphan children whose parents had died on the journey.[42]

Provisions, beds, and tempers had been short at Waiilatpu during the previous winter, when the Whitmans seated more than twenty indigent overlanders at the mission table. Whitman once estimated that he butchered no fewer than thirty-two horses over the years; horsemeat became staple fare during the austere winter of 1843–1844. Mrs. Whitman accepted new emotional burdens, too, assuming the role of chief comforter to Adaline Littlejohn; the melancholy-mad moods of her husband, Philo, ranged from highs of ecstatic piety to lows of extreme dejection, an inability to work, and a desperate longing to return to the United States. "I have more around me and within, to make me cry than to make me laugh," Narcissa wrote in response to a sister's efforts to cheer her up.[43]

By the middle of 1844 the Whitmans were making preparations for the arrival of another migration and, perhaps, another season of scarcity. Both fully comprehended the destabilizing and even revolutionary impact of the caravans. "The influx is not going to let us live in as much quiet, as it regards the people, as we have done," Mrs. Whitman wrote her friend Laura Brewer at Wascopam. "We are all of us, I suppose, on the eve of another scene of last fall—the passing of the emigrants." Determined not to be caught short again and to do as much as he could to promote settlement, the doctor cleared new fields for wheat and potatoes; rebuilt the burned-out gristmill; and established a sawmill twenty miles distant in the Blue Mountains to turn spruce and fir into fencing, shingles, and clapboards.[44]

The van of the '44 migration fetched the mission in early October with the report that the main columns were much delayed in the mountains. There was widespread sickness, and stocks of provisions, clothing, and other essentials were all but used up. The Whitmans braced for the onslaught. "Here we are, one family alone, a way mark, as it were, or center post, about which multitudes will or must gather this winter," Narcissa wrote her parents. "And these we must feed and warm to the extent of our powers." The mission and outbuildings already were filled nearly to capacity, with more than five hundred migrants yet to cross the Blue Mountains. Still, she felt more equal to the task this winter. For one thing, the disruptive Littlejohn and his long-suffering wife had left for the Willamette in September. For another, her health had improved; she now weighed a prosperous 167 pounds.[45]

The settlers' demands energized Whitman. He now wrote as though he had called the 1843 caravan into existence rather than attached himself to it for traveling convenience. "As I hold the settlement of this Country by Americans rather than by any English Colony most important I am happy to have been the means of landing so large an Immigration onto the Shores of the Columbia with their Waggons, Families & Stock, all in safety," he wrote Narcissa's parents. True, his labors over the summer led him to slight the Cayuses. Nevertheless, he believed he had done all he could; he had extended the natives the offer of salvation through the gospel and civilization through settled farming; if they refused these, they must accept their fate. Whitman went on to adumbrate a chilling future for the tribe.

"I am fully convinced that when a people neglect or refuse to fill the designs of Providence they ought not to complain at the results & so it is equally useless for Christians to be anxious on their account," he wrote Narcissa's parents. "The Indians have in no case obeyed the command to multiply and replenish the earth & they cannot stand in the way of others in doing so."[46]

The arrival of the migrants in October and November could hardly assuage the anxieties of the Cayuses, as Whitman freely acknowledged. Yet he waxed proud over the growth in numbers and complexity of the Waiilatpu settlement. He contemplated sending the seven orphans north to Tshimakain, then decided they would be useful in his own kitchen. The harvest was bountiful, and food supplies would be sufficient this winter. "We cannot be eaten out as we must have a hundred bushels of wheat, two or more of corn kept yet & more than a thousand bushels of potatoes & plenty of beef & hogs," he wrote Elkanah Walker in mid-November.[47] Whitman reported early in the new year that the season had been mild so far, with grass as thick and green as in the spring; that the orphans, even the babe who had come to them sickly and malnourished, were thriving; and that the school operated full bore with twenty-six scholars, all of them white.

"We have no Indian schools this winter," he admitted to Walker, "but hope to have one in the spring."[48]

Downstream, Vancouver braced for the new migration; John McLoughlin strained, too, to adapt to changing political circumstances. At McLoughlin's request, a British warship called in midsummer and anchored off the fort, the *Modeste* sloop, 18 guns, carrying 15 officers, 18 marines, 13 boys, and a crew of 115, whose "moral and political effect," the chief factor predicted, doubtless would be salutary.[49] McLoughlin also moved to strengthen Vancouver's defenses, ostensibly in reaction to settler-provoked Indian unrest in the upper country. But the doctor believed he had cause to fear the settlers as well. Americans were squatting on company lands; one new arrival avowed that he had come to Oregon with the express purpose of reducing Vancouver to ashes.

"If we made ourselves unpopular, and such a thing happened," he wrote the company directors, "where could we get redress? I do not apprehend such an event, in the least, but still we must be prudent."[50]

The company's caution stirred the suspicions of the Willamette colony. Perhaps McLoughlin's moves were a reaction, too, to political developments in the United States. James Polk's ascension made the *Tribune*'s call for Oregon independence about as likely of fulfillment as William Miller's prediction of the end of the world in the autumn of 1844. The time appointed for the millennium came and went, the globe continued to spin, and the chiliastic excitement waned. In January 1845 the British plenipotentiary Richard Pakenham formally proposed arbitration of the Oregon question. The United States just as formally declined; even more emphatically, the House passed a bill calling for American territorial government to latitude 54° 40'. President Polk elaborated his own view from the steps of the Capitol in a cold, driving rain on March 4, 1845.[51]

"Our title to the country of the Oregon is clear and unquestionable, and already our people are preparing to perfect that title by occupying it with their wives and children," Polk declared in his inaugural address. "The world beholds the peaceful triumphs of the industry of our emigrants. To us belongs the duty of protecting them adequately wherever they may be upon our soil."[52]

Polk made no direct mention of 54°40', but British opinion judged the speech inadmissible all the same. According to the *Times of London*, the new president's "pretensions amount, if acted upon, to the clearest *causa belli* which has ever yet arisen between Great Britain and the American Union."[53] Hard words; and the diplomats had cause to wonder whether Polk had left them anything to *negotiate*.

JESSIE FRÉMONT'S SICK HEADACHES persisted. She had heard nothing from Frémont over the winter of 1843–1844; whooping cough confined little Lily to the sickroom and, in March, news arrived of Senator Benton's wounding in a dreadful explosion aboard the USS *Princeton*. The navy had arranged a gala cruise on the Potomac for cabinet members and senior congressional leaders to show off the powerful new frigate and demonstrate a brace of experimental great guns denominated "Peacemaker" and "Oregon." Guests assembled in *Princeton's* bow for a test firing, Benton standing six feet or so from the gun's breech. The hammer drew back, he heard a tap and saw a flash, and then lost consciousness. The gun burst into a thousand deadly wrought iron fragments, killing eight people, among them the secretaries of state and the navy, and tearing away twenty feet of the warship's hull. "I had heard no noise—no more than the dead," Benton recalled. He regained consciousness amid a scene of carnage, dead and maimed lying about, Robert Stockton, *Princeton's* commander, standing hatless, stupefied, his face black with powder.[54] Benton suffered a ruptured eardrum that left him permanently deaf in one ear. Beset with anxiety about Frémont, Jessie allowed her invalid mother to return to Washington alone to attend to the recovering senator. She now looked for Frémont by the middle of May 1844.

"The advancing season cannot fail to bring them," Jessie wrote Adelaide Talbot. "The locust trees by my windows are covered with white blossoms. They look as if they had come forth to meet a bridegroom. I am sure I feel more like a bride than I ever expected to do again only Lily makes an unusual addition to the wedding party."[55]

She learned from a returned traveler in mid-June that Frémont had elected to winter over at Nathaniel Wyeth's Fort Hall. That would put back the earliest date of his arrival by another month or so. Then, at the end of June, the State Department reported that the expedition had gained Sutter's principality safely, rested and reprovisioned there, and recrossed the California mountains via the southern passes.[56] So he was en route anyway. She now had firm ground to anticipate him before autumn. Jessie wished she could flash the news, once the expedition finally arrived, to Mrs. Talbot by Morse's new electrical telegraph, which had gone into operation between Washington and Baltimore earlier in the year.

"It would surely be a better use than disappointing presidential candidates, and bothering the country about the Texas treaty," she wrote.[57]

In the event, the Frémont expedition raised "the little town of Kansas, on the banks of the Missouri," on the last day of July, embarked in the steamboat *Iatan* on August 1, and arrived in St. Louis late on the sixth.[58] Jessie had absented herself for a few days to comfort a cousin whose husband was slowly dying of consumption, and only the servants were at home at the Bentons' place. Frémont turned back for the city center and spent a lonely night at Barnum's Hotel. Jessie quickly learned of the moonlight appearance of the thin, spectral lieutenant, and she hurried home. They were reunited at last, after a separation of fully fourteen months, on the morning of the seventh.

Frémont fleshed out narrative of the second expedition over the next few days. The concluding stages had begun inauspiciously, with the retributive murder and scalping of two Mojave Indians. Two Mexicans—a man and a boy—appeared in camp along the Old Spanish Trail on the afternoon of April 24 to report that four of their party (including the boy's parents) had been killed in a Mojave ambush and their herd of thirty horses driven off. Kit Carson and Alexis Godey set off the next day in hot pursuit. Covering a hundred miles out and back in thirty hours, they returned in triumph, driving the Mexicans' horses before them, two bloody scalps dangling from the barrel of Godey's rifle.

With Jessie's eager connivance, Frémont's published report would present the revenge killings as an epic of knight-errantry. Following the Mojaves' trail, Carson and Godey came upon the horses at sunrise and, just beyond, an Indian camp of four lodges. The fattest horses had been destroyed at once and butchered, and the pieces were stewing slowly in large earthen pots. The others grew restive at the approach of strangers and alerted the Indians. Surprise in forfeit, Carson let out a war whoop and charged the camp. The Mojaves launched a flight of arrows, one of which pierced Godey's shirt collar. Thoroughly aroused, the Americans fired into crowd, killing two Indians. The others fled. Carson and Godey proceeded methodically to relieve the casualties of their scalps. As they sliced, one of the victims sprang to his feet, howling with rage and pain. The heroes swiftly terminated him—humanity required it, according to Frémont—and returned to their grisly work.

"The time, place, object, and numbers considered, this expedition may be considered among the boldest and most disinterested which the annals of western adventure, so full of daring deeds, can present," Frémont wrote. "Two men, in a savage desert, pursue day and night an unknown body of Indians—attack them on sight, without counting numbers—and defeat them in an instant—and for what? To punish the robbers of the desert, and to avenge the wrongs of Mexicans whom they did not know."[59]

As so often, Charles Preuss's account offers a corrective to Frémont's, or anyhow an alternative view. Preuss claimed that Carson shot the retreating Mojaves in the back. The scalping of the victims and Frémont's excited reaction to the vigilantes' swaggering return sickened him.

"Are these whites not much worse than the Indians? Godey rode into camp with a yelling war cry, both scalps on a rod before him. To me, such butchery is disgusting, but Frémont is in high spirits. I believe he would exchange all [scientific] observations for a scalp taken by his own hand."[60]

Carson and Godey reprieved a Mojave boy who had been unable to escape with the others. On his release, the captive turned impassively to a breakfast of boiled horse's head. Frémont and his wife liberally salted the second report with such details in a renewed collaboration that began not long after they returned to Washington at the end of August. The second expedition confirmed Frémont's celebrity, and the steady stream of callers at the Bentons' C Street house made sustained effort difficult there. He rented a *pied-à-terre* near the Bentons for a workshop, installing his astronomical assistant, Joseph Hubbard, on the first floor. John Kirk Townsend, the ornithologist who had recorded his own Oregon adventures with Wyeth in a spirited narrative published in 1839, had fallen on temporary hard times, and he signed on to help prepare tables and astronomical observations at a salary of $3 a day. The Frémonts settled into a second-floor room for day-long dictation sessions that continued through the autumn and into the winter. Preuss assembled the maps in his own

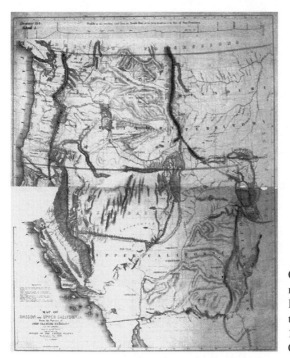

Charles Preuss prepared this map based on surveys with Frémont's second expedition to Oregon and California in 1843–1844. (Library of Congress)

newly purchased house (he had abandoned the notion of migrating to New Helvetia) near the Washington Arsenal.

Poring over the expedition notebooks, the Frémonts outlined each day's installment the night before. Jessie joined her husband in the upstairs workroom at nine o'clock in the morning. Frémont paced and Jessie wrote until one o'clock, when they broke for lunch and a reinvigorating walk down to the Potomac. They resumed writing until dusk descended on the short winter afternoon. Frémont delivered "A Report of the Exploring Expedition to Oregon and North California in 1843–44" to Colonel Abert on March 1. Livelier and much longer than the first report (299 printed pages to 117 in the 1970 edition), the account immediately found a respectful, attentive, and eager audience.

"Frémont deserves to have a monument erected to his memory upon the peak of the highest mountain he has or shall attain, for the light he has already shed upon the world, from those heretofore unexplored recesses, projections, reservoirs, and other wonders of our planet," observed *Niles' National Register* in introducing an extract from the report.[61]

Brigham Young would read it and launch thousands of Mormons along the Oregon Trail to the Salt Lake country. In an unintended consequence, it evidently caused a spike in unemployment among mountain men. With the collapse of the fur market, many western veterans sought work as emigrant guides. Frémont's reports and accompanying maps were so detailed that such costly services were often dispensed with, leading some old trappers—or so the overlanders charged—to exaggerate Indian dangers as a means of artificially inflating demand. Finally, and perhaps most significantly, the nineteenth-century historian Josiah Royce credited Frémont with "a kind of discovery of California" by means of a narrative that "brought the fair land before the eye of numberless readers."[62] Long afterward, Jessie credited the second report's account of the interlude in the California Eden with accelerating the U.S. move to seize the province from Mexico.

"Upon this second expedition hinged great results," she wrote in her dramatic style. "It made California known in a way which roused and enlisted our people and led directly to its being acquired during the third expedition."[63]

Never Frémont's favorite place, Washington had changed in ways personal and political during his extended absences. His mentor Joseph Nicollet had died in September 1843, breaking down badly at the last, becoming "morbid and solitary," in Frémont's phrase. He gave up the ghost alone and unfriended in a Washington hotel.[64] Benton's Senate colleague and Oregon boomer Lewis Linn died in October of the same year, and Ferdinand Hassler, owner of the singular vehicle that had carried the Frémonts to their first postelopement appearance in society, followed in November.

In a noticeable shift of interest, Washingtonians now asked Frémont more often about California than Oregon. There had been, too, an administration change—eager and unapologetic western expansionists were now in power. The dour Tennessean Polk won a narrow victory on an aggressively imperialist platform that demanded "the whole of the Territory of Oregon" and the "reoccupation of Oregon and the reannexation of Texas at the earliest practicable period." Polk's triumph ought to have pleased Senator Benton, but in fact, in company with fellow Democrat Martin Van Buren, he had developed a powerful aversion to Texas annexation. By contrast with the president's crowd, Benton sounded moderate expansion themes. Besides, he felt a genuine affection and respect for Mexico. Like Van Buren, Benton believed that annexation would lead to war. Perhaps surprisingly as a representative of Missouri, a slave state, he opposed it, too, on grounds that it would increase the political power of Southern politicians determined to extend the Peculiar Institution. Benton's stand baffled and outraged his Democratic allies, including the party patriarch Andrew Jackson, who speculated that the *Princeton* disaster had addled the brain of his onetime protégé.[65]

However they felt about the Missouri senator and his independent views, the great and near-great were avid to meet Frémont. "Spent an hour with Benton and his most interesting son-in-law Lieutenant Frémont," historian, Polk loyalist, and soon-to-be navy secretary George Bancroft wrote his wife. Bancroft's account of the evening suggests that the color and dramatic intensity of the expedition narratives may not have been largely Jessie's doing after all. He went on, "To hear him talk of the Oregon country seemed like being carried among snowcapped mountains of Switzerland, and his account of the valleys and beautiful runs of water were almost enough to make you think that the Garden of Eden was the other side of the mountains." Frémont dined, too, with Daniel Webster, who, no longer so dismissive of the Pacific, wanted to hear all about California, and with the Briton Pakenham, who winced at the prospect of the Mexican province falling into the hands of any power but England.[66]

In company with Benton, Frémont paid a courtesy call on Polk. One of the new president's intimates had speculated that a Benton speech against Texas annexation the previous October cost Polk a hundred thousand votes, so the reception may have been chilly. Frémont tried to set the president straight on the matter of the Buenaventura, explaining that his explorations proved conclusively that no such river flowed from the Great Basin to the sea. Polk's rejoinder: He refused to allow "the impulsiveness of young men" to weaken his faith in the old maps painstakingly assembled since Escalante's time.[67]

The American expansion juggernaut, already rolling, gathered momentum in the early months of Polk's presidency. In one of his last presidential acts, John Tyler on March 1 signed a joint congressional resolution for Texas annexation. Four weeks later, Mexico broke off diplomatic relations with the United States. American obstinacy over the Oregon boundary—54°40', Polk insisted—continued to complicate Richard Pakenham's diplomatic mission. George Bancroft's hour with Frémont had opened new democratic and imperial vistas to the historian. "I had no idea that there were so many ranges of mountains, or so beautifully picturesque and inviting a region; destined to be sure to be filled by Yankees," he wrote.[68] And over the summer, a phrase-making magazine editor named John L. O'Sullivan offered a sanctification of the American advance to the Pacific.

No nation, O'Sullivan declared, could be allowed to hamper or thwart American policy and power, or check "the fulfillment of our *manifest destiny* to overspread the continent allotted by Providence for the free development of our yearly multiplying millions."[69] Whether by happenstance or design, the essay introducing O'Sullivan's rallying cry appeared in the same number of the *United States Magazine and Democratic Review* that contained a fulsome notice of the just-published combined reports of Frémont's first and second exploring expeditions.

IN ONE LAPIDARY PHRASE, the British army subalterns Henry Warre and Mervin Vavasour delivered a judgment on the Methodist enterprise in the Willamette Valley. "They quarreled among themselves," wrote Warre and Vavasour, "and sold the greater part of their land and improvements to Dr. McLoughlin." So ended Jason Lee's dream after nine years of effort agonizing to body and spirit alike: an illusory mission to the "Flathead" Indians, the collapse of the missionary republic, Methodist commercial operations absorbed into the Hudson's Bay Company monolith.[70]

Events had overtaken Lee; they outpaced his rival John McLoughlin, too, leaving the chief factor's personal and professional affairs a sad shambles. For the third time in three years the Oregon provisional government re-formed and reconstituted itself, this time with the company as a partner. McLoughlin's decision to enter into a coalition with the American colonists would perplex his superiors, intensify an already bitter feud with Sir George Simpson, and alienate his countrymen. At a time when the Oregon boundary dispute approached a crisis and tensions between the United States and Britain seemed to threaten war, the doctor allied himself with the American settlers, accepting the provisional government's tender to become party "to the Articles of Compact by the payment of taxes and in other respects complying with the laws." McLoughlin argued, passionately and persuasively, that circumstances—"the danger to which the large property of the Company was exposed in the midst of a hostile population living without the restraint of laws"—left him no choice in the matter.[71]

The emigrants' two-year takeover gambit thus achieved a victorious denouement with the reluctant entry of the Hudson's Bay Company into the provisional government. Lee's forces were routed, the company neutralized. In a bid to consolidate their triumph, the Americans drew up yet another in a long series of memorials petitioning Congress for direct territorial government. They sought protection from Indians, security for their land titles, and freedom from the Hudson's Bay Company's commercial monopoly; they asked, too, in their pragmatic and matter-of-fact way, for a postal service between Oregon City and Independence, local mail routes, and a naval shipyard on the Columbia. Should Congress decline to grant territorial status, the colonists pleaded for the extension of "adequate military and naval protection so as to place us at least upon a par with other occupants of this country"—presumably the company and its Indian allies, backed by the power of the British Empire.[72] Sooner or later, every right-thinking American believed, the United States would act. In the meantime, the settlers trumpeted their ascendancy in the summer of 1845.

"Both the Methodist Mission and the Hudson's Bay Company ceased to be political powers either to be courted or feared in the colony," observed the provisional legislator and 1843 arrival Jesse Applegate.[73]

It remained only for the bumptious Britons with the Gilbert & Sullivan surnames to attempt the demolition of John McLoughlin's reputation. Lieutenants Warre and Vavasour reached Vancouver overland from Canada in late August on a secret mission to gather intelligence on British-American affairs in Oregon. There is a supposition, too, that Simpson, the longtime head of company operations in western Canada, had instructed them to spy on McLoughlin. Simpson and the doctor had disagreed with increasing rancor on business strategy for the Columbia Department. McLoughlin favored one approach, the Little Emperor another; and Simpson suspected the chief factor of profiting from questionable deals with the Americans in land and wheat. A deep personal antagonism developed, too, in the aftermath of the 1842 killing of McLoughlin's son in the remote company outpost of Stikine. McLoughlin charged Simpson with dereliction in failing to aggressively investigate the murder. Indeed, the killer, a company *engagé*, remained at large, and Simpson had declared the case closed.[74]

British diplomats and colonial officials concerned themselves with larger issues involving the Oregon Country. U.S. House passage in February 1845 of a call for American territorial government in Oregon set off a flurry of activity in London. The foreign secretary, Lord Aberdeen, sent to the Admiralty for a heavy warship to reinforce the little *Modeste*, "with a view to give a feeling of security to our own settlers in the country and to let the Americans see clearly that Her Majesty's Government are alive to their proceedings and are prepared, in case of necessity, to oppose them."[75] Then word of Polk's inaugural address reached the Foreign Office. Aberdeen and the prime minister, Sir Robert Peel, called in Simpson, who had settled in London on company business over the winter of 1845, for consultations that led to the decision to carry out a "military reconnaissance" of the Oregon Territory.

The commander of British forces in Canada detailed Warre, a line officer, and Vavasour, an engineer, for the assignment. Simpson sailed for Canada on April 4. After a detour to Washington for discussions with Richard Pakenham, Simpson briefed the soldiers, then assembled his own recommendations for facing down the Americans. The Admiralty should dispatch two sailing warships and two steamships to the North Pacific coast. On the outbreak of war, the British should move swiftly to fortify Cape Disappointment, at the entrance to the Columbia. The company could assist with the enrollment of natives, "who from their activity and habits of life, are admirably adapted for guerrilla warfare," in a militia corps under British officers.[76]

Simpson briefed Warre and Vavasour, then entrusted them to Peter Skene Ogden, the veteran trapper, with instructions to push the pace so as to reach Oregon ahead of Lieutenant Frémont, whose third expedition had been rumored (inaccurately, as it happened) to be headed for the Columbia. Minister Pakenham had deflected Simpson from his original plan to plant great guns on Cape Disappointment. Instead, Simpson told Ogden to claim the headland for the company, throw up a house, hedge in the property with a fence, and give Vavasour an opportunity to survey the ground for battery sites in case of need. Simpson cautioned Ogden against jumping any prior American claim to the cape.

Traveling in the character of private gentlemen "for the pleasure of field sports and scientific pursuits," Warre and Vavasour arrived at Vancouver on August 26. They had been exasperating company, according to Ogden, complaining ceaselessly about the fare, the discomforts of the route, and Simpson himself. "I shall not trouble you with the particulars," he wrote Simpson, "suffice it to say I would rather forever forgo the pleasure of seeing my Friends than submit to travel over the same road with the same companions." Warre and Vavasour equipped themselves at Vancouver with beaver hats, frock coats, figured waistcoats, tweed and buckskin trousers, fine handkerchiefs, nail brushes and toothbrushes, and extract of roses. The confidential agents could have assembled no outfit better calculated to call attention to themselves.[77]

If the soldiers' purchases from McLoughin's stores were frivolous, their observations of the country, contained in a preliminary report compiled in October 1845 and a final survey completed the following June, were superficial. Warre and Vavasour visited all the usual outposts and settlements: Fort George, Oregon City, Champoeg, The Dalles, Walla Walla, Nisqually. Despite Peter Burnett's boasts, the townlet of Linnton wore an abandoned aspect, with only one family in residence there. (The "village of Portland," between the Falls and Linnton, would prove a better site, with easier access to the backcountry.) Desperate and lawless characters among the Americans were persecuting British subjects. The Roman Catholic mission prospered, with four priests, six nuns, and sixty Canadian children in school. The Methodist schoolhouse had deteriorated badly, and hardly anyone showed up for lessons. Although certainly idyllic, the Willamette Valley failed to meet the expectations of some Americans; they "become dissatisfied," Warre and Vavasour reported, "and remove to California, where the climate is more salubrious and their possessions unlimited." That said, wheat and potatoes flourished in Oregon, salmon fisheries were inexhaustible, the hills were richly timbered, the country well watered. The provisional government now fielded a militia, a volunteer cavalry troop of fifty men.[78]

Warre and Vavasour concluded in the first report that McLoughlin had acted judiciously in joining the provisional government compact. In the second, they were highly censorious of the chief factor. This shift doubtless reflected the views of Simpson, who had been skeptical from the start of McLoughlin's openhanded dealings with the Americans and with his willingness to carry their debts. (By the spring of 1844, McLoughlin had extended some $31,000 in credit to four hundred settlers.[79]) An unhappy combination of good nature and greed in McLoughlin abetted American settlement. The doctor extended aid and credit when the miserable caravans straggled into Vancouver in 1842; and with the arrival of the industrious Americans he anticipated bumper harvests of wheat for profitable export to the Russian outposts in Alaska and the Sandwich Islands. McLoughlin's policy encouraged the mass migrations of 1843 and 1844. Without the Hudson's Bay Company safety net, the report asserted, there would have been scarcely thirty American families in the Willamette Valley in 1845.

The Americans not only survived, they flourished; and so McLoughlin unwittingly had created a diplomatic and military conundrum for Britain. "Their lands are invaded—themselves insulted," Warre and Vavasour wrote of the company and its officers, "and they now require the protection of the British Government against the very people to the introduction of whom they have been more than accessory." Fortunately, *Modeste* returned to the river in October 1845 to project British power and prevent the Americans from taking the law into their own hands. To further protect the outnumbered Britons, the soldiers' final report recommended excavating a moat around Fort Vancouver, constructing a blockhouse at the southeast angle of the stockade, and siting three batteries totaling ten heavy guns on Cape Disappointment and a six-gun battery on the opposite headland, Cape Adams. Oregon City could be profitably fortified, too—especially Dr. McLoughlin's squared-timber mills from which the loophole fire of well-disciplined British marksmen would overawe the Americans.[80]

As it happened, the Oregon question was moot by the time the Warre-Vavasour report reached London in mid-1846. The outlines of a settlement had been faintly visible at least since 1843, when President Tyler signaled privately that the United States would accept a boundary at latitude 49°. It remained for President Polk to creep back from the ledge of 54°40′ with his dignity unimpaired. Crisis with Mexico and an imminent change of administration in Britain lent urgency to the matter. In mid-May Lord Aberdeen responded to a conciliatory note from Washington with a revised boundary offer: the forty-ninth parallel to the Strait of Juan de Fuca, leaving Vancouver Island to the British, and navigation rights on the Columbia for the Hudson's Bay Company. The Senate approved the boundary treaty on June 18, 1846.[81]

With California and Mexico looming large, the Americans welcomed a rapprochement with Britain. In late April, Mexican cavalry attacked a U.S. patrol operating in disputed territory north of the Rio Grande, killing eleven American dragoons. By mid-May Congress had given Polk a declaration of war. A few days later, American forces crossed the Rio Grande and invaded northern Mexico. The June boundary settlement subtracted the British from the military-diplomatic equation.

"We can now thrash Mexico into decency at our leisure," observed the expansionist *New York Herald*.[82]

Caught between two fires, McLoughlin resigned under pressure after nearly twenty-two years as chief factor of the Hudson's Bay Company Columbia Department. The doctor defended himself vigorously, insisting he had acted throughout from motives of humanity and sound business practice. The Americans would discharge their debts; they would help the Oregon Country prosper. True, the Methodists incited the settlers against him; the Americans reprobated him while accepting as an entitlement his offer of provisions, seed wheat, livestock, and tools. He bore no grudge; he had done his best to balance the interests of the company with the dictates of his conscience. In the end, Simpson left him no choice but to go.

With the threat of war with Britain removed, McLoughlin resettled in Oregon City in 1846, continued to press his private land claims through legal channels, converted to Roman Catholicism, and became an American citizen. To the Americans, McLoughlin was dictatorial and monopolistic; to his own people his prosettler orientation doomed British interests in Oregon. The outcome, McLoughlin argued, had been foreordained as long ago as the 1820s, when Jedediah Smith's trapping brigades spilled out of South Pass and pushed west to Oregon and California, the vanguard of the American ascendancy. For as Dr. Whitman had so shrewdly observed, what the Americans desired they obtained, and no mortal power could thwart them.

"I HAD RETURNED inspired with California," Frémont would write of the second exploring expedition. "My wish when I first saw it settled into intention, and I determined to make it my home."[83]

Carrying a miniature of herself Jessie had given him, he set out from the Missouri frontier on the third expedition in the late spring of 1845. There remains some mystery about his purpose. He would say later that his chief object had been to survey the shortest overland route from Independence to the Pacific. Colonel Abert instructed him merely to "strike the Arkansas as soon as practicable, survey the Red River without our boundary line . . . [and] determine as nearly as practicable the points at which the boundary line of the U.S. the 100th degree of longitude west of Greenwich strikes the Arkansas, and the Red River." He should, the colonel added, take care to conclude the expedition by the end of the year. Follow-up orders authorized him to augment his forces if necessary, explore the southern Rockies (Mexican territory, presumably), and reconnoiter with a view to future military operations in the country. They also alluded to "more distant discoveries, which will probably keep you some time longer in the field." But Abert made no mention of traversing the Great Basin to California.[84]

Broad hints from Frémont and his supporters implied a secret service connection. The Polk administration coveted California with a lust exceeding even the burning desire it had felt for Texas. An internal revolt left a squabbling, semiautonomous band of *Californios* nominally in power, and Polk and his leading advisers concluded that Mexico had little chance of retaining control of the province. Even— or perhaps especially—after the Oregon boundary settlement, the Americans remained wary of the British on the Pacific Coast. To the president, Secretary of the Navy Bancroft, Senator Benton, and other expansionists, the crisis was at hand. Britain and the United States would contest for California. According to Frémont, Polk meant to acquire it by negotiation and purchase if possible, by other means, including war, if necessary. Frémont at his court-martial and later in his memoirs recalled discussing all this with his father-in-law and "other governing men" in Washington. And his wife would claim that she had heard her father, in the name of the Senate War Committee, authorize his entry into California.

"I was given discretion to act," he wrote.[85]

Polk moved decisively on multiple fronts in 1845, ordering Commodore John D. Sloat's Pacific Squadron to sail at once to seize the California ports in the event of war with Mexico and instructing Thomas Larkin, the American consul at Monterey, to agitate the American settlers on behalf of the United States. He also dispatched a young marine, Lieutenant Archibald Gillespie, to search out Frémont in California. Gillespie, Frémont claimed afterward, carried letters from his wife and Benton in "family cipher" and a memorized dispatch from Secretary of State James Buchanan, a Benton friend and political ally.[86]

Dividing the band, Frémont led an advance party of ten across the Sierra Nevada at Donner Pass, now the main emigrant gateway to California, in early December and descended into the Sacramento Valley. By December 14, after a few days for rest and refit in the old camp on the American River near Sutter's Fort, he struck southeast up the San Joaquin Valley for a rendezvous with the main party. A misunderstanding with the guide, the veteran mountain man Joseph Walker, made this an aimless journey. Frémont spent several days in the Tulare Lake–Kings River country, botanizing and admiring the wildlife, before returning to Sutter's estate in mid-January. The two detachments would finally reunite a month later in the San José Valley, sixty miles northeast of Monterey.

Bearing a passport from Sutter, the New Helvetia *alcalde*, Frémont sailed in one of Sutter's launches down the Sacramento and across San Francisco Bay to Yerba Buena for a conference with the U.S. consul there, then continued on to Monterey, where Larkin introduced him to the local commandant, José Castro, and a former governor, Juan Bautista Alvarado. Frémont offered the survey mission as the pretext for his incursion, assuring Castro that the expedition traveled in "the interests of science and commerce" exclusively and consisted of civilians, not soldiers. Accepting this explanation, General Castro granted Frémont permission to pass the rest of the winter in California and to extend his explorations south and east to the Colorado River.[87]

In the event, Frémont marched west instead, through the most thickly settled districts of the province into the valley of the Salinas. This too-close approach to the capital aroused Castro's suspicions, and he sent an officer to Frémont with an ultimatum to leave California forthwith or face arrest. The Pathfinder found the young Mexican cavalryman who delivered the message "rude and abrupt," chose to take offense at what he construed as Castro's peremptory tone, and withdrew in dudgeon to the heights of a spur of the Gabilan Mountains known as Wildcat Ridge. Wood, water, and grass were plentiful there, and the summit commanded a broad prospect of the Salinas plain, with a secure line of retreat into the San Joaquin Valley. Frémont threw up a log breastwork, pinned the U.S. colors to the tapered end of a trimmed sapling, and awaited Castro's pleasure.[88]

The Mexican forces—three hundred or four hundred men and three fieldpieces in Frémont's estimate—massed on the plain. With the spyglass he could follow their every movement. Living on his nerves, wrought up to a state of extreme tension, Frémont invested this slapstick confrontation with high romantic import. In a rather hysterical note to Larkin, he vowed that he and his band would defend their "entrenched camp" to the last, "every man of us," refusing quarter and "trusting to our country to avenge our death." For his part, Castro published a windy proclamation labeling Frémont's expedition "a band of robbers" and urging *Californios* to "lance the ulcer" of the American visitation.[89]

Thinking matters over, Frémont opted to retreat from Wildcat Ridge. Interpreting the toppling over of the frail sapling flagpole on the afternoon of the third day as an omen, he rang down the curtain anticlimactically on this latest of his psychodramas. He had given Castro three days to attack him; he now felt released from his obligation. "My sense of duty did not allow me to fight them," he explained to Jessie. His was, after all, a scientific expedition.[90]

The Americans withdrew in easy stages to Sutter's Fort, then advanced up the Sacramento Valley to the ranch of Peter Lassen sixty miles north of New Helvetia. Frémont surveyed the country thereabouts, returned to Lassen's for a week or so, then resumed the trek toward his ultimate destination, the Klamath country of southern Oregon. He encamped upon the shore of Klamath Lake, important to the natives for its fishery, on May 6. Two nights later, scouts turned up with word that Archibald Gillespie was on his trail. Frémont backtracked the next day, met Lieutenant Gillespie at about sundown, and greedily devoured the letters he carried from Benton and from Jessie.

Details of Gillespie's mission to Frémont remain speculative. Frémont wrote long afterward that he decoded Benton's cipher letter to read: "The time has come. England must not get a foothold, we must be first. Act; discreetly but positively." Gillespie certainly passed on Thomas Larkin's forecast that confirmation of war between Mexico and the United States would reach Monterey inside of two weeks. What else did he say? He had, after all, met privately with Polk before he set out for California. Frémont evidently told the people that Gillespie carried orders recalling them to California for some larger purpose. In the memoirs he remarked that Gillespie "absolved me from my duty as an explorer" and supplied the "further authoritative knowledge that the Government intended to take California." By implication, Gillespie delivered verbal instructions for Frémont to whip the American settlers into revolt, goad the Mexicans into attacking him, or both.[91]

Three decades later, in an interview in December 1884, Frémont told the historian Josiah Royce that he had intended to return to California in any event, but that Gillespie's appearance prompted him to move south at once. He also implied that the message from Buchanan gave him discretionary authority to touch off an American uprising in the province.

"It is not to be supposed that an officer of the government would act as I did unless he had the sense that his authority for his act was sufficient under the circumstances," Royce quoted Frémont as saying. "I felt that the certainty of war would place me in a position to have the government behind me in all that I might do; but that if no war took place I would so assume the responsibility as to leave the government free to disavow me if it was needed."[92]

In fact, fighting already had broken out along the Rio Grande; Congress would declare war on Mexico on May 11–12. Frémont's command, though small, "constituted a formidable nucleus for frontier warfare," he believed, and he expected to pick up as many recruits from the American settlements as he could equip and maintain.

"The decision" to go, Frémont would write, "was the first step in the conquest of California."[93]

Perhaps it was excitement at the prospect of conquest that led Frémont to neglect the simple expedient of a mounting a guard on the camp the night of his encounter with Gillespie. The sound of an ax being driven into Basil Lajeunesse's head roused Carson, who sounded the alarm; the *voyageurs* drove off the assault at a cost of three men killed. One of the Klamath chiefs fell at the edge of the camp; Frémont's Delaware Indian auxiliaries lifted his scalp. Frémont was curiously reticent about the death of the highly competent Lajeunesse, who had served him faithfully on the two previous exploring expeditions. But the Americans exacted their revenge the next day. Frémont led the assault on a Klamath village along the lakeshore—not, so it appears, the home place of the band responsible for the attack of the night before, but no matter.[94] The Americans drove the Indians from the village and into a field of sagebrush. Their rifles easily outranged the Indians' poison-tipped arrows, and fourteen Klamaths were killed before the survivors melted away into the pinewoods. Frémont ordered quantities of salmon and the scaffolds on which the fish were drying destroyed and the rush and willow huts of the deserted village put to the torch.

Frémont read into the Klamath confrontations the lesson that the Indians were hostile to the Americans and friendly to Britain, and that the British, operating from the Hudson's Bay Company post on the Umpqua River, would raise the tribes against the American settlers in the event of war. He returned to the lower Sacramento Valley toward the end of May to find a series of messages and updates of California political intelligence awaiting him. Sutter reported that General Castro had sent an agent to the California tribes to mobilize them for frontier war, with instructions to burn the settlers' wheat in the fields and drive them from their homes. One of the settler leaders, Samuel Hensley, told Frémont that northern *Californio* delegates had declared themselves in favor of separating from Mexico and placing the province under the protection of a foreign power, presumably Britain. Hensley went on to say that the eight hundred or so Americans in the valley looked to the Pathfinder and his little army for protection, and had concluded they would either have to fight for their homes or leave the country. Frémont entertained a stream of Americans at his camp on the Marysville Buttes—respectable settlers and hunters along with, according to John Bidwell, "about as rough specimens of humanity as it would be possible to find anywhere."[95]

To Frémont, the alarms suggested a pattern and an opportunity. The settlers were affrighted; the settlers were besieged. He sent Gillespie to arrange for a resupply of ammunition, medicine, and provisions from the sloop USS *Portsmouth* lying off Sausalito, for he had resolved to take "decided action" to seek out "any contingency which I could turn in favor of the United States." In Bidwell's recollection, though, settler fears were a phantom, the Mexican-Indian threat non-existent. The Americans enjoyed a numerical advantage; three successive emigrations had seen to that. "We felt entirely secure, even without the presence of a United States officer and his exploring force of sixty men," wrote Bidwell.[96] General Castro lacked the resources—money, arms, troops—to make serious mischief for the Americans.

Frémont, Bidwell went on, only wanted a pretext for a preemptive war. Why? As a fresh act in the psychodrama? Because his ambiguous instructions posed a kind of test of his judgment and courage? Because he was impulsive, impatient, and—where his own interests were involved—unscrupulous? According to a rumor circulating among the bluejackets in *Portsmouth*, Frémont's motives were personal—he had "determined to chastise Castro for his insolence" in chasing him out of the province in March. In the 1884 interview with Royce, Frémont never mentioned a Mexican plot to rout the settlers, still less a desire to reprove Castro for his offhand manners, saying only that he acted on his own initiative in accord with his duty as a confidential agent. The Pathfinder dismissed Bidwell as incompetent to evaluate his conduct. He was, after all, only a settler.[97]

The Bear Flag Revolt opened on about June 10 with the rustling of a herd of horses Lieutenant Francisco Arce and his dragoons were driving to Castro's command at Monterey. A settler named Ezekiel Merritt led the cattle raid. He was "fearless and simple," according to Frémont, "taking delight in incurring risks, but tractable and not given to asking questions when there was something he was required to do." Bidwell remembered Merritt differently, as one of the rough specimens. Royce profiled him as "a frontiersman of no great reputation for all virtues." Frémont's lapse into the passive voice in his recollections makes it unclear whether Merritt acted on the Pathfinder's direct order. Bidwell claimed that Frémont, learning Arce's horses were in the neighborhood, sent Merritt and his confederates to chase off the guard and *vaqueros* and deliver the herd into the Americans' camp.[98]

As for the next move, Frémont expressed himself without equivocation: "I sent Merritt into Sonoma instructed to surprise the garrison at that place." As a preliminary, he turned his attention to the supposed Indian threat. Frémont may have decided to go over to the offensive against the natives for the record, figuring that a short, sharp raid would be taken as outward evidence that "the hostiles" were preparing to strike. "The scouts reported the Indians with feathers on their heads," he wrote, "and faces painted black, their war color; and in the midst of their war ceremonies." Frémont's pocket army swept down the valley, attacking the native *rancherias* along the route, dispersing the villages, and killing a number of inhabitants—"a rude but necessary measure," in his words, for the settlers' protection.[99]

Merritt and his band of twenty-five men (mostly vagabonds and rogues, in Royce's view) slipped into defenseless Sonoma before daybreak on June 14, found the lone sentinel asleep on a bench, and induced General Mariano Vallejo, the paramount *Californio* leader north of Monterey, to surrender the town. A detachment carried Vallejo and three others off to Frémont's camp as prisoners; John Bidwell later took charge of them at New Helvetia. In the meantime, the main insurgent body under William B. Ide ran up a homemade flag— a brown cloth with the figure of a grizzly bear roughly approximated in brown or red paint, in Bidwell's recollection; something resembling a bear stained in berry juice onto a white cloth, according to Royce. The *Californios* mistook the device for a *coche*.

The Bear Flaggers hunkered down to await Frémont's arrival. Ide, fifty years old, a native New Englander, delivered a long, confused harangue on the Sonoma square, concluding with a reference to George Washington that left his hearers with the impression that he, Ide, regarded himself as the father of the California Republic. Ide wrote proclamations nearly every day, signing himself as "Commander in Chief of the Fortress of Sonoma," and posted them on the old Mexican flagstaff. But matters soon took a serious turn. *Californios* captured two of the Bears and murdered them, allegedly cutting them up with knives. A small force of insurgent militia clashed with one of General Castro's columns at Olompali on June 23; one or two *Californios* were killed before their commander broke off the action and withdrew.

Perhaps fearful that events would outpace him, Frémont now decided that his moment had come. He would respond to the Bears' "urgent appeals" for aid; he would "govern events rather than be governed by them." Gillespie's errand had yielded powder, lead, percussion caps, and provisions from *Portsmouth*'s stores, so the expedition marched heavily armed and fully equipped. Reaching Sonoma on June 25, Frémont admonished the light-fingered insurgents, who prated about the sanctity of private property even as they helped themselves liberally to Vallejo's brandy, provender, and livestock. Meanwhile, one of the Pathfinder's patrols killed three Mexicans in reprisal for the execution of the two Bears. Royce claimed that the victims—an elderly "ranchman" (perhaps only a *vaquero*) and his twin nephews—had no involvement in the outrage. He called the episode a lynching. Frémont remarked only that "three of Castro's party . . . were killed on the beach"; one of his men characterized them as spies. Kit Carson, a hard man who tended to wax psychopathic in times of stress, and two others carried out the executions.[100]

The cycle of violence here came to an end. U.S. naval forces under Commodore Sloat raised the Stars and Stripes over the *presidio* of Monterey on July 7. Sloat, though, had been a late arrival, hanging on his anchor in the Mexican West Coast port of Mazatlán for weeks while events unfolded in Texas and California. He commanded a powerful squadron, the frigates *Savannah* and *Constitution* together with light forces, and Secretary of the Navy Bancroft's orders were clear and direct: He was to seize the California ports immediately on the outbreak of war. Sloat had sent *Portsmouth* north in early April after hearing of Frémont's confrontation with Castro in the Salinas Valley. In mid-May, when unofficial word of the first clash along the Rio Grande reached him, he dispatched a second sloop to California waters. But even though he had learned of the opening battles and the U.S. occupation of Matamoros as early as May 31, still Sloat delayed for another week or so. Notice that U.S. warships had blocked up the port of Veracruz finally prompted him to sail.[101]

Savannah came to anchor in Monterey Harbor on July 2. Sloat found the situation murky; Larkin cautiously advised him to allow the fog of war to disperse before he acted. Frémont and the Bears finally forced his hand; he had a full report of their escapades on July 5 via dispatches from *Portsmouth*'s commander, John B. Montgomery.

"I have determined to hoist the flag of the U. States at this place tomorrow," Sloat wrote Montgomery, "as I would prefer being sacrificed for doing too much than too little."[102]

Sloat landed 250 bluejackets and marines and seized the undefended town. Within a day or two, details from *Portsmouth* occupied Sonoma and Yerba Buena. A sailor detachment marched into the latter place with a fife chirping "Yankee Doodle" and bent the national flag on the halyards in the presence of "some 25 or 30 souls, dogs and all"; the flag stretched out in the breeze, the bystanders cheered, the dogs howled, and the sloop fired a twenty-one-gun salute.[103] Word of

Sloat's coup reached Frémont at his old camp on the American River on July 9. He raised the American color over Sutter's Fort on the eleventh. The next day he received an express from Montgomery with Sloat's request that he join him in Monterey.

Frémont marched at once, reaching the yellow hills behind Monterey on July 19 to find Castro's forces in retreat toward Los Angeles and five warships in the harbor—four U.S. men-of-war (including the frigate *Congress*, just arrived from the Sandwich Islands) and a British line-of-battle ship, the eighty-gun HMS *Collingwood*. The British had missed the moment. The corvette *Juno* rushed up from Santa Barbara to investigate reports of the Bear Flag uprising, but by the time she cleared the Golden Gate, the Stars and Stripes were afloat over Yerba Buena. The visit of *Collingwood*, the flagship of the British naval commander in the Pacific, Sir George Seymour, thus turned out to be a courtesy call with no political implications. His orders anyhow warned him off a confrontation with the United States over California. Seymour lingered for a week, acknowledged the American *fait accompli*, and sailed away to Oahu.

With his highly developed sense of occasion (his "passion for seeming," as Emerson had put it), Frémont made the most of the expedition's arrival at the capital of Mexican California. "A vast cloud of dust appeared first," wrote one of *Collingwood's* officers, Lieutenant Frederick Walpole, "and thence in a long file emerged this wildest wild party." Frémont rode out front, accoutered in leggings, blouse, and a felt hat, with an exotic escort of five Delawares just behind. The main column followed, the people riding two and two, each man with one hand loosely holding the reins, the other steadying a rifle across the saddlehorn. "Here were true trappers," Walpole wrote, "the class that produced the heroes of Fenimore Cooper's best works." His eye lighted on Carson, as well-known on the prairies, he remarked, as a duke would be in Europe.[104]

For all practical purposes, the conquest of California was complete. There was no valor in it. In retrospect, Frémont's presence seems hardly to have been required. "The natural progress of events will undoubtedly give us that province just as it gave us Texas," the *American Whig Review* had observed six months earlier. Settlers, silent emigrants (another fifteen hundred Americans arrived in 1846), fossickers, drifters, beached sailors, main chancers, and *pistoleros* were available in sufficient quantity to execute a takeover without Frémont's meddling, or without Commodore Sloat's marines, for that matter, although doubtless the acquisition would have happened later than it did in the absence of official American power. Then again, Frémont had been fortunate, perhaps, not to have deranged things with his intervention. Consul Larkin certainly thought that the Bears had disrupted a delicate diplomacy and threatened mayhem. "I can hardly believe it and do not understand the affair," he had responded when the news reached him.[105] More energetic Mexican leaders—or anyhow men less obsessed with political intriguing than were Castro and his superior, Governor Pío Pico—might have bestirred the *Californios* and perhaps the Indians, too, to rise up and smash the American rowdies and their *opera buffa* republic.

The closing scenes yet remained to be enacted. The settlers' California Battalion would march south under Frémont's command in search of fame, fortune, and someone to shoot. "We tried to find an enemy, but could not," Bidwell would write. In November, General Stephen Kearny's column of regulars arrived overland from New Mexico to occupy the province. Mexicans in the south mounted a short-lived rebellion and chased the Americans out of Los Angeles before Frémont, Commodore Robert Stockton, and Kearny restored order and forced the final capitulation at Cahuenga in January 1847.

Frémont, briefly the civil governor of California, would be court-martialed for refusing to acknowledge Kearny's authority. The Pathfinder had dominated the province; it stood to reason he would rule it, or so he argued before a military court. Unimpressed, the court found him guilty. The president pardoned him, but Frémont dreamed of greater triumphs. He quit the army and realized his intention of settling in California, where he became briefly gold-rich. He had seen the province "all unused; lying waste like an Indian country," its wealth neglected.[106] Within a few years thousands of American gold-hunters would swarm over the lovely foothills the second and third expeditions had tramped, leaving a literal wasteland, slopes stripped of pine and live oak, streams silted up, grassy meadows pockmarked and scarred—the legacy of a conquest.

HER MISSIONARY VOCATION long since abandoned, Narcissa Whitman settled into the role of foster mother, matron of an orphanage of eleven boys and girls. Mrs. Whitman's biographer, Julie Roy Jeffrey, would call the years of the middle 1840s the happiest of her life in

Oregon. Relations with the Indians had never been better, Narcissa insisted. Her health had improved; she would travel 180 miles to the Tshimakain mission station on horseback without ill effect. Her husband flourished as agent and outfitter for the Oregon migrants and as the increasingly prosperous master of Waiilatpu.

Wifely and maternal responsibilities and a developing friendship with one of the mission schoolmasters seemed to fulfill her, though she brooded often about her isolation and about the mission's insignificance under the boundless Oregon sky. But she could glimpse a future now. In sunny hours she imagined her family coming to her at remote Waiilatpu. "Take the map, if you please," she wrote home, "and just look at our situation on this western coast. The Sandwich Islands and China are our next door neighbors."[107] All the Prentisses would find useful work there in a mild and healthy climate: sister Jane, brother Edward, brother Harvey and his wife, Lavinia, and her parents, too—above all her parents, still young and vigorous enough, she insisted, to make the long trek and start anew in the Oregon Country.

Seven of Narcissa's foster children were siblings, orphaned in 1844 when their parents, Henry and Naomi Sager, died on the Oregon Trail. They came to her an unruly and ill-conditioned septet. The three oldest, John (fifteen in 1846), Francis (thirteen), and Catherine (eleven), could barely read. In the Whitmans' view, they were heathens in the full meaning of the term. Narcissa and their tutors, Alanson Hinman, and later Andrew Rodgers, assumed responsibility for "breaking them in to habits of obedience and order." The youngest, Henrietta Naomi, born on the Platte River on the last day of May 1844, reached Waiilatpu sickly, emaciated, and near death. Narcissa set herself the task of redeeming the babe, investing the project with a tremendous weight of emotional meaning. "I wanted her as a charm to bind the rest to me," she wrote her sister Harriet. A milk-and-water diet and a daily bath gradually brought the girl up to strength. Now, as she approached her second birthday, she was strong, fleshy, and full of health and mischief.[108]

"We have as happy a family as the world affords," she wrote home.[109]

The Holy Spirit retained its power to move her profoundly, only now her ecstasies had nothing to do with missionary life. She dissolved into raptures over the coming to Jesus of Joseph L. Finley, a thirty-two-year-old Illinois bachelor who arrived with the 1845 emigration penniless, alone, and in an advanced state of consumption. From mid-January 1846, he was bedfast. Narcissa and Andrew Rodgers nursed Finley, read to him, prayed with him. At the end of February he entered formally into their church, Rodgers and others assembled at his bedside. Finley struck her as curiously calm, with an incapacity to rejoice that for a moment led her to question his conviction. She attributed it finally to his upbringing. His mother had died when he was young, and he had never received much in the way of religious training.

Finley's spiritual and temporal condition reached a crisis on the forenoon of a late March day. "I went to him and told him that I thought Jesus was about to take him away, and asked him if he did not rejoice," she wrote her mother. "He said he did, if he knew what rejoicing was." Henry Spalding had come down from Lapwai; he seemed more at ease in the Whitmans' company, suggesting that if he had not forgotten his ancient grievances, at least they were muted now. At any rate, Spalding joined Narcissa and Rodgers at the deathbed that morning.

"Lord help me now," Finley said after a while. "Thy will be done."

A moment later he whispered, "Farewell to this world."

Hovering, Spalding leaned toward him and asked whether his savior was with him. "I think so," Finley answered, and then called out: "Jesus, save me." Rodgers took his hand. "Sweet Jesus," Finley rasped. "Sweet Jesus! Sweet Jesus!" His breathing became labored and heavy. His sunken chest heaved. He asked them to shift his wasted body in the bed; this brought him no relief. He continued to whisper "Sweet Jesus" at intervals, his voice an agony of suffering.

"Sweet Jesus, sweet Redeemer," Finley said indistinctly. "Farewell, farewell, farewell. I am going."[110]

And so Joseph Finley yielded up his immortal soul. To Narcissa it had been a transcendent experience, "a glorious sight." To her mother she wrote blissfully of "having been permitted to accompany a fellow travaler down to the gates of death and to see him pass the dark waters triumphantly and enter joyfully into the New Jerusalem above." And she congratulated herself for the generosity of her own unquenchable maternal spirit.

"He felt that I had been a mother to him," she wrote, "for he never received such attention before from anyone."[111]

Judging from Mrs. Whitman's correspondence, little other than Finley's long good-bye occurred to disturb the monotony of life at Waiilatpu. The routines were often cheerless, even grim, though from time to time Narcissa would arrange all eleven children by height and, with Rodgers, her particular friend, lead them in a hymn sing. She wrote of subduing the children's spirits, of the eternal vigilance required "in a heathen land, where every influence tends to degrade rather than elevate."[112] She forbade them to study the Nez Perce language and tried to keep them away from the Indians entirely.

Narcissa doted upon Rodgers. He was twenty-five and had studied for the ministry before his health broke down. Evidently a certain amount of teasing, banter, was customary between them. Rodgers managed to get himself talked about not only for his sweet singing voice and his passion for the violin, but also on account of his eccentric appearance. "As to the matter of my not wearing my hat I can only say that I am not conscious of doing it for the sake of being considered odd," he wrote Mary Walker at Tshimakain. "I sometimes step out of doors thinking of going only a step or two from the house when something calls me a little farther than I at first expected and then I think it is not worth while to return for my hat for that distance. That's about all the explanation I am able to give of it." Narcissa must have teased him about his absentmindedness, a sign of intimacy. Other than her husband, she wrote her sister Jane, she had never had—nor did she again expect to have—a more agreeable companion than Rodgers.

The 1846 caravans brought mail from the States, enlivening the autumn at Waiilatpu. Narcissa received letters from her parents, her first since Marcus's return with the Great Migration late in 1843. Sent from Boston, they reached Westport, Missouri, on March 26, 1846, and came into her hands five months later. She learned, too, of discussions in Congress about establishing a monthly overland mail, a development that she felt certain would inaugurate "a new era in our western world."[113]

The Cayuses were an afterthought in this new world. Narcissa had as little as possible to do with them; Whitman dealt with the Indians in a business way—crop and livestock matters, mostly—and continued to provide medical attention when consulted. But he conceded that he had given up any substantial effort at religious instruction. There were "praying Indians," Catholic as well as Protestant, but no actual converts. Whitman had ceased to brood about this. And his wife now felt that she could contribute most effectively by the maternal example she set for the Cayuses.

"So far as the Indians are concerned our prospects of permanently remaining among them were never more favourable than at present," she wrote Laura Brewer at The Dalles in July. "I feel distressed sometimes to think I am making so little personal effort for their benefit, when so much ought to be done, but perhaps I could not do more than I am through the family."[114]

Still, there were ominous signs that Narcissa chose to ignore. The Whitmans, in Mrs. Victor's phrase, lived over "a smouldering volcano" at Waiilatpu. An older generation of Cayuse leaders was passing away, younger chiefs coming into power. Tensions had run high the previous autumn. What Narcissa characterized as Indian "commotions" grew out of yet another large migration, an estimated twenty-five hundred overlanders to Oregon in 1845, some fifty of whom would winter over at Waiilatpu. The natives perfectly kenned Whitman's role as a promoter of white settlement, and they remained resentful of his refusal to pay them for use of their lands. Internal disputes between the praying Indians and those who followed traditional religious practices further stirred the Cayuses and allied tribes. A faction wanted the Whitmans to leave, some on account of the doctor's role in the emigration, others who suspected him of witchcraft with his potions and treatments. Archibald McKinlay, the Hudson's Bay Company factor at Fort Walla Walla, warned Whitman "that the Indians hated him, and that he had better go away, because he was afraid they would kill him."[115] Dr. McLoughlin took the disturbances seriously enough to advise the Whitmans to retire to Vancouver for a season.

Whitman took matters seriously, too, so much so that his hand trembled when he came to set down the case on paper. He had received death threats. Tautai, the young chief, accused him of poisoning one of the senior headmen. Another of the younger Cayuses, Tomahas, brandished a war club in his direction and ordered him to leave Waiilatpu. In late November the young chief confronted Whitman with a long list of grievances. "He spoke of the Americans as having a design to obtain their country and property," he wrote his associates Walker and Eels. The American newcomers drove the game out of the country, they used up firewood, their livestock ravaged the grasslands and polluted the watercourses. They brought diseases that infected the Indian people. Whitman himself had connived in all this.[116]

"I have only given you a faint idea of the matter as it occurred and by no means a full account," he went on. "I have written with such interruptions & while I am so nervous that I cannot govern my hand."[117]

Whitman told the young chief and the Nez Perce with him that he did not believe they would arrange for his murder. But their accusations would inflame the reckless men, he said, and "I would have no assurance but that I might be killed on the most slight or sudden occasion." Abruptly ending the interview, Whitman informed the young chief that he would give the tribe until the following spring to decide whether the missionaries should stay or leave.[118]

Why did Whitman stay? What led him to dismiss the omens? He had a lot invested: time, labor, money, and sentiment as well—the Walla Walla Valley, after all, had been his home for eleven years. Perhaps, too, he shrank from the prospect of ceding the mission field to the papists. Whitman was a stubborn man. When tensions subsided over the winter, he put the threats out of mind. Narcissa, remote, detached, unwilling or unable to probe beneath the placid surface of events, persuaded herself that all was well. "The Indians are very quiet now and never more friendly," she wrote Laura Brewer in July 1846. "The Indians are kind and quiet and very much attached to us," she wrote her mother in November 1846. The wagons rolled past in a steady stream that autumn, bringing another twelve hundred emigrants to Oregon.[119]

Some seventy settlers wintered at the mission in 1846–1847. Whitman sought to employ as many as possible. "The doctor was a man of affairs," wrote Mrs. Victor; "he loved work, and he liked to see others work." The men worked in the gristmill and smithy and tended the stock. The women assisted Narcissa in household affairs. Their children attended the mission school. In the interests of good diplomatic relations, Whitman strove to make himself useful to the Cayuses, too. "I have been doing a good deal for the Indians this past winter & this spring by way of providing nails & breaking land & sawing lumber for coffins & to build store houses," he wrote Elkanah Walker in May. "We have had a spring of great harmony & good feeling on the part of the Indians." He began to think of expansion. The Methodists were selling off Jason Lee's mission station at The Dalles, and he moved to acquire the property for the Presbyterian cause—and possibly, too, as a potential haven should the Cayuses force him out after all.[120]

The antimission faction in the tribe observed the thriving white settlement sullenly from a distance. The younger chiefs increasingly resented and mistrusted the Americans; they feared them, too. The Canadian artist Paul Kane, stopping at Waiilatpu for a few days in the summer of 1847, sketched Tomahas in his lodge, Whitman providing the entrée. After a while Tomahas asked the artist whether he planned to give the sketch to the Whitmans, "superstitiously fancying that their possessing it would put him in their power." Tomahas lunged for the drawing, intending to throw it into the fire. Kane held on and retreated, escaping the lodge without further incident.[121]

The first cases of measles had broken out among the Cayuses in the spring of 1847 with the return of a raiding party from northern California. The virus claimed some thirty Cayuses and their Wallawalla Indian allies. Then dysentery appeared in the Cayuse encampments. By late August the first of the 1847 migration began to pass, eighty or so wagons; according to Mrs. Whitman, there were said to be a thousand wagons on the road still. In fact, the 1847 emigration would total a record-to-date four thousand settlers.

"The poor Indians are amazed at the overwhelming numbers of Americans coming into the country," she wrote home. "They seem not to know what to make of it. . . . They do not wish to see any *Sniapus* (Americans) settle among them here; they are willing to have them spend the winter here, but in the spring they must all go on."[122]

So the fateful autumn advanced. Fifty-four overlanders elected to pass the winter at Waiilatpu; the Cayuses suspected them of plotting to homestead permanently in their country. Word filtered in from Lapwai that disaffected Nez Perces had knocked down Spalding's fences and damaged the mill there. "They are threatening to turn us out of these missions," Spalding said.[123] Seemingly heedless of the peril, Mrs. Whitman sent another appeal to her sister Jane to join her in Oregon, adding the homely detail that she had reserved a fine mule for her use, one Uncle Sam, so named because Lieutenant Frémont had made the mission a present of him when the exploring expedition passed through in 1843. With the first of the '47 emigrants came a renewed outbreak of measles among the Cayuses, perhaps an eruption of the earlier strain, perhaps something the Americans introduced. Whatever the cause, the antimission Indians blamed the epidemic on Whitman.

The doctor reported a great demand for his services, and in consequence a serious shortage of medicines. A six-year-old white child died of measles at the mission. The virus claimed another thirty or more Cayuses near Waiilatpu in October and November. Overall estimates of Cayuse deaths ranged as high as two hundred, close to half the tribe's population. Spalding would write that he had entered a lodge of ten fires to find twenty or twenty-five people in various stages of critical illness. "They were dying every day, one, two and sometimes five, with the dysentery, which very generally followed the measles," he recalled. "Everywhere the sick and dying were pointed to Jesus, and the well were urged to prepare for death." Whitman's prescriptions were no more effectual than prayer; some of the Cayuses revived the old accusation of witchcraft. Whitman surely knew they sometimes followed a practice of putting their shamans to death when spells, charms, and medicines went awry. One of the Cayuses told him the "bad Indians" were going to kill him.[124]

Significant numbers of Cayuses believed they had grounds for their suspicions about Whitman's prescriptions. The doctor had poisoned wolves; he had poisoned melons in his garden to deter thieves. Three Cayuse men incautiously consumed poisoned meat set out for the wolves and fell violently ill. John Young, a laborer at Whitman's sawmill, recalled that the doctor had told him, laughing, that "they would have certainly have died if they had not drunk a great quantity of warm water to excite vomiting." As for the melons, they had been but lightly poisoned—only just enough to make a poacher a little sick.[125]

Such stories, perhaps exaggerated, lent plausibility to two part-Indian provocateurs. Among the combustible Cayuses they were, in Mrs. Victor's words, "like fire in tow." Tom Hill warned the Indians that the Americans would treat them as they had his own Delawares; that is to say, they would swarm over their land and drive them away. "Look how they are selling everything they raise on your own lands," he said; "you cannot get anything from them without paying for it; not so much as a piece of meat when you are hungry." Joe Lewis reminded the Indians how an American trapper in 1837 had deliberately spread smallpox among the Blackfeet. Now he broadcast the charge that the Whitmans and Henry Spalding were conspiring to kill off the Cayuses so they could seize their land and horses.[126]

Lewis met with Cayuse elders in council on November 27, a Saturday, telling them that Whitman and Spalding had sent to their friends in the East for poison and that it had arrived in late summer with the caravans. The results were plain enough: disease, death, destitution. They had seen that whites recovered from the sickness and Indians died; these were white men's troubles, and a white medicine man ought to be able to cure them. The Cayuses thus arraigned Dr. Whitman, the white shaman.

Whitman returned from a two-day medical circuit among the lodges late on Sunday. The next day—Monday the twenty-ninth— the doctor, weary from his travels, lingered in the sitting room through the morning, reading and resting. Otherwise the Waiilatpu workweek began much as usual, with school in session and Mrs. Whitman supervising the younger children's baths. One of the hands dressed a beef in the mission yard. Narcissa left the children for some errand into the kitchen, where she found a group of Cayuses crowding in. She withdrew in alarm and bolted the door behind her. A moment later she heard her husband's voice, then many raised voices. A firearm discharged with the impact of a thunderbolt.

It happened this way: One of the Cayuses distracted Whitman by asking for medicine while another, Tomahas, slipped behind the doctor and struck him two tomahawk blows in the head. Then a third, Tilokaikt, rushed into the room and slashed at his face with a long knife. Whitman slumped to the floor, mortally wounded. Narcissa reentered the kitchen to find her husband bleeding and insensible and her foster son John Sager lying near death close by. With the help of another woman, Narcissa carried the doctor into the parlor and tried to stanch the bleeding. Barely conscious, he whispered there was nothing she could do.

The attacks continued out of doors, the whites penned up for the slaughter. From the window, Narcissa could see Cayuse men in their black-and-white war paint, with eagle feathers in their headdress; women were singing and dancing, acting out their roles in Cayuse battle ritual. The butcher and two or three others lay dead near their places of work. Narcissa was hit as she approached the door, shot in the breast or upper arm. Her blouse, hands, and copper-colored hair smeared with her husband's blood and her own, she retreated up the stairs with Andrew Rodgers and several of the children. On the first floor, Indians broke in and disfigured the faces of Whitman and John Sager. One of their number, Tamsucky, came to the foot of the stairs and pleaded with Rodgers to descend, saying he would lead the women and children to safety before the others set fire to the house.

Trembling and in shock, Narcissa followed Rodgers unsteadily down the stairs and into the parlor. She lay down upon a wooden settee. Then Rodgers and one of the mission women lifted the ends of the settee and carried her outside. Renewed firing broke out. Rodgers, Francis Sager, and Mrs. Whitman were hit; she tumbled to the ground in a pool of fresh blood. Survivors remembered seeing one of the Cayuses repeatedly strike the dying Narcissa in the face with a war club or possibly a whip. Night closed in on a scene of devastation. At dawn the attackers chanted a Cayuse death song.

There were more killings over the next few days, bringing the death toll to fourteen altogether. The Cayuses took forty women and children captive; they would add seven others from Whitman's sawmill in the Blue Mountains a few days later. Some of the women were raped; three young women would be assigned to Cayuse warriors as wives. Narcissa Whitman was the only woman to be put to death. For the Cayuses—some of them, anyhow—rough justice had been served.

A Roman Catholic priest, Jean Baptiste Brouillet, learned of the murders when he rode out from Fort Walla Walla to Tilokaikt's camp on the thirtieth. Father Brouillet continued on to Waiilatpu on December 1. He spoke briefly with the prisoners, then inquired about the dead. They lay about unburied, though one of the surviving mission hands, Joseph Stanfield, had washed some of the corpses. Brouillet counted ten bodies around the mission house. He read a funeral service in Latin for the Whitmans and the others and saw them buried in a common grave that Stanfield had hollowed out. Brouillet learned later that wolves disturbed the grave and gnawed at the corpses. In the end the Whitmans' bones, in Henry Spalding's lament, lay scattered upon the plains.[127]

Epilogue

The Country of the Setting Sun

Marcus and narcissa whitman had borne the Cayuses no animus. Yet their good intentions and invincible incomprehension set in motion the process of destruction of the Cayuse way of life. The Whitmans and the others at Waiilatpu fell victim to their fatal meddling in a culture they did not understand, made scant effort to understand. Their appearance in the Oregon Country proved catastrophic for themselves and for the people they had come to enlighten. The process had operated wherever Euroamericans met native peoples, in seventeenth-century Virginia and New England, along the Ohio River Valley in the eighteenth century, in the mountains of North Carolina, Georgia, and Tennessee and the rich bottomlands of Alabama and Mississippi in the 1830s, and now, in midcentury, in Oregon and California: the seductive approach of the traders, with firearms, clothing, beads, and liquor; the introduction of destabilizing new ideas and devastating new diseases; the steady encroachment of homesteaders; and accelerating conflict over land and resources.

With the corpses insecurely buried in their shallow graves, the Reverend Jean Baptiste Brouillet rode out of Waiilatpu on the foggy afternoon of December 1, 1847, bound for the Catholic mission on the Umatilla River with an escort of an Indian interpreter and one of the sons of the Cayuse chief Tilokaikt. Father Brouillet met Henry Spalding as he approached the mission unaware of the killings there and of the fact that his daughter Eliza had been taken captive. The priest interceded with the chief's son on Spalding's behalf; briefly undecided about how to dispose of him, the two Indians moved a short distance off to smoke and ponder, giving Spalding his chance to slip away under cover of the fog. He carried only the short rations Brouillet had been able to transfer to him. After six days' hard travel, physically eroded, in a state of extreme psychological and spiritual strain, Spalding reached the mission station at Lapwai.

Spalding found the valley of the Clearwater peaceful, the Nez Perces reassuring. "They pledged to protect us from the Cayuses," he wrote on December 10, "if we would prevent the Americans from coming up to avenge the murders."[1] Spalding reasoned that he had little choice but to fall in with their wishes, and that any attempt to leave would be dangerous. With the mission more or less under siege for the time being, he wrote to alert Elkanah Walker and Cushing Eels at Tshimakain of the troubles and to warn them not to allow themselves to be isolated there.

"Let me *repeat*," Spalding advised, "make no proposition to your Indians in regard to your remaining or leaving, or promises to return, and *by all means* secure the assistance of the Canadians in transporting your effects to Colville—when I *advise you as you value your lives* to repair as soon as circumstances of your families will admit."[2]

Word of the Whitman killings reached James Douglas, Dr. McLoughlin's successor at Fort Vancouver, on the evening of December 6. Douglas alerted the American provisional governor, George Abernethy, the next day, and Abernethy delivered the news to the Oregon legislature on December 8. Governor and assembly moved at once to raise money and men for a punitive expedition into the upper country and to send a messenger across the mountains to plead for U.S. protection.

The initial response fell short of Abernethy's expectations. About 230 men answered the call for 500 militia volunteers. And Douglas refused Abernethy's request for a $100,000 loan to finance the campaign, citing a post-McLoughlin company policy of denying substantial credit to individual settlers or the provisional government. Besides, on grounds of trade and general principle, Douglas objected to making war on an entire Indian nation. The murderers, if they could be found, should be punished individually, rather than the Cayuses collectively.

While the Americans beat the drums for war—"Fifty well-fed and mounted riflemen could massacre with the best of them, not omitting the women and children, or even the time-honored custom of scalping," observed Frances Fuller Victor—Douglas at once readied a mission to the Cayuses to negotiate the release of the forty-seven captives. The veteran trader Peter Skene Ogden left Vancouver on December 7, fetched Fort Walla Walla after a journey of twelve days, and learned there that all the whites—five men, eight women, and thirty-four children—were still alive.[3]

Ogden met in council with the Cayuse chiefs two days before Christmas. The chiefs proposed that the Americans send "two or three great men" to negotiate a peace treaty, after which the hostages would be released. Essentially the Cayuse elders offered to let bygones be bygones; the tribe would forgive the whites for trespass and for the introduction of fatal poisons if the whites would forgive the Whitman murders. They asked, too, that "the Americans may not travel any more through their country, as their young men might do them harm."[4] Ogden replied bluntly that the Americans would be in no mood for the finer points of diplomacy. The Cayuses had no choice but to return the hostages and surrender the killers. And even those measures might not suffice.

"If the Americans begin war," Ogden told the chiefs, the fighting "will not end until every man of you is cut off from the face of the earth. I am aware that many of your people have died; but so have others. It was not Dr. Whitman who poisoned them, but God who has commanded that they should die."[5]

He offered a ransom, and promised to "see what can be done for you"; he did not, could not, undertake to prevent a war. The Cayuses thought it over and agreed to exchange the 47 captives for 62 three-point blankets, 63 cotton shirts, 12 guns, 600 loads of ammunition, 37 pounds of tobacco, and 12 flints—for a total value of $500, or a few cents more than $10 a head. Accompanied by 50 Nez Perces, Henry and Eliza Spalding reached Fort Walla Walla safely on January 1, 1848, and were reunited with their daughter Eliza. Skeletal, undernourished, too weak to stand without assistance, Eliza told her parents she had stopped up her ears when she heard the first shrieks of terror and pain that November day. The Spaldings bundled the little girl into a canoe and set off downriver with Ogden and the other refugees the next day.[6]

THE OREGON MILITIA marched for The Dalles on January 8, the same day Ogden's flotilla reached Vancouver with the Waiilatpu refugees. The American colonel-commandant, Cornelius Gilliam, carried orders to proceed with caution and to make every effort to distinguish between friendly and unfriendly Indians. A slash-and-burn type, Gilliam—so a rumor went—had contemplated seizing Fort Vancouver when Douglas refused to finance the expedition, figuring he would simply help himself to what he needed to provision and equip his army; Governor Abernethy hastened to assure an alarmed Douglas that Gilliam harbored no such intention. The colonel's notions were brutally direct: he meant to drive the Indians out of the country or exterminate them. Contemptuous of the three-man peace commission that accompanied the militia, he reacted with Old Testament ferocity to a brief, inconclusive negotiating session with the Cayuses' Nez Perce allies. "Col. Gilliam left the council in a huff and declared he has come to fight and he will," remarked one of the commissioners.[7]

With Ogden's mission complete, Gilliam could advance into the upper country without endangering any whites. Word of his initial operations reached the Willamette in mid-February. "The army have passed The Dalles, had fighting with the Indians, killed some 24, took considerable property and lost three white men and one friendly Indian," Henry Spalding wrote Walker and Eels. "Have taken up the march for Waiilatpu."[8] Gilliam's point, however, may have been lost on the Cayuses; the militia had assailed a village of friendly Indians who had taken no part in the Whitman murders.

Gilliam's march had the effect of uniting the fractious Cayuses, whose praying and traditional factions now mobilized to defend their country. The Americans marched here and there without achieving much, unable to bring the Cayuses to a decisive battle. The troops did, however, round up or rustle livestock they suspected of belonging to the enemy. In fact, the cattle were the property of a band of innocent Palouse Indians. One such operation, in February, touched off an all-day running skirmish with a party of 250 Palouses that left 10 of the militiamen wounded and added another upper country tribe to the roll of America's enemies.

Gilliam withdrew to Waiilatpu, where he had made his headquarters in the mission ruins, a devastation of scorched adobes, broken wagons, shattered glass and pottery, knocked-down fences, and felled orchard trees. The scene fueled the colonel's rage, but fate decreed that he should meet his end before he could expend his pent-up fury in a battle. As he prepared to tether his horse, Gilliam caught the rope on the trigger of a gun and it discharged, killing him instantly. Anyhow, by then the Cayuse remnant and their herds had melted into Nez Perce country, out of the Americans' reach. The militia returned to the Willamette Valley in June with the Whitmans unavenged.

THE WHITMAN MURDERS accelerated the establishment of U.S. territorial government in Oregon, Congress moving to pass legislation organizing the territory in August 1848. Five Cayuses implicated in the Waiilatpu killings surrendered to U.S. authorities early in 1850. By then Oregon's new rulers had declared Cayuse lands forfeit and encouraged veterans of the 1848 militia campaign to homestead in the Walla Walla Valley. Joseph Lane, the territorial governor, pressed negotiations for the voluntary handover of the killers. In due course, the tribe agreed to extradite Tilokaikt and Tomahas, who had touched off the uprising at the mission, and three others. The five consented to face trial, offering fifty horses to their counsel should they be acquitted.

Lane himself went up to The Dalles to take custody of the accused. Suspects, dignitaries, and a heavy guard then retraced the route to the territorial capital at Oregon City, the venue of the trial. The police guard expressed curiosity about why the Cayuses had agreed to abbreviate their lives. After all, the outcome was foregone: in the unlikely event of a sentence short of death, or the still more unlikely event of an acquittal, the settlers were prepared to take justice into their own hands and carry out a lynching. The guards' barrage of questions elicited an embittered reply from Tilokaikt:

"Did not your missionaries teach us that Christ died to save his people? So we die to save our people."

The trial opened on May 22. In this case the wheels of justice positively whirred: the Cayuses were convicted and sentenced to death on June 3. The judge denied their request for a retrial, and they were led to the gibbet on schedule before an eager hanging-day crowd estimated at four hundred. U.S. Marshal Joseph Meek, the veteran mountain man who had danced attendance on Narcissa Whitman at the 1836 trapper rendezvous, sustained the role of hangman. A Roman Catholic priest administered the sacraments; Tilokaikt and the others brusquely refused Henry Spalding's offer of Presbyterian consolation.

"Onward, onward to heaven, children, into thy hands I commend thy spirit," Father Veyret called out at the moment the five condemned men swung into the air.[9]

His duty done, Governor Lane moved south to California in search of gold. Finding none, or anyhow not enough to permanently enrich him, he returned to Oregon in 1851 to seek election as the territory's delegate to the U.S. Congress. By then the Cayuses had ceased to exist as an independent nation.

LIEUTENANT FRÉMONT'S GOLDEN DREAMS evaporated, too. He achieved a temporary fortune in gold along the American River, won a U.S. Senate seat from the newly admitted state of California in 1850, and leveraged his fame as the Pathfinder to the nascent Republican Party's nomination for the presidency in 1856. Frémont lost the election and retired from politics, lost the fortune and eventually his renown as well. Jessie Frémont soldiered on as the keeper of his faded legacy: where his campfires once flickered, she would write in the 1890s, towns and cities flourished.

Part of Frémont's legacy, and the legacy, too, of the Astorians, Hall Kelley, Nathaniel Wyeth, Jason Lee, and the Whitmans, was a cosmic upheaval among the first nations of the Pacific slope. California's Indian population totaled about a hundred thousand in 1846, the year of the Bear Flag revolt. Within a decade, malnutrition, disease, and prospector violence had reduced it to a demoralized remnant of about thirty thousand. A series of frontier wars displaced the Nisenan, the Klamaths, and the Modocs of California, and the Rogue River bands and the Yakimas of the Oregon Territory. Finally, in the years after the Civil War, their unappeasable earth hunger led the Americans into the remote Idaho recesses of the Nez Perces.

The Americans offered no apology, then or later. Indian war, the Treasury agent J. Ross Browne wrote in 1857, "is the natural result of immigration and settlement. . . . The history of our Indian wars will show that the primary cause is the progress of civilization, to which the inferior races, from their habits and instincts, are naturally opposed."[10] In Oregon in the aftermath of the Whitman killings, the territorial legislature, with its Land Donation Law of 1850, in effect issued an invitation to settlers to seize Indian lands. The tribes of the Willamette Valley, Browne conceded, were simply informed that the country no longer belonged to them. The natives were as powerless to prevent this as they were conceptually unequipped to understand how it all could have happened.

"They could never be taught to comprehend that subtle species of argument by which another race could come among them, put them aside, ignore their claims, and assume possession, on the grounds of being a superior people," wrote Browne.[11]

By 1890 two million Americans had migrated to the Country of the Setting Sun. Just as they arranged for most of the original inhabitants to disappear, the Americans in their furious energy reshaped the landscape of the conquered lands, from the pristine hinterland of Charles Wilkes's Puget Sound south to John Muir's California bee garden. They hacked wagon roads through the mountains, burrowed into hillsides in quest of mineral wealth, cut down pine and oak forests, dredged harbors, rerouted rivers, excavated canals, plowed under bunch-grass and sage prairies for wheat, turned livestock loose to range where they allowed the grasslands to survive, and laid down iron ribbons of railroad track that stretched beyond the horizon.

The Americans were relentless in their efforts to control nature and adapt it to their purposes; technological innovation extended their power in new and transfiguring ways. The state of Oregon cut the first wagon road through the Columbia River Gorge in 1872. Four years later, the U.S. Congress approved construction of a canal portage around the Cascades; a three-thousand-foot-long ditch with locks opened in 1896. The northern transcontinental railroad reached Portland in 1883, reducing cross-country travel time from three or four months to five or six days. Railroads brought half a million emigrants to the Pacific Northwest in the 1880s, a third again as many as traveled the Oregon Trail over three mid-century decades. Federal fisheries experts issued warnings of serious declines in salmon stocks as early as 1894. Below Vancouver, diking and filling dried up the riparian lands where Townsend and Nuttall had stalked the Oregon Country's exotic plant and bird specimens. The three-hundred-mile-long Columbia River Highway opened for internal combustion vehicles in 1915.[12]

Then, in a colossal act of ecological degradation, American energy caused the turbulent Great River of the West to go slack and still. In four decades beginning in the 1930s with the Bonneville project (it flooded the terrible and magnificent Cascades) and concluding in 1975 with the Lower Granite Dam on the Snake River, the U.S. government

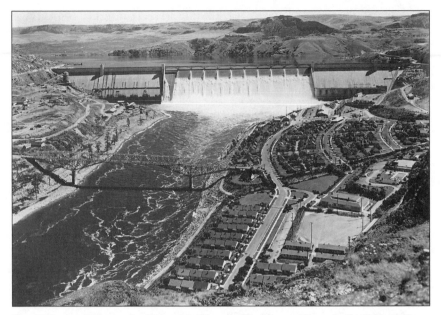

Grand Coulee Dam on the Columbia River in Washington State, built 1933–1942, stands as a mighty symbol of New Deal–era progress. With other dams of the Columbia River Basin Project, it converted the once free-flowing Columbia into a slackwater barge highway and generator of cheap electrical power for the Pacific Northwest. (Library of Congress)

built thirteen big dams on the Columbia and twenty on the Snake. With astonishing impertinence, they named one of the Columbia dams after Chief Joseph, who had led the Nez Perces on their harrowing forced march out of the Wallowa Valley in 1877. This massive development project created Depression-era jobs, 10,000 at the peak of construction at the Bonneville and Grand Coulee dams alone. In time, it bestowed water on farmers, low transport rates on shippers, and cheap electricity on factories and homes, and it built the old Oregon Territory, with the Canadian province of British Columbia added, into the tenth-ranking economy in the world.[13]

The dams tamed and sterilized the once wild and bountiful Columbia, converting its tumult of rapids and cascades into "a chain of slow-moving puddles," in journalist Blaine Harden's phrase, and decimated a salmon population that the awestruck Astorians had judged inexhaustible. Backed-up waters flooded Indian reservation lands, fishing sites, and sacred places. The great impoundments touched off climate changes, making winters warmer and summers cooler. Silt bottoms replaced gravel beds, trapping pollutants. Carp replaced salmon. Early in the nineteenth century, an estimated two million adult salmon returned to the Snake River spawning grounds annually. Salmon stocks averaged a hundred thousand adults as late as the 1960s, before the last of the Snake River barrages were built. In the first years of the twenty-first century, fewer than four thousand returned.[14]

The river tribes arranged their lives and rituals around salmon, especially the wondrous chinook—in Astorian Robert Stuart's view, "by far the finest fish I ever beheld." Federal government treaties granted the Columbia and Snake River Indian nations perpetual fishing rights. The dams effectively abrogated those treaties. The great spring and summer runs are a historical curiosity now, soon to be lost to the memories of living men. The canoes of fur trader/explorer David Thompson swept down toward the Pacific on rivers thick with leaping, flashing salmon. In our time, perhaps one in every *ten thousand* chinooks manages to evade the turbines and scale the fish ladders to reach the spawning ground a thousand miles from the Pacific: progress.

Notes

Prologue: *Columbia*'s River

1. "John Boit's Log of the Second Voyage of the *Columbia*," in *Voyages of the Columbia to the Northwest Coast in 1787–1790 and 1790–1793*, ed. Frederick W. Howay (Boston: Massachusetts Historical Society, 1941), 390.

2. "Robert Haswell's Log of the Second Voyage of the *Columbia*," in Howay, ed., *Voyages of the Columbia*, 251; "John Boit's Log," 383.

3. "John Hoskins' Narrative of the Second Voyage of the *Columbia*," in Howay, ed., *Voyages of the Columbia*, 196; "John Boit's Log," 385.

4. Ibid., 377.

5. "Robert Haswell's Log," 313; "John Boit's Log," 389.

6. "John Boit's Log," 390–391.

7. "John Hoskins' Narrative," 272.

8. Joseph Barrell to Robert Gray, September 25, 1790, *Columbia* Papers, Oregon Historical Society (hereafter, OHS).

9. Ibid. "John Hoskins' Narrative," 161; "John Boit's Log," 298.

10. Ibid.

11. Ibid., 391–392.

12. George Vancouver, *Voyage of Discovery to the North Pacific Ocean and Round the World*, vol. 1 (1798; reprint, New York: Da Capo Press, 1967), 213.

13. Ibid., 215, 224.

14. Quoted in Barry M. Gough, *Distant Dominion: Britain and the Northwest Coast of North America, 1579–1809* (Vancouver: University of British Columbia Press, 1980), 119.

15. "John Boit's Log," 393–394; "Remnant of Official Log of the *Columbia*," *Oregon Historical Quarterly* [hereafter *OHQ*] 22 (1921): 352.

16. "John Boit's Log," 394.

17. Ibid., 395–396.

18. "Remnant of Official Log of the *Columbia*," 353; "John Boit's Log," 396–397.

19. "John Boit's Log," 397; "Remnant of Official Log of the *Columbia*," 353.

20. "John Boit's Log," 397–399, 398n.

21. "Remnant of Official Log of the *Columbia*," 354–355.

22. "John Boit's Log," 399.

23. John Hoskins to Joseph Barrell, December 13, 1792, *Columbia* Papers, OHS; "John Boit's Log," 421.

24. Vancouver, *Voyage of Discovery to the North Pacific*, vol. 2, 52–53.

25. Ibid., 77.

26. Ibid., 59.

27. Ibid., 63.

28. Ibid., 66.

29. J. Neilsen Barry, "Broughton on the Columbia in 1792," *OHQ* 26 (1927): 406; Vancouver, *Voyage of Discovery to the North Pacific*, vol. 2, 66.

30. Ibid., 75.

31. Ibid., 77.

1. Ways West

1. Washington Irving, *Astoria* (1836; reprint, Portland, Ore.: Binford & Mort, 1967), 23; quoted in Henry Nash Smith, *Virgin Land* (Cambridge, Mass.: Harvard University Press, 1950), 9.

2. Irving, *Astoria*, 24; J. J. Astor to Thomas Jefferson, February 27, 1808, Thomas Jefferson Papers, Series 1: General Correspondence, 1751–1827. Library of Congress http://memory.loc.gov/ammem/mtjhml/mtjhome.html; Thomas Jefferson to J. J. Astor, April 13, 1808, Jefferson Papers, Library of Congress.

3. Alexander Ross, *Adventures of the First Settlers on the Columbia River* (1849; reprint, Ann Arbor, Mich.: University Microfilms, 1966), 4, 7; Irving, *Astoria*, 25, 27.

4. Gabriel Franchère, *Adventure at Astoria*, 1810–1814, trans. and ed. by Hoyt C. Franchère (Norman: University of Oklahoma Press, 1967), 9.

5. Ibid., 19; Irving, *Astoria*, 35.

6. Irving, *Astoria*, 34; Ross, *Adventures on the Columbia*, 15.

7. According to historian James P. Ronda, there is no documentary evidence that *Constitution* left port on September 8, 1810. See Ronda, *Astoria and Empire* (Lincoln: University of Nebraska Press, 1990), 102.

8. Franchère, *Adventure at Astoria*, 13.

9. Ibid., 18; Ross, *Adventures on the Columbia*, 22.

10. Franchère, *Adventure at Astoria*, 20; Ross, *Adventures on the Columbia*, 25.

11. Irving, *Astoria*, 43.

12. Ibid., 55.

13. Ross, *Adventures on the Columbia*, 57.

14. Robert Stuart, *On the Oregon Trail*, ed. Kenneth A. Spalding (Norman: University of Oklahoma Press, 1953), 41; Irving, *Astoria*, 65.

15. Ross, *Adventures on the Columbia*, 67.

16. Franchère, *Adventure at Astoria*, 46.

17. Stuart, *On the Oregon Trail*, 30–31.

18. Franchère, *Adventure at Astoria*, 106.

19. David Thompson, *Travels in Western North America, 1784–1812*, ed. Victor G. Hopwood (Toronto: Macmillan of Canada, 1971), 281–283.

20. Ibid., 296.

21. Ibid., 297–298.

22. Ibid., 299.

23. Arthur S. Morton, "The North West Company's Columbia Enterprise and David Thompson," *The Canadian Historical Review* 17 (September 1936): 279, 287.

24. Ronda, *Astoria and Empire*, 232–233; Ross, *Adventures on the Columbia*, 85; 154. Thompson, *Travels in Western North America*, 299.

25. Franchère, *Adventure at Astoria*, 57; William Dietrich, *Northwest Passage: The Great Columbia River* (New York: Simon & Schuster, 1995), 142; Irving, *Astoria*, 97.

26. Ross, *Adventures on the Columbia*, 142.

27. Stuart, *On the Oregon Trail*, 42.

28. Ross, *Adventures on the Columbia*, 88; Stuart, *On the Oregon Trail*, 41; Franchère, *Adventure at Astoria*, 122.

29. Stuart, *On the Oregon Trail*, 38; Ross, *Adventures on the Columbia*, 89.

30. Franchère, *Adventure at Astoria*, 115.

31. Ibid., 91.

32. Ibid., 93, 117.

33. Ross, *Adventures on the Columbia*, 99–100.

34. Thompson, *Travels in Western North America*, 245–246.

35. Stuart, *On the Oregon Trail*, 32.

36. Franchère, *Adventure at Astoria*, 108.

37. Ross, *Adventures on the Columbia*, 97; Franchère, *Adventure at Astoria*, 121.

38. Ross, *Adventures on the Columbia*, 172.

39. Irving, *Astoria*, 146.

40. John Bradbury, *Travels in the Interior* (1817; reprint, Ann Arbor, Mich.: University Microfilms, 1966), 72.

41. Ibid., 126 (a spencer was a close-fitting bodice women commonly wore early in the nineteenth century); Ronda, *Astoria and Empire*, 163.

42. Unless otherwise noted, the account of Hunt's overland journey follows Irving, *Astoria*.

43. Wilson Price Hunt Diary, in Philip Ashton Rollins, *The Discovery of the Oregon Trail* (1935; reprint, Lincoln: University of Nebraska Press, 1995), 292.

44. Ibid., 295–296.

45. Ibid.

46. Ibid., 301.

47. Ross Cox, *The Columbia River*, ed. Edgar I. Stewart and Jane R. Stewart (Norman: University of Oklahoma Press, 1957), 73.

48. Ross, *Adventures on the Columbia*, 142, 146.

49. Ibid., 146.

50. Stuart, *On the Oregon Trail*, 49, 50, 54; Robert Stuart, "Journal of a Voyage across the Continent of North America from Astoria to the City of New York," Western Americana Collection, Beinecke Library, Yale University, 37; Cox, *The Columbia River*, 77–78.

51. Stuart, *On the Oregon Trail*, 64, 66; Cox, *The Columbia River*, 83.

52. Stuart, "Journal," 62–64.

53. Irving, *Astoria*, 335–336.

54. Stuart, *On the Oregon Trail*, 88; Stuart, "Journal," 86.

55. Stuart, *On the Oregon Trail*, 91.

56. Ibid., 97; Irving, *Astoria*, 341.

57. Stuart, *On the Oregon Trail*, 103–104.

58. Ibid., 109.

59. Ibid., 114.

60. Ibid., 115; Irving, *Astoria*, 360–361.

61. Stuart, *On the Oregon Trail*, 118; Irving, *Astoria*, 363.

62. Stuart, *On the Oregon Trail*, 130.

63. Ibid., 141.

64. Stuart, "Journal," 211.

65. Cox, *The Columbia River*, 119; Ross, *Adventures on the Columbia*, 245.

66. Franchère, *Adventure at Astoria*, 87; Ross, *Adventures on the Columbia*, 275.

67. Irving, *Astoria*, 438–439; Ronda, *Astoria and Empire*, 291.

68. J. J. Astor to Thomas Jefferson, October 18, 1813, Thomas Jefferson Papers, Library of Congress.

69. Irving, *Astoria*, 438–439; Ross, *Adventures on the Columbia*, 254.

70. Franchère, *Adventure at Astoria*, 91.

71. Ibid., 91; "Captain Black's Report on Taking of Astoria," *Oregon Historical Quarterly* 17 (1916): 147–148; Irving, *Astoria*, 441.

72. Ross, *Adventures on the Columbia*, 283.

73. J. J. Astor to Thomas Jefferson, October 18, 1813, Thomas Jefferson Papers, Library of Congress.

2. The Road to India

1. *Register of Debates*, 18th Cong., 2nd sess., March 1, 1825, 706; T. C. Elliott, "The Surrender at Astoria in 1818," *Oregon Historical Quarterly* [hereafter *OHQ*] 19 (1918): 272.

2. George Simpson, *Fur Trade and Empire: George Simpson's Journal*, ed. Frederick W. Merk (Cambridge, Mass.: Harvard University Press, Belknap Press, 1968), xix–xxi; R. Harvey Fleming, ed., *Minutes of Council of Northern Department of Rupert's Land*, Hudson's Bay Company Series III (Toronto: Champlain Society, 1940), 302, 328.

3. Quoted in James Morris, *Heaven's Command* (San Diego: Harcourt, Brace, 1973), 216.

4. Ibid., 120.

5. Fleming, ed., *Minutes of Council*, 297–298.

6. Ibid., 71.

7. Simpson, *Journal*, 23, 16.

8. Ibid., 23.

9. Ibid., 132.

10. Ibid., 7, 43, 57–58, 46.

11. Ibid., 64–65.

12. Ibid., 65, 49.

13. Ibid., 87, 124.

14. Ibid., 71–72.

15. J. H. Pelley to George Canning, December 9, 1825, *OHQ* 20 (1919): 25–34.

16. George Simpson to H. U. Aldington, December 28, 1825, in Simpson, *Journal*, 265–266.

17. John McLoughlin to George Simpson, March 20, 1827, in Simpson, *Journal*, 291–292.

18. Governor and Committee to George Simpson, March 10, 1827, in Fleming, ed., *Minutes of Council*, lxviii.

19. Governor and Committee to George Simpson, January 16, 1828, in Simpson, *Journal*, 294–295.

20. William H. Goetzmann, *Exploration and Empire: The Explorer and the Scientist in the Winning of the American West* (New York: Alfred A. Knopf, 1966), 130–136.

21. Ibid., 138.

22. George Simpson to Jedediah Smith, December 26, 1828, in Simpson, *Journal*, 305.

23. Jedediah Smith, David Jackson, and William Sublette to John H. Eaton, October 29, 1830, in U.S. Senate, 21st Cong., 2nd sess., Document 39, December 6, 1830, 39–40; Goetzmann, *Exploration and Empire*, 140.

24. George Simpson to John McLoughlin, March 15, 1829, in Simpson, *Journal*, 308; Simpson, *Journal*, 106.

25. John McLoughlin to the Governor and Committee, October 11, 1830, in Simpson, *Journal*, 337; William Dietrich, *Northwest Passage: The Great Columbia River* (New York: Simon & Schuster, 1995), 139.

26. Jesse Benton Frémont, "Sketch of the Life of Senator Benton," in John C. Frémont, *Memoirs of My Life*, vol. 1 (Chicago: Bedford, Clarke, 1887), 2.

27. Quoted in Elbert B. Smith, *Magnificent Missourian: The Life of Thomas Hart Benton* (Philadelphia: J. B. Lippincott, 1958), 68; Thomas Hart Benton, *Thirty Years' View*, vol. 1 (New York: D. Appleton, 1854), 110.

28. *Annals of Congress*, 17th Cong., 2nd sess., December 17, 1822, 407.

29. Archer B. Hulbert and Dorothy P. Hulbert, eds., *The Oregon Crusade: Across Land and Sea to Oregon*, vol. 5 of *Overland to the Pacific* (Denver: Colorado College and Denver Public Library, 1935), 23–24.

30. *Annals of Congress*, 17th Cong., 1st sess., March 25, 1822, 329.

31. Ibid., 420.

32. Register of Debates, 18th Cong., 2nd sess., March 1, 1825.

33. Quoted in Smith, *Magnificent Missourian*, 84; Register of Debates, 18th Cong., 2nd sess., February 26, 1825, 691.

34. Ibid., 689, 712.

35. John Quincy Adams to Richard Rush, July 22, 1823, in *John Quincy Adams and American Continental Empire: Letters, Papers and Speeches*, ed. Walter LaFeber (Chicago: Quadrangle Books, 1965), 91.

36. William R. Manning, ed., *Diplomatic Correspondence of the United States: Canadian Relations, 1784–1860*, vol. 2 (Washington, D.C.: Carnegie Endowment for World Peace, 1940–1945), 613–14; Benton, *Thirty Years' View*, 50.

37. Quoted in F. W. Power, ed., *Hall Kelley on Oregon* (Princeton, N.J.: Princeton University Press, 1932), ix.

38. John B. Wyeth, *Oregon: or a Short History of a Long Journey* (1833; reprint, Ann Arbor, Mich.: University Microfilms, 1966), 4.

39. Nathaniel J. Wyeth to Leonard Jarvis, February 6, 1832, in "The Correspondence and Journals of Captain Nathaniel J. Wyeth, 1831–36," in *Sources in the History of Oregon*, ed. F. G. Young (Eugene, Ore.: University Press, 1899), 33; Nathaniel J. Wyeth to Hall J. Kelley, August 30, 1831, "Correspondence and Journals," 1; Nathaniel J. Wyeth to Leonard Wyeth, November 14, 1831, "Correspondence and Journals," 6.

40. Nathaniel J. Wyeth to Robert H. Gardner, January 31, 1832, "Correspondence and Journals," 29; Nathaniel J. Wyeth to Solomon K. Livermore, February 13, 1832, "Correspondence and Journals," 32.

41. *New England Christian Herald*, June 6, 1832, in Hulbert and Hulbert, eds., *The Oregon Crusade*, 100.

42. Nathaniel J. Wyeth to Leonard Wyeth, March 15, 1832, "Correspondence and Journals," 49.

43. Washington Irving, *The Adventures of Captain Bonneville*, vol. 1 (New York: G. P. Putnam's Sons, 1895), 69–70; John Wyeth, *Oregon*, 26.

44. Nathaniel Wyeth's journal, June 16, 1832, "Correspondence and Journals," 157.

45. John Wyeth, *Oregon*, 43–44.

46. Ibid., 57.

47. Ibid., 60, 87.

48. John McLoughlin to the Governor and Committee, October 29, 1832, in *The Letters of John McLoughlin from Fort Vancouver to the Governor and Committee*, First Series, 1825–1838, ed. E. E. Rich (London: Champlain Society, 1941), 109.

49. Nathaniel Wyeth's journal, November 15 and 29, 1832, "Correspondence and Journals," 178–179.

50. *Missionary Herald*, December 1827, in Hulbert and Hulbert, eds., *The Oregon Crusade*, 28.

51. G. P. Disosway, *Christian Advocate*, March 1, 1833, in Hulbert and Hulbert, eds., *The Oregon Crusade*, 92–93.

52. G. P. Disosway to Willbur Fisk, June 21, 1833, Willbur Fisk Papers, Wesleyan University.

53. Quoted in Frederick A. Norwood, *The Story of American Methodism* (Nashville, Tenn.: Abingdon Press, 1974), 49.

54. *The Christian Advocate*, August 7, 1833, in Fisk Papers.

55. Ibid., October 12, 1832, in Fisk Papers.

56. *The Christian Advocate*, June 17, 1833, in Fisk Papers.

57. Goetzmann, *Exploration and Empire*, 148–149, 156, 158; Alexander Macomb to Benjamin Bonneville, July 29, 1831, in Washington Irving, *The Adventures of Captain Bonneville*, ed. by Edgley U. Todd (Norman: University of Oklahoma Press, 1961), appendix A, 379.

58. Benjamin Bonneville to Alexander Macomb, July 29, 1833, in Irving, *Adventures of Bonneville*, ed. Todd, appendix B, 381–382.

59. Nathaniel Wyeth to Leonard Jarvis, November 12, 1833, in Wyeth, "Correspondence and Journals," 83.

60. *Zion's Herald*, December 4, 1833, in Hulbert and Hulbert, eds., *The Oregon Crusade*, 117–121.

61. Willbur Fisk to Ruth Fisk, n.d. (by contents, early December 1833), Fisk Papers.

62. Nathaniel Wyeth to Elizabeth Wyeth, February 26, 1834, in Wyeth, "Correspondence and Journals," 118.

63. Cyrus Shepard's journal, William Robertson Coe Collection, Beinecke Library, Yale University, iv–vi.

64. Cyrus Shepard's journal, March 4–6, 1834.

65. Ibid., March 9–13, 1834.

66. Ibid., March 16, 1834.

67. Ibid., March 19, 1834.

68. *Zion's Herald*, April 30, 1834, in Hulbert and Hulbert, eds., *The Oregon Crusade*, 125.

69. Nathaniel Wyeth to Thomas Nuttall, July 4, 1833, in Wyeth, "Correspondence and Journals," 67.

70. John Kirk Townsend, *Narrative of a Journey across the Rocky Mountains, to the Columbia River*, ed. George A. Jobanek (Corvallis: Oregon State University Press, 1999), 1.

71. Ibid., 10.

72. Cyrus Shepard's journal, April 4, 15, 16, 20, 22, 1834.

73. Nathaniel Wyeth to Elizabeth Wyeth, March 31, 1834, in Wyeth, "Correspondence and Journals," 128.

74. Nathaniel Wyeth to Messrs. Tucker and Williams, April 17, 1834, in Wyeth, "Correspondence and Journals," 130.

75. Jason Lee to the *Christian Advocate*, July 1, 1834, in Hulbert and Hulbert, eds., *The Oregon Crusade*, 146–147.

76. Townsend, *Narrative of a Journey*, 12.

77. "Diary of Rev. Jason Lee," *OHQ* 17 (1916): 117.

78. Cyrus Shepard's journal, May 1, 1834; "Diary of Jason Lee," 118.

79. Cyrus Shepard's journal, May 1, 1834.

80. Ibid., May 4, 1834.

81. Townsend, *Narrative of a Journey*, 32.

82. Ibid., 27.

83. "Diary of Jason Lee," 125.

84. Townsend, *Narrative of a Journey*, 34.

85. Cyrus Shepard's journal, May 22, 1834.

86. "Diary of Jason Lee," 126.

87. Ibid.

88. Townsend, *Narrative of a Journey*, 42; Cyrus Shepard's journal, May 30, 1834.

89. "Diary of Jason Lee," 130.

90. Ibid., 138.

91. Townsend, *Narrative of a Journey*, 53; Jason Lee to the *Christian Advocate*, September 26, 1834, in Hulbert and Hulbert, eds., *The Oregon Crusade*, 145.

92. Irving, *Adventures of Captain Bonneville*, vol. II, 153.

93. Nathaniel Wyeth to Leonard Jarvis, June 20, 1834, in Wyeth, "Correspondence and Journals," 134; ibid., 138.

94. Benjamin Bonneville to Alexander Macomb, July 29, 1833, in Irving, *Adventures of Bonneville*, ed. Todd, appendix B, 384.

95. "Diary of Jason Lee," 138.

96. Ibid., 141.

97. Jason Lee to the *Christian Advocate*, September 26, 1834, in Hulbert and Hulbert, eds., *The Oregon Crusade*, 145.

98. "Diary of Jason Lee," 142; Townsend, *Narrative of a Journey*, 56.

99. Cyrus Shepard's journal, July 19, 1834.

100. Nathaniel Wyeth to Frederic Tudor, October 6, 1834, in Wyeth, "Correspondence and Journals," 143; Cyrus Shepard's Journal, July 26, 1834.

101. Townsend, *Narrative of a Journey*, 76–77; Cyrus Shepard's Journal, July 28, 1834.

102. Townsend, *Narrative of a Journey*, 77.

103. Cyrus Shepard's journal, August 3 and 7, 1834.

104. Ibid., August 11, 1834.

105. "Diary of Jason Lee," 254; "Lee's Original Diary, July 2, 1834–February 6, 1835," in Hulbert and Hulbert, eds., *The Oregon Crusade*, 178.

106. Cyrus Shepard's journal, September 1, 1834.

107. "Jason Lee's Diary," 258; Cyrus Shepard's Journal, September 3, 1834.

108. Townsend, *Narrative of a Journey*, 122; "Lee's Original Diary," in Hulbert and Hulbert, eds., *The Oregon Crusade*, 180.

109. Cyrus Shepard's journal, September 15, 1834.

3. Arcadia

1. "Diary of Rev. Jason Lee," *Oregon Historical Quarterly* [hereafter *OHQ*] 17 (1916): 262.

2. Ibid., 264.

3. Samuel Parker, *Journal of an Exploring Tour beyond the Rocky Mountains* (Ithaca, N.Y.: privately printed, 1838), 179; "Slacum's Report on Oregon, 1836–7," *OHQ* 13 (1912): 189; Daniel Lee and John Frost, *Ten Years in Oregon* (New York: privately printed, 1844), 108.

4. Ibid., 265.

5. E. E. Rich, ed., *The Letters of John McLoughlin from Fort Vancouver to the Governor and Committee*, First Series, 1825–1838 (London: Champlain Society, 1941), cvii; Nathaniel Wyeth's journal, September 23, 1834, in "The Correspondence and Journals of Captain Nathaniel J. Wyeth, 1831–36," in *Sources in Oregon History*, ed. F. G. Young (Eugene, Ore.: University Press, 1899), 233.

6. "Lee's Original Diary," September 29, 1834, in Archer B. Hulbert and Dorothy P. Hulbert, eds., *The Oregon Crusade: Across Land and Sea to Oregon*, vol. 5 of *Overland to the Pacific* (Denver: Colorado College and Denver Public Library, 1935), 181.

7. Cyrus Shepard's journal, October 3, 1834, William Robertson Coe Collection, Beinecke Library, Yale University.

8. "Lee's Original Diary," October 29, 1834, 182; Robert J. Loewenberg, *Equality on the Oregon Frontier: Jason Lee and the Methodist Mission* (Seattle: University of Washington Press, 1976), 79.

9. "Lee's Original Diary," October 29, 1834, 183; "Diary of Jason Lee," 401; "Slacum's Report on Oregon," 210.

10. "Lee's Original Diary," October 29, 1834, 182–183.

11. Cyrus Shepard's journal, October 16–18, 1834.

12. Ibid., October 19, 1834.

13. John Kirk Townsend, *Narrative of a Journey across the Rocky Mountains, to the Columbia River*, ed. George A. Jobanek (Corvallis: Oregon State University Press, 1999), 132–133.

14. Nathaniel Wyeth's journal, December 25, 1834, and January 11, 1835, "Correspondence and Journals," 241–243.

15. Ibid., January 29, 1835, 247.

16. Ibid., February 12, 1835, 258.

17. "Narrative of Events and Difficulties in the Colonization of Oregon," in *Hall J. Kelley on Oregon*, ed. F. W. Powell (Princeton, N.J.: Princeton University Press, 1932), 186.

18. Townsend, *Narrative of a Journey*, 254.

19. Ibid., 162; William Dietrich, *Northwest Passage: The Great Columbia River* (New York: Simon & Schuster, 1995), 137.

20. Ibid., 161.

21. Cyrus Shepard's journal, June 17, August 19, and August 25, 1835; Cyrus Shepard to a church colleague, Cyrus Shepard's journal, October 28, 1836.

22. Samuel Parker to American Board of Commissioners for Foreign Missions, April 10, 1833, in Samuel J. Parker, "Article," September 7, 1882, Beinecke Library, Yale University. The author was the son of the missionary.

23. Parker, *Journal of an Exploring Tour*, 73.

24. Ibid., 142.

25. Ibid., 164–165.

26. Jason Lee to Nathan Bangs, December 8, 1837, Letters of the Oregon Methodist Missions, University of Puget Sound, Tacoma, Wash.

27. Washington Irving, *The Adventures of Captain Bonneville,* vol. 2 (New York: G. P. Putnam's Sons, 1895), 231, 233.

28. Richard Henry Dana Jr., *Two Years before the Mast: A Personal Narrative* (1839; reprint, Boston: Houghton Mifflin, 1923), 360.

29. Joshua Paddison, ed., *A World Transformed: Firsthand Accounts of California before the Gold Rush* (Berkeley, Calif.: Heyday Books, 1999), 172–173.

30. Hubert H. Bancroft, *California Pastoral, 1769–1848* (San Francisco: The History Company, 1888), 180.

31. Paddison, ed., *A World Transformed,* 177.

32. Ibid., 182–183.

33. Ibid., 194.

34. John C. Ewers, ed., *Adventures of Zenas Leonard* (Norman: University of Oklahoma Press, 1959), 94.

35. Ibid., 67, 68.

36. Ibid., 70.

37. Ibid., 72.

38. William Goetzmann, *Exploration and Empire* (New York: Alfred A. Knopf, 1966), 153.

39. Ewers, ed., *Adventures of Zenas Leonard,* 91.

40. Ibid., 95.

41. Paddison, ed., *A World Transformed,* 199–200, 202.

42. Dana, *Two Years before the Mast,* 72.

43. Ibid., 87.

44. Ibid., 94.

45. Ibid., 189.

46. Ibid., 211, 216, 219.

47. Ibid., 216.

48. Parker, "Article."

49. Julie Roy Jeffrey, *Converting the West: A Biography of Narcissa Whitman* (Norman: University of Oklahoma Press, 1991), 24.

50. Ibid., 27–28.

51. Parker, "Article."

52. Parker, *Journal of an Exploring Tour,* 44, 76–77.

53. Clifford M. Drury, ed., *Where Wagons Could Go: Narcissa Whitman and Eliza Spalding* (Lincoln: University of Nebraska Press, 1997), 34, 184.

54. Quoted in Edward Bourne, *Essays in Historical Criticism* (1901; reprint, Freeport, N.Y.: Books for Libraries Press, 1967), 55n.

55. Narcissa Whitman to her family, March 30, 1836, in *The Letters of Narcissa Whitman, 1836–1847* (Fairfield, Wash.: Ye Galleon Press, 1996), 11.

56. Ibid., April 7, 1836, 14.

57. Ira Pettibone to the Prudential Committee, American Board of Commissioners for Foreign Missions, February 1836, William H. Gray Papers, Oregon Historical Society [hereafter OHS].

58. Henry H. Spalding, "Narrative of an Overland Journey to Ft. Vancouver and Lapwai in 1836," Beinecke Library, Yale University, 22.

59. Narcissa Whitman to her family, June 3, 1836, and to Augustus and Julia Whitman, June 27, 1836, in *Letters of Narcissa Whitman*, 17, 21.

60. Eliza Spalding Diary, June 21, 1836, in Drury, ed., *Where Wagons Could Go*, 192.

61. Spalding, "Narrative of an Overland Journey," 37.

62. Osborne Russell, *Journal of a Trapper*, ed. Aubrey L. Haines (Portland: OHS, 1953), 41; Narcissa Whitman Diary, July 16, 1836, in Drury, ed., *Where Wagons Could Go*, 58.

63. Quoted in Jeffrey, *Converting the West*, 21.

64. Spalding, "Narrative of an Overland Journey," 57.

65. Ibid., 58.

66. Quoted in Drury, *Where Wagons Could Go*, 194n.

67. Narcissa Whitman Diary, July 18 and 25, 1836, in Drury, ed., *Where Wagons Could Go*, 73–74.

68. Narcissa Whitman to her family, July 27 and 28, 1836, in *Letters of Narcissa Whitman*, 23–24.

69. Ibid., 24.

70. Ibid., July 28, 1836, 24; Narcissa Whitman Diary, August 7, 1836, in Drury, ed., *Where Wagons Could Go*, 81.

71. Eliza Spalding Diary, August 6, 1836, in Drury, ed., *Where Wagons Could Go*, 195; Narcissa Whitman to her family, August 12, 1836, in *Letters of Narcissa Whitman*, 27.

72. Narcissa Whitman to her family, August 22, 1836, in *Letters of Narcissa Whitman*, 28.

73. William Gray to "Dear Friends," September 9, 1836, Gray Papers, OHS; Narcissa Whitman to her family, August 29, 1836, in *Letters of Narcissa Whitman*, 31.

74. Narcissa Whitman to her family, September 1, 1836, in *Letters of Narcissa Whitman*, 32.

75. William Gray to "Dear Friends," September 9, 1836, Gray Papers, OHS.

76. Narcissa Whitman to her family, September 9, 1836, in *Letters of Narcissa Whitman*, 35–36.

77. Eliza Spalding Diary, September 14, 1836, in Drury, ed., *Where Wagons Could Go*, 196.

78. Narcissa Whitman to her family, September 16, 1836, in *Letters of Narcissa Whitman*, 38.

79. Quoted in Drury, ed., *Where Wagons Could Go*, 105n.

80. Narcissa Whitman's Diary, November 1, 1836, in Drury, ed., *Where Wagons Could Go*, 111.

81. Narcissa Whitman to her family, December 26, 1836, in *Letters of Narcissa Whitman*, 47.

82. Ibid., March 30, 1837, 47.

83. Narcissa Whitman's Diary, January 2, 1836, in Drury, ed., *Where Wagons Could Go*, 123.

84. "Diary of Jason Lee," 408.

85. Anna Maria Pittman to her brother, July 1836, Anna Maria Pittman Letters and Poems, Beinecke Library, Yale University.

86. Anna Maria Pittman to her mother, July 12, 1836, Pittman Letters and Poems.

87. Ibid.

88. Anna Maria Pittman to her parents, July 17, 1836, Pittman Letters and Poems.

89. Ibid., December 8, 1836.

90. Anna Maria Pittman to her sisters and brothers, May 11, 1837, Pittman Letters and Poems.

91. Ibid.

92. Ibid., May 15, 1837.

93. Ibid., May 18, 1837.

94. "Diary of Jason Lee," 409.

95. Anna Maria Pittman to her parents, June 5, 1837, Pittman Letters and Poems.

96. Ibid.

97. Ibid.

98. "Diary of Jason Lee," 409–410.

99. Lee and Frost, *Ten Years in Oregon*, 149; quoted in introduction, Pittman Letters and Poems, 27.

100. Lee and Frost, *Ten Years in Oregon*, 150.

101. Ibid.

102. Anna Maria Pittman to her mother, March 28, 1838, Pittman Letters and Poems. Anna Maria Pittman to Jason Lee, April 14, 1838, Pittman Letters and Poems.

103. *The Congressional Globe*, 1838–1839, 141; C. J. Pike, "Petitions of Oregon Settlers," *OHQ* 34 (1933): 219.

104. "Slacum's Report," 177–178.

105. Dana, *Two Years before the Mast*, 75; "Slacum's Report," 182.

106. Ibid., 181.

107. Ibid., 196; Hubert H. Bancroft [Frances Fuller Victor], *History of Oregon*, vol. 1, 1834–1848 (San Francisco: The History Company, 1886), 140.

108. "Slacum's Report," 197–199.

109. Bancroft [Victor], *History of Oregon*, vol. 1, 166; quoted in Loewenberg, *Equality on the Oregon Frontier*, 108.

110. Pike, "Petitions of Oregon Settlers," 219; Anna Maria Pittman to Jason Lee, April 6, 1838, Pittman Letters and Poems.

111. Anna Maria Pittman to Jason Lee, April 15, 1838, Pittman Letters and Poems; Anna Maria Pittman to Hester Ann Pittman, April 16, 1838, Pittman Letters and Poems.

112. Anna Maria Pittman to her mother, July 12, 1836, Pittman Letters and Poems.

113. Elvira Johnson to George and Mary Pittman, July 5, 1838, Pittman Letters and Poems.

4. The Missionary Impulse

1. Asa Bowen Smith to his parents, March 14, 1838, Asa Bowen Smith Letters, Beinecke Library, Yale University.

2. Cushing Eels to Elkanah Walker, December 27, 1837, Walker Family Papers, Beinecke Library, Yale University.

3. Diary of Myra Eels, April 10–12, 1838, Oregon Historical Society (hereafter, OHS); Asa Bowen Smith to his sisters, April 6, 1838, Smith Letters; Asa Bowen Smith to his brother, April 22, 1838, Smith Letters.

4. Ibid.

5. Diary of Myra Eels, May 3, 1838.

6. Ibid., June 2, 1838.

7. Diary of Mary Richardson Walker, June 10, 1838, Walker Papers.

8. Ibid.; Asa Bowen Smith to his family, May 18 and July 6, 1838, Smith Letters.

9. Ibid., April 16 and 28, 1838.

10. Diary of Mary Walker, June 11, 1838, Walker Papers.

11. Ibid., June 15, 1838.

12. Ibid., July 5, 1838; Diary of Myra Eels, July 5, 1838, OHS.

13. Diary of Mary Walker, July 7, 1838, Walker Papers; Asa Bowen Smith to his family, July 9, 1838, Smith Letters.

14. Ibid., July 27, 1838.

15. Diary of Mary Walker, August 16, 23, 25, and 26, 1838, Walker Papers.

16. Narcissa Whitman to her sister, September 18, 1838, in *The Letters of Narcissa Whitman*, 1836–1847, ed. Glen Adams (Fairfield, Wash.: Ye Galleon Press, 1996), 61.

17. Diary of Myra Eels, August 29, 1838, OHS.

18. Diary of Mary Walker, August 30, 1838, Walker Letters; Asa Bowen Smith to his parents, September 15, 1838, Smith Letters.

19. Diary of Elkanah Walker, September 10, 1838, OHS.

20. Diary of Mary Walker, September 2, 1838, Walker Papers.

21. Daniel Lee and John Frost, *Ten Years in Oregon* (New York: privately printed, 1844), 153, 216; quoted in Robert J. Loewenberg, *Equality on the Oregon Frontier* (Seattle: University of Washington Press, 1976), 100; Jason Lee to David Leslie, November 21, 1838, in Cornelius J. Brosnan, *Jason Lee: Prophet of the Old Oregon* (New York: Macmillan, 1932), 106.

22. Ibid.

23. Jason Lee to Nathan Bangs, December 8, 1837, Oregon Methodist Mission Letters, University of Puget Sound.

24. Daniel Lee to Nathan Bangs, April 30, 1838, Oregon Methodist Mission Letters.

25. Ibid.

26. David Leslie to Willbur Fisk, March 24, 1838, Oregon Methodist Mission Letters.

27. Ibid., 104, 143–44, 149.

28. Ibid., 108.

29. *Congressional Globe*, 1838–1839, 141; quoted in H. H. Bancroft [Frances Fuller Victor], *History of Oregon*, vol. 1, 1834–1848 (San Francisco: The History Company, 1886), 173; *Congressional Globe*, 1838–1839, 141.

30. Quoted in Loewenberg, *Equality on the Oregon Frontier*, 181.

31. Brosnan, *Jason Lee*, 114, 128.

32. Lucy Thomson to her brother and sister, October 8, 1839, quoted in Brosnan, *Jason Lee*, 154.

33. Jason Lee to Mary Pittman, November 24, 1839, Anna Maria Pittman Lee Papers, Beinecke Library, Yale University.

34. Loewenberg, *Equality on the Oregon Frontier*, 72 and n.

35. Lucy Thomson to her brother and sister, October 8, 1839, quoted in Brosnan, *Jason Lee*, 153.

36. Elvira Perkins to Mary Walker, n.d., 1838, Walker–Whitman Papers, Beinecke Library, Yale University.

37. Mary Walker Diary, October 4 and September 29, 1838, Walker Family Papers.

38. Ibid., September 10, 1838.

39. Diary of Elkanah Walker, September 12, 1838, OHS.

40. Ibid., September 15 and 16, 1838.

41. Ibid., September 17, 1838.

42. Ibid., September 22, 1838.

43. Ibid.

44. Ibid., September 24, 1838.

45. Ibid., October 5, 1838.

46. Diary of Mary Walker, November 16 and December 3, 1838, Walker Papers.

47. Narcissa Whitman to her sister Jane, September 18, 1838, in Adams, ed., *Letters of Narcissa Whitman*, 61.

48. Ibid., 63.

49. Asa Smith to his parents, September 15, 1838, Smith Letters.

50. Ibid., October 29, 1838.

51. Ibid., December 18, 1838.

52. Ibid.

53. Ibid., September 15, 1838; ibid., September 8, 1839.

54. Ibid., December 18, 1838; Diary of Mary Walker, December 7, 1838, Walker Papers.

55. Ibid., November 18 and 21, 1838.

56. Ibid., December 12 and 29, 1838.

57. Ibid., December 31, 1838.

58. Asa B. Smith to Elkanah Walker, March 28, 1839, Smith Letters.

59. Quoted in Cecil P. Dryden, *Give All to Oregon! Missionary Pioneers of the Far West* (New York: Hastings House, 1968), 147.

60. Asa B. Smith to Elkanah Walker, April 20, 1839, Smith Letters; Edwin O. Hall to Elkanah Walker and Cushing Eels, May 5, 1839, Walker Family Papers.

61. Thomas Farnham, *Travels in the Great Western Prairies*, 2 vols. (New York: Da Capo Press, 1973), 2, 50.

62. Ibid., 131.

63. Narcissa Whitman to Elvira Perkins, June 25, 1839, in Adams, ed., *Letters of Narcissa Whitman*, 79.

64. Ibid.; Clifford M. Drury, *Where Wagons Could Go: Narcissa Whitman and Eliza Spalding* (Lincoln: University of Nebraska Press, 1997 ed.), 146; Narcissa Whitman to Clarissa Prentiss, October 9, 1839, in Adams, ed., *Letters of Narcissa Whitman*, 86.

65. Narcissa Whitman to Elvira Perkins, June 25, 1839, and to Stephen Prentiss, September 30, 1839, in Adams, ed., *Letters of Narcissa Whitman*, 79, 83.

66. Narcissa Whitman to Clarissa Prentiss, October 9, 1839, in Adams, ed., *Letters of Narcissa Whitman,* 87.

67. Farnham, *Travels in the Great Western Prairies,* 2, 169.

68. Ibid., 209.

69. Asa B. Smith to his family, March 11, 1839, Smith Letters.

70. Farnham, *Travels in the Great Western Prairies,* 2, 210.

71. C. J. Pike, "Petitions of the Oregon Settlers, 1838–1848," *Oregon Historical Quarterly* 34 (1933): 221.

72. Farnham, *Travels in the Great Western Prairies,* 2, 213.

73. Ibid.; Loewenberg, *Equality on the Oregon Frontier,* 146.

74. Pike, "Petitions of the Oregon Settlers," 223.

75. Farnham, *Travels in the Great Western Prairies,* 2, 214.

76. Lee and Frost, *Ten Years in Oregon,* 167.

77. Ibid., 173.

78. Loewenberg, *Equality on the Oregon Frontier,* 71; 117.

79. Brosnan, *Jason Lee,* 266; Jason Lee, "Diary," *Oregon Historical Quarterly* 17 (1916): 402–403.

80. Loewenberg, *Equality on the Oregon Frontier,* 73.

81. Elijah White to Jason Lee, July 31, 1840, Oregon Methodist Mission Letters.

82. Ibid.

83. Jason Lee to Elijah White, August 3, 1840, Oregon Methodist Mission Letters.

84. "Diary of Wilkes in the Northwest," ed. Edmond S. Meany, *Washington Historical Quarterly* 16 (1925): 55–56; Charles Wilkes, *Narrative of the United States Exploring Expedition during the Years 1838, 1839, 1840, 1841, 1842,* vol. 4 (Philadelphia: Lea & Blanchard, 1845), 296.

85. *North American Review* 61 (July 1845): 105.

86. Ibid., 99, 105.

87. "Diary of Wilkes in the Northwest," 58–61; Wilkes, *Narrative of the Exploring Expedition,* vol. 4, 303–304.

88. "Diary of Wilkes in the Northwest," 137, 139.

89. Ibid., 57, 137.

90. John K. Richmond to G. P. Disosway, August 18, 1841, Oregon Methodist Mission Letters; Jason Lee to corresponding secretary, June 18, 1841, Oregon Methodist Mission Letters; "Diary of Wilkes in the Northwest," 139.

91. Wilkes, *Narrative of the Exploring Expedition,* vol. 4, 307; John Richmond to G. P. Disosway, August 18, 1841, Oregon Methodist Mission Letters.

92. "Diary of Wilkes in the Northwest," 140.

93. Wilkes, *Narrative of the Exploring Expedition,* vol. 4, 311; 358; "Diary of Wilkes in the Northwest," 142.

94. Wilkes, *Narrative of the Exploring Expedition,* Vol. 4, 317.

95. Ibid., 321.

96. Ibid.; "Diary of Wilkes in the Northwest," 213–214; 291; Bancroft [Victor], *History of Oregon,* vol. 1, 195.

97. Asa Bowen Smith to Marcia Smith, September 8, 1839, Oregon Methodist Mission Letters; "Diary of Wilkes in the Northwest," 213–214.

98. "Diary of Wilkes in the Northwest," 301.

99. Quoted in William Stanton, *The Great United States Exploring Expedition of 1838–1842* (Berkeley: University of California Press, 1975), 256.

100. Jason Lee to corresponding secretary, September 23, 1841, Oregon Methodist Mission Letters.

101. Loewenberg, *Equality on the Oregon Frontier*, 143–44.

102. Wilkes, *Narrative of the Exploring Expedition*, vol. 4, 355; Jason Lee to corresponding secretary, June 18, 1841, Oregon Methodist Mission Letters.

103. Stanton, *Great United States Exploring Expedition*, 250.

104. Wilkes, *Narrative of the Exploring Expedition*, vol. 4, 491–92; Stanton, *Great United States Exploring Expedition*, 250.

105. Stanton, *Great United States Exploring Expedition*, 250–253; Jason Lee to corresponding secretary, September 23, 1841, Oregon Methodist Mission Letters.

106. Stanton, *Great United States Exploring Expedition*, 259; William J. Morgan, ed., *Autobiography of Rear Admiral Charles Wilkes, U.S. Navy, 1798–1877* (Washington, D.C.: U.S. Department of the Navy, Naval History Division, 1978), 502, 505.

107. Morgan, ed., *Autobiography of Rear Admiral Charles Wilkes*, 505.

108. Jason Lee to corresponding secretary, June 18, 1841, Oregon Methodist Mission Letters.

109. Bancroft [Victor], *History of Oregon*, vol. 1, 192, 247n; Wilkes, *Narrative of the Exploring Expedition*, Vol. 4, 353.

110. Jason Lee to George and Mary Pittman, September 23, 1841, Anna Maria Pittman Lee Papers.

111. John Bidwell, "The First Emigrant Train to California," *Century* 41 (November 1890): 107–108.

112. Ibid., 109.

113. Ibid., 129; John Bidwell, "Life in California before the Gold Discovery," *Century* 41 (December 1890): 163.

114. George Simpson, "An Overland Journey around the World," in *A World Transformed: Firsthand Accounts of California before the Gold Rush*, ed. Joshua Paddison (Berkeley, Calif.: Heyday Books, 1999), 256–257.

115. Ibid., 259.

5. The Great Migration

1. Henry David Thoreau, "Walking," in *Collected Essays and Poems* (New York: Library of America, 2001), 234.

2. "Discovery beyond the Rocky Mountains," *North American Review* 50 (January 1840): 79.

3. Ibid., 123.

4. Ibid., 132.

5. Quoted in John D. Unruh, *The Plains Across: The Overland Emigrants and the Trans-Mississippi West, 1840–60* (Urbana: University of Illinois Press, 1979), 43.

6. Daniel Waldo, "Critiques: Narrative and Remarks," n.d., Beinecke Library, Yale University.

7. "Irving's Astoria," *North American Review* 44 (January 1837): 200, 234.

8. "John Charles Frémont," *Littell's Living Age* 26 (July 27, 1850): 207; Unruh, *The Plains Across*, 119.

9. Joaquin Miller, *Overland in a Covered Wagon*, ed. Sidney G. Firman (New York: D. Appleton, 1930), 42–43.

10. Frederick Merk, *History of the Westward Movement* (New York: Alfred A. Knopf, 1978), 255; Samuel J. Parker, unpublished manuscript, September 7, 1882, Beinecke Library, Yale University.

11. Biographical details are drawn from Patricia Herr, *Jessie Benton Frémont* (New York: Franklin Watts, 1987) and Donald Jackson and Mary Lee Spence, eds., *The Expeditions of John Charles Frémont*, vol. 1 (Urbana: University of Illinois Press, 1970).

12. John Charles Frémont, *Memoirs of My Life* (Chicago: Belford, Clarke, 1887), 19.

13. Quoted in Jackson and Spence, eds., *Expeditions of John Charles Frémont*, vol. 1, xxv; Frémont, *Memoirs*, 19.

14. Frémont, *Memoirs*, 18, 21.

15. Ibid., 25.

16. Ibid., 24.

17. John C. Frémont to Joel Poinsett, June 8, 1838, in Jackson and Spence, eds., *Expeditions of John Charles Frémont*, vol. 1, 12.

18. John C. Frémont to Joel Poinsett, September 5, 1838, in Jackson and Spence, eds., *Expeditions of John Charles Frémont*, vol. 1, 23–24.

19. Frémont, *Memoirs*, 30.

20. Ibid., 65.

21. Ibid., 67.

22. Ibid., 68.

23. Jessie Benton Frémont to Elizabeth Blair Lee, July 23, 1856, in *The Letters of Jessie Benton Frémont*, ed. Pamela Herr and Mary Lee Spence (Urbana: University of Illinois Press, 1993), 118.

24. Ferdinand H. Gerdes to John C. Frémont, November 7, 1841, in Jackson and Spence, eds., *Expeditions of John Charles Frémont*, vol. 1, 102.

25. Herr, *Jessie Benton Frémont*, 65; Jackson and Spence, eds., *Expeditions of John Charles Frémont*, vol. 1, 103n.

26. Quoted in Herr, *Jessie Benton Frémont*, 72.

27. Frémont, *Memoirs*, 71.

28. Ralph Waldo Emerson, *The Journals and Miscellaneous Notebooks of Ralph Waldo Emerson*, ed. William H. Gilman, vol. 9, 1843–1847 (Cambridge, Mass.: Harvard University Press, 1971), 431.

29. Quoted in Peter Wolf, *Land in America* (New York: Pantheon Books, 1981), 64–65.

30. Jessie Benton Frémont, "The Origin of the Frémont Explorations," *Century* 41 (March 1891): 766.

31. Frémont, *Memoirs*, 69, 70.

32. Thomas Hart Benton, *Thirty Years' View*, vol. 2 (New York: D. Appleton, 1856), 474.

33. J. J. Abert to John C. Frémont, April 25, 1842, in Jackson and Spence, eds., *Expeditions of John Charles Frémont*, vol. 1, 121–122.

34. "Report of the First Expedition," March 1, 1843, in Jackson and Spence, eds., *Expeditions of John Charles Frémont*, vol. 1, 170.

35. Ibid., 178.

36. Charles Preuss, *Exploring with Frémont*, trans. and ed. Erwin G. and Elisabeth K. Gudde (Norman: University of Oklahoma Press, 1958), 3–5.

37. Rufus B. Sage, *Rocky Mountain Life* (1857; reprint, Lincoln: University of Nebraska Press, 1982), 197.

38. Preuss, *Exploring with Frémont*, 21.

39. "Report of First Expedition," 197–198.

40. Ibid., 201.

41. Ibid., 203.

42. Preuss, *Exploring with Frémont*, 26.

43. Lansford W. Hastings, *The Emigrants' Guide to Oregon and California* (1845; reprint, Bedford, Mass.: Applewood Books, n.d.) 6; Hubert H. Bancroft [Frances Fuller Victor], *History of Oregon*, vol. 1 (San Francisco: The History Company, 1886), 258.

44. "Report of First Expedition," 222.

45. Preuss, *Exploring with Frémont*, 47; "Report of First Expedition," 224.

46. "Report of First Expedition," 233.

47. Ibid., 240.

48. Preuss, *Exploring with Frémont*, 31–32. In fact, one of the White party had been shot and killed by accident.

49. "Report of First Expedition," 253.

50. Ibid.

51. Preuss, *Exploring with Frémont*, 37; "Report of First Expedition," 255.

52. Preuss, *Exploring with Frémont*, 41.

53. Ibid., 43.

54. "Report of First Expedition," 269–270.

55. Ibid., 270, 273.

56. Frémont, *Memoirs*, 162.

57. Jessie Benton Frémont, "Memoirs," in Herr and Spence, eds., *Letters of Jessie Benton Frémont*, 12; Frémont, *Memoirs*, 163.

58. Frémont, *Memoirs*, 163; Jessie Benton Frémont, "Origin of the Frémont Expeditions," 768.

59. Frémont, *Memoirs*, 162–163.

60. "Report of the Secretary of War," *United States Magazine and Democratic Review* 28 (April 1846): 294.

61. Henry Wadsworth Longfellow, *Life of Henry Wadsworth Longfellow with Extracts from His Journal and Correspondence*, vol. 1, ed. Samuel Longfellow (Boston: Ticknor & Fields, 1886), 65–66.

62. Jason Lee to Charles Pitman, April 23, 1842, Oregon Methodist Mission Letters, University of Puget Sound, Tacoma, Wash.

63. Charles Pitman to Jason Lee, February 28, 1842, Oregon Methodist Mission Letters.

64. Ibid.

65. Jason Lee to Charles Pitman, April 8, 1842, Oregon Methodist Mission Letters.

66. Mary August Dix Diary, September 9, 19, and 21, 1842, William H. Gray Papers, Oregon Historical Society, Portland.

67. Bancroft [Victor], *History of Oregon*, vol. 1, 263–264.

68. Jason Lee to Charles Pitman, October 18, 1842, Oregon Methodist Mission Letters.

69. Jason Lee to George and Mary Pittman, August 2, 1842, Anna Maria Pittman Lee, Letters and Poems, 1813–1842, Beinecke Library, Yale University.

70. Henry Kirk White to Charles Pitman, December 4, 1843, quoted in Robert J. Loewenberg, *Equality on the Oregon Frontier* (Seattle: University of Washington Press, 1976), 91; Jason Lee to Charles Pitman, October 18, 1842, Oregon Methodist Mission Letters.

71. Cornelius Brosnan, *Jason Lee: Prophet of the New Oregon* (New York: Macmillan, 1932), 268; Alvan Waller to his brother, April 6, 1842, quoted in Loewenberg, *Equality on the Oregon Frontier*, 219.

72. Quoted in Loewenberg, *Equality on the Oregon Frontier*, 191.

73. Bancroft [Victor], *History of Oregon*, vol. 1, 296; Robert Clark, "How British and American Subjects Unite in a Common Government for Oregon Territory in 1844," *Oregon Historical Quarterly* [hereafter *OHQ*] 13 (1912): 145.

74. Bancroft [Victor], *History of Oregon*, vol. 1, 300–301; Clark, "How British and American Subjects Unite," *OHQ* 13 (1912): 146.

75. Loewenberg, *Equality on the Oregon Frontier*, 161; *Congressional Globe* (February 7, 1844): 237.

76. C. J. Pike, "Petitions of Oregon Settlers, 1838–48," *OHQ* 34 (1933): 224–225; *Congressional Globe*, February 7, 1844, 237.

77. Bancroft [Victor], *History of Oregon*, vol. 1, 303–304; Frederick V. Holman, "A Brief History of the Oregon Provisional Government and What Caused Its Formation," *OHQ* 13 (1912): 111–113.

78. Bancroft [Victor], *History of Oregon*, vol. 1, 311–312.

79. Ibid., 313–314.

80. Jason Lee to Charles Pitman, March 30, 1843, Oregon Methodist Mission Letters.

81. Ibid.

82. Ibid.; Charles Pitman to Jason Lee, March 18, 1843, Oregon Methodist Mission Letters.

83. Ibid.

84. Narcissa Whitman to Jane and Edward Prentiss, September 29, 1842, in *The Letters of Narcissa Whitman, 1836–1847*, ed. Glen Adams (Fairfield, Wash.: Ye Galleon Press, 1996), 138; Julie Roy Jeffrey, *Converting the West: A Biography of Narcissa Whitman* (Norman: University of Oklahoma Press, 1991), 160; Edward G. Bourne, *Essays in Historical Criticism* (1901; reprint, Freeport, N.Y.: Books for Libraries Press, 1967), 55.

85. Ibid., 59.

86. Elkanah Walker to David Greene, October 3, 1842, Walker Family Papers, Beinecke Library, Yale University.

87. Narcissa Whitman to her parents, October 6, 1841, in Adams, ed., *Letters of Narcissa Whitman*, 115.

88. Marcus Whitman to David Greene, n.d. (copy in Narcissa Whitman to her parents, November 18, 1841), in Adams, ed., *Letters of Narcissa Whitman*, 122, 125.

89. Ibid., 126; Narcissa Whitman to Jane and Edward Prentiss, March 1–26, 1842, in Adams, ed., *Letters of Narcissa Whitman*, 128.

90. Narcissa Whitman to her husband, October 4–17, 1842, in Adams, ed., *Letters of Narcissa Whitman*, 142.

91. "Always anxious about sleeping alone, she could have dreamed the incident." Jeffrey, *Converting the West*, 176.

92. Narcissa Whitman to her husband, October 4–17, 1842, in Adams, ed., *Letters of Narcissa Whitman*, 144–45.

93. Narcissa Whitman to her parents, February 7, 1843, in Adams, ed., *Letters of Narcissa Whitman*, 150.

94. Cornelius Rogers to Elkanah Walker, December 8, 1842, Walker-Whitman Papers, Beinecke Library, Yale University.

95. John McLoughlin to George Simpson, March 20, 1844, *OHQ* 17 (1916): 233; Cornelius Rogers to Elkanah Walker, December 13, 1842, Walker-Whitman Papers.

96. Narcissa Whitman to her brother, March 31, 1843, in Adams, ed., *Letters of Narcissa Whitman*, 157.

97. Narcissa Whitman to Galusha Prentiss, April 14, 1843, in Adams, ed., *Letters of Narcissa Whitman*, 158.

98. Elvira Perkins to Mary Walker, April 11, 1843, Walker-Whitman Papers.

99. *New York Weekly Tribune*, March 11, 1843.

100. *New York Weekly Tribune*, April 1, 1843.

101. Bancroft [Victor], *History of Oregon*, vol. 1, 343–344; Waldo, "Critiques: Narrative and Remarks."

102. Marcus Whitman to Edward Prentiss, May 27, 1843, in Adams, ed., *Letters of Narcissa Whitman*, 160.

103. "Archives of the American Board of Commissioners for Foreign Missions, April 4, 1843," *OHQ* 22 (December 1921): 357–358; Marcus Whitman to Galusha Prentiss, May 28, 1843, in Adams, ed., *Letters of Narcissa Whitman*, 161; Elkanah Walker to David Greene, October 3, 1842, Walker Family Papers.

104. Quoted in Bourne, *Essays in Historical Criticism*, 90.

105. Marcus Whitman to Galusha Prentiss, May 28, 1843, in Adams, ed., *Letters of Narcissa Whitman*, 161.

106. Preuss, *Exploring with Frémont*, 82; Theodore Talbot, *The Journals of Theodore Talbot*, ed. Charles H. Carey (Portland, Ore.: Metropolitan Press, 1931), 25; "The Second Expedition to Oregon and California, 1843–44," in Jackson and Spence, eds., *The Expeditions of John C. Frémont*, vol. 1, 454–455.

107. *New York Weekly Tribune*, July 19, 1843.

108. "The Second Expedition to Oregon and California," 472.

109. Ibid., 473–474.

110. *New York Weekly Tribune*, December 28, 1843.

111. Waldo, "Critiques: Narrative and Remarks"; P. L. Edwards, "Instructions to immigrants," May 25, 1843, handscript and typescript copy, Oregon Historical Society.

112. John Zachary to Henry H. Spalding, February 1868, Beinecke Library, Yale University.

113. Preuss, *Exploring with Frémont*, 86.

114. "The Second Expedition to Oregon and California," 484–485; 490.

115. Ibid., 501.

116. Ibid., 516.

117. Talbot, *Journals*, 47; "The Second Expedition to Oregon and California," 530.

118. "The Second Expedition to Oregon and California," 543–544.

119. Ibid., 550, 553.

120. Preuss, *Exploring with Frémont*, 97; Bancroft [Victor], *History of Oregon*, vol. 1, 413.

121. "The Second Expedition to Oregon and California," 562; Bancroft [Victor], *History of Oregon*, vol. 1, 413–415.

122. Narcissa Prentiss to Harriet Jackson, March 11, 1843, and to Jane Prentiss, July 11, 1843, in Adams, ed., *Letters of Narcissa Whitman*, 155, 163.

123. Narcissa Whitman to her parents, August 11, 1843, in Adams, ed., *Letters of Narcissa Whitman*, 165.

124. John Zachary to Henry H. Spalding, February 1868, Beinecke Library, Yale University; Marcus Whitman to Stephen and Narcissa Prentiss, May 16, 1844, Whitman-Walker Papers.

125. Narcissa Whitman to Laura Brewer, January 30, 1844, in Adams, ed., *Letters of Narcissa Whitman*, 166.

126. Jason Lee to Charles Pitman, October 13, 1843, Oregon Methodist Mission Letters.

6. Manifest Destiny

1. J. J. Abert to John C. Frémont, March 10, 1843, in *The Expeditions of John Charles Frémont*, vol. 1, ed. Donald Jackson and Mary Lee Spence (Urbana: University of Illinois Press, 1970), 160.

2. "The Expedition to Oregon and California in 1843–44," in Jackson and Spence, eds., *The Expeditions of John Charles Frémont*, vol. 1, 604.

3. Ibid., 609–610.

4. Charles Preuss, *Exploring with Frémont*, trans. and ed. Erwin G. and Elisabeth K. Gudde (Norman: University of Oklahoma Press, 1958), 93.

5. Jessie Benton Frémont to Adelaide Talbot, February 1, 1844, in Pamela Herr and Mary Lee Spence, eds., *The Letters of Jessie Benton Frémont* (Urbana: University of Illinois Press, 1993), 16.

6. "Expedition to Oregon and California," 619–621.

7. Ibid., 621.

8. Ibid., 622.

9. Ibid., 623.

10. Ibid., 626.

11. Preuss, *Exploring with Frémont*, 106.

12. "Expedition to Oregon and California," 631.

13. Preuss, *Exploring with Frémont*, 107–109.

14. "Expedition to Oregon and California," 635n.

15. Ibid., 637–638.

16. Preuss, *Exploring with Frémont*, 114.

17. Ibid., 116–117.

18. Ibid., 117–118.

19. "Expedition to Oregon and California," 652.

20. Preuss, *Exploring with Frémont*, 119; "Expedition to Oregon and California," 654–655.

21. "Expedition to Oregon and California," 653n.; *Niles' National Register* 66, June 29, 1844.

22. "Expedition to Oregon and California," 659–660.

23. Preuss, *Exploring with Frémont*, 120.

24. Ibid., 121.

25. "Expedition to Oregon and California," 662.

26. Ibid., 668n, 670.

27. Ibid., 671.

28. Ibid., 673.

29. *New York Weekly Tribune*, December 28, 1843.

30. *Niles' National Register* 65, December 9, 1843.

31. *Niles' National Register* 68, May 17, 1845; *Niles' National Register* 65, November 11, 1843.

32. Ibid.

33. *Congressional Globe*, February 7, 1844, 226; *Niles' National Register* 65, December 9, 1843; David M. Pletcher, *The Diplomacy of Annexation: Texas, Oregon, and the Mexican War* (Columbia: University of Missouri Press, 1973), 218–219.

34. *Niles' National Register* 67, November 2, 1844.

35. Ibid.

36. Marcus Whitman to Stephen and Clarissa Prentiss, May 16, 1844, Whitman-Walker Papers, Beinecke Library, Yale University.

37. Daniel Waldo, "Critiques: Narrative and Remarks," Beinecke Library, Yale University.

38. Robert C. Clark, "How British and American Subjects Unite in a Common Government for Oregon Territory in 1844," *Oregon Historical Quarterly* [hereafter *OHQ*] 13 (1912): 156.

39. Frederick V. Holman, "A Brief History of the Oregon Provisional Government and What Caused Its Formation," *OHQ* 13 (1912): 124; Hubert H. Bancroft [Frances Fuller Victor], *History of Oregon*, vol. 1 (San Francisco: The History Company, 1886), 428–431.

40. Ibid.; Clark, "How British and American Subjects Unite in a Common Government," 157.

41. *Niles' National Register* 66, June 22, 1844.

42. Ibid.

43. Narcissa Whitman to Clarissa Kinny, May 20, 1844, in *The Letters of Narcissa Whitman*, 1836–1847, ed. Glen Adams (Fairfield, Wash.: Ye Galleon Press, 1996), 178.

44. Narcissa Whitman to Laura Brewer, April 24 and August 5, 1844, in Adams, ed., *Letters of Narcissa Whitman*, 175, 180.

45. Narcissa Whitman to her parents, October 9 and 25, 1844, in Adams, ed., *Letters of Narcissa Whitman*, 181.

46. Marcus Whitman to Stephen and Clarissa Prentiss, May 16, 1844, Whitman-Walker Papers.

47. Marcus Whitman to Elkanah Walker, November 11, 1844, Whitman-Walker Papers.

48. Marcus Whitman to Elkanah Walker, January 27, 1845, Whitman-Walker Papers.

49. John McLoughlin to the Governor and Committee, November 20, 1845, ed. Katharine B. Judson, *American Historical Review* 21 (October 1915): 132.

50. John McLoughlin to the Governor and Committee, November 18, 1843, in *The Letters of John McLoughlin*, Second Series, 1839–1844, ed. E. E. Rich (London: Champlain Society, 1943), 160.

51. Pletcher, *Diplomacy of Annexation*, 223.

52. *Niles' National Register* 68, March 8, 1845.

53. Quoted in Pletcher, *Diplomacy of Annexation*, 238.

54. Thomas Hart Benton, *Thirty Years' View*, vol. 2 (New York: D. Appleton, 1856) 568.

55. Jessie Benton Frémont to Adelaide Talbot, April 21, 1844, in Herr and Spence, eds., *Letters of Jessie Benton Frémont*, 21.

56. *Niles' National Register* 66, June 29, 1844.

57. Jessie Benton Frémont to Adelaide Talbot, June 15, 1844, in Herr and Spence, eds., *Letters of Jessie Benton Frémont*, 23.

58. John Charles Frémont, *Memoirs of My Life*, vol. 1 (Chicago: Bedford, Clarke, 1887), 409.

59. "Expedition to Oregon and California," 681.

60. Preuss, *Exploring with Frémont*, 127–129.

61. *Niles' National Register* 68, August 30, 1845.

62. John D. Unruh Jr., *The Plains Across: Overland Emigrants and the Trans-Mississippi West, 1840–60* (Urbana: University of Illinois Press, 1979), 111; Josiah Royce, *California: From the Conquest of 1846 to the Second Vigilance Committee in San Francisco* (Boston: Houghton Mifflin, 1881), 54.

63. Jessie Benton Frémont, "The Origin of the Frémont Explorations," *Century* 41 (March 1891): 770.

64. Frémont, *Memoirs*, vol. 1, 413.

65. Benton, *Thirty Years' View*, vol. 2, 600; Wayne Cutler, ed., *Correspondence of James K. Polk*, vol. 8 (Nashville, Tenn.: Vanderbilt University Press, 1989). 356; J.

George Harris to James K. Polk, June 25, 1844, in Cutler, ed., *Correspondence of James K. Polk*, vol. 7, 282.

66. M. A. DeWolfe Howe, *The Life and Letters of George Bancroft*, vol. 1 (1908; reprint, New York: Da Capo Press, 1970), 259–260; Pamela Herr, *Jessie Benton Frémont* (New York: Franklin Watts, 1987), 106.

67. Frémont, *Memoirs*, 418–419.

68. Howe, *Life and Letters of George Bancroft*, 259–260.

69. "Annexation," *United States Magazine and Democratic Review* 17 (July–August 1845).

70. "Report of Lieutenants Warre and Vavasour, 26 October 1845," ed. Joseph Shafer, *OHQ* 10 (March 1909): 47.

71. Ibid., 110, 114.

72. *Congressional Globe* (December 8, 1845): 24.

73. Hubert H. Bancroft [Frances Fuller Victor], *History of Oregon*, vol. 1 (San Francisco: The History Company, 1886), 479–480.

74. John McLoughlin to Sir George Simpson, *OHQ* 17 (1916): 221.

75. "Warre and Vavasour's Military Reconnoissance in Oregon, 1845–6," ed. Joseph Shafer, *OHQ* 10 (March 1909): 5.

76. Sir George Simpson to Henry Warre and Mervin Vavasour, May 30, 1845, in "Warre and Vavasour's Military Reconnoissance," 28.

77. Sir George Simpson to Peter Skene Ogden, May 30, 1845, in "Warre and Vavasour's Military Reconnoissance," 35; Peter Skene Ogden to Sir George Simpson, March 20, 1846, in *The Letters of John McLoughlin*, Third Series, 1844–1846, ed. E. E. Rich (London: Champlain Society, 1944), 147n.

78. Report of October 26, 1845, in "Warre and Vavasour's Military Reconnoissance," 53.

79. Unruh, *The Plains Across*, 358–359.

80. Report of June 16, 1846, in "Warre and Vavasour's Military Reconnoissance," 82, 86–91.

81. Pletcher, *Diplomacy of Annexation*, 414.

82. Ibid.

83. Frémont, *Memoirs*, 419.

84. J. J. Abert to John C. Frémont, February 12, April 10, and May 14, 1845, in "Report of the Exploring Expedition to Oregon and California," 396, 407.

85. Frémont, *Memoirs*, 423.

86. Pletcher, *Diplomacy of Annexation*, 421; Royce, *California*, 115–116.

87. Frémont, *Memoirs*, 454.

88. José Castro to John C. Frémont, March 5, 1846, in *The Expeditions of John Charles Frémont*, vol. 2, *The Bear Flag Revolt and the Court-Martial*, ed. Mary Lee Spence and Donald Jackson (Urbana: University of Illinois Press, 1973), 74, 75; Frémont, *Memoirs*, 459.

89. John C. Frémont to Thomas O. Larkin, March 9, 1846, in Spence and Jackson, eds., *Expeditions*, vol. 2, 81–82, and José Castro's Proclamation, March 8, 1846, 81.

90. Frémont, *Memoirs*, 460; John C. Frémont to Jessie Benton Frémont, April 1, 1846, in Spence and Jackson. eds., *Expeditions*, vol. 2, 130.

91. Frémont, *Memoirs*, 489; Spence and Jackson, eds., *Expeditions*, vol. 2, xxviii–xxix.

92. Royce, *California*, 119–20.

93. Frémont, *Memoirs*, 490.

94. Spence and Jackson, eds., *Expeditions*, vol. 2, 128n.

95. Frémont, *Memoirs*, 502, 506; John Bidwell, "Frémont in the Conquest of California," *Century* 41 (February 1891): 519.

96. Bidwell, "Frémont in the Conquest of California," 522.

97. Joseph T. Downey, *The Cruise of the Portsmouth, 1845–1847: A Sailor's View of the Conquest of California*, ed. Howard Lamar (New Haven, Conn.: Yale University Library, 1958), 127–128; Frémont, *Memoirs*, 508; Royce, *California*, 121.

98. Frémont, *Memoirs*, 509; Bidwell, "Frémont in the Conquest of California," 519; Royce, *California*, 59.

99. Frémont, *Memoirs*, 517.

100. Ibid., 520, 522–523; John C. Frémont to Thomas H. Benton, July 25, 1845, in Spence and Jackson, eds., *Expeditions*, vol. 2, 183, 186n.

101. Pletcher, *Diplomacy of Annexation*, 431, 433.

102. John D. Sloat to John B. Montgomery, July 6, 1846, in Spence and Jackson, eds., *Expeditions*, vol. 2, 164.

103. Downey, *Cruise of the Portsmouth*, 132.

104. Quoted in Frémont, *Memoirs*, 533.

105. *American Whig Review* 3 (January 1846): 82; quoted in Herr, *Jessie Benton Frémont*, 144.

106. Frémont, *Memoirs*, 420.

107. Narcissa Whitman to Harvey and Livonia Prentiss, September 11, 1846, in Adams, ed., *Letters of Narcissa Whitman*, 208.

108. Narcissa Whitman to Laura Brewer, February 10, 1845, in Adams, ed., *Letters of Narcissa Whitman*, 187; Narcissa Whitman to Harriet Prentiss, April 13, 1846, in Adams, ed., *Letters of Narcissa Whitman*, 200.

109. Ibid., 201.

110. Narcissa Whitman to Clarissa Prentiss, April 9, 1846, in Adams, ed., *Letters of Narcissa Whitman*, 194–195.

111. Narcissa Whitman to Jane Prentiss, April 2, 1846, ibid., 193; Narcissa Whitman to Clarissa Prentiss, April 9, 1846, ibid., 195.

112. Narcissa Whitman to Stephen Prentiss, April 10, 1846, in Adams, ed., *Letters of Narcissa Whitman*, 197.

113. Andrew Rodgers to Mary Walker, June 26, 1847, Walker Family Papers, Beinecke Library, Yale University; Narcissa Whitman to Clarissa Prentiss, November 3, 1846, in Adams, ed., *Letters of Narcissa Whitman*, 211.

114. Narcissa Whitman to Laura Brewer, July 17, 1846, in Adams, ed., *Letters of Narcissa Whitman*, 207.

115. J. B. A. Brouillet, "True Causes of the Massacre at Waiilatpu," in "Indian War in Oregon and Washington Territories," U.S. House Doc. 38, 35th Cong., 1858, 16.

116. Marcus Whitman to Elkanah Walker and Cushing Eels, November 25, 1845, Walker-Whitman Letters.

117. Ibid.

118. Ibid.

119. Narcissa Whitman to Laura Brewer, July 17, 1846, 207, and Narcissa Whitman to Clarissa Prentiss, November 3, 1846, 214, in Adams, ed., *Letters of Narcissa Whitman*.

120. Bancroft [Victor], *History of Oregon*, vol. 1, 648; Marcus Whitman to Elkanah Walker, May 17, 1847, Walker-Whitman Papers.

121. Paul Kane, *Wanderings of an Artist among the Indians of North America* (Toronto: The Radisson Society of Canada, 1925), 195.

122. Narcissa Whitman to her mother, August 23, 1847, in Adams, ed., *Letters of Narcissa Whitman*, 225.

123. Brouillet, "True Causes of the Massacre at Waiilatpu," 17.

124. Ibid., 32; Jeffrey, *Converting the West*, 216.

125. John Young's and Augustin Raymond's statement, September 12, 1848, in "Indian War in Oregon and Washington Territories," U.S. House Doc. 38, 23.

126. William Craig's statement, July 11, 1848, in "Indian War in Oregon and Washington Territories," U.S. House Doc. 38, 26–27.

127. The account of the Whitman killings is drawn from the following: Jeffrey, *Converting the West*, 217–219; Henry H. Spalding to Stephen and Clarissa Prentiss, April 6, 1848, in Adams, ed., *Letters of Narcissa Whitman*, 230–235; Brouillet, "True Causes of the Massacre at Waiilatpu," 37–38; Bancroft [Victor], *History of Oregon*, vol. 1, 658–664.

Epilogue: The Country of the Setting Sun

1. J. B. A. Brouillet, "True Causes of the Massacre at Waiilatpu," in "Indian War in Oregon and Washington Territories," U.S. House Doc. 38, 35th Cong., 1858, 42.

2. Henry H. Spalding to Elkanah Walker and Cushing Eels, January 1, 1848, H. H. Spalding Letters, Beinecke Library, Yale University.

3. Hubert H. Bancroft [Frances Fuller Victor], *History of Oregon*, vol. 1 (San Francisco: The History Company, 1886), 669, 689.

4. Brouillet, "True Causes of the Massacre at Waiilatpu," 45.

5. Bancroft [Victor], *History of Oregon*, vol. 1, 693.

6. Ibid., 694; Henry H. Spalding to Stephen and Clarissa Prentiss, April 6, 1848, in *The Letters of Narcissa Whitman*, 1836–1847, ed. Glen Adams (Fairfield, Wash.: Ye Galleon Press, 1996), 232.

7. Bancroft [Victor], *History of Oregon*, vol. 1, 681; quoted in Robert M. Utley and Wilcomb E. Washburn, *Indian Wars* (Boston: Houghton Mifflin, 1977), 164.

8. Henry H. Spalding to Elkanah Walker and Cushing Eels, February 17, 1848, Spalding Letters.

9. Bancroft [Victor], *History of Oregon*, vol. 2 (San Francisco: The History Company, 1888), 99.

10. J. Ross Browne, "Indian War in Oregon and Washington Territories," U.S. House Doc. 38, 35th Cong., 1858, 2–3.

11. Ibid., 4.

12. William Dietrich, *Northwest Passage: The Great Columbia River* (New York: Simon & Schuster, 1995), 188, 214–215.

13. Blaine Harden, *A River Lost: The Life and Death of the Columbia* (New York: W. W. Norton, 1996), 18.

14. Ibid., 17; Dietrich, *Northwest Passage*, 310; *New York Times*, April 2, 2000.

Bibliography

Unpublished Sources

Nathan Bangs Letters, Wesleyan University, Middletown, Connecticut.

Willbur Fisk Letters, Wesleyan University.

William H. Gray Papers, Oregon Historical Society, Portland.

Jason Lee Letters, University of Puget Sound, Tacoma, Washington.

Letters of H. K. W. Perkins and wife, Beinecke Library, Yale University, New Haven, Connecticut.

Cyrus Shepard Journal (March 1834–December 1835), Beinecke Library, Yale University.

Asa Bowen Smith, Oregon Mission Letters, Beinecke Library, Yale University.

Elkanah Walker Diary, Oregon Historical Society.

Elkanah Walker, Oregon-Hawaii Mission Papers, Beinecke Library, Yale University.

Elkanah Walker, Oregon Mission Papers, Beinecke Library, Yale University.

Walker (Elkanah) Family Papers, Beinecke Library, Yale University.

Whitman Family Papers, Beinecke Library, Yale University.

Published Sources

Ackerknect, Erwin H. *History and Geography of the Most Important Diseases*. New York: Hafner, 1965.

Adams, Glen, ed. *The Letters of Narcissa Whitman, 1836–1847*. Fairfield, Wash.: Ye Galleon Press, 1996.

Bancroft, Hubert H. *California Pastoral, 1769–1848*. San Francisco: The History Company, 1888.

————— [Frances Fuller Victor]. *History of Oregon*. 2 vols. San Francisco: The History Company, 1886–1888.

Benton, Thomas Hart. *Thirty Years' View*. 2 vols. New York: D. Appleton, 1854–1856.

Bidwell, John. "Bidwell-Bartleson Journey," in *First Three Wagon Trains*. Portland, Ore.: Binford & Mort, 1993.

————. "Life in California before the Gold Discovery." *Century* 41 (December 1890).

Billington, Ray A. *The Far Western Frontier*. New York: Harper & Brothers, 1956.

Billington, Ray A., and Martin Ridge. *Westward Expansion: A History of the American Frontier*, 5th ed. New York: Macmillan, 1982.

Bourne, Edward. *Essays in Historical Criticism*. 1901. Reprint, Freeport, N.Y.: Books for Libraries Press, 1967.

Bradbury, John. *Travels in the Interior of America*. 1817. Reprint, Ann Arbor, Mich.: University Microfilms, 1966.

Brosnan, Cornelius J. *Jason Lee: Prophet of the New Oregon*. New York: Macmillan, 1932.

Carey, Charles, ed. "Diary of Rev. George Gary." *Quarterly of the Oregon Historical Society* 24 (March 1923): 68–105; part 2 (June 1923): 153–185; part 3 (September 1923): 269–333; part 4 (December 1923): 386–433.

Chittenden, Hiram Martin. *The American Fur Trade of the Far West*. 2 vols. New York: F. P. Harper, 1902.

Clark, Robert. "How British and American Subjects Unite in a Common Government for Oregon Territory in 1844." *Oregon Historical Quarterly* 13 (1912).

Cox, Ross. *The Columbia River*. Edited by Edgar I. Stewart and Jane R. Stewart. Norman: University of Oklahoma Press, 1957.

Dana, Richard Henry Jr. *Two Years before the Mast: A Personal Narrative*. 1839. Reprint, Boston: Houghton Mifflin, 1923.

Davies, John D. *Phrenology Fad and Science: A 19th-Century American Crusade*. New York: Archon Books, 1971.

DeVoto, Bernard. *Across the Wide Missouri*. Boston: Houghton Mifflin, 1947.

————. *The Year of Decision: 1846*. Boston: Houghton Mifflin, 1943.

"Diary of Wilkes in the Northwest." Edited by Edmond S. Meany. *Washington Historical Quarterly* 16 (1925).

Dietrich, William. *Northwest Passage: The Great Columbia River*. New York: Simon & Schuster, 1995.

"Document: Slacum's Report on Oregon, 1836–1837." *Oregon Historical Quarterly* 13 (1912).

Downey, Joseph T. *The Cruise of the Portsmouth, 1845–1847*. Edited by Howard Lamar. New Haven, Conn.: Yale University Library Press, 1958.

Drury, Clifford M., ed. *Where Wagons Could Go: Narcissa Whitman and Eliza Spalding*. Lincoln: University of Nebraska Press, 1997.

Dryden, Cecil P. *Give All to Oregon: Missionary Pioneers in the Far West*. New York: Hastings House, 1968.

Duniway, David C., and Neil R. Riggs, eds. "The Oregon Archives, 1841–1843." *Oregon Historical Quarterly* 60 (1959): 211–280.

Egan, Ferol. *Frémont: Explorer for a Restless Nation*. Garden City, N.Y.: Doubleday, 1977.

Elliot, T. C. "The Earliest Travelers on the Oregon Trail." *Oregon Historical Quarterly* 13 (1912).

————. "The Surrender at Astoria in 1818." *Oregon Historical Quarterly* 19 (1918).

Ewers, John C., ed. *Adventures of Zenas Leonard*. Norman: University of Oklahoma Press, 1959.

Farnham, Thomas J. *Travels in the Great Western Prairies*. 1843. Reprint, New York: Da Capo Press, 1973.

Fleming, R. Harvey. *Minutes of Council Northern Department of Rupert's Land, 1821–1831*. Hudson's Bay Company Series III. Toronto: The Champlain Society, 1940.

Franchère, Gabriel. *Adventure at Astoria, 1810–1814*. Translated and edited by Hoyt C. Franchère. Norman: University of Oklahoma Press, 1967.

Frémont, Jessie Benton. "The Origin of the Frémont Explorations." *Century* 41 (March 1891).

Frémont, John C. *Memoirs of My Life*. Vol. 1. Chicago: Bedford Clarke, 1887.

Garraty, John A., and Mark C. Carnes, eds. *American National Biography*. New York: Oxford University Press, 1999.

Goetzmann, William H. *Army Exploration in the American West, 1803–1863*. New Haven: Yale University Press, 1959.

————. *Exploration and Empire*. New York: Alfred A. Knopf, 1966.

Gough, Barry M. *Distant Dominion: Britain and the Northwest Coast of America, 1579–1809*. Vancouver: University of British Columbia Press, 1980.

Graustein, Jeanette. *Thomas Nuttall, Naturalist: Explorations in America, 1808–1841*. Cambridge, Mass.: Harvard University Press, 1967.

Guthrie, A. B. *The Way West*. Boston: Houghton Mifflin, 1949.

Harden, Blaine. *A River Lost: The Life and Death of the Columbia*. New York: W. W. Norton, 1996.

Hastings, Lansford W. *The Emigrants' Guide to Oregon and California*. 1845. Reprint, Bedford, Mass.: Applewood Books, n.d..

Herr, Pamela. *Jessie Benton Frémont: A Biography*. New York: Franklin Watts, 1987.

Herr, Pamela, and Mary Lee Spence. *The Letters of Jessie Benton Frémont*. Urbana: University of Illinois Press, 1993.

Holman, Frederick V. "A Brief History of the Oregon Provisional Government and What Caused Its Formation." *Oregon Historical Quarterly* 13 (1912).

Hulbert, Archer B., and Dorothy Hulbert, eds. *The Oregon Crusade: Across Land and Sea to Oregon*. Vol. 5 of *Overland to the Pacific*. Denver: Colorado College and Denver Public Library, 1935.

Irving, Washington. *Adventures of Captain Bonneville*. Vol. 16, *The Complete Works of Washington Irving*. Boston: Twayne, 1977.

————. *Astoria*. Clatsop Edition. Portland, Ore.: Binford & Mort, 1967.

Jackson, Donald, and Mary Lee Spence. *The Expeditions of John Charles Frémont*. Vol. 1. Urbana: University of Illinois Press, 1970.

Jackson, Helen. *A Century of Dishonor*. Boston: Roberts Brothers, 1895.

"Jason Lee Diary." *Oregon Historical Quarterly* 17 (1916).

Jeffrey, Julie Roy. *Converting the West: A Biography of Narcissa Whitman*. Norman: University of Oklahoma Press, 1991.

Johnston, Johanna. *The Heart That Would Not Hold: A Biography of Washington Irving*. New York: M. Evans, 1971.

"Journal of John H. Frost, 1840–1843." Edited by Nellie B. Pipes. *Oregon Historical Quarterly* 35 (1934).

Kane, Paul. *Wanderings of an Artist among the Indians of North America.* Toronto: Radisson Society of Canada, 1925.

LaFeber, Walter. *John Quincy Adams and American Continental Empire: Letters, Papers, and Speeches.* Chicago: Quadrangle Books, 1965.

Lavender, David. *Westward Vision: The Story of the Oregon Trail.* New York: McGraw-Hill, 1963.

Leader, Herman A. "McLoughlin's Answer to Warre Report." *Oregon Historical Quarterly* 33 (September 1932): 214–229.

Lee, Daniel, and John Frost. *Ten Years in Oregon.* New York: Privately printed, 1844.

Lee, Willis T., et al. *Guidebook of the Western United States.* United States Geological Survey, Bulletin 612. Washington, D.C.: U.S. Government Printing Office, 1916.

Loewenberg, Robert J. *Equality on the Oregon Frontier: Jason Lee and the Methodist Mission, 1834–43.* Seattle: University of Washington Press, 1976.

Lyons, L. M. *Francis Norbert Blanchet and the Founding of the Oregon Missions.* Washington, D.C.: Catholic University of America Press, 1940.

Martin, Thomas S. *With Frémont to California and the Southwest, 1845–1849.* Edited by Ferol Egan. Ashland: Lewis Osborne, 1975.

Mattes, Merrill J. *The Great Platte River Road: The Covered Wagon Mainline via Fort Kearny to Fort Laramie.* Lincoln: University of Nebraska Press, 1969.

McDermott, John Francis, ed. *Travelers on the Western Frontier.* Urbana: University of Illinois Press, 1970.

Merk, Frederick. *Fur Trade and Empire: George Simpson's Journal.* Cambridge, Mass: Harvard University Press, Belknap Press, 1968.

———. *History of the Westward Movement.* New York: Alfred A. Knopf, 1978.

———. *Manifest Destiny and Mission in American History.* New York: Alfred A. Knopf, 1963.

———. *The Oregon Question.* Cambridge, Mass: Harvard University Press, Belknap Press, 1967.

Morgan, Dale L. *Jedediah Smith and the Opening of the West.* Indianapolis, Ind.: Bobbs-Merrill, 1953.

Morgan, William J., et al., eds. *Autobiography of Rear Admiral Charles Wilkes, U.S. Navy, 1798–1877.* Washington, D.C.: U.S. Department of the Navy, Naval History Division, 1978.

Nixon, Oliver W. *How Whitman Saved Oregon.* Chicago: Star, 1895.

Norwood, Frederick A. *The Story of American Methodism.* Nashville, Tenn.: Abingdon Press, 1974.

Paddison, Joshua. *A World Transformed: Firsthand Accounts of California before the Gold Rush.* Berkeley, Calif.: Heyday Books, 1999.

Palmer, Joel. *Journal of Travels over the Rocky Mountains; to the Mouth of the Columbia River, Made during the Years 1845 and 1846.* 1847. Reprint, Ann Arbor, Mich.: University Microfilms, 1996.

Parker, Samuel. *Journal of an Exploring Tour.* Ithaca, N.Y.: Privately printed, 1838.

Peterson, Norma L. *The Presidencies of William Henry Harrison and John Tyler.* Lawrence: University Press of Kansas, 1989.

Pike, C. J. "Petitions of Oregon Settlers, 1838–1848," *Oregon Historical Quarterly* 34 (1933): 216–235.

Pletcher, David M. *The Diplomacy of Annexation: Texas, Oregon, and the Mexican War.* Columbia: University of Missouri Press, 1973.

Powell, Fred Wilber, ed. *Hall J. Kelley on Oregon.* Princeton, N.J.: Princeton University Press, 1923.

Preuss, Charles. *Exploring with Frémont.* Translated and edited by Edwin G. and Elizabeth Gudde. Norman: University of Oklahoma Press, 1958.

Pritzker, Barry M., ed. *Native Americans: An Encyclopedia of History, Culture, and Peoples.* Santa Barbara, CA: ABC-CLIO, 1998.

Rich, E. E., ed. *The Letters of John McLoughlin from Fort Vancouver to the Governor and Committee.* First Series, 1825–1838. London: The Champlain Society, 1941.

——————. *The Letters of John McLoughlin from Fort Vancouver to the Governor and Committee.* Second Series, 1839–1844. London: The Champlain Society, 1943.

——————. *The Letters of John McLoughlin from Fort Vancouver to the Governor and Committee.* Third Series, 1844–1846. London: The Champlain Society, 1944.

Roberts, David. *A Newer World: Kit Carson, John Charles Frémont, and the Claiming of the American West.* New York: Simon & Schuster, 2000.

Rollins, Philip Ashton. *The Discovery of the Oregon Trail: Robert Stuart's Narratives of His Overland Trip Eastward from Astoria in 1812–13.* 1935. Reprint, Lincoln: University of Nebraska Press, 1995.

Ronda, James P. *Astoria and Empire.* Lincoln: University of Nebraska Press, 1990.

Ross, Alexander. *Adventures of the First Settlers of the Columbia River.* 1849. Reprint, Ann Arbor, Mich.: University Microfilms, 1966.

——————. *The Fur Hunters of the Far West.* Edited by Kenneth A. Spalding. Norman: University of Oklahoma Press, 1956.

Royce, Josiah. *California: From the Conquest of 1846 to the Second Vigilance Committee in San Francisco.* Boston: Houghton, Mifflin, 1886.

Ruby, Robert H. and John A. Brown. *A Guide to the Indian Tribes of the Pacific Northwest,* rev. ed. Norman: University of Oklahoma Press, 1992.

Russell, Osborne. *Journal of a Trapper.* Edited by Aubrey L. Haines. Portland: Oregon Historical Society, 1955.

Sage, Rufus B. *Rocky Mountain Life.* 1857. Reprint, Lincoln: University of Nebraska Press, 1982.

Sellers, Charles. *James K. Polk, Continentalist.* Princeton, N.J.: Princeton University Press, 1966.

——————. *The Market Revolution: Jacksonian America, 1815–1846.* New York: Oxford University Press, 1991.

Spence, Mary Lee, and Donald Jackson. *The Expeditions of John Charles Frémont.* Vol. 2. Urbana: University of Illinois Press, 1973.

Stanton, William. *The Great United States Exploring Expedition of 1838–1842.* Berkeley: University of California Press, 1975.

Stegner, Wallace. *The Gathering of Zion*. New York: McGraw-Hill, 1964.

Stewart, George R. *The California Trail*. New York: McGraw-Hill, 1962.

Stuart, Robert. *On the Oregon Trail: Robert Stuart's Journey of Discovery*. Edited by Kenneth A. Spalding. Norman: University of Oklahoma Press, 1953.

Talbot, Theodore. *The Journals of Theodore Talbot, 1843 and 1849–52*. Edited by Charles H. Carey. Portland, Ore.: Metropolitan Press, 1931.

Taylor, Alan. *American Colonies: The Settling of North America*. New York: Penguin Books, 2001.

Terrell, John Upton. *Furs by Astor*. New York: William Morrow, 1963.

Thompson, David. *Travels in Western North America, 1784–1812*. Edited by Victor G. Hopwood. Toronto: Macmillan, 1971.

Townsend, John Kirk. *Narrative of a Journey across the Rocky Mountains, to the Columbia River*. Edited by George A. Jobanek. Corvallis: Oregon State University Press, 1999.

Tyrell, J. B., ed. *David Thompson's Narrative of His Explorations in North America, 1784–1812*. Toronto: The Champlain Society, 1916.

Unruh, John D. Jr. *The Plains Across: The Overland Emigrants and the Trans-Mississippi West, 1840–60*. Urbana: University of Illinois Press, 1979.

Utley, Robert M., and Wilcomb E. Washburn. *Indian Wars*. Boston: Houghton Mifflin, 1977.

Vancouver, George. *Voyage of Discovery to the North Pacific Ocean and Round the World*. Vol. 1. 1798. Reprint, New York: Da Capo Press, 1967.

Voyages of the "Columbia" to the Northwest Coast 1787–1790 and 1790–1793. Edited by Frederick W. Howay. Boston: Massachusetts Historical Society, 1941.

Wilkes, Charles. *Narrative of the United States Exploring Expedition during the Years 1838, 1839, 1840, 1841, 1842*. Vol. 4. Philadelphia, 1849.

Wyeth, John B. *Oregon*. 1833. Reprint, Ann Arbor, Mich.: University Microfilms, 1966.

Young, F. G., ed. "The Correspondence and Journals of Captain Nathaniel J. Wyeth, 1831–36." In *Sources in the History of Oregon*. Eugene, Ore.: University Press, 1899.

Index

Page numbers in *italic* indicate illustrations.